DEFLATION

Until recently, fears of deflation seemed nothing more than a relic of the Great Depression. However, beginning in the 1990s, persistently falling consumer prices emerged in Japan, China, and elsewhere. Deflation is also a distinct possibility in some of the major euro area economies, especially Germany, and became a concern of the U.S. Federal Reserve in 2003. Deflation may be worse than inflation, not only because the real burden of debt rises but also because firms would confront rising real wages in a world where nominal wage rigidity prevails. This volume explores some key themes regarding deflation including: (i) how economic agents and policy makers have responded to deflation; (ii) the links between monetary policy, goods price movements, and asset price movements; (iii) the impact of deflation under different monetary policy and exchange rate regimes; and (iv) stock market reactions to deflation.

Richard C. K. Burdekin is Jonathan B. Lovelace Professor of Economics at Claremont McKenna College, Claremont, California. His areas of interest include monetary and financial economics, Chinese economic reforms, and inflation and deflation. Professor Burdekin has published four books: *Budget Deficits and Economic Performance* (with Farrokh K. Langdana), *Confidence, Credibility and Macroeconomic Policy* (with Farrokh K. Langdana), *Distributional Conflict and Inflation* (with Paul Burkett), and *Establishing Monetary Stability in Emerging Market Economies* (edited with Thomas D. Willett, Richard J. Sweeney, and Clas Wihlborg). He has also authored more than forty refereed journal articles that have been published in the *American Economic Review;* the *Journal of Economic History*; the *Journal of International Money and Finance*; the *Journal of Money, Credit, and Banking*; and the *Review of Economics and Statistics*, among other leading publications.

Pierre L. Siklos is Professor of Economics at Wilfrid Laurier University, Waterloo, Ontario, Canada, and Associate Director of its Viessmann Centre for the Study of Modern Europe. He specializes in macroeconomics with an emphasis on the study of inflation, central banks, and financial markets and also conducts research in applied time series analysis. Professor Siklos has been a consultant to a variety of institutions and central banks. He is the author of several books, including the leading textbook in Canada on money and banking, and *The Changing Face of Central Banking: Evolutionary Trends Since World War II* (Cambridge University Press, 2002). He has also published numerous articles in eminent economics journals such as the *Journal of Money, Credit, and Banking*, the *Journal of Econometrics*, the *Journal of Business and Economic Statistics*, the *Journal of International Money and Finance*, and the *Journal of Applied Econometrics*. Professor Siklos has been a visiting lecturer or fellow at several universities in Europe, North America, New Zealand, and Australia. In 2000–2001 he was Wilfrid Laurier University's University Research Professor.

STUDIES IN MACROECONOMIC HISTORY

SERIES EDITOR: Michael D. Bordo, *Rutgers University*

EDITORS: Forrest Capie, *City University Business School, U.K.*
Barry Eichengreen, *University of California, Berkeley*
Nick Crafts, *London School of Economics*
Angela Redish, *University of British Columbia*

The titles in this series investigate themes of interest to economists and economic historians in the rapidly developing field of macroeconomic history. The four areas covered include the application of monetary and finance theory, international economics, and quantitative methods to historical problems; the historical application of growth and development theory and theories of business fluctuations; the history of domestic and international monetary, financial, and other macroeconomic institutions; and the history of international monetary and financial systems. The series amalgamates the former Cambridge University Press series *Studies in Monetary and Financial History* and *Studies in Quantitative Economic History*.

Other books in the series:

Howard Bodenhorn, *A History of Banking in Antebellum America* (0-521-66999-5)

Michael D. Bordo, *The Gold Standard and Related Regimes* (0-521-55006-8)

Michael D. Bordo and Forrest Capie, editors, *Monetary Regimes in Transition* (0-521-41906-9)

Michael D. Bordo and Roberto Cortés-Conde, editors, *Transferring Wealth and Power from the Old to the New World* (0-521-77305-9)

Trevor J. O. Dick and John E. Floyd, *Canada and the Gold Standard* (0-521-40408-8)

Barry Eichengreen, *Elusive Stability* (0-521-44847-6)

Barry Eichengreen, editor, *Europe's Postwar Recovery* (0-521-48279-8)

Michele Fratianni and Franco Spinelli, *A Monetary History of Italy* (0-521-44315-6)

Continued on page 361

DEFLATION

Current and Historical Perspectives

Edited by

RICHARD C. K. BURDEKIN
Claremont McKenna College

PIERRE L. SIKLOS
Wilfrid Laurier University

CAMBRIDGE
UNIVERSITY PRESS

CAMBRIDGE UNIVERSITY PRESS
Cambridge, New York, Melbourne, Madrid, Cape Town, Singapore,
São Paulo, Delhi, Dubai, Tokyo, Mexico City

Cambridge University Press
The Edinburgh Building, Cambridge CB2 8RU, UK

Published in the United States of America by Cambridge University Press, New York

www.cambridge.org
Information on this title: www.cambridge.org/9780521153560

First published 2004
First paperback printing 2010

A catalogue record for this publication is available from the British Library

Library of Congress Cataloguing in Publication data
Deflation : current and historical perspectives / edited by Richard C. K. Burdekin,
    Pierre L. Siklos.
        p.   cm. – (Studies in macroeconomic history)
    Includes bibliographical references and index.
    ISBN 0-521-83799-5
    1. Deflation (Finance).   2. Monetary policy.   3. Prices.   I. Burdekin, Richard C. K.
(Richard Charles Keighley), 1958–   II. Siklos, Pierre L., 1955–   III. Series.
    HG229.D384   2004
    332.4'1 – dc22   2003069669

ISBN 978-0-521-83799-6 Hardback
ISBN 978-0-521-15356-0 Paperback

From RCKB to Yanjie, Eileen, Emma, and my mother

From PLS to H.B., and here's hoping for the best for the boys

Contents

Tables and Figures

FIGURES

Contributors

MARTIN T. BOHL
European University Viadrina, Frankfurt

MICHAEL D. BORDO
Rutgers University

RICHARD C. K. BURDEKIN
Claremont McKenna College

FORREST CAPIE
City University Business School, London

LANCE DAVIS
California Institute of Technology

MICHELE FRATIANNI
Indiana University

KLAS FREGERT
Lund University, Sweden

CHARLES GOODHART
London School of Economics

BORIS HOFMANN
Center for European Integration Studies, University of Bonn, Germany

MICHAEL HUTCHINSON
University of California, Santa Cruz

OLIVIER JEANNE
International Monetary Fund

LARS JONUNG
European Commission and Stockholm School of Economics

LARRY NEAL
University of Illinois, Urbana-Champaign

ANGELA REDISH
University of British Columbia, Canada

HUGH ROCKOFF
Rutgers University

PIERRE L. SIKLOS
Wilfrid Laurier University, Canada

FRANCO SPINELLI
Università di Brescià, Italy

MARC D. WEIDENMIER
Claremont McKenna College

EUGENE WHITE
Rutgers University

GEOFFREY WOOD
City University Business School, London

Preface

Both of us, independently and jointly, have devoted many years to studying inflation and hyperinflation and analyzing central banking institutions. Indeed, it was our shared interests in these areas that led us to engage in joint research. In 1998, we began to think seriously about whether the incipient deflations in Asia, most notably in China and Japan, amounted to something other than simply the flip side of inflation. It quickly became apparent to us there was, potentially at least, something substantially different about studying an economy in the throes of a deflation. We also decided, early on, that the best way to proceed would be to call upon several interested academics to engage in research that would parallel our own interests, enabling us to provide a much broader perspective on historical and modern experiences with deflation. The end result is the present edited volume. The contributed papers were presented at two major conferences on the topic. One was held in April 2000 at Claremont McKenna College. We also organized a session at the XIIIth International Economic History Congress in Buenos Aires in 2002 that was devoted to deflation.

The rather long gestation period for this project partly reflects the fact that the study of deflation is, in many ways, in its infancy, especially regarding the conduct of monetary policy in such an environment. We were also determined to take the time to hone our ideas through seminar and conference participation, and in other ways to seek out respected colleagues' opinions. We trust that the end product will serve as a useful starting point for academics and policy makers wishing to learn more about the economics of deflation.

Richard Burdekin is very grateful to President Pamela Gann and Dean Bill Ascher of Claremont McKenna for supporting this project and funding the 2000 Claremont Conference on Deflation. He also extends a special thanks to the many contributors and discussants, who made sometimes very long trips to come to the conference – with Charles Goodhart not only cheerfully enduring the long trip from England but also serving with such aplomb as our dinner keynote speaker. Pierre Siklos thanks Wilfrid Laurier University, the Social Sciences and Humanities Research Council of Canada, and the German-American Academic Council for financial support. He is also grateful for the many invitations received to discuss the issues and to his family for their constant support, even when he was far away or, as he much preferred, when they were able to tag along. Deflation need not be all that bad. However, we hope no one has to go through situations similar to some of the worst deflations studied here.

Both editors are also grateful to Elsie Grogan for her invaluable help in the preparation of the manuscript.

1 Fears of Deflation and the Role of Monetary Policy

Some Lessons and an Overview

Richard C. K. Burdekin and Pierre L. Siklos

INTRODUCTION

Episodes of sustained declines in consumer prices have been rare since the 1930s. Recently, however, in addition to Japan's well-known ongoing experience with deflation, persistently falling consumer prices have been seen in other countries, such as Argentina, China, Hong Kong, Singapore, and Taiwan. Indeed, international success in reducing inflation by the mid-1990s was quickly followed by fresh fears of deflation.[1] Deflation may be "worse" than inflation because of firms confronting rising real wages should nominal wage rigidity prevail.[2] In the United States, Federal Reserve Bank of Richmond President J. Alfred Broaddus, having cast more dissents than anyone else in favor of tighter monetary policy in Federal Open Market Committee (FOMC) meetings in the past decade, recently stated that it would be "ironic to have fought all this time to bring the inflation rate down ... and then lose price stability on the down side" (see Ip 2002: p. A1). Meanwhile, the FOMC meeting of May 6, 2003, gave official notice of the Fed's concern that "the probability of an unwelcome substantial fall in inflation, though

[1] Norton (1997), *The Economist* (November 15, 1997, pp. 77–78; February 20, 1999a, pp. 19–22; September 25, 1999b, pp. 26–30; November 15, 1999c; September 14, 2002a; October 12, 2002b), Lushkin (2001), and Wanniski (2001) are just some who have raised fears over the specter of deflation. The latest expression of rising interest, if not concern, over the prospects of deflation is reflected in the D-word index produced by *The Economist* (2002c) meant to parallel the magazine's R-word recession indicator that has apparently signaled the onset of earlier recessions. Although the D-word index " ... is spreading like a plague" it has yet to meet Goodhart's Law that, in the present context, might imply that publicity given to the potential for deflation might well ensure that it never occurs.

[2] There remains lively disagreement among academics, however, over the extent to which wages would in fact remain rigid downward if sustained deflation set in (see, for example, King 1999).

1

minor, exceeds that of a pickup in inflation from its already low level." As
Ip (2003: p. A1) points out, this represented "a profound shift from half a
century of preoccupation with fighting inflation."

In the euro area, deflation is a distinct possibility in some of the major
economies, especially in Germany (International Monetary Fund 2003).[3]
The very low inflation rates in Germany (1 percent or less, at the time of
writing, based on the consumer price index [CPI]) have led to complaints
that the policy of the European Central Bank has been too tight. Another
culprit is the potential role played by the Stability and Growth Pact, which
is currently seen as an excessively binding constraint on the fiscal policy of
several member countries. Inflexible labor markets pose yet another threat.
But while real interest rates have risen sharply in Germany and certain other
parts of the euro area, elsewhere in Euroland we see negative real interest
rates. And, even though several central bankers have become concerned
about the possibility of deflation, many are also keen to point out that such
fears are overblown (Bernanke 2002a; Stevens 2002). For example, low inflation in Germany could be a reflection of relative price changes within the
euro area (Bean 2002).

The present chapter explores some key themes regarding deflation. First,
we review past and present macroeconomic concerns over the causes and
consequences of deflation. Next, we examine various perspectives about
what deflation means and why policy makers and academics have worried,
and continue to worry, about the emergence of deflation. A separate section
considers some international evidence that attempts to tease out certain
stylized features that can be drawn from the historical evidence on deflation from the nineteenth and first half of the twentieth centuries. Next, we
provide an overview of the two deflations in China and Japan. The chapter
concludes by providing a summary of the remaining contributions to this
volume.

---

[3] Although the European Central Bank has shied away from expressing concerns over deflation ("So our analysis does not show any tendency for deflation. I want to remove that fear"
[Duisenberg 2002: p. 9]), members of the European Parliament have repeatedly expressed
such fears partly in light of the lack of clarity over the inflation objective (the so-called
second pillar of monetary policy). A case in point is the recent testimony of the ECB president: "The monetary strategy that we have pursued has been to aim for price developments
of basically between 0.5 and 2 percent" (Duisenberg 2002: p. 9). Later on, the president
adds: "I can confirm that, if the outlook for inflation were to go in the direction below
1 percent, ... the prospects of deflation, alluded to earlier, would become more threatening"
(op. cit., p. 17).

FEARS OF DEFLATION THEN AND NOW

With much of the developed world currently facing near-zero inflation, it is useful to reexamine the channels through which deflation may influence aggregate economic performance. Fisher's (1933) debt-deflation mechanism suggests that declines in goods prices would be closely linked to declines in asset prices, with higher real debt burdens leading to rising default rates and bankruptcy. High debt levels during the 1920s, followed by an unprecedented deflation, which was unanticipated when the debt was issued, may have allowed this mechanism to play an important role in the United States during the Great Depression (Parker and Fackler 2001). There is also the potential for "reverse causation" running from asset prices to goods prices, whereby a severe asset price decline, as in the October 1929 crash, may trigger deflationary pressures in the economy as a whole. Collateral constraints may well also play a role here. In Japan, as land prices and share prices plunged, not only was loan collateral wiped out but bank balance sheets also suffered from direct bank exposure to the stock market, thereby magnifying the developing bad debt problem and making banks still less willing to make new loans.

Until international stock markets began their sharp drop in early 2000, few outside Japan worried about the feedback from asset prices to consumer prices. Today, however, more are inclined to echo the sentiments of Roach (2002: p. 13): "The equity bubble helped create other bubbles – most notably in the housing market and in consumer spending. Their continued existence poses a serious threat to lasting expansion and yet puncturing them raises the grave risks of deflation."

The growing share of wealth in the form of financial assets, as well as large swings in asset prices at the end of the twentieth century, have highlighted the potential for wealth effects on goods prices, in particular, and the economy more generally. Although these effects have yet to be satisfactorily quantified, Shilling (2001) argues that the sudden negative effect on household net wealth in the face of stock market losses in 2000 could have important effects on savings-consumption patterns. Indeed, Shilling (2001: p. 43) asserts that even a relatively moderate switch from the recent two-thirds of a percentage point decline in the savings rate to a one percentage point increase "will virtually ensure deflation." Although we do not know at this point whether any such effect will actually emerge in the United States or elsewhere, the post-2000 period of stock market weakness in the United States and in other countries has certainly been followed by rising default rates on corporate debt and a number of high-level bankruptcies. This has helped fuel concern that the United States may be at risk of emulating Japan's recent period of economic decline whereby, as in the case of the Great Depression, declines in both goods and asset prices are combined with a slumping real economy.

Although it is unclear just how much monetary policy makers should fear deflation today, influential individuals at the U.S. Federal Reserve did not worry enough about deflation in the 1920s and early 1930s. Indeed, the competence of the interwar Fed has been the subject of considerable ongoing debate throughout the decades (see, for example, Friedman and Schwartz 1963; Meltzer 2003). Disagreements over the role of credit in deflation and concerns as to how to reinvigorate the economy were, of course, also expressed in public at the time. Strikingly, the relationship between deflation and central bank policy was often entirely missing from the discussion, however. For example:

Governor Harding [of the Federal Reserve] said: "We have heard much complaint of constant deflation, which some allege has been the cause of the depression, but it is evident that the deflation which has taken place has not been a deflation of credit or currency." (*New York Times*, January 19, 1921, p. 10, col. 4)

A few days later, a former Chancellor of the Exchequer argued,

This policy of gradual monetary deflation, but deflation so guarded as to not interfere with production, is a policy impossible of execution.... A fall in wholesale prices will follow, due to goods being thrown upon the market by traders who are unable to carry their stocks or have failed in business. There will be a diminution in production, profits will be greatly lessened and unemployment will grow.... (*New York Times*, January 29, 1921, p. 2, col. 2)

While not all deflationary episodes have been associated with overall declines in economic activity (Bank for International Settlements 1999: pp. 78–80), Sylla (1991) does suggest that nineteenth-century U.S. evidence offers further examples of widespread speculative excesses apparently triggering a cycle of boom and bust that produced not only financial disturbances (or "panics") but full-blown economic depression. In addition to the potential threat of Fisher's debt-deflation mechanism, another reason to fear deflation in consumer prices is that, if it is expected that such declining prices will continue in the future, there is an incentive to delay purchases. This then leads to a further decline in aggregate demand, putting further downward pressure on prices and suggesting that deflation could be at least partially

self-sustaining. This helps explain why Keynes (1923), for example, emphasized that deflation was more dangerous than inflation (see also Laidler 1999:
p. 109; Meltzer 1988: p. 47).

Monetary policy makers must also confront the zero lower bound on
nominal interest rates. Once rates have been cut to zero, as in Japan, real
interest rates remain positive in the face of deflation; yet there is no scope
for providing any further boost through interest-rate policy alone. Concerns
over avoiding deflation are reflected in a statement made by David Dodge
shortly before he assumed the office of Governor of the Bank of Canada in
2001 (as quoted in Thorsell 2001: A15): "I think the costs of going down to
[zero inflation] are high, and there are real asymmetries when you get into
price deflation. We haven't got much evidence that things work a lot better
at zero than they do at one or two."

Meanwhile, in the United States, Treasury official John Taylor, reflecting
on the current Japanese experience with deflation, stated: "I get worried
about deflation and that is another reason to have an inflation target" (see
Snowdon and Vane 1999: p. 201). This begs the question of how deflation
arises in the first place and why it appears to have " ... a frightening history"
(Poole and Rasche 2002: p. 1). Policy makers in the 1930s, while facing an
unprecedented decline in overall economic activity, did nevertheless have
plenty of past experiences with deflation upon which to draw. As Mundell
(2000: pp. 329–330) puts it, "Deflation was already in the air ... the deflation
of the 1930s has its precedents in the 1780s, the 1820s, and the 1870s." Snyder
(1935: p. 202) draws the following conclusion from these earlier episodes:
"Periods of serious price disturbances are periods of industrial and financial
disturbance and social unrest. Practically never one without the other. And
periods of price stability are periods of industrial and social equilibrium and
sanity."

Contemporary observers recognized that financial distress occasioned by
falling prices, and the belief that these conditions would continue, was exacerbating deflationary pressures:

The continuous expectation of a further fall in prices has had a very restricting
influence on the buying power of the public. The steady reduction in prices has
made it impossible in a great many cases to pay back money borrowed at a
time when prices were higher.... Further, restriction of credit has followed, with
the result that prices have been forced down still more.... (*New York Times*,
November 27, 1921, p. 8, col. 1)

Keynes had also long recognized that expectations could only be affected if the policies put in place were credible: "For my part, I believe that confidence in the price level is the biggest practical help which the official would give to the business world." (as quoted in *The Times* August 7, 1923) Falling goods prices could be triggered by any number of factors, including not only a drop in asset prices but also positive supply shocks that shift the economy's aggregate supply curve to the right, thereby putting downward pressure on prices even as output increases. Although this allows for the possibility of "good" deflation rather than "bad" deflation, it is still true that sustained deflation is only possible when the rate of money growth falls behind the rate of growth of output and money demand. Just as the inflation of the 1970s could not be ascribed to supply shocks alone, but rather required central bank accommodation of these supply shocks through loose monetary policy, sustained deflation must surely imply a similar failure of central bank policy in the opposite direction. According to Federal Reserve Chairman Alan Greenspan (1998): "While asset price deflation can occur for a number of reasons, a persistent deflation in the prices of currently produced goods and services – just like a persistent increase in these prices – necessarily is, at its root, a monetary phenomenon." Contrasting with this position is the view expressed by former Bank of Japan Governor Hayami (2001) that, "at a time when prices decline on account of productivity gains based on rapid technological innovation, a forceful reduction in interest rates with a view to raising prices may amplify economic swings."[4]

Japan's recent experience actually reveals abundant evidence of a chronic shortfall of aggregate demand, and the long-lived period of decline dates back to the abrupt tightening in Japanese monetary policy at the end of the 1980s. Using a quantity-theory-based approach, Hetzel (1999) points to a sudden shift from excess money creation in the 1980s to an overly restrictive monetary policy that lagged behind growth in money demand in the early 1990s. Miyao's (2002) empirical analysis supports the importance of this "deflationary shock" and Miyao points to persistent effects of monetary shocks on real output during the rise and fall of the "bubble economy." It is certainly hard to see why monetary expansion would hurt Japan's supply-side performance today. After all, the problem is that of a downturn, not an upturn, in the real economy. Nor does there seem to be any clear reason

---

[4] This view might be more defensible if aggregate price movements were actually being explained by movements in the prices of goods influenced directly by technological change (e.g., computers). But, as Kuttner and Posen (2001) point out, until recently, Japan's CPI excluded products undergoing significant productivity improvements.

why expansionary policies would delay or impede any needed structural adjustments in the Japanese economy – a perspective that would have us embracing the "'liquidationist' views of then–Treasury Secretary Andrew Mellon and others who opposed macroeconomic stimulus during the Hoover administration in the United States" (Kuttner and Posen 2001: p. 103).[5] It is probably just as well that the Bank of Japan did an about-face in late 2001 and concluded, in agreement with the government, that deflation is enemy number one. By that time, at least one member of the Policy Board of the Bank of Japan was seriously contemplating the possibility of a deflationary spiral (Takebe 2001a, 2001b; Bank of Japan 2001).

WHAT IS DEFLATION ANYWAY? HISTORICAL
AND INTERNATIONAL PERSPECTIVES

Deflation occurs only when there is a general fall in some aggregate price level. As several observers have pointed out, however, this does not preclude the possibility of *relative* price changes wherein some components of the price level fall while others keep rising. Although most discussions about the role of monetary policy focus on the behavior of headline price indices, deflation in certain key components of aggregate prices can be just as worrisome if the effects of deflation in some sectors of the economy eventually spill over onto the rest of the economy. Hence, in what follows, we shall treat deflation as a sustained fall in some aggregate price level that has demonstrable macroeconomic implications. In this fashion, our definition covers not only prices for goods and services but it can also include asset prices more generally.

The prewar view that any plans to stabilize goods prices must make allowance for productivity improvements is perhaps exemplified by Viner's (1933) reference to a productivity-induced deflation as "balanced deflation." Furthermore, many policy makers and academics in the 1920s and 1930s believed that the occasional deflation was actually a necessary spur

---

[5] In this regard, Fisher (1935: p. 265–266) also quotes Federal Reserve Board Governor Miller as rejecting Congressional proposals to stabilize prices because "the thing to be expected in this country if we operated under a stabilization philosophy would be inflation." On the otherhand, Hayek (1931) claimed that opponents of deflation focused too strongly on aggregate price movements, neglecting the role of relative price changes and the role of productivity changes in directing economic resources to their best uses. According to Hayek (1931: p. 7), contemporary views of deflation led to "... very erroneous opinions ... that a rising price level tends always to cause an increase in production, and a falling price level always a decrease in production."

for economic growth and therefore a symptom of economic health, not economic malaise (see DeLong 1997).[6] Dickey (1977) offers some support for this perspective, arguing that the U.S. deflation of 1869–1896 was primarily of the "good" variety since relative price changes, profit expectations, and bond yields all implied that supply-side influences dominated price movements over demand-side effects.[7] Another way of addressing this issue is to assess how much of a deflation (or, for that matter, an inflation) is monetary in nature (i.e., demand-pull). More recently, Greenspan (1998) has recognized the advisability of falling prices in the face of productivity improvements while also warning that "...when the characteristics of products and services are changing rapidly, defining the unit of output, and thereby adjusting an item's price for improvements in quality, can be exceptionally difficult."

The conflict between "demand-pull" and "cost-push" views of deflation harks back to controversies in the late nineteenth and early twentieth centuries over the causes of inflation and deflation. Laughlin (1933: p. 225) defended the costs of production view while simultaneously denigrating the theories associated with Fisher and others. However, it is the views of Fisher (e.g., Fisher 1911) and others, including Keynes, that triumphed because it was eventually recognized that nominal interest rates do not fully adjust to falling prices, except in the long run. Therefore, the distinction between anticipated and unanticipated deflation is critical to an understanding of the potential consequences of a deflation. Nevertheless, it ought to be emphasized once more that even fully anticipated deflation can have negative economic consequences if, for example, the sector of the economy that experiences lower prices suffers from wages that are downward inflexible.

In an exhaustive review of the causes and consequences of the ongoing deflation in Japan, Ahearne et al. (2002) conclude that unanticipated shocks and insufficiently aggressive policies have been the main problem in that country.[8] The idea of an expectations trap has also resurfaced amid calls for

---

[6] See also Selgin (1995).

[7] Dickey (1977: p. 5), in fact, characterizes this 1869–1896 period as one of "dramatic changes in production functions."

[8] Much of the evidence presented by the authors is based on forecasts from Consensus Economics. However, they never compare the forecasting performance in Japan with the experience in other industrial countries such as the United States. Siklos (2002: ch. 6) argues, based on the monthly forecasts of inflation and real GDP growth in *The Economist*, while the inflation rate was poorly forecasted in Japan in 1997–1998 the resulting forecast errors were not larger than, say, the errors in forecasting U.S. inflation in the early 1990s when the economy was in a recession. On the other hand, it is true that forecast errors were far more volatile in Japan than in the United States and this may be taken as causal evidence that the economic environment more generally was considerably more uncertain in Japan.

the Bank of Japan to deliberately engineer expectations of inflation while expanding the money supply through the monetization of government debt (Krugman 1998). Exactly how such a policy would convince the public that future deflation will evaporate, especially when the lever of interest rates has vanished, is left unexplained. Nevertheless, this is exactly what the Bank of Japan *did* do after leaving the gold standard in 1931 – at which time Japan's response to the onset of the Great Depression appears to have been much more aggressive than the widely studied Federal Reserve (non)response. Large-scale government debt purchases helped facilitate robust economic growth in Japan through most of the 1930s and "allowing the exchange rate to depreciate effectively stopped domestic deflation" (Cargill, Hutchison, and Ito 2000: p. 140).[9]

As was clearly true in the 1930s, the choice of exchange rate regimes remains a key question that continues to be debated today. Whereas there was no fixed exchange rate constraint in the case of post-bubble Japan, other recent deflations in Argentina and Hong Kong involved policy makers applying deflationary policies to maintain their fixed exchange rate with the strong U.S. dollar. The desire to escape the external constraint limiting policy makers' ability to counter deflationary pressures during the Great Depression led the United Kingdom and Japan in 1931, and later the United States in 1933, to abandon the prewar international gold standard. Hong Kong's deflationary trend after November 1998 could not be readily countered by expansionary monetary policy because of the continued exchange rate commitment, however, and when "U.S. monetary policy tightened in the summer of 1999 . . . Hong Kong had to follow suit" (Jao 2001: p. 164). Hong Kong's consumer price index has continued to fall every year since 1999 and, by the fall of 2002, property values were down 65 percent from 1997 levels. Hong Kong's adherence to the currency board arrangement vis-á-vis the U.S. dollar contrasts, of course, with Argentina's December 2001 move to float its exchange rate after being mired in a four-year recession.

China's deflation, unlike that of Hong Kong, predated the Asian Financial Crisis of 1997–1998 and began in the midst of extremely tight monetary policy aimed at combating an inflationary spike in 1993–1994. Although some observers like Bernanke (2002b) and Stevens (2002) contend that the ensuing

---

[9] This accords with Viner's (1933: p. 26) more general observation that the "countries which went off the Gold Standard have . . . weathered the economic storm much better than we." And at this time, Sweden in the 1930s even pioneered the use of price level targeting as an explicit policy objective (Berg and Jonung 1999; Fregert and Jonung: in this volume).

deflation may be one of the few to fall into the good category (that is, driven by productivity improvements), this perspective is controversial. It has also been alleged that cheap Chinese exports have been putting downward pressure on prices elsewhere in Asia. For example, Lehman Brothers economist Graham Parry argues that this effect will be especially strong "for countries that compete on price rather than technology.... Because of it, Asia will remain a source of deflation for the rest of the world" (see Booth and Pottinger 2001: p. A2). As concerns with deflation continue to mount today, we should not forget that scope for international transmission of deflationary pressures remains an important policy issue.

To sum up, good or productivity-generated deflations are the exception. In general, most deflations reflect an expectational trap assisted by poor policy choices. Few today would see deflation as the normal, if not inevitable, cyclical counterpart of inflationary tendencies in the economy. Deflation could initially reflect supply-side technological improvements. But, as the Japanese example amply demonstrates, persistent deflation eventually exposes poor policy choices and, in this respect, raises fears of deflation on a global scale.

HISTORICAL EVIDENCE ON DEFLATIONARY EPISODES

This section explores the properties of annual price level data extending back into the nineteenth century (see also the extended version of this chapter available at www.wlu.ca/~wwwsbe/faculty/psiklos/deflation.htm). Whereas sustained inflation is the hallmark of the post-1945 period, the earlier era offers a mix of inflation and deflation. Table 1.1 presents some international evidence concerning the frequency of deflationary episodes in 20 countries (including the United States). The data suggest that, while most of the foreign deflations occurred at the same time as in the United States, the fraction of deflationary years that overlap with the U.S. experience drops sharply if we exclude the Great Depression. This episode was clearly an international phenomenon. Nevertheless, deflations were frequent prior to 1945 in many countries, even though, with the exception of the United Kingdom and France, they did not occur as frequently as in the United States, especially if the years of the Great Depression are excluded.

If we examine simple pair-wise cross-correlations between deflations in the United States and elsewhere in our 20-country sample, we usually find

Table 1.1. *The historical experience with deflation: pre-1945*

Country	No. of years of deflation pre-1945	Percent of time common with U.S.	Excluding great depression (1928–1933)		
			Number of episodes of deflation	No. years of deflation	Percent of time common with U.S.
Australia	33	76	5	13	30
Austria	11	45	1	2	5
Belgium	32	78	10	21	49
Canada	10	80	2	4	9
Denmark	31	87	7	22	51
Finland	12	50	2	1	2
France	34	82	4	24	56
Germany	27	59	7	18	42
Ireland	8	75	4	2	5
Italy	34	85	7	24	56
Japan	9	56	1	1	2
Netherlands	39	72	5	22	51
Norway	18	67	2	6	14
New Zealand	12	83	1	5	12
Portugal	7	86	2	2	5
Spain	11	36	3	2	5
Sweden	33	82	9	21	49
Switzerland	26	69	5	13	30
U.K.	40	80	5	26	60
U.S.	43	—	4	24	—

Periods of deflation include years when the year-over-year change in consumer prices is zero or negative. All data are annual. Episodes of deflation refer to the number of years of consecutive deflation interrupted by inflation. Samples are not the same for all countries.

Sources: See Appendix available at www.wlu.ca/~wwwsbe/faculty/psiklos/deflation.htm.

that U.S. deflations either *lead* deflations elsewhere or are coincident.[10] Only the Australian and Italian experiences reveal no apparent statistically significant cross-correlations. Also, it is worth noting that, while the peaks in the cross-correlation functions are usually positive, an indication that price declines in the United States are correlated with similar reductions in prices in other countries, the opposite is found for Austria, Denmark, and Germany. Austria and Germany experienced hyperinflation during the sample considered, which may explain this result, while the deflation in Denmark during the 1920s was both sharper and more persistent than in the United States. Table 1.1 also notes the number of episodes of deflation evaluated as the

[10] It was suggested to us that, over part of the sample considered, the U.K. might be a better candidate as a basis of comparison. However, the essentials of our arguments are unchanged if we use U.K. data.

instances of consecutive years of deflation separated by at least one year of inflation. Generally, deflations occur fairly infrequently – though, in several European countries, multiple episodes of deflation were experienced.

A way of thinking about the consequences of deflation versus inflation is to examine their persistence properties. Burdekin and Siklos (1999) find, using a data set similar to the one being used here, that an AR(1) model of inflation, augmented with other variables, adequately explains the evolution of inflation over long periods. However, this earlier work makes no distinction between inflation and deflation episodes for the four countries examined (United Kingdom, United States, Canada, and Sweden). In an AR(1) model, inflation persistence is estimated by the coefficient on the lagged inflation rate from the following expression:[11]

$$\pi_t = \alpha_0 + \alpha_1 \pi_{t-1} + \varepsilon_t \tag{1.1}$$

where π is the annual rate of inflation and α_1 is the measure of inflation persistence. Based on equation (1.1), we find that inflation is easier to predict, based on its past history, than deflation and this may be one reason for the unease with policies or events that lead to falling prices. Why does this matter? An important argument in modern macroeconomics is that economic "shocks," that is, unexpected movements in economic variables, create fluctuations in economic activity. If deflation is more difficult to predict, then unexpected movements are likely to have a larger economic impact.[12] This is, of course, simply an argument for stability in the movement of prices.

Persistence, as defined here, while a function of the particular monetary regime in place, also serves another function. Assuming the Fisher relationship between nominal interest rates and inflation holds approximately, highly persistent inflation will translate into highly persistent interest rates, another well-known feature of post–World War II data. The likelihood of reaching the zero bound of interest rates may very well be a function of the level of

---

[11] Needless to say, more complicated models can be developed to address the question (e.g., Benati 2002; Cogley and Sargent 2002). Nevertheless, these approaches do not arrive at fundamentally different conclusions, concurring that inflation persistence is not an intrinsic property of all monetary regimes.

[12] Whether policy makers or agents learn from these errors depends, however, on the size of such shocks. If the shock is large, learning about such an event will likely be faster than where there is a succession of small shocks. It should be added, however, that recognizing a large shock does not guarantee that the right policies will be put in place to deal with its consequences.

inflation persistence, since, for example, higher interest rates can be used to maintain positive inflation expectations. Unfortunately, sticky inflationary expectations may also pose considerable difficulties for the conduct of monetary policy if deflation is persistent.[13] A separate question then, and one that is outside the scope of this chapter, is what level of inflation is consistent with some notion of price stability and thereby can prevent a deflationary trap.[14]

Figure 1.1 provides forecasts of CPI inflation over two centuries of data for three cases. The top figure shows the case in which the data are "uncensored," which means that we implicitly assume agents make no separate allowance in their forecasts for inflation or deflation.[15] The remaining two figures are for the cases in which there is a memory of only inflation or only deflation, respectively, but not both. Root-mean-square-error estimates reveal that the case in which memory of deflation is excluded (middle figure) produces the best forecasts followed by the case in which both inflation and deflation data are incorporated into the model (top figure). Not surprisingly, the least successful forecasting model is the one that relies on effectively deflation data alone.

There are some interesting additional observations that can be made about the results shown in Figure 1.1. First, censoring inflation implies that the Great Depression could not have been anticipated despite the deflation of the 1920s. Second, even if agents use all available information (as in the top entry in Figure 1.1), they will consistently underestimate the *severity* of sharp inflations or deflations. Finally, a model that is based solely on what we might call "fears" of deflation (bottom Figure 1.1) may imply that the deflation will end up becoming uncontrollable. Overall, the evidence suggests that the prior emphasis on whether price level changes before World War II can be forecasted (Barsky and DeLong 2000; Summers 1983) may be

---

[13] Besides inflation persistence, the speed with which shocks are transmitted also has important implications for interest rate adjustment (Yates 2002). If an interest rate change proceeds quickly through the transmission process, smaller changes will be required to achieve a desired inflation and output outcome and, consequently, there is a reduced probability of hitting the zero bound for nominal interest rates.

[14] The theoretical literature (e.g., see Orphanides and Wieland 1998; Amirault and O'Reilly 2001), however, finds that the likelihood of a deflationary spiral is much greater at inflation rates below 1 percent. Hence, one is likely to want to exclude 0 percent from an inflation target. By 2002, no industrial country with an explicit inflation target included 0 percent as a lower bound.

[15] The AR(1) case is equation (1.1). The AR(1) + WPI is equation (1.1) augmented with lagged inflation in the wholesale price index (WPI). Kahneman and Tversky (1979) argue that "editing" of information is actually more the rule than the exception – as is consistent with the literature on "bounded rationality."

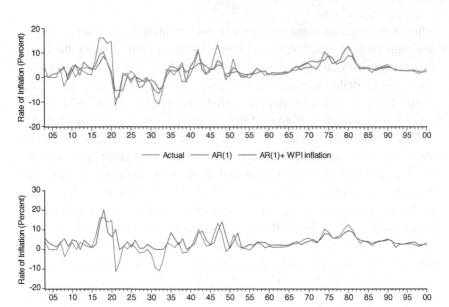

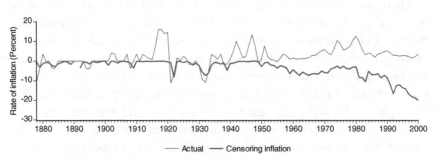

Figure 1.1. Alternative Forecasting Models of Inflation: Annual U.S., 1800–2000
Note: In the case of censored inflation, Tobit estimation is used. In the top figure, the entire history of inflation is used. In the middle figure, only the history of positive inflation is used, while in the bottom figure, only the history of zero or negative inflation is used.

misplaced. The key point is not to separate episodes of inflation. It seems more important that episodes of inflation be separated from instances of deflation.[16]

Clearly, aggregate demand and supply disturbances jointly determine inflation and output performance. Following Bayoumi and Eichengreen

[16] Whereas the foregoing analysis is that inflation forecasts are based on a purely backward-looking model, Fuhrer (1997) argues that the behavior of actual U.S. inflation is best described using a mix of backward- and forward-looking features. Re-estimation allowing for both forward-looking and backward-looking behavior does not significantly improve our ability to forecast deflation, however, especially during the 1895–1920 period.

Table 1.2. *Pair-wise correlations between aggregate demand and aggregate supply shocks: historical evidence*

	Aggregate demand (U.S.)			Aggregate supply (U.S.)		
Country	Full sample	Inflation only	Deflation only	Full sample	Inflation only	Deflation only
Austria	−.13	−.56	.32	−.19	.02	.60
Australia	.02	−.57	.13	−.09	−.01	−.20
Canada	−.07	−.38	−.61	.45	.16	.28
Denmark	.07	−.13	.11	.34	.05	−.30
Finland	−.66	−.85	−.18	.31	−.29	.11
France	−.16	−.30	−.19	.40	.24	.16
Germany	.24	.21	.22	−.16	−.23	.13
Italy	−.36	−.50	−.16	.06	.30	−.27
Japan	−.26	−.46	−.45	−.16	.93	−.07
Netherlands	.11	−.04	.08	.05	.02	.03
New Zealand	.01	−.11	−.41	.17	.32	−.11
U.K.	−.04	−.20	.03	.35	.08	.22
U.S. deflation	.92	—	—	.75	—	—
U.S. inflation	.83	—	—	.57	—	—

Note: A VAR of order 2 of the rate of change in real GDP and inflation was estimated and the restriction that the long-run impact of inflation on real GDP growth is zero was then imposed. The resulting structural shocks were extracted, and the simple correlation between those shocks is evaluated in the table for the cases shown.

(1993), we address this by estimating an unrestricted bivariate vector autoregression (VAR) of the output gap and inflation on which we then impose the condition that, in the long run, aggregate demand shocks are neutral with respect to the output gap while aggregate supply shocks are not constrained to have a zero long-run output effect.[17] We then consider how aggregate demand and supply shocks are pair-wise correlated across countries to assess the degree of symmetry in these types of shocks and, hence, the extent to which output and inflation responses are similar under inflation and deflation. As shown in Table 1.2, there is a striking difference between inflation-only and deflation-only samples in the correlations between U.S. demand shocks and other countries' aggregate demand shocks. In the inflation-only sample, aggregate demand shocks are, with the exception of Germany, negative. This may indicate that monetary and fiscal policies become more restrictive in the face of such shocks. By contrast, aggregate demand shocks are positive for half of the pairs considered in the deflation-only sample, also an indication that aggregate demand policies have the desired effect

[17] The output gap is estimated by applying a one-sided Hodrick-Prescott filter to Balke and Gordon's (1989) real gross national product (GNP) data series.

on inflation. Nevertheless, these results do not tell the whole story about inflation versus deflationary episodes.

These results may reflect differences, not only in inflationary or deflationary experiences but also in exchange rate regimes, as the deflation-only sample overlaps with much of the gold standard era. For example, the Netherlands and Denmark either remained on the gold standard until 1931 or switched toward a floating regime late in the deflationary sample. This accounts for the (small) positive correlations. Only Canada, New Zealand, and Japan display negative correlations that can be explained by the ability of the exchange rate to partially insulate the transmission of deflationary shocks from the United States. Meanwhile, for the inflation-only sample, the correlation coefficients reflect some of the influence of the managed floating regimes that dominate the post-war period. It is possible then that, in addition to a role for the exchange rate, the transmission of aggregate demand shocks is fundamentally different under deflation from that in inflationary periods. This, in turn, suggests a greater variety of policy responses to each of these events. Finally, it is worth noting that aggregate demand shocks over inflationary regimes, in the United States at least, are highly correlated with full-sample estimates. This suggests some symmetry in the inflation response to aggregate demand shocks whether the U.S. economy was in an inflationary or a deflationary state.

Correlations in aggregate supply shocks are typically positive (for 7 of 12 countries in the deflation-only sample and 9 of 12 in the inflation-only sample). However, with the notable exception of Japan in the inflation-only sample, the correlations are typically low. Hence, to the extent that such supply shocks reflect productivity shocks, these do not appear to be strongly correlated with the U.S. experience. This result appears to corroborate Bernanke's (2002a: n. 1) contention: "I don't know of any unambiguous example of a supply-side deflation...." The resulting asymmetry in aggregate supply shocks across countries does, however, suggest that productivity shocks are country-specific.

DEFLATION TODAY IN CHINA AND JAPAN

Our interest here is to illustrate potential links among monetary policy, asset prices, and output for China and Japan, two notable examples of countries that have suffered from persistent deflation in recent years. As discussed earlier, one way that asset price declines can exacerbate, or even initiate, a deflationary process is through wealth effects that reduce consumer spending. In the specific case of Japan, Miyao (2002) points to possible transmission of higher stock prices through consumption via a wealth effect and/or through real investment – including a credit channel effect involving collateral constraints of the type considered by Bordo and Jeanne in this volume. The recent Japanese case, therefore, not only offers an example of a modern-day deflation in a mature economy but also presents a case in which major asset price declines appear to have been a crucial element.[18]

China, like Japan, experienced deflation in the second half of the 1990s. In addition to sharing Japan's bad debt problems, the Chinese deflation was itself preceded by a major stock market decline in 1994 – albeit for a stock market considerably smaller, in relation to gross domestic product (GDP), than Japan's. Both the Chinese and Japanese deflations emerged after a period of severe monetary tightening. In Japan's case, the major monetary tightening seemed to coincide more with the decline in stock prices in 1990 than with the more recent deflation of consumer prices, however. In China the sharp tightening of monetary policy in 1994 coincides closely with the stock market decline but precedes the onset of deflation in goods prices. Continued disinflation after 1994 in China turned into outright deflation in consumer prices in 1998. Although the overall rate of consumer price decline has been quite mild, averaging around 1 percent in the first half of 2002, for example, other price indices slipped much more – with commodity prices declining at a near 2 percent rate and raw material prices falling at a near 5 percent rate over that same period (see Yuan 2002).

Although the 1990 collapse of Japanese asset prices was, in part, an inevitable correction to the extreme speculative run-up of the latter half of the 1980s, there is general agreement that the asset price decline was triggered by sharp monetary tightening – with the Bank of Japan raising the official discount rate from 2.5 percent to 6 percent between May 1989 and August 1990 (see Cargill, Hutchison, and Ito 2000: p. 20). And Japanese policy remained tight even after the bubble burst. Overall, the rate of money growth declined from an annual rate of 9.5 percent over the 1980s to just 1.1 percent between the first quarter of 1991 and the second quarter of 1994 (see Hetzel 1999:

---

[18] Share prices in other countries have also previously been found to be significant both in the monetary transmission mechanism (Lastrapes 1998) and as a determinant of long-run money demand (Choudhri 1996).

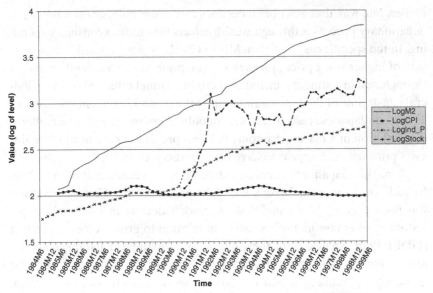

Figure 1.2. Money Supply, Goods, and Asset Price Levels in China, 1984:2–1999:4

p. 16). The Japanese experience seems, in fact, to have many parallels with that of the United States around the time of the Wall Street Crash of 1929. The Federal Reserve tightened in 1928 and maintained its contractionary stance in 1930 in spite of the calamitous decline in asset prices and evidence that the economy had moved into recession. A difference, however, is that it is less clear that there was an asset price bubble when U.S. monetary policy began to tighten (Cogley 1999) than is true of the Japanese case (Ito and Iwaisako 1996).

Overall trends in output, money, goods prices, and shares prices in China and Japan are laid out in Figures 1.2 and 1.3. In the case of China, Figure 1.2 shows the declining trend in goods prices in the latter half of the 1990s along with the 1994 stock market drop. The reduction in money growth in the second half of the 1990s is also evident and represented a response to the inflationary surge of 1993–1994 – during which the rate of growth of consumer prices peaked at 24.1 percent in 1994. Unlike the earlier brief tightening of monetary policy in response to the 1988–1989 inflation peak, in this case, reduced inflation rates evolved into actual deflation as the rate of money supply growth continued to decline. Broad money (M2) growth fell every year, dropping from 42.8 percent in 1993 to 14.9 percent in 1998, the first full

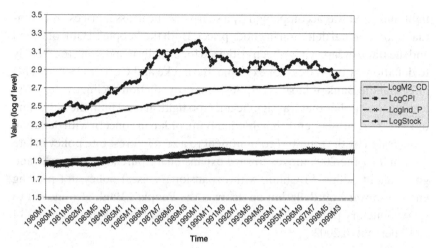

Figure 1.3. Money Supply, Goods, and Asset Price Levels in Japan, 1980:1–1999:12

year of deflation.[19] Along with the reduced rates of money supply growth, the rate of growth of real output, as measured by industrial production, is seen to flatten out after 1994 – suggesting that monetary tightening may also have hurt the real economy in China.

Meanwhile, the dramatic run-up in Japanese stock prices over the 1980s is evident in Figure 1.3 followed, of course, by the collapse that occurred at the end of the decade. The Nikkei 225 fell by more than 60 percent between December 1989 and August 1992 and ultimately lost more than 75 percent of its value, falling below the 10,000 level in 2001. The stock market decline was accompanied by a precipitous drop in land values – and a standout 90 percent drop in the price of golf club memberships. Although Japanese consumer prices continued to rise mildly until the mid-1990s, this is predated by the marked leveling off of the money supply around the time that the asset price bubble burst in late 1989. There is then little indication of any renewed acceleration in money supply growth through the 1990s, even as Japan slipped into full-fledged deflation in goods prices as well as asset prices.

Although the trends described remain no more than suggestive, it does seem clear that both China and Japan featured significant monetary

---

[19] Although even this reduced rate of money growth exceeded the rate of income growth in 1998, the rising appetite for real money balances in China greatly boosts the rate of monetary expansion consistent with price stability. There was a near quadrupling of the M2/GNP ratio between 1979 and 1997, for example (also see Burdekin 2000).

tightening that was accompanied by a sharp decline in asset prices and eventually some actual deflation in goods prices. Both the People's Bank of China and the Bank of Japan have been criticized for initially responding too weakly to deflationary pressures. For example, Bernanke and Gertler (1999: p. 114) infer that the Bank of Japan's responsiveness to inflation declined after 1990, leading to a "policy that was significantly too tight, at least until the beginning of 1996."[20] A subsequently heightened Bank of Japan concern with deflation is suggested by the renewed commitment to a zero interest rate policy in late 2001 and by the 2003 moves toward expansionary purchases of stocks and government bonds. In China, with expansionary fiscal policy not proving enough to ward off deflation on its own, the People's Bank also moved to relax monetary policy, raising the target rate of M2 money growth from 14 to 17 percent in 2002.[21]

OVERVIEW OF THE CONTRIBUTIONS TO *DEFLATION*

This opening chapter is followed by three others, which consider how economic agents have adjusted to deflation during different historical episodes and whether fears of deflation were justified. A case study of the bank runs and monetary contraction in the United States in the 1930s is followed by an analysis of the adjustment of expectations in the prewar British economy and, finally, by a contrast of wage setting and monetary policymaking during two different deflationary episodes in Sweden. The second part of the book contains two chapters offering both theoretical and empirical analyses of the links among monetary policy, goods price movements, and asset price movements. The theoretical modeling follows Kiyotaki and Moore's (1997) emphasis on the connection between asset prices and firms' collateral. International evidence is presented on the possible link between bank credit and housing prices as well as on the relationship between bank credit and share prices in the post-1985 period. It is also argued that monetary policy might have effectively offset asset price run-ups in the United States in the 1920s and in Japan in the 1980s if action had been taken early enough.

[20] Bernanke and Gertler's (1999) related argument that the Bank of Japan focused on asset price stability to the detriment of the overall price level during 1989–1997 may itself have a historical precedent in the nineteenth-century Confederate experience (Burdekin and Weidenmier 2003).

[21] See "China Still Troubled by Deflation in October" (2002).

The third part of the book has three chapters that offer comparative international perspectives on the impact of deflation under different monetary policy and exchange rate regimes. The first study looks at the extended period of deflation that occurred under the gold standard in the latter part of the nineteenth century. The focus here is on the experiences of Canada and the United States and on the potentially contrasting effects of "good deflation" associated with expansions in aggregate supply and "bad deflation" associated with contractions in aggregate demand. The second chapter examines the Italian deflation from 1927 to 1933 and compares the Italian experience to that of Britain and the United States. A further comparison is made with the Italian disinflationary programs of the late 1980s and 1990s and the role of the fixed exchange rate imposed under the European Monetary System. The overall conclusion of this work is that fixed exchange rates were not credible precommitment devices in either the prewar or the postwar episodes. The final chapter in this section compares the ongoing Japanese deflation with the experience of the 1930s. The more moderate consequences of deflation in Japan are ascribed to a more expansionary fiscal policy, a more stable banking and financial sector, and a more favorable external environment.

The book concludes with analysis of stock market reactions to deflation. The deflation in worldwide commodity prices in the late nineteenth century helped fuel financial innovation as traders produced new assets for investors searching for higher returns. The responses of the stock exchanges in London, New York, Paris, and Berlin are examined in detail. There is also a case study of stock price movements in Germany during deflation (interrupted by hyperinflation) in the Weimar era between the wars. Finally, the special role that may be played by gold at times of major asset price declines is examined in a comparative analysis of the 1929, 1987, and 2000 stock market crashes in the United States.

Part 1: Fears of Deflation and the Role of Monetary Policy

In "Deflation, Silent Runs, and Bank Holidays in the Great Contraction," Hugh Rockoff shows that there was substantial capital flight (or "silent runs") from rural areas to financial center banks during the Great Depression in the United States. This, combined with the more familiar attempts of depositors to convert their deposits into cash, put increasing pressures on the banking system. Silent runs and traditional bank runs reflected individual depositors' panic at the growing wave of bank closures. Meanwhile, the regional nature of the crisis, whereby deposits tended to be shifted out of the rural banks first, may have contributed to the Federal Reserve's failure to respond more effectively to the crisis. Although the Federal Reserve Bank of New York urged more aggressive action, other regional Federal Reserve Banks perhaps looked upon the proposed open market purchases as a "region-specific medicine, likely to re-ignite speculation on the stock market, but unlikely to pay real dividends elsewhere" (Rockoff, this volume).

In "Price Change, Financial Stability, and the British Economy, 1870–1939," Forrest Capie and Geoffrey Wood compare the relevance of Irving Fisher's "debt-deflation" theory to two British historical experiences: 1873–1896 and 1920–1939. Some aspects of the British case were similar and even parallel to those seen in the prewar U.S. economy, with which Fisher was primarily concerned. For example, there was a strong bull market in the late 1920s and then a collapse in the early 1930s. But there is little evidence that deflation transmitted adverse effects to the real economy through the channels suggested by Fisher's theory. The authors find that both interest rate and price series were quite predictable over the two deflationary episodes in Britain, seemingly leaving little room for unanticipated deflationary "shocks." There also seems to have been little disturbance to financial markets and, in contrast to the U.S. experience, no strong evidence of financial instability. This may help explain why, even during the Great Depression itself, relatively little concern about debt-deflation was expressed in countries other than the United States.

In "Deflation Dynamics in Sweden: Perceptions, Expectations, and Adjustment During the Deflations of 1921–1923 and 1931–1933," Klas Fregert and Lars Jonung examine how the attitudes of wage bargainers and of policy makers explain the outcomes of two different deflationary episodes in Sweden. The first of these episodes covers the resumption of the gold standard in Sweden after World War I, whereas the second involves Sweden's exit from the gold standard and switch to a policy of price level targeting. In both cases, nominal wages were reduced, thus apparently denying the existence of an absolute floor for wage adjustment. The adjustment, though, varied in speed and size across the two episodes. One feature of the chapter is the use of a comprehensive set of data on collective agreements to discuss the validity of some popular theories of wage stickiness. The authors also provide a rich body of evidence on the beliefs and expectations espoused by economists and policy makers over the course of these deflationary episodes. The importance of uncertainty is clearly demonstrated, and the authors assess to what extent the deflations were unanticipated by contemporary observers and market participants.

Part 2: Deflation and Asset Prices

In "Boom–Busts in Asset Prices, Economic Instability, and Monetary Policy," Michael Bordo and Olivier Jeanne provide a theoretical perspective on whether it is appropriate for monetary authorities to pay attention to the movements of asset prices in charting their policy. Economists have debated these issues for years, and two views predominate: the orthodox view, that asset prices are determined by fundamentals and are related in a predictable manner to the macro variables (prices and aggregate output) on which monetary policy should focus, and the revisionist view, that asset market reversals (whether determined by fundamentals or by possible bubbles) can have very serious effects on the real economy and hence need to be clearly addressed by policy makers. Whereas Bernanke and Gertler (1999) make the orthodox case that a central bank dedicated to a policy of flexible inflation targeting should pay little attention to asset price movements, their approach severely limits the extent to which plausible ranges of asset price movements can affect the real economy. Bordo and Jeanne instead develop a simple model that can encompass potentially large macro effects from plausible asset price shocks. It is based in a nonlinear way on the connection between asset prices and firms' collateral posited by Kiyotaki and Moore (1997). The authors believe that this model captures an important connection between asset markets and the real economy that may be relevant for the setting of monetary policy and understanding the great asset price debacles of the past.

In "Deflation, Credit, and Asset Prices," Charles Goodhart and Boris Hofmann emphasize that deflationary episodes, such as the Great Depression in the 1930s and the recent Japanese deflation, have often been preceded by asset price collapses. One rationale for a linkage between asset prices and goods prices is provided by the credit view, whereby borrowing by firms and households may be constrained because of asymmetric information in credit markets, giving rise to adverse selection and moral hazard problems. A fall in asset prices lowers the borrowing capacity of firms and households by reducing the value of collateral. The resulting credit crunch reduces the demand for goods and services and may thus lead to lower price inflation and even deflation. At the same time, the credit crunch reduces the demand for assets, pushing asset prices even further down, so that a self-reinforcing process can evolve. The authors identify a consistent relationship between bank credit and house prices since the mid-1980s for 10 of the 12 countries they examine. Although there is less widespread evidence of a link between bank credit and share prices, such a relationship is found for four countries, including Japan and the United States. The potential role for monetary policy in reacting to asset prices is also addressed. Using U.S. data from 1925 to 1934 and Japanese data from 1985 to 2001, the authors conclude that, in each case, monetary policy makers could have been successful in heading off asset price bubbles if they had tightened early enough – say in 1927 and 1987–1988, respectively.

Part 3: International Perspectives on Deflation

In "Is Deflation Depressing? Evidence from the Classical Gold Standard," Michael Bordo and Angela Redish focus on the deflations experienced during the heyday of the classical gold standard prior to World War I. Although most analyses of the Great Depression have focused on the role played by demand shocks, historical data suggest that output may have been driven more by supply shocks in the United States and Canada over the 1870–1913 period. Slower economic growth in each country does not yield strong evidence of a causal relationship between falling prices and falling output. Unlike the U.S. case, Canada's experience does not reveal persistent positive effects on output arising from money supply shocks, however. The authors suggest that this contrast with the neutrality of money supply shocks in the United States may reflect the different structure of the banking system in the two countries. Canadian banks held more loans in their portfolios than was true of U.S. banks, for example, perhaps making the credit channel for the transmission of monetary policy more important in Canada. Overall, the authors reject any simple demarcation between "good" and "bad" deflations and argue that prices fell as the combined result of negative money supply shocks *and* positive supply shocks.

In "The Strong Lira Policy and Deflation in Italy's Interwar Period," Michele Fratianni and Franco Spinelli focus on the policy implications in Italy from 1927 to 1933. This period is coincident to a large extent with the Great Deflation of the 1930s. The authors' analysis underscores the peculiarities of the Italian Great Deflation in relation to deflations elsewhere. The chapter, however, also notes the common elements between Italian deflation and deflation abroad, particularly the U.S. experience over the same period. The authors undertake an empirical analysis of the nominal and real exchange rate appreciations of 1927 and 1931–1933, the second of these episodes following the exit of Britain and the United States from the gold standard. The authors also compare the Italian experience in the 1930s to the disinflationary program of the late 1980s and 1990s. A main lesson of the chapter is that fixed exchange rates, whether in the days of the gold standard or after, may well not be a credible precommitment device for deflation or disinflation.

In "Deflation and Stagnation in Japan: Collapse of the Monetary Transmission Mechanism and Echo from the 1930s," Michael Hutchison addresses Japan's economic performance in the post-bubble era. In addition to problems posed by the rising debt burden, the author provides empirical evidence that asset price declines have been a major factor in the continued slump in Japan's economy. Monetary policy, meanwhile, has been handicapped by not only the zero floor on nominal interest rates but also by a downward shift in the money multiplier and a weakened monetary transmission mechanism in the latter half of the 1990s. For these reasons, even quite rapid growth in the monetary base may still not produce much of an increase in the broad money supply – and further money supply increases become less effective in boosting real output over the deflation period. Japan's economic situation remains much better than the 1930s experience with deflation, however, thanks in part to more stimulative fiscal policies, less severe banking and financial problems, and a more benign external environment.

Part 4: Stock Market Adjustments to Deflation

In "Deflation, the Financial Crisis of the 1890s, and Stock Exchange Responses in London, New York, Paris, and Berlin," Lance Davis, Larry Neal, and Eugene White examine the period starting with the Baring crisis of 1890 in London and ending with the passage of the Gold Standard Act of 1900 in the United States. The stock exchanges that created the first global market in financial capital responded in different ways to continued deflation and to a series of financial crises. Responses varied according to differences in the political and legal environments and the persistence of the exchanges' microstructures. The organizational reforms or regulation by government in each of the major exchanges of the world – London, New York, Paris, and Berlin – fundamentally changed the operations of the global market of the time. As interest yields fell on high-quality bonds, whether government gilts in London and Paris or railroad bonds in New York and Berlin, traders produced new assets for investors who were searching for higher returns. From brewery and mining stocks in London to industrial securities in New York, specialized securities appeared in each exchange. Financial crises often, but not always, fell most heavily on the newest, most speculative securities. Government inquiries that followed resulted in different reforms for each exchange.

In "The Stock Market and the Business Cycle in Periods of Deflation, (Hyper-) Inflation, and Political Turmoil: Germany, 1913–1926," Martin Bohl and Pierre Siklos show that, quite unlike the pre–World War I experience, the period from 1913 to 1926 in Germany was marked by enormous political instability, leading up to the collapse of the Weimar regime and Hitler's accession to power in 1933. This politically turbulent period offers a unique opportunity to investigate stock market dynamics under extreme conditions. As was the case elsewhere in the world, there were powerful deflationary tendencies. The authors conclude that stock prices are driven by the expected present value of dividends as fundamentals, in spite of ongoing political turbulence, but the underlying relationships might differ as between inflation and deflation in goods and equity prices. The empirical evidence is accompanied by an analysis of the institutional factors that were important for the stock market behavior between 1913 and 1926. DeLong and Becht (1992) previously argued that the role of the German big banks in the pre–World War I stock market might be the cause of the low volatility of stock prices before 1914 in Germany. But Bohl and Siklos suggest that institutional factors must also have been relevant as the behavior of goods prices cannot explain asset prices nor economic performance adequately during the 1913–1926 period in Germany.

In "Deflationary Pressures and the Role of Gold Stocks: 1929, 1987, and Today," Richard Burdekin and Marc Weidenmier point out that, although there is extensive literature on the role played by the international gold standard in contributing to the Wall Street Crash of October 1929 and the Great Depression, much less attention has been paid to the performance of gold mining shares at the time of the crash. Gold prices and share prices of gold mining companies served as a hedge against assist price declines during the 1930s and have risen sharply after the market decline that set in during 2000. Although the 1987 experience shows that gold stocks do not consistently move opposite to broad market averages, significant positive excess returns have been generated under the more extreme and prolonged financial difficulties after 1929 and 2000. Moreover, these gains have been secured at times when fears of deflation were almost certainly greater than the risks of inflation. Declines in the external value of the dollar during the 1930s and after 2000 imply that gold stocks served not only as a hedge against domestic asset prices but also against a loss of purchasing power abroad.

PART ONE

FEARS OF DEFLATION AND THE ROLE
OF MONETARY POLICY

2 Deflation, Silent Runs, and Bank Holidays in the Great Contraction

Hugh Rockoff

SEPARATE REGIONS WITH SEPARATE BANKING SYSTEMS[1]

The Great Contraction of 1929 to 1939, as Friedman and Schwartz (1963) designated it, must surely be the most carefully studied episode in American monetary history. Their work, and that of Kindleberger (1973), Temin (1976, 1989), Eichengreen (1992a), and many other scholars focusing on particular aspects of the contraction, has done much to clarify the causes and consequences of the collapse, and to clarify the policy mistakes made by the Federal Reserve System. Nevertheless, the flood of books and papers on monetary problems during the Depression shows no signs of abating, suggesting that we have not yet reached the point where we believe that existing explanations are entirely sufficient. Moreover, as this is written, the renewed threat of falling prices makes it more important than ever to examine how financial system performance may be affected by deflationary pressures.

Important advances have been made in assessing contagion effects, as opposed to the role of fundamentals, in causing the collapse of a banking system. In this chapter, I will argue that the banking crises of the early 1930s were similar to the "twin crises" – banking and balance of payments crises – that have occurred in developing countries in recent years. The rural regions of the United States were like the developing countries today: dependent on the export of a few commodities in which they had a comparative advantage and with independent and relatively weak banking systems. Declining demand and export prices after 1929 weakened the banking systems in rural regions because they raised doubts about the ability of bank borrowers to repay their loans and led to balance of payments deficits. Because the banks

---

[1] Michael Bordo, Richard Burdekin, Kerry Odell, Pierre Siklos, and Eugene White graciously provided comments on a previous draft. They are not to blame for the mistakes that remain.

31

in rural regions were linked by fixed exchange rates to separate banking systems in more developed regions, there was a natural desire, moreover, on the part of people who had deposits in rural banks to move their funds to stronger banks in the financial centers, a capital flight. The interregional movement of funds further weakened the banking system in the regions experiencing the "external" drain. Eventually, as bank failure rates rose, runs developed. In the end, governments intervened by imposing restrictions on withdrawals.[2]

To be sure, the analogy between the twin crises in developing countries and the banking crises of the 1930s can be taken only so far. The crises in developing regions today have involved elements, such as short-term capital flows and currency mismatches, that we do not find among regions of the United States in the 1930s. Most developing countries, moreover, can devalue their currencies relative to others. This option was not open to regions within the United States. Minnesota dollars were not going to be reduced to .75 in New York dollars. Nevertheless, the analogy with the twin crises of recent years, helps provide a vocabulary for understanding the banking crises in the early 1930s.

This chapter, examines the banking crises from a regional perspective. It attempts to demonstrate that there were important forces at work that have been somewhat neglected because they do not show up clearly when the problem is viewed from a purely macroeconomic or purely microeconomic perspective.[3]

Although regional aspects of the Depression have been neglected in recent discussions of the monetary side of the contraction, with the important exception of Wicker (1996), regional differences were important to people at the time for a number of good reasons. (1) During the 1930s, there were important cultural barriers to the mobility of labor. African Americans faced enormous racial discrimination wherever they went, and even white southerners were branded as lazy and inferior workers. As Wright (1996) has shown, although the labor markets of Birmingham, England, and Pittsburgh, Pennsylvania, were integrated, those of Birmingham, Alabama, and Pittsburgh, Pennsylvania, were not. (2) Banks were not permitted to branch

---

[2] There is a large literature on the "twin crises." Some papers that started me thinking about the analogy between the regional crises in the United States in the 1930s and more recent crises were Kaminsky and Reinhart (1998), Miller (1998), and Kaminsky and Reinhart (1999).

[3] Scholars addressing real as opposed to monetary aspects of the Depression, however, have frequently adopted a regional perspective: Wallis (1987), Rosenbloom and Sundstrom (1997), and Heim (1998).

across state lines and often were prohibited from branching within states. Many banks in rural areas, therefore, had most of their resources tied up in assets that depended on the price of a single agricultural product. (3) Federal programs that transfer income from regions that are doing well to regions that are not, such as agricultural price support programs, did not exist on a modern scale when the Depression began. (4) Monetary policy was influenced strongly by the individual Governors of the Federal Reserve Banks. By design, the District Banks represented the interests of separate regions and were given far more power to adopt independent policy actions than is the case today. This was changing. Indeed, soon after the Federal Reserve was established, it was recognized that open market purchases had to be co-ordinated by a systemwide committee because the interests of a particular district (to avoid the drain of reserves to central money markets produced by a purchase of securities) might differ from the interests of the system as a whole. But the tendency of governors from predominantly rural districts to see a conflict between what was good for their district and what was good for the eastern money markets persisted.

The experience of the United States during the early 1930s is unlikely to be repeated in detail. Nevertheless, it does throw into sharp relief some of the problems that face a monetary authority that must find the right path for a group of diverse regions when things go bad. Certain rural regions of the United States were hit especially hard by the downturn of 1929 because the prices of food, fibers, and minerals fell especially rapidly. The banking systems in those regions experienced a silent, but nonetheless destructive, loss of deposits because their rudimentary banking systems were linked by a common currency to powerful financial centers. Had policy makers been alert to the signs of interregional capital flight, they might have intervened successfully. Instead, the banking crisis was allowed to fester. Hopefully, this chapter will be of some relevance to the current debate over whether to extend existing monetary unions and possibly to future debates about how to conduct monetary policy within a monetary union, especially when the spectre of deflation haunts some members but not others.

THE ROLE OF DEFLATION

The cyclical downturn that began in late 1929 (August, according to the National Bureau of Economic Research [NBER] chronology) ushered in a strong downward trend in prices and income: The Net National Product

Table 2.1. *Real prices of agricultural commodities and real farm and mineral income, 1925–1932*

	Price of wheat per bushel	Price of cotton per pound	Price of raw corn per bushel	Price of beef steers per pound	Net income of farm operators from farming per farm	Total value of mineral products
1925	100	100	100	100	100	100
1926	89	74	105	93	88	110
1927	84	77	124	114	87	100
1928	80	86	122	139	90	95
1929	72	82	114	134	92	104
1930	57	61	91	115	67	88
1931	44	44	55	96	59	65
1932	40	37	63	90	40	57

Note: The NNP deflator was used to deflate all prices and farm and mineral incomes.
Sources: U.S. Bureau of the Census (1975): series E123 (wheat), E126 (cotton), K504 (corn), K585 (beef), K260 (farm income), and Friedman and Schwartz (1983: table 4.8, column 4, p. 124) (NNP deflator).

(NNP) deflator fell 4.6 percent between 1929 and 1930, and nominal NNP fell 16.1.[4] The deflation, of course, was far from uniform. The prices of some of the major agricultural products dropped steeply in real terms.[5] This is shown in Table 2.1, which reports the real prices of some of the important agricultural products, real net farm income, and real value of mineral products, starting in 1925 when the real prices of a number of these crops and real net farm income reached their postwar peaks. The real price of wheat experienced the most dramatic decline. It fell steadily year after year until, by 1932, it had lost 60 percent of its 1925 value. The other series showed a rebound in the late 1920s. So real net farm income reached another peak in 1929, although at a lower level than in 1925. Between 1929 and 1930, however, all of the key farm prices dropped in real terms, and real net farm income declined about 29 percent. Between 1929 and 1932, real farm income declined about 60 percent. Such a decline was bound to have enormous consequences for regions that were highly specialized in the production of basic agricultural products and for banks in those regions because it raised serious questions about the ability of farmers to service their debts.

[4] The data are from Friedman and Schwartz (1982: p. 124).
[5] Bank failure rates were high in rural regions in the 1920s, partly as a result of agricultural distress (Alston, Grove, and Wheelock 1994; Wheelock 1992).

The impact of these movements in real prices can be seen in the regional terms of trade shown in Table 2.2. The West North Central division, a wheat-growing region, and the West South Central, division, a cotton-growing region, were hard hit. Perhaps somewhat more surprising are the substantial declines in the terms of trade of the Pacific and Mountain regions. The fall in mineral prices may be the reason. The price of silver fell from $.53 per fine ounce in 1929 to $.28 in 1932, a fall of 64 percent in nominal terms and 38 percent in real terms (using the gross national product [GNP] deflator).[6] The price of lead fell from about $.068 per pound in 1929 to $.032 in 1932, a fall of 68 percent in nominal terms and 53 percent in real terms. The price of copper fell from $.184 per pound in 1929 to $.058 in 1932, a staggering fall of 68 percent in nominal terms and 53 percent in real terms. There are, however, some surprises in the table. The South Atlantic region, for example, actually experienced an improvement in its terms of trade.

What caused the relative price shocks of the early 1930s? A boom-and-bust cycle associated with World War I is one candidate. The war added greatly to the demand for these basic commodities while destroying productive capacity in Europe. Farmers and businessmen in neutral countries, such as the United States, went into debt to expand capacity. Later demand declined to more normal levels, and supply expanded as European producers came back on line. The result was a decline in commodity prices that became a rout in the early 1930s. Barry Eichengreen's (2002) argument that the monetary shock was worldwide provides a second candidate: If the world shock, was greater initially than the U.S. shock, it would explain why the prices of internationally traded goods fell faster and farther than the prices of domestically traded goods. But to explain the origins of these relative price shocks in adequate detail would take us far afield. Kindleberger (1973: p. 83–107) provides a detailed commodity-by-commodity account going back to World War I. For our purpose, it is sufficient to take these shocks as given.

How did the deterioration in the terms of trade and the contraction in income affect the stability of the banking system? Table 2.3 summarizes

---

[6] Roosevelt's Silver Purchase Program reversed the plunge in silver prices. This Program, which began in December 1933 and was accelerated under the Silver Purchase Act of June 1934, was intended to raise the price of silver, a boon to western silver-producing states, and to increase the stock of money through Treasury purchases of silver. As a result, the price of silver rose to a temporary peak of $.64 per fine oz. in 1935. The price then slumped once more, although it remained above the depths of 1930–1932 in both nominal and real terms. It has been claimed that the purchase program had a deleterious effect on China. (Friedman and Schwartz 1963: p. 483–90; Brandt and Sargent 1989; Friedman 1992; Rawski 1993).

Table 2.2. *Terms of trade by census divisions of the United States, 1925–1932 (1925 = 100)*

	New England	Middle Atlantic	East north central	West north central	South Atlantic	East south central	West south central	Mountain	Pacific
1925	100	100	100	100	100	100	100	100	100
1926	96	97	100	105	96	94	102	102	105
1927	98	97	105	106	101	99	89	102	96
1928	99	94	105	112	101	102	89	104	90
1929	98	95	110	109	96	98	87	107	91
1930	99	94	117	106	102	97	81	95	91
1931	103	96	136	98	103	93	61	82	78
1932	95	99	148	86	125	86	73	74	86
1933	105	103	136	84	115	94	65	79	86

Note: The regions are defined as follows. **New England:** Maine, New Hampshire, Vermont, Massachusetts, Rhode Island, and Connecticut. **Middle Atlantic:** New York, New Jersey, and Pennsylvania. **East North Central:** Ohio, Indiana, Illinois, Michigan, and Wisconsin. **West North Central:** Minnesota, Iowa, Missouri, North Dakota, South Dakota, Nebraska, and Kansas. **South Atlantic:** Delaware, Maryland, District of Columbia, Virginia, West Virginia, North Carolina, South Carolina, Georgia, and Florida. **East South Central:** Kentucky, Tennessee, Alabama, and Mississippi. **West South Central:** Arkansas, Louisiana, Oklahoma, and Texas. **Mountain:** Montana, Idaho, Wyoming, Colorado, New Mexico, Arizona, Utah, and Nevada. **Pacific:** Washington, Oregon, and California.
Source: Waite (1942).

Table 2.3. *Suspended deposits, terms of trade, and personal income by region,*
1930–1933

	Suspended deposits (as a percentage of 1929 deposits)	Terms of trade (percentage change from 1929)	Total personal income (percentage change from 1929)
New England	6.00%	6.94%	−48.76%
Middle Atlantic	5.67	8.31	−55.61
East North Central	25.17	21.76	−73.33
West North Central	16.97	−26.72	−70.37
South Atlantic	20.91	17.98	−44.97
East South Central	19.89	−4.04	−63.34
West South Central	17.04	−29.78	−61.33
Mountain	11.65	−30.01	−60.21
Pacific	4.87	−5.46	−54.69
Correlation	—	0.15	−0.50

Note: See Table 2.2 for the regions.
Sources: Suspended Deposits: U.S. Board of Governors (1943: p. 25–33, 285). Export Prices: Waite (1942: table 10, p. 30). Personal Income: Schwartz and Graham (1956). Correlation shown is with suspended deposits.

suspended deposits, terms of trade, and personal income by region. The first column of data shows the cumulated amount of suspended bank deposits as a percentage of 1929 deposits. In other words, the figure for New England shows total suspended deposits from 1930 through 1933 as a percentage of total deposits in all commercial banks in the region in 1929. This column illustrates the wide regional differences in the experience of the crisis. Evidently, the regions containing the Eastern financial centers (New England and Middle Atlantic) along with the Pacific Coast suffered the least damage.

The second column of data shows the percentage change in the terms of trade of each region – "the prices of goods sold by census divisions to other parts of the United States" divided by "the prices of goods bought by census divisions from other parts of the United States" – based on Warren Waite's (1942) estimates. This column shows that movements in interregional terms of trade were dramatic, but not always in the same direction as suspended deposits.[7] In fact, the simple correlation between changes in the terms of trade and the amount of suspended deposits, shown in the last row of the column, goes the "wrong" way.[8]

[7] Paul Rhode brought this data to my attention.
[8] Calomiris and Mason (2000: p. 24), using their rich microeconomic data set, found mixed results from their agricultural variables. For example, monthly agricultural price change was significant in some, but not all regressions explain bank survival rates. A greater presence of small farms had a negative effect on bank survival, but, in their words, the effect was not "highly significant or robust."

The change in total personal income, shown in column 3, goes directly to the question of how much income borrowers had with which to repay loans. This variable is correlated in the right direction with the amount of suspended deposits. The correlation, however, is far from perfect. The simple correlation between suspended deposits and personal income change, $-.50$, is not statistically significant in such a small sample. Over all four years, for example, the South Atlantic region experienced the smallest fall in personal income, "only" 44.97 percent, but it experienced the second highest level of bank suspensions, 20.91 percent. The institutional advantage of containing the large money center banks evidently could offset, in some measure, the disadvantage of a large decline in personal income.

There were precedents for the deflation of the early 1930s. Prices and real incomes, including farm prices and real incomes, fell dramatically in the 1890s and after World War I. The deflation of the 1890s was associated with banking crises, particularly the crisis of 1893. The depression associated with the deflation and banking crises of the 1890s was severe in terms of output and employment, although as Davis et al. (this volume) point out, the deflation and banking crises may have produced reforms in the financial system that set the stage for more rapid economic growth. The post–World War I deflation, on the other hand, did not produce anything like the crack-ups in the 1890s and early 1930s. One difference may be that rural regions were coming off of a long period of prosperity, so the rural banking problems and capital flight observed in the early 1930s did not emerge following World War I.

SILENT RUNS AND NOISY RUNS

There has been a tendency in the literature to focus on what might be called "noisy runs." Depositors literally run down to the bank, stand in line with their scared fellow depositors, and withdraw cash, perhaps forcing the bank to close its doors. Equally damaging to banks, and to the economy in a particular region, was a "silent run." Depositors simply write checks on a bank they consider weak and deposit them in another bank they consider stronger. Noisy runs lead naturally to a decline in the deposit currency ratio. This is one reason why Friedman and Schwartz, and subsequent authors, tended to focus on the deposit currency ratio as an indicator of distrust of the banking system.[9] A silent run, by way of contrast, need not produce any

---

[9]   The deposit currency ratio is also, of course, a determinant of the stock of money, which
      Friedman and Schwartz consider the key variable.

change in the aggregate deposit-currency ratio. As I will try to show, silent runs of substantial magnitude seem to have preceded the noisy runs of the early 1930s. Silent runs are familiar from more recent banking crises, such as the savings and loan crisis, but their role in the Great Contraction has been neglected compared with the attention paid to noisy runs.

A silent run could be intraregional (the transfer of deposits from a small local bank to a bigger bank in a nearby city) or interregional (the transfer of deposits from a small bank in the interior of the country to a large bank in the Eastern financial centers). Both drains create a liquidity problem for the bank losing deposits, and both types of runs were important during the contraction. I will focus on the interregional runs, however. First, interregional runs probably created more economic distress in the region losing funds. Borrowers, for example, may have been able to follow depositors when the run was intraregional, but not when it was interregional. Second, monetary policy during the contraction was controlled by the Governors of the Federal Reserve banks. Finally, focusing on the interregional runs may provide some useful examples for current debates about dollarization and monetary unions.

There has been a good deal of attention paid in the literature to whether bank runs were sometimes the result of a "contagion of fear," that is, a panic, or whether they always resulted from rational concerns about the solvency of banks. The latest research by Calomiris and Mason (1997, 2000), based on a large microeconomic sample of banks, suggests that a contagion of fear may not have been very prominent – that the weakest banks experienced the most intense runs. A silent interregional run, almost by definition, is up to a point at least, a measured and rational response to concerns about the solvency of the banking system and, therefore, also inconsistent with a contagion of fear. It could be that fundamentals were misjudged, although given the subsequent course of events, this would be a hard position to defend. It could also be that the people making the decision to move deposits were taking their cues from other people they regarded as informed and prudent, rather than looking themselves at fundamentals. Still, a run based on these considerations would be better described as a "demonstration effect," than as a contagion of fear.

At times, the term panic is used to refer not so much to the behavior of individuals as to the behavior of the group. One can imagine events in which the behavior of each individual separately is rational, even though the behavior of the group as a whole is self-destructive. Someone yells fire in a crowded auditorium. Each individual separately takes the rational action of running straight for the exit. No one is running around in a random fashion. But the aggregate effect is to create a dangerous congestion at the exit. If people were disciplined and filed out in order, more lives could be saved. Perhaps this definition of a panic applies to the runs of the early 1930s. The decision to remove deposits from rural areas in the face of a sharp downturn in real agricultural prices and incomes may have been prudent from the point of view of each depositor taken separately, but the aggregate effect was to undermine the banking system in those regions.

To get a sense of the magnitude of silent interregional runs, we can turn to the Gold Settlement Fund. The Fund (its name was changed to the Interdistrict Settlement Fund after the United States went off the gold standard) was the set of accounts that recorded the flow of funds among Federal Reserve districts. If a check was drawn on a bank in San Francisco and deposited in New York, the Gold Settlement Account would record the increase in the assets of the Federal Reserve Bank of New York and the decrease in the assets of the Federal Reserve Bank of San Francisco. The accounts also showed, on separate lines, the effects of federal government transfers and external gold flows.

The accounts of the Gold Settlement Fund do not provide a complete record of interdistrict movements of funds because some interregional transactions might have been completed by shipping gold or cleared through private clearing arrangements. Although the Federal Reserve had hoped that its clearing facilities would quickly supplant private clearinghouses and correspondent relationships, private arrangements remained important in the 1920s and 1930s. In 1929, for example, clearings through private clearinghouses were nearly double clearings through the Federal Reserve System (White 1983: pp. 108–10). Many of the private clearings through clearinghouses, however, must have involved local transactions. In the long run, moreover, transactions that produced sustained increases or decreases in correspondent balances would probably give rise, as Hartland-Thunberg (1949: p. 396) contended, to clearings through the Gold Settlement Fund. So it is safe to assume that the Fund provides a clear picture of the direction that private funds were moving, at least for the period we are examining. It should also be kept in mind that changes in the Gold Settlement Fund do not correspond directly to changes in bank reserves because other variables, such as bank borrowing from the Federal Reserve, will affect bank reserves.

Figure 2.1 shows a summary measure of the extent of interregional gold flows from 1926 to 1937: the sum of all regional gold outflows (equal to the

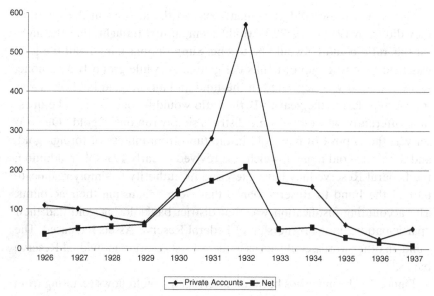

Figure 2.1. Interregional Gold Flows, 1926–1937 (as a Percentage of Total Gold Held by the Gold Settlement Fund)

sum of gold inflows from regions gaining gold) divided by the average of amount of gold in the Gold Settlement Fund. For example, if Minnesota and other rural districts lost $10 in gold (while New York and other eastern districts gained $10) and if there was, on average, $100 in the gold settlement fund, the figure plotted would be 10 percent. In other words, 10 percent of the gold stock had moved from one region to another during the year.

It is clear from the figure that there were extraordinary interregional movements of gold during the Great Contraction. There was little change in the denominator during the early years of the Depression, so the spike is largely due to interregional gold flows. The picture in the post-1934 figure is complicated by the influx of European gold. The low level of the ratio in these years compared with those immediately preceding reflects an increase in the denominator.[10]

[10] We see some large private flows in the 1920–1921 recession if we extend the figure back to the early 1920s. These flows, however, appear to be a winding down of flows produced by the war. The net figures, moreover, show distinctly smaller interregional movements of gold, relative to the existing stock, than in the early 1930s. The form of the accounts was changed, however, in 1926. I have not found a discussion of the pre-1926 accounts as thorough and authoritative as Hartland-Thunberg's (1949) discussion of the post-1926 accounts. So my reading of the early accounts is tentative.

How could these gold movements exceed the amount in the Fund, as they did from 1930 to 1932? It would seem, at first thought, that the highest this ratio could go would be to one. Suppose that initially all the gold was held by one group of banks designated A, while group B held none. If no new gold was deposited in the fund and all the gold held by A was transferred during the year to B, the ratio would be one. To put the question differently, why didn't some districts simply run out of gold? One offset was the deposit of new gold in the fund from inflows of foreign gold, and domestic gold mining, which was revived in early 1930s.[11] In addition, the Federal Reserve may have exercised its authority to simply reallocate part of the Fund to Reserve banks that were exhausting their accounts. The accounting justification was that district banks losing gold had their "participation" in the ownership of Federal Reserve Assets increased. The Fund, in other words, could act as lender of last resort to individual Reserve banks.[12]

Figure 2.1 distinguishes between interregional gold flows resulting from private transactions and net gold flows, the sum of private and Federal government transactions. Clearly, net gold flows were always less than private gold flows. This means that, in general, gold flows produced by Federal government transactions tended to offset private gold flows and preserve the internal balance of payments. I had expected to find this result only during the later years of the Depression. New Deal programs, such as agricultural price supports that produced transfers to rural areas, became important after 1933. The data show, however, that interregional Federal transfers helped to preserve the internal monetary union, even in the period 1930 to 1932; Federal transfers were simply insufficient to offset the other forces undermining the banking system.[13]

What was causing these interregional gold flows? I believe that, in large part, they reflected the transfer of funds from banks in the interior to banks in the traditional financial centers, most importantly New York, but also Boston and Philadelphia, by deposit holders seeking greater safety for their funds. In some cases, the flow might have been the result of someone writing

[11] Gold mining was an exception to the general trend in mining because the government fixed the nominal price. Thus, the real price of gold rose while the real price of other minerals fell.

[12] The Settlement Fund accounts do not distinguish among the sources of additional gold. It is known that the Federal Reserve changed participations regularly to maintain district gold balances.

[13] This point was noted by Fels (1950), and Hartland (1950a, 1950b).

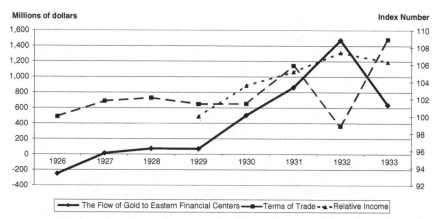

Figure 2.2. The Flow of Gold to Eastern Financial Centers on Private Accounts, 1926–1933

a check on a bank in one region and depositing it in a bank in another region. In other cases, the flow might have been the result of someone writing a check to purchase a security owned in another region. In either case, the transfers could be termed a silent run, or to use a term more familiar from discussions of international crises, a capital flight.

Some additional evidence is provided in Figure 2.2, which shows the flow of gold into the Eastern financial centers (the all-important New York District, Boston, and Philadelphia) from 1926 to 1933. Figure 2.2 places the influx of funds in 1930, 1931, and 1932 in dramatic relief. Some inflow might have been expected because of changes in the terms of trade. If rural regions had to pay only slightly less for their imports, but got substantially less for their exports, they would, other things equal, run a balance of payments deficit. Figure 2.2, therefore, shows the terms of trade between the Eastern financial centers and the rest of the country as an index, to be read against the right-hand axis, with 1926 = 100.[14] The Eastern terms of trade did improve somewhat during 1930 and 1931, and that might account for some of the inflow, although there was a sharp drop in 1932, while gold continued to flow in. Figure 2.2 also shows total personal income in the Eastern financial centers relative to total personal income in the remainder of the country,

---

[14] Trade weighted terms of trade by census region were computed by Waite (1942). I calculated the terms of trade for the Eastern financial districts by weighting his indexes for New England and the Middle Atlantic states by their shares in regional personal income. I have not found the explanation for the sharp drop in the terms of trade in 1932.

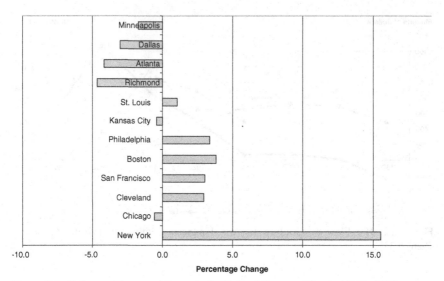

Figure 2.3. Gains and Losses of Deposits by Federal Reserve District, 1929–1930

beginning in 1929 when the figures become available.[15] This is also an index (1929 = 100) to be read against the right-hand side. Eastern incomes, it turns out, rose steadily relative to those in the rest of the country during 1930–1932. Other things equal, the relative strength of income in the East would have drained funds from the East because Eastern exports would have fallen more than imports. This factor was working in opposition to the dominant flows and cannot explain them.

The effect of these movements, along with other factors such as the lending by Federal Reserve district banks to their members, can be seen in Figure 2.3, which shows the growth of deposits by district between June 1929 and June 1930.[16] The dates here are important. The Gold Settlement Fund data show end-of-year figures, and things were to deteriorate substantially between June and December 1930. Evidently, the experience varied dramatically from district to district during the first year of the contraction.[17] Some had experienced substantial contraction; others had experienced substantial

---

[15] The per capita income figures by state are widely available. I created federal district estimates simply by adding the personal incomes of each state in the district. Where only a part of a state was included in a district, I had to guesstimate the fraction of the state's economic activity that occurred in a particular district. Overall, the estimates do not appear sensitive to these guesses.

[16] A chart of reserve growth is similar.

[17] More precisely, the first 10 months of the contraction. The NBER business cycle peak occurred in August 1929.

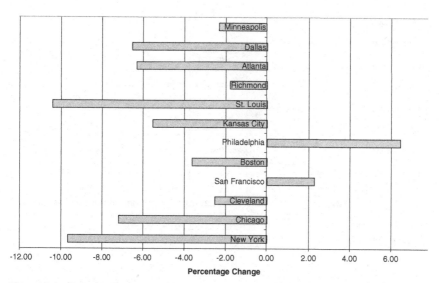

Figure 2.4. Gains and Losses of Deposits by Federal Reserve District, 1930–1931

growth. New York, in particular, had experienced a 15 percent gain in deposits. The districts have been arranged by total 1929 deposits from smallest (Minneapolis) to largest (New York). The chart illustrates the tendency of deposits to move from the smaller, and therefore weaker, banking systems to larger, and therefore stronger, systems.

Figure 2.4 shows the change in deposits the following year, from June 1930 to June 1931, by region. The picture was very different. What had been a retreat in some regions and an advance in others had become a general rout. Only San Francisco and Philadelphia were able to keep their heads above water. In most cases, the decline in deposits was due to both a decrease in reserves and a fall in the deposit-currency ratio. New York, however, was an exception. It experienced a small increase in reserves.

We can also see the redistribution of funds if we look at the balance sheets of the four largest New York national banks – First, National City, Chase, and Public. End-of-year values for deposits, loans, and reserves of the Big Four are shown in Figure 2.5. All three categories were higher at the end of 1930 than at the end of 1929. The gains started in the late 1920s and were probably produced during that period by the boom in the stock market rather than banking difficulties in the interior. This may mean that there was an organic link between the stock market boom and the deterioration of the condition of the banks in the interior.

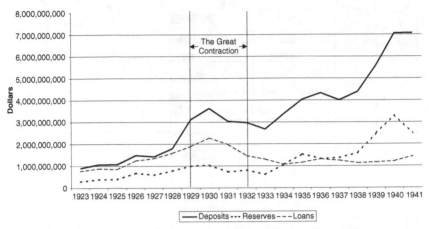

Figure 2.5. The Big-Four New York Banks

Who was moving their funds? It seems unlikely that individual depositors contributed very much to the interregional capital flight of the early 1930s by directly moving funds from one bank to another. Individuals might move their funds to a larger bank in the same city, divide their funds among several banks, purchase financial assets, or withdraw cash. They were unlikely, one would think, to move their funds to a bank in another district. It seems more likely that when funds were moved directly to a bank in a different district, they were in the main business or bank funds. It would be sensible for the chief financial officer of a nationwide corporation to move the working funds at a small local bank to a larger bank in a financial center, especially if that is where the corporate headquarters were located. It is possible that some of the funds in flight were bank funds. A bank that had traditionally divided the funds it held in other banks between regional centers and the Eastern financial centers might have shifted more of its funds to the latter as local conditions worsened.

Individuals would be involved, however, when the interregional transfer resulted from the purchase of financial assets on the stock exchange. The purchase of a government bond, for example, might lead to the removal of funds from a bank in the interior by the individual purchasing the bond and their redeposit in a bank in the East by the person selling the bond. World War I, by creating a large, widely held public debt and by creating familiarity with the government bond market, may have contributed to the development of this channel for disintermediation and capital flight.

Although the capital flight has not received much attention in recent years, careful observers noted it at the time. E. A. Goldenweiser was the director of the Division of Research and Statistics of the Board of Governors of the Federal Reserve System during the contraction. In his retrospective assessment of the period, Goldenweiser (1951: p. 164) cites two factors to explain the tide of bank failures: (1) "commodity price declines [which we will discuss in more detail] and shrinkage of real-estate values" and (2) "lack of confidence in the solvency of banks [that] resulted in large-scale withdrawals of deposits and in transfers of funds from smaller to larger banks, particularly to banks in reserve and central reserve cities." Although Goldenweiser tends to discount actions that the Federal Reserve might have taken to end the crisis (and so to make the case for the advice that he gave at the time?), there is no reason to think that his account of the causes of the crisis was biased. James W. Angell (1969 [1936]: pp. 66–8), who examined regional deposit data, noted the rise in New York and Philadelphia's shares of total deposits and attributed the increases to "interior funds seeking safety after 1929."

Hoover and Ratchford (1951: p. 171) claimed that large insurance and railroad companies transferred working balances from small local banks in the South to larger, safer banks nearer their home offices. More recently, Elmus Wicker (1996: p. 102) describes the problem under the term "seepage." He notes: "Data on bank deposits show a general movement of funds from agricultural to financial and industrial centers during the Great Depression." As evidence, he offers the decline in the ratio of nonmember bank total deposits to total deposits of all commercial banks and the increase in the ratio of total deposits of 101 weekly reporting member banks to total deposits of all commercial banks. One advantage of the Gold Settlement Fund data is that, rather than simply showing the ratio of deposits in two different kinds of banks, or two different areas, it shows dollars that were actually transferred from one region to another.

The evidence, although admittedly sketchy, suggests that we are dealing with a substantial drain of gold from the interior motivated by the search for deposit safety. From the point of view of the banks and regions losing the gold, of course, the liquidity problems are the same, whether the loss was due to a capital flight or a balance of trade deficit.

A capital flight to the East is the opposite of the traditional picture of drain on the East produced by banks in the South and West drawing on Eastern correspondents, the picture made famous by Sprague (1968 [1910]) in his classic history of bank failures under the National Banking Act. It would be surprising if we could not find individual examples of banks in the interior that were under pressure from depositors liquidating deposits held in Eastern banks during 1929 to 1932. Again, the Eastern movement of funds remains hard to explain in the absence of a capital flight. Perhaps what had changed from an earlier day was the growth of national corporations with the ability to move funds from one region to another and growth of widespread holdings of government bonds that could be liquidated (on Eastern markets) in an emergency, a point I will return to later.

How significant were these flows for the system as a whole? One metric is bank reserves. In 1929, bank reserves outside New York totaled $1.405 billion. The net flow of gold toward New York averaged about 36 percent of this amount. Partly, these private flows were offset by gold flows resulting from federal taxes and expenditures. Then, as now, more taxes were collected in the Eastern financial centers than were spent there. These flows were also offset by loans extended by the various Federal Reserve banks. Nevertheless, the net flow of gold must have placed a severe burden on banks in other regions and helped to intensify the crisis.

To clinch the argument that silent runs undermined the banking systems in the interior regions and contributed to the banking crises, it would be necessary to show in detail how losses of deposits due to interregional transfers affected individual banks. This, I must confess, I have not done. That real harm was done is, I would argue, plausible. The story would be, essentially, the usual textbook story of a multiple contraction of loans and deposits. Borrowers who could not renew loans or borrow working capital would be forced to default, undermining the solvency of their lender, and creating deterioration in local economic conditions that would undermine other banks. But I have no ground-level examples of banks that actually experienced this sequence of events. It is possible, as a matter of arithmetic, that the banks that lost reserves due to the interregional capital flows were the ones that survived the crisis.

For someone seeking confirmation that the capital flight mattered, a natural question to ask is whether the interregional gold flows produced liquidity effects on interest rates. In other words, did rates rise in regions losing gold relative to regions gaining gold? The answer, it must be admitted, is no. Gene Smiley (1981) and Howard Bodenhorn (1995) estimated bank loan rates by region, and their series do not reveal distinct liquidity effects from the gold flows in the first half of 1930. On a regional level, this is the same finding – declining interest rates in the face of a declining stock of money – that was at the center of Temin's (1976, 1989) critique of Friedman and Schwartz's (1963, 1982) interpretation of the Depression. Evidently, the demand for loans was declining rapidly, even as losses of deposits deprived banks of the ability to make them. Real rates, of course, were rising rapidly. For example, the nominal loan rate for country national banks in the West North Central region, a wheat-growing region, was 7.58 percent in 1929 and 7.04 percent in 1930. No evidence here of a liquidity effect.[18] But the "wheat rate of interest" was 3.65 percent in 1929 and 51.96 percent in 1930![19]

To form a complete picture of the banking crisis, one must move from the silent runs to the noisy runs and the bank failures. This part of the story, however, has been well told elsewhere, most recently and most thoroughly by Wicker (1996). The first banking crisis, according to Wicker, was associated with the failure of a chain of banks, the Caldwell banks, headquartered in St. Louis. The St. Louis district was hit hard by the deflation and the collapse of agricultural incomes. But the high rate of failure in this region was also due to factors specific to the Caldwell banks, and it would not do to exaggerate the correlation that existed at this stage in the crisis between specific events and the deflation. Although the St. Louis district experienced a momentous decline in personal income between 1929 and 1930, other districts, such as Dallas, experienced a similar decline but did not suffer to the same extent in the first noisy crisis. The right metaphor might be a cloth stretched to the breaking point. All of the cloth is under pressure, but where the first tear occurs will depend on particular structural weaknesses.

Wicker (1996) details the growing crisis, but the exact roles played by deflation, declining income, bank insolvency, fear itself, and other factors are in doubt. Wicker (2000), for example, suggests that Britain's departure from gold in September 1931 might have undermined confidence in the U.S. banking system by creating the fear of an external drain of gold, the more familiar analog of the interregional drains highlighted here. But in the nature of things, he is unable to uncover evidence of a direct link between that event and the particular failures that followed in the United States on the heels

---

[18] I examined the state-level data that underlie Bodenhorn's (1995) regional estimates, but failed to turn up obvious increases due to banking panics or liquidity shortages. I am grateful to Professor Bodenhorn for sharing his state-level estimate.

[19] The nominal rates are from Smiley (1981: p. 897). The wheat rate of interest was computed by subtracting the percentage change in the price of a bushel of wheat (U.S. Bureau of the Census [1975], 511, series K508) between 1928 and 1929 from the 1929 nominal loan rate, and the percentage change between 1929 and 1930 from the 1930 nominal loan rate.

of the British decision. Although there was some improvement in 1932 over 1931, bank failures and deposits in failed banks remained at very high levels, and the supply of money and bank credit contracted dramatically.

THE BANKING HOLIDAYS

Inevitably, governments intervene when financial crises become sufficiently severe. On the international scene, intervention may take various forms: central banks may act as lenders of last resort, currency pegs may be abandoned, and capital controls may be imposed. In the early 1930s, local and state government intervened by declaring "bank holidays." During the holidays, depositors were prevented from making withdrawals from banks or the amount that they could withdraw at one time was limited in some fashion, say to 5 percent of the account per month.[20] There were several rationales. In most cases, the banks were suffering heavy withdrawals. The goal was to protect the remaining assets while loans were arranged from the Reconstruction Finance Corporation, the Federal Reserve, or private lenders. In many cases, state and local officials also felt pressured into declaring holidays because holidays had already been declared in neighboring states. If depositors could not get cash in one state, they might turn to banks in neighboring states. The earlier discussion of silent runs suggests that this was a reasonable fear. There was probably also the hope that a "cooling off" period would allow the banks to reopen without suffering panicky withdrawals.

The rash of bank holidays was clearly a sign of how bad things had become. Whether the holidays made things better or worse is a difficult question. With a more conventional bank panic, an action that is separately sensible – getting money out of a weak bank – leads to actions that in the aggregate undermine the system. The same was true with the bank holidays. Actions that were rational in a given state had an external effect and led to a rash of holidays, accurately labeled a panic, which undermined the payments system in the aggregate.

Table 2.4 chronicles the state and local bank holidays. I do not make any claim that this list is complete. It was compiled mainly from a perusal of the *New York Times* and the *Financial Chronicle* simply to give a sense of the timing and regional diffusion of the crisis. It is clear from the table that the holidays began in the regions that had lost reserves earlier because of price

---

[20] Similar restrictions were adopted in Argentina in December 2001 during its financial crisis.

Table 2.4. *State and local bank holidays in 1932–1933*

Date	State	Action taken
October 17, 1932	Minnesota	Municipal holidays declared
November 1	Nevada	12-Day moratorium; twice renewed
January 1933	Illinois, Iowa	Small towns declare local holidays
January 20	Iowa	One-day holiday
February 4	Louisiana	One-day holiday
February 14	Michigan	8-Day holiday, renewed until federal holiday
February 20	New Jersey	Legislature authorizes banking commission to declare a moratorium on February 21; this power is exercised for one bank
	Missouri	One bank restricts withdrawals after mayor declares moratorium
February 23	New Jersey	Limited withdrawals authorized at two banks
February 25	Maryland	3-Day holiday, subsequently extended
	Ohio	Banks self-declare holidays
	Missouri	Banks granted right to restrict withdrawals
February 28	Indiana, North Kentucky, Ohio	Banks restrict withdrawals under the authority of new banking laws
February 28	Arkansas, Pennsylvania	Banks initiate restrictions
March 1	Philadelphia, Pittsburgh	Individual banks self-declare holidays
	Kentucky, Mississippi, Tennessee	Bank holidays
March 2	Alabama, California, Georgia, Louisiana, Mississippi, Nevada, Oklahoma, Oregon, Texas, Utah, Washington, Wisconsin	Bank holidays
March 3	Arizona, Georgia, Idaho, Illinois, New Mexico, North Carolina, Oklahoma, Virginia, Wyoming	Bank holidays
March 4	Colorado, Delaware, District of Columbia, Florida, Georgia, Illinois, Kansas, Maine, Massachusetts, Minnesota, Missouri, Montana, Nebraska, New Hampshire, New Jersey, New York, North Dakota, South Dakota, Vermont	Virtually all remaining banks closed by governor's proclamations at the request of Treasury officials
March 6	United States	Bank holiday

Sources: Commercial and Financial Chronicle (various issues), the *New York Times* (various issues), and Kennedy (1973), passim. The list is probably not complete, but it is probably sufficient for a broad-brush picture of the extent and timing of the holiday movement.

and confidence shocks. The first signs were municipal holidays declared in
the upper Midwest. The first statewide moratorium was on November 1,
1932 in Nevada. The next one was a one-day holiday on February 4, 1933
in Louisiana.[21] The final dissolution of the banking system was ushered in
by the holiday declared in Michigan in mid-February. Most of the larger
Michigan banks belonged to one of two holding companies. The smaller, the
Guardian Detroit Union Group, was teetering on the edge of bankruptcy. A
desperate effort was launched to save this group through a Reconstruction
Finance Corporation loan combined with aid from the Ford interests. But the
plan foundered on demands that the Reconstruction Finance Corporation
hold adequate collateral for its loan and the unwillingness of Henry Ford to
take part (Ballantine 1948).[22]

The final spurt of holidays was caused, in part, by the fear in some states
that holidays in neighboring states would lead to unsustainable withdrawals
in those states that dared to keep their banks open. Governor Ruby Laffoon
of Kentucky, obviously a politician of some imagination, spoke for many
when he declared a bank holiday on March 1, 1933. His proclamation also
describes the nature of the restrictions typically imposed,

Whereas many banks in the cities and towns contiguous to the borders of the
State of Kentucky are closed or are only permitting limited withdrawals of their
deposits.

Whereas a result of this situation will be that the funds of the banks of
Kentucky will be withdrawn to supply the needs of these other communities,
thus weakening the resources of the people of the Commonwealth, and...

Whereas legal holidays may only be declared in the State of Kentucky by the
Governor appointing certain days as days of thanksgiving.

Now, therefore in consideration of the nation-wide banking situation and in
view of the fact that the people of the State of Kentucky, though suffering from
the general depression, may perhaps in comparison with the people of other
states have reason for thanksgiving.

I as Governor of the State of Kentucky, appoint the days of March 1, 2, 3 and
4 1933, as days of thanksgiving in the State of Kentucky and declare such days
legal holidays and do further provide as follows:

[21] The holiday was declared to give the state's largest bank time to apply for a Reconstruction
Finance Corporation Loan, a consideration that was also behind some of the other holidays.
The pressure on the bank determined the date; the occasion was found afterwards – the
anniversary of the severance of diplomatic relations with Germany prior to World War I
(Chandler 1970: p. 120)!

[22] Ballantine, the Under Secretary of the Treasury, took part in the negotiations with Henry
Ford.

(1) That during said holidays all banks and trust companies shall be closed in the State of Kentucky for the regular transaction of business except.

(a) Said banks and trust companies may during the ordinary business hours of said holiday pay to their depositors (whether time or demand) not exceeding an aggregate of 5% of the respective deposits of such depositors at close of business on Feb. 28, 1933, provided that such payments shall only be made on checks, drafts or receipts dated subsequent to Feb. 28, 1933.

(b) During the banking hours of the last three days of the holiday period, said banks and trust companies may accept new deposits but such deposits shall be held in trust funds and may be insofar as they are represented by deposits of cash, withdrawn in full during said period.

(c) During said holiday period, said banks and trust companies, may transact any and all other business which does not involve the paying out of deposited funds other than herein authorized. . . . (*Commercial and Financial Chronicle*, March 4, 1933, 1484–5).

It is obvious from Table 2.3 that by late February or early March 1933 a large fraction of deposits had been restricted by official actions and a good portion of the remainder had been restricted in some measure by individual bank actions. Table 2.4 makes this point in a different way by showing a snapshot of the banking system on the eve of President Roosevelt's announcement of the national banking holiday: Virtually all deposits in the country were subject in some measure to restriction.

The rapid diffusion of the bank holidays also raises the question of whether it would be correct to speak of a bank-holiday panic or a contagion of fear. Again, much depends on how these terms are defined. If panic is defined as simply foolish unreasoning behavior, then this was not the case. Governor Laffoon, at least, was clearly nobody's fool. His concern, that banks in Kentucky would be drained of gold if they remained open while other systems closed, was reasonable in the circumstances, although whether this drain would actually have happened is hard to say. On the other hand, if panic is defined as a situation in which people are making rational decisions that create negative externalities and that could be channeled into a more socially responsible direction by alternative institutional arrangements, then it is reasonable to speak of a bank-holiday panic. If Governor Laffoon and the other politicians declaring holidays could have been dissuaded from issuing these proclamations by promises of lender of last resort loans to the banks in their jurisdiction from the Federal Reserve, the ultimate breakdown of the payments mechanism might have been avoided. The chain leading from deflation, to silent runs, to noisy runs, to bank holidays might have been interrupted by the Federal Reserve at many points. Early on, the Federal Reserve could be excused for failing to act because the underlying process was hard to recognize, but when bank holidays erupted, the case for vigorous action was clear.

Wigmore (1987) suggests that the final denouement, the national bank holiday, was also due to the fear that President Roosevelt would take the United States off the gold standard. This fear, according to Wigmore, produced an external gold drain, which determined, at the least, the timing of the national holiday. As with Wicker's (1996) suggestion that Britain's departure from gold in September 1931 had repercussions for American banks, the external drain in 1933 created problems for Eastern banks similar to those faced earlier by banks in the interior experiencing a drain to the Eastern financial centers.

REGIONAL ASPECTS OF THE CONFLICT OVER MONETARY POLICY

As is well known, there was a divide, partly along regional lines, within the Federal Reserve between those who favored aggressive open market operations and those who thought that large-scale open market purchases would be futile or counterproductive. The former group included, at times, the governor of the influential Federal Reserve Bank of New York, and the latter included most of the governors of the other district banks, including the governor of the influential Chicago bank. It is natural, therefore, to ask whether the interregional balance of payments problems discussed above played a role in undermining support for open market purchases.

The opposition to open market operations undoubtedly reflected psychological predispositions and political infighting. As Friedman and Schwartz (1963: p. 415) astutely noted: "The other Banks [other than New York] were much more parochial in both situation and outlook, more in the position of reacting to financial currents originating elsewhere, more concerned with their immediate regional problems, and hence more likely to believe that the Reserve System must adjust to other forces than that it could or should take the lead." And as Friedman and Schwartz also noted, regional banks could assert their independence by opposing the policies advocated by the New York Federal Reserve.

But the governors did have to provide an intellectual justification of some sort for the positions they took, and they were influenced in some measure by ideas. One episode discussed at length by Friedman and Schwartz

(1963: pp. 370–4) is particularly revealing. In July 1930, George L. Harrison, Governor of the Federal Reserve Bank of New York, wrote to the governors of the other district Banks asking for support for a policy of open market purchases.[23] The reason he needed their support is simply that the power to make decisions regarding open market operations had recently been placed in the hands of the Open Market Policy Committee, which consisted of the 12 Governors of the Federal Reserve banks. The Committee had held its first meeting in May 1930. Harrison, in other words, had to persuade a majority of his fellow governors to support a policy of buying government bonds in the open market if the United States was to follow an expansionary open market policy.

Only two governors supported open market purchases: the Governors of the Richmond and Atlanta Banks. Those happened to be the two districts that had witnessed the largest decreases in deposits, so to this limited extent, there is some support for the notion that opposition or support was based on the district level experience. (Figure 2.3 shows the picture of the districts shortly before Harrison called on the other governors for support.) But the list of opponents of open market purchases also included Governors in districts that had already begun to experience a loss of deposits, including Chicago, the second largest bank in the system. Most of the opponents justified their opposition to open market operations with what might be characterized as versions of the real bills doctrine: the idea that monetary policy should simply accommodate to the needs of trade. This doctrine, always congenial to bankers, had to some extent been institutionalized at the Federal Reserve Board, as Meltzer has shown in a relatively sophisticated version that Meltzer dubbed the Burgess-Riefler doctrine (Meltzer 2003; Wheelock 1998). The views of some of the Governors, however, seemed to reflect relatively primitive versions of the doctrine: (1) that low levels of nominal interest rates were proof that credit was already abundant, or simply (2) that open market operations intended to buoy the economy were attempts at tampering with supply and demand.[24]

Several of the governors expressed concerns that open market operations at that time would reignite speculation. Frederic H. Curtiss, the chairman of the Boston Bank "expressed strong opposition to further purchases on the grounds that they were likely to feed the stock market rather than the bond market" (as summarized by Friedman and Schwartz 1963: p. 373).

---

[23] This section is based on Friedman and Schwartz (1963: p. 370–4).

[24] The failure to distinguish between nominal and real rates was stressed by Brunner and Meltzer (1968).

James McDougal, Governor of the Chicago Bank, the second largest in the system, warned that if open market purchases were made, "speculation might easily arise in some other direction" (as quoted by Friedman and Schwartz 1963: p. 371). Lynn P. Talley of the Dallas Bank seemed to refer with some bitterness to the failure of the Federal Reserve to stop speculation in 1929. Fear of reigniting speculation may seem fanciful in retrospect. The stock market (measured by the Dow Jones average) was then about 70 percent below its peak and was about back to where it was in 1924. Nevertheless, it is clear that, if one is willing to take these Governors at face value, this is what they believed (Calomiris and Wheelock 1998).

As the contraction worsened, and as deposits in all regions began to shrink, support for open market operations grew among the governors, but McDougal of Chicago remained a persistent opponent. In one famous episode in 1932 he refused to allow the Federal Reserve Bank of Chicago to join in open market purchases. Since the New York Federal Reserve might then have run short of gold, McDougal's intransigence undermined the effort to continue open market operations begun in 1932 (Eichengreen 1992b: pp. 30–1).

The fear of reigniting speculation may have been based simply on a general feeling that speculation was bad and had produced the downturn. But it is possible that the fear of speculation was based on an understanding, perhaps intuitive, that a boom on Wall Street would attract funds from the interior, as had happened in 1928 and 1929, further weakening banks in the interior. One is then led to ask whether the Governors would have been more receptive to another policy, for example, cuts in required reserve ratios, that was less biased toward New York and Wall Street. Given their general conservatism and their reliance on interest rates as the ultimate test of the ease or tightness of monetary policy, it seems unlikely. Nevertheless, it is probably fair to say that open market purchases, which were perceived as attracting money from the interior into New York, may have faced more difficulties in winning support than a policy that promised a more even geographical distribution of the benefits.

THE BANKING CRISES OF THE EARLY 1930s FROM
A REGIONAL PERSPECTIVE

The banking crises of the early 1930s seem to have much in common with the twin crises of recent years. In 1929–1930, the United States experienced a sharp cyclical decline in income that was especially severe in some of the agricultural regions because of decreases in the real prices of foods, fibers, and minerals. There was, moreover, a silent run on the interior banks, as corporations and banks moved funds to the Eastern financial centers for precautionary purposes and as institutions and individuals purchased nonbank assets held in the east. Banks in the rural regions, therefore, came under intense pressure. A number of failures, some of them large, occurred, but because the failures were concentrated among the banks that had taken undue risks in the 1920s, their regional locus was somewhat idiosyncratic. Eventually, silent runs were joined by noisy runs as individual depositors, alarmed by the growing tide of bank closures and by the continual decline in economic activity, began converting deposits into cash. This produced a catastrophic contraction in the number of banks and in the supply of money and credit. The final denouement was produced by a rash of bank holidays declared by local and state governments that restricted the convertibility of deposits into cash.

The absence of nationwide branch banking, as shown in Table 2.5, has been pointed to as an important structural weakness that lay behind the banking crisis (White, 1984). The analysis presented here strengthens that conclusion. If the banks in the interior had been branches of major banks with home offices in the Eastern financial centers, the story might have been very different. Lending might have been curtailed in the interior and branches closed, as in Canada (Bordo, Rockoff, and Redish 1994).[25] But there would have been no incentive for corporations to move working balances from the interior to the financial centers. In developing this argument, it is important to distinguish between intraregional branching and interregional branching. The problem for the interior banks was not so much that they were small banks, although that did not help, but rather, that they were separated from the banks in the financial centers. When fears of bank illiquidity and insolvency increased, depositors tried to protect themselves by moving funds outside the affected regions. The decision to move funds must have been partly based on the assumption that banks in the financial centers held safer, better diversified portfolios of assets. But the decision may also have been based simply on the assumption that banks in the financial centers were more sophisticated about financial matters and, therefore, better able to cope with uncertain times. The banking situation, to put it somewhat differently, would

---

[25] The success of the Canadian banking system in avoiding a U.S.-style collapse does not mean that Canada avoided the Great Contraction. Industrial production in Canada followed the same downhill path as in the United States.

Table 2.5. *State bank restrictions, Sunday, March 5, 1933*

State	Description of restrictions
Alabama	Closed until further notice
Arizona	Closed until March 13
Arkansas	Closed until March 7
California	Almost all closed until March 9
Colorado	Closed until March 8
Connecticut	Closed until March 7
Delaware	Closed indefinitely
District of Columbia	Three banks limited to 5%; nine savings banks invoke sixty days' notice
Florida	Withdrawals restricted to 5% plus $10 until March 8
Georgia	Mostly closed until March 7, closing optional
Idaho	Some closed until March 18, closing optional
Illinois	Closed until March 8, then to be opened on 5% restriction basis for seven days
Indiana	About half restricted to 5% indefinitely
Iowa	Closed "temporarily"
Kansas	Restricted to 5% withdrawals indefinitely
Kentucky	Mostly restricted to 5% withdrawals until March 11
Louisiana	Closing mandatory until March 7
Maine	Closed until March 7
Maryland	Closed until March 6
Massachusetts	Closed until March 7
Michigan	Mostly closed, others restricted to 5% indefinitely; upper peninsula banks open
Minnesota	Closed "temporarily"
Mississippi	Restricted to 5% indefinitely
Missouri	Closed until March 7
Montana	Closed until further notice
Nebraska	Closed until March 8
Nevada	Closed until March 8, also schools
New Hampshire	Closed subject to further proclamation
New Jersey	Closed until March 7
New Mexico	Mostly closed until March 8
New York	Closed until March 7
North Carolina	Some banks restricted to 5% withdrawals
North Dakota	Closed temporarily
Ohio	Mostly restricted to 5% withdrawals indefinitely
Oklahoma	All closed until March 8
Oregon	All closed until March 7
Pennsylvania	Mostly closed until March 7, Pittsburgh banks open
Rhode Island	Closed yesterday
South Carolina	Some closed, some restricted, all on own initiative
South Dakota	Closed indefinitely
Tennessee	A few closed, others restricted, until March 9

State	Description of restrictions
Texas	Mostly closed, others restricted to withdrawals of $15 daily until March 8
Utah	Mostly closed until March 8
Vermont	Closed until March 7
Virginia	All closed until March 8
Washington	Some closed until March 7
West Virginia	Restricted to 5% monthly withdrawals indefinitely
Wisconsin	Closed until March 17
Wyoming	Withdrawals restricted to 5% indefinitely

Source: Commercial and Financial Chronicle, March 11, 1933: p. 1670.

not have been very different even if there had been widespread intraregional branching; only interregional branching would do. Even a large bank with branches throughout the wheat-growing region of the Middle West, for example, might have fallen under a cloud and been subject to runs in the early 1930s when the real price of wheat was falling 60 percent. Only a bank with branches in both the Middle West and the Eastern financial centers could hope to whether the storm.

It is always possible, one must admit, that if interregional branching had been widespread, things might have gone wrong in another way. Recent evidence (Carlson 2001) suggests that in the 1930s, banks with branches were more likely to fail rather than less likely because the banks with branches had assumed more risk than banks without branches. There was no banking across state lines in the 1930s, but Carlson's data include California, where banks could branch across different economic regions. Therefore, it is possible that, had cross-state branching been permitted, banks would have assumed riskier postures in the 1920s and concern about bad loans in the interior in the early 1930s might have undermined confidence in and led to the closure of some very large banks. One cannot be sure. But the collapse of the system might have been avoided had interregional branch banking been the norm, and if the collapse had occurred, it would have followed a very different path from the one actually followed and might have generated a more appropriate policy response.

The regional nature of the crisis, especially during the early period, may have contributed to the failure of the Federal Reserve to respond effectively to the crisis. The one plan then seriously under consideration that might have alleviated the pressure on the banking system was the proposal by the Federal Reserve Bank of New York that the Federal Reserve System buy bonds on the open market. The Governors of the other district banks, however, vetoed large-scale open market operations. Their opposition stemmed from a variety of factors, including their reliance on a version (in some cases a rather crude version) of the real bills doctrine. From their viewpoint, moreover, open market purchases may have appeared to be a region-specific medicine, likely to reignite speculation on the stock market but unlikely to pay real dividends elsewhere. Although one can fault the Federal Reserve for failing to engage in open market operations in response to the general contraction of income, it would be unreasonable to criticize it for failing to see the warning signs in the interregional gold flows. The Federal Reserve was a young institution, and these were unprecedented gold movements. Nevertheless, it is interesting to recognize that, had these been international rather than interregional flows, they would have excited considerable interest.

There was a time when it would have appeared foolish to worry about the recurrence of a crisis caused by a combination of depression, deflation, and a balkanized banking system. In recent years, however, deflation – already a fact of life in Japan – has loomed on the horizon for the United States and the European Monetary Union. And, although the banking system of the United States has been increasingly linked together through nationwide branching, the European Monetary Union is still far from having a unified banking system. The present analysis then, may serve as a cautionary tale showing how a banking-balance-of-payments crisis can develop with great rapidity and virulence within what seems on the surface to be a sound, progressive banking system.

3 Price Change, Financial Stability, and the British Economy, 1870–1939

Forrest Capie and Geoffrey Wood

INTRODUCTION

For much of the last quarter-century, a principal focus of economists' attention has been inflation and, to some extent, disinflation and the associated costs. More recently, deflation has attracted some interest, although only its possible harmful consequences have been discussed; there has been no mention of deflation as the by-product of increased economic growth interacting with unchanged money growth. Concern over deflation has been prompted by some sharp rises and falls in asset prices in Japan and, more recently, in the United States and to a lesser extent the United Kingdom, and the interest taken in the relationship between these and the general price level. But also important are the actual deflations in prices in Japan, China, Hong Kong, Singapore, and Taiwan, and the near-zero inflation in the United States and Europe. But what, do we know about deflation? It is necessary to go back to before World War II to find episodes in almost any Organisation for Economic Co-Operation and Development (OECD) country except Japan. The purpose of this chapter is to begin to investigate the effects of deflation in the British economy.

The depression of the 1930s stimulated many developments in economic analysis. But Keynes's (1936) ideas on deflation in the *General Theory* and Irving Fisher's debt-deflation theory have been, at least by comparison, neglected. These ideas suggest that debt-deflation causes, or at least worsens, depressions. Our aim in this chapter is to explore what these ideas can contribute to understanding the behaviour of the British economy both in the late nineteenth century and in the interwar years.

We first describe the debt-deflation ideas of Keynes and Fisher (the models are far from identical) and then examine whether any of the key variables in these models moved as the models require for there to be debt-deflation at work. We seek to evaluate what contribution the debt-deflation models make to understanding the behaviour of the British economy in the two periods. We examine, 1873–1896 and 1920–1939.

The first section of the chapter outlines briefly the course of the British economy in the two periods. Then, the debt-deflation ideas of Keynes and Fisher are outlined, and the variables crucial to those debt-deflation models are identified. As will emerge, price expectations, albeit different aspects of them, are central to both views; therefore, the following section considers informally how these might be identified in the two periods. After modelling price expectations, we provide differently constructed real interest rates and examine the informational content of the bond market. We then consider the behaviour of bond spreads as a possible route to understanding the role of debt-deflation, before finishing by noting the role of intertemporal substitution.

THE BRITISH ECONOMY[1]

Our principal focus is on the interwar years in Britain, and the behaviour of the economy during this period is outlined first. Following a boom at the end of World War I, there was a period that ran until the early 1930s when prices were either falling or flat. They fell most sharply in the recession at the end of the 1920s. Interestingly, asset prices rose quite consistently throughout, and in the later 1920s, they rose quite rapidly. They then fell steeply in the recession years of 1929 to 1932 and beyond. In the closest preceding period of falling prices, the long deflation of the late nineteenth century (1873–1896), the economy, although continuing to grow, was doing so at an ever-slowing pace. In the 1920s and 1930s, in contrast, the economy performed much better than in the nineteenth century deflation – at least from peak to peak to peak, 1924–1929–1937. There have been no deflations since then, although there have been several occasions when asset prices have moved in a manner dramatically different from the general price level.

Price experience is our key concern. In the interwar period, it followed a pattern that was not greatly out of line with what it had been in the past. But it should not be surprising that, to a certain extent, it also reflected the attempts at restoring monetary order following war. Thus, there were fluctuations but there was also a slight downward trend. Examining the cost

[1] Appendix 1 provides information about data sources.

of living index reveals the following picture. After considerable inflation in the war, prices continued rising and then rose sharply in the immediate postwar boom. They then collapsed from a peak of 154 in October 1920 to 99 in March 1923, as Britain sought to rejoin the international gold standard at sterling's old parity. They drifted down further until 1925 and were then more or less flat until 1929. They fell still further in the worldwide depression, levelled out in 1933, and from then on drifted up slightly in the upswing of the 1930s. At the end of the period, they were a little lower than they had been at the beginning. How much expectation of this general deflationary path there might have been is an important question to which we return later.

Over the years 1873 to 1896, the previous period of deflation, the behaviour of the British economy was much less dramatic. That period was at one time described as the Great Depression. But that was a misnomer, derived partly from the association of falling prices with relatively declining economic performance and partly from the deteriorating position of agriculture (in the face of severe competition from the New World) and the voice that landowners had in parliament. In fact, the trend rate of growth was not out of line with previous periods. Real output (gross domestic product [GDP]) rose from £1,177 m in 1873 to £1,776 m in 1896, a growth of over 50 percent in a twenty-three-year period (Figure 3.1). There were some falls along the way, the worst of them occurring in 1879 and the mid-1880s. Unemployment, as captured in the percentage of insured workers unemployed, fluctuated broadly in line with output. Unemployment averaged

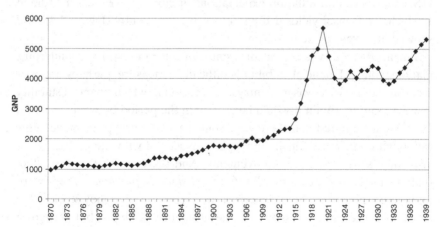

Figure 3.1. Gross National Product (£m), 1870–1939
Sources: See Appendix 1.

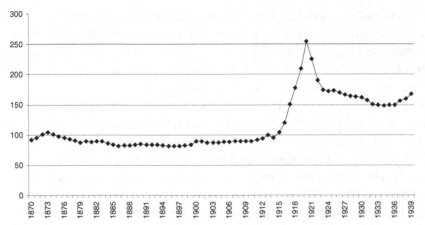

Figure 3.2. Level of Gross National Product Deflator, 1870–1939 (1913 = 100)
Sources: See Appendix 1.

5 percent per year across the whole period. There were three years in which
it went above 9 percent and four in which it fell below 2.2 percent.

Prices fell, on average, from 1873 to 1896. An index of the GDP deflator
(with 1913 = 100) began the period in 1873 at 109.2 (a peak) and finished it
in 1896 at 86.2, an average decline of exactly 1 percent deflation per annum
(Figure 3.2). The decline, of course, was not smooth, but rather a fluctuating
path with a downward trend. Prices did, however, move fairly modestly year
by year. The biggest fall in the period was 4.7 percent in 1879, and the biggest
rise was 4.3 percent in the following year. Short-term interest rates fluctuated
substantially but showed no signs of any trend (Figure 3.3), consistent with
U.S. experience and inflation expectations of close to zero (see Friedman
1992: ch. 2). Consol yields drifted downward very gently (Figure 3.4) and
showed little year-by-year movement.

Financial stability is also at the centre of our interest, for it underpins
macro-stability. Financial stability is difficult to measure, perhaps impossible. But if ever there was a country and a period in which financial stability
could be said to obtain it would be Britain in the period between 1870 and
1939. We have noted that there were some sharp general price movements
(although these were, for the most part, associated with war). There were
also some sharp asset price movements. And there were, of course, fluctuations in the real economy. *But financial stability prevailed.* There were
no banking panics, no financial crises (no threat to the money stock).[2] No
single measure can express the degree of financial stability, but perhaps a

2   The nominal quantity of money was not threatened and trust in it held, for there was no
    flight to gold, even when the gold standard was abandoned.

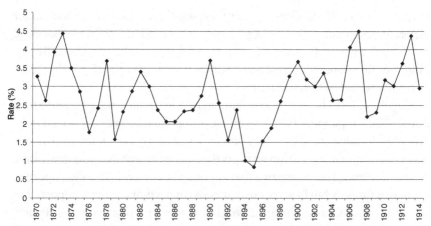

Figure 3.3. U.K. Interest Rates: Average Annual Prime Bank Bill Rate, 1870–1914
Sources: See Appendix 1.

good guide can be found in commercial bank profitability, which remained remarkably stable across the whole period (Capie 1988; Capie and Billings 2001). The behaviour of components of the money multiplier supports that view; there was no example of a rush to cash or a collapse in the multiplier (Capie and Webber 1985).

HYPOTHESES

The two basic approaches to debt-deflation are those of Keynes and Fisher. We first describe the approach that originated with Keynes, and then turn

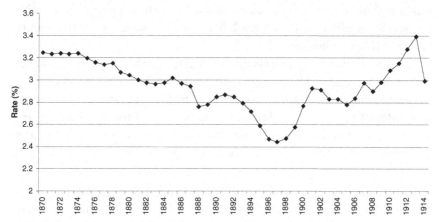

Figure 3.4. U.K. Interest Rates: Average Annual Yield on Consols, 1870–1914
Sources: See Appendix 1.

to that of Fisher. In developing their theories, Keynes and Fisher had rather different objectives. Keynes was primarily concerned with showing that wage flexibility (a particular form of price flexibility) would not necessarily stabilise output. Fisher was concerned with a stronger proposition – that price flexibility would destabilise output.

Keynes (1936: ch. 19) argued that changes in money wages could affect output (and employment) only by changing aggregate demand. He listed several ways by which money wage falls could shift aggregate demand. The first was a transfer of income from workers to rentiers; this would, he conjectured, reduce demand. Then came two that applied to open economies with pegged exchange rates. A fall in wages would boost exports and reduce imports, but the resulting fall in real income would cut consumption spending. Fourth was intertemporal substitution: If money wages fell relative to expected future money wages, current spending would be boosted, whereas if the fall led to expectations of further falls, spending would itself also fall. Investment was the part of total spending Keynes expected to be affected by this channel. Fifth was a monetary channel; the fall in wages and prices would produce a fall in interest rates due to a rise in money supply relative to money demand. Sixth was an anticipation of Lucas. Businessmen may mistake a general wage fall for one specific to them, hire more labour in consequence and thus break the cycle of depression. Last was the effect on indebtedness.

According to Keynes (1936: p. 264), "On the other hand, the depressing influence on entrepreneurs of their burden of debt may partly offset any cheerful reactions from the reduction of wages. Indeed, if the fall of wages and price goes far, the embarrassment of those entrepreneurs who are heavily indebted may soon reach the point of insolvency – with severely adverse effects on investment."

Keynes placed greatest stress on the intertemporal substitution channel and on interest rates. He thought that effects through interest rates would be weak. Small falls in prices would have small effects and only on short-term interest rates, whereas large price falls would disturb confidence. He set out in some detail the possibility that a fall in money wages could raise the expected real rate of interest (Keynes 1936: p. 265):

The most favourable contingency is that in which money wages are slowly sagging downwards and each reduction in wages serves to diminish confidence in the prospective maintenance in wages. . . . For example, the effect of an expectation that wages are going to sag by say 2 percent in the coming year will be roughly equivalent to the effect of a rise of 2 percent in the amount of interest payable for the same period.

His analysis plainly suggests that wage (price) flexibility cannot cure depressions; but he does not suggest, as Fisher did, that such flexibility can cause depressions.

Fisher's views are described clearly in his 1933 *Econometrica* article. For Fisher, debt and deflation were key ingredients in recessions. We have to start from a situation of "overindebtedness." Nine factors then come into play. An initial shock causes a change in confidence and produces distress selling; therefore, bank loans are repaid and the money supply falls. This leads, in turn, to a fall in prices (a "swelling of the dollar" in the U.S. case) and a decline in net worth and profits. These lead to falls in output and employment, followed by increased pessimism, hoarding of money, and decreases in nominal interest rates along with increases in real rates.

As Fisher suggests, the overindebtness, which is a key ingredient, can arise through a route such as the following. A technological breakthrough fuels borrowing. This leads to speculative enthusiasm, followed by criminality: "Probably no great crash has every happened without shady transactions" (Fisher 1933: p. 40). Inflation can lead to similar results by creating the illusion of easy profits. It is the interaction of debt and deflation that is crucial in Fisher's analysis: "The very effort of individuals to lessen their burden of debt increases it, because of the mass effect of the stampede to liquidate in swelling each dollar owed. Thus we have the great paradox which, I submit is the chief secret of most, if not all, great depressions: the more debtors pay, the more they owe" (Fisher 1933: p. 344).

The very process of liquidating debt leads to a fall in bank deposits and thus prices; prices fall faster than debt, real debt rises, and "good risks" are thus exposed to problems. Not only does the real value of debt rise; the real interest rate payable on it also rises. In deflations, there is a ". . . fall in the nominal or money, rates, and a rise in the real, or commodity rate of interest" (Fisher 1933: para 19, p. 341).

A key point distinguishing Keynes from Fisher is that Keynes saw expected real rates as important, whereas Fisher saw an increase in realised real rates as having a damaging effect on existing debtors.

PRICE EXPECTATIONS

In modern macroeconomics, inflation expectations are recognised as having an important role to play. In modelling, different kinds of expectations, from extrapolative, to adaptive, to rational, have been employed. Currently, with a range of interpretations, rational behaviour is assumed. This is broadly taken to mean expectations formed on a rational basis using the best information that is freely available and based on the best economic model of price behaviour. Expectations now focus directly on changes in government policy.

Life was simpler in the nineteenth century in this important respect. Adherence to the gold standard largely removed monetary policy from government control. Thus, price expectations were formed differently. In the nineteenth century, at least among the more advanced economies, there developed a respect and admiration for the gold standard. Britain was the strikingly successful economy of the time and had adopted the standard at an early date. Countries that followed that path had stable price experience in accord with the theory of the standard. Prices continued to move with the economic cycle but were flat on trend. More and more countries opted to adopt this regime in the 1870s, and it has since been argued that there was a relative shortage of gold, which exerted a downward pressure on prices. In the period from 1873 to 1896, there was a long decline in prices. Gold discoveries and improved technology produced the subsequent reversal in the trend.

Might this deflation have been foreseen? Was it anticipated? That is difficult to establish. There were certainly those at the time who warned that the shrinkage in the supply of high-powered money, which would result from abandoning silver and moving to gold, would produce deflation. In addition, there was the huge extension of primary production in the new world and, via the simultaneous transport revolution, the arrival of these products in northwest Europe. The prices of these primary products fell and must have been expected to fall further. Although these price falls were not the cause of the deflation, they did influence some contemporaries and must have contributed to a weakening of pressure on prices. One can conclude that there must have been widespread expectation of price falls in the period. There were, as usual, different explanations for the deflation (real versus monetary again), but there now seems little doubt that gold was the cause. New gold discoveries in the 1890s helped alleviate the gold shortage, and prices began to rise again.

During World War I, when the standard was abandoned, there were widespread and differential rates of inflation. At the end of the war, there was an almost equally widespread desire to restore the monetary order of the late nineteenth century. Because Britain had been at the centre of that system, attention focussed heavily on British actions. The story of Britain's return to gold is well known. From soon after the war, price expectations were clearly on a downward course. There was no other possibility. The intention had been clearly announced (Mundell 2000). All parties were agreed on what was necessary, and the appropriate policies were introduced.

Soon after restoration was achieved in 1925, it became clear that there was still work to be done in Britain. High interest rates persisted over the next few years to protect the parity chosen – the one that had held in the nineteenth century. Therefore, price expectations probably continued to have been negative.

Mundell (2000) has recently restated the view that this price expectation must have been much more widely held, indeed, held by all those considering a return to gold. The United States had taken over Britain's role of major economy and had experienced inflation during the war. The Federal Reserve had then engineered a recession in 1920–1921 that brought the dollar price level, "60 percent of the way back to the pre-war equilibrium" (op. cit.: p. 328). But that still left prices 40 percent higher than they had been and gold reserves correspondingly lower. The increased demand for gold as restoration was pursued would inevitably bring deflation. Mundell argues that this was understood at the time by the leading monetary economists. He cites Cassel, who had been explicit on the point even before Britain had returned to gold in 1925:

The gold standard, of course, cannot secure a greater stability in the general level of prices than the value of gold itself possesses. . . . With the actual state of gold production it can be taken for certain that after a comparatively short time, perhaps within a decade, the present superabundance of gold will be followed, as a consequence of increasing demand, by a marked scarcity of this precious metal tending to cause a fall in prices" (Mundell 2000: p. 329).

So deflation was already expected in the 1920s. Mundell (2000: p. 329) goes on to say, ". . . the theory that deflation was caused by the return to the gold standard was not only predictable, but was actually, as we have noted above, predicted." Prices were to fall much more in the depression of the 1930s and Mundell further states that the deflation was a consequence of not returning to the pre-1914 price level in 1920–1921. That was not achieved until 1934 when the dollar price level was the same as it had been in 1914.

Further evidence of the mood of deflation can be found in Britain at the turn of the decade. In 1930, when prices had fallen sharply again after a decade of sluggishness, attention focussed on measures that might be adopted to raise prices. When, for example, there was discussion of the introduction of a tariff in 1931 (a dramatic proposal, given Britain's history as the great upholder of free trade), great play was made of the fact that this was a policy that would raise prices. That on its own was advanced as a powerful recommendation for the policy (Capie 1983).

In other words, the whole climate of this period was one in which the expectation of price rises must have been exceptionally low and, indeed, expectation of price falls was quite likely. There seemed, certainly in Britain at least, little prospect of prices rising before the early 1930s.

PROXYING THE KEYNES AND FISHER EFFECTS

Plainly, the crucial variables in the Keynes and Fisher models are, the expected real rate and the realised real rate, respectively. The first is defined in the normal way,

$$Re_t = r_t - Ae_t$$

where Re is the expected real rate over the expected length of the loan, r_t the nominal rate over that period, and r_t the expected inflation rate over the same period. The real rate for Fisher is slightly nonstandard. In his model, problems emerge because an individual or firm has signed up to a nominal rate contract expecting a certain inflation rate, but the actual rate of inflation turns out to be lower, even negative. Hence, the real rate for Fisher at time t is as follows:

$$R_t = r_{t-1} - A_t$$

where

$$A_t < Ae_{t-1}$$

R_t is the realised real rate, r_{t-1} the nominal rate when the loan was taken on, A_t the inflation rate, and Ae_{t-1} the expected inflation rate when the loan was taken on.

Some of these variables are, at any rate in principle, observable. These are r_t, r_{t-1}, and A_t. The others can be calculated from these three observable variables if we can somehow devise a measure for A_t – that is, for expected inflation. Before discussing sources for the other three variables, we consider this problem.

Hamilton (1987) tackled this problem for the period of the Great Depression in the United States. He first looked at predepression statements of expectations: indicative, but of no quantitative help. Then he used time series models to predict prices and compared forecasts with actual price outturns. Finally, he looked at commodities futures prices. He calculated the difference between one-month and seven-month futures prices and compared this with the difference between two one-month future prices, six months apart.

He found that the variability of the expected series was greater than that of the actual and that the expected series was an unbiased (although noisy) predictor of the actual. On average, over each six-month period, the market expected 9.4 percent inflation; the comparable outturn was 39 percent. This bears on prices in general, for knowledge of commodity prices helps predict the consumer price index (CPI). He concluded that the interaction of nominal rates with expectations of deflation (the Keynes effect) could not have contributed to the depression, for deflation was not expected. It is not clear whether or not this contradicts Mundell, for he was discussing the need to restore the 1914 gold price over a fairly long period.

What about the Fisher effect? Fisher (1933: pp. 346–7) wanted price rises because he thought they would help recovery. Friedman and Schwartz (1963) and Weinstein (1981), however, reject the claim that the National Industrial Recovery Act (NIRA) was beneficial through its effects on raising prices. As they point out, by raising prices, it reduced the *real* increase in the money stock. According to Weinstein (1981), it reduced this real increase to zero because from 1933 to 1935 prices rose by 14 percent in the United States and so did the nominal stock of money. Friedman and Schwartz (1963) argue likewise for the years 1933–1937.

But this does not allow for the harmful effects on the real burden of debt and on the financial system via deterioration in asset values (Bernanke 1983) that might have been alleviated by the price rise. Thus, there is the possibility that the price rises might have been of benefit despite the monetary constraint (see Bordo and Jeanne, this volume).

PRICE LEVEL AND PRICE LEVEL CHANGE EXPECTATIONS

Price expectations are important in both Keynes's and Fisher's debt-deflation theories. For Keynes, they could affect both interest rates (although he did not expect this channel to be of great significance) and work through intertemporal substitution leading to deferral of spending. Fisher, meanwhile, feared that falsified expectations, price falls being greater than expected, could raise the burden of existing debt. How did price expectations actually behave during this period? Earlier, we discussed some qualitative assessments of this. Now we turn to simple quantification.

An efficient forecasting method (provided there is no change in the process generating the series to be modelled) is to use a time series model. We do this, acknowledging the limitation imposed by the modest number of data points for both the price level (as measured by the GNP deflator; see Figure 3.1) and for the year-by year change of the price level (measured, of course, by the year-by-year change in the GNP deflator). This is done for both periods. The models are shown in Appendix 2. As will be seen, they are both simple and fit well; this is to be expected, given the small amount of variation in the series to be modelled. Simple autoregressive models fit the data well.

Plots of actual and predicted series are shown in Figures 3.5a, 3.5b, 3.6a, and 3.6b. The levels and rates of change are given for both periods. (The rate of change plots for the second period omit the postwar boom because we left that atypical period out of the estimation.)

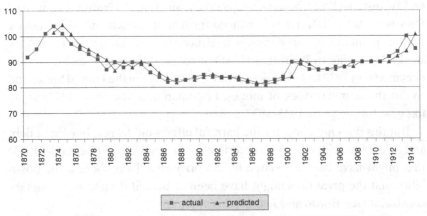

Figure 3.5a. Actual and Predicted level of GNP Deflator, 1870–1914 (1913 = 100)

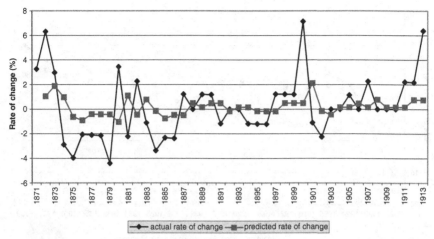

Figure 3.5b. Year-by-Year Rates of Change in GNP Deflator, 1870–1913
Sources: See Appendix 1.

As is clear, both the actual and predicted series track closely together in each period. The level series move so closely together that no comment on them is necessary. The year-by-year change series do, however, merit comment. Looking first at the early period, although the series move along together, the "actual" series is much more variable. That is, of course, consistent with the extensively documented observation on the gold and presumably other commodity standards that long-run movements are constrained,

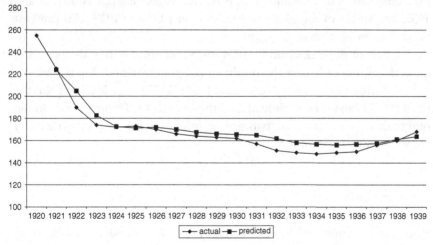

Figure 3.6a. Actual and Predicted Level of GNP Deflator, 1920–1939 (1913 = 100)

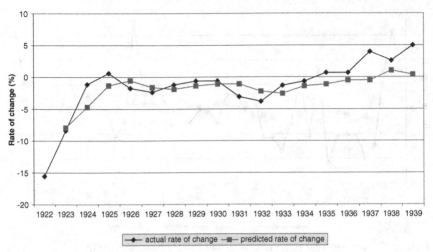

Figure 3.6b. Year-by-Year Rates of Change in GNP Deflator, 1921–1939
Sources: See Appendix 1.

but there is greater scope for short-run variability (Schwartz 1991). This was known at the time and thereby influenced expectations, as of course did actual experience of long run stability. (For a comparatively recent discussion, see Mills and Wood 1992.)

In the later period, there were no years when the difference between actual and predicted rates of change were sufficiently large to be statistically significant. But if we look at the larger deviations, we find actual exceeding predicted values in 1924 and 1925, predicted exceeding actual in 1931 and 1932, and spikes of actual above predicted in 1937 and 1939. This can best be seen by inspection of the graph.

The first of these deviations (1924–1925) occurred during the period of monetary squeeze before the return to the gold standard, the second occurred during the period of relaxation (1931–1932) after leaving gold, the third (1937) cannot be explained, and the fourth (1939) corresponds to the outbreak of war. The first two are of interest because they go exactly the wrong way for debt-deflation!

REAL INTEREST RATES

Price expectations lead to real interest rates. We consider the behaviour of four different series for real interest rates in each of the two periods: a

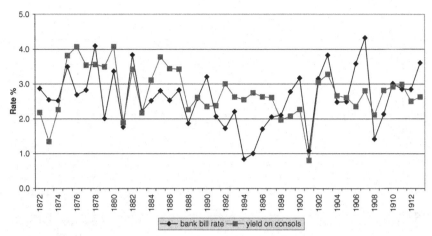

Figure 3.7a. Expected Real Rate, 1872–1913

real short rate and a real long rate, first calculated according to the Keynes method, taking account expected inflation, and then according to Fisher, taking account actual inflation.

To illustrate, we provide an annual observation for interest rates, calculated by averaging monthly data (Capie and Webber 1985), as shown in Figures 3.7a, 3.7b, 3.8a, and 3.8b. We also provide an annual GNP deflator. For the Keynes series, for example, the change in the GNP deflator expected

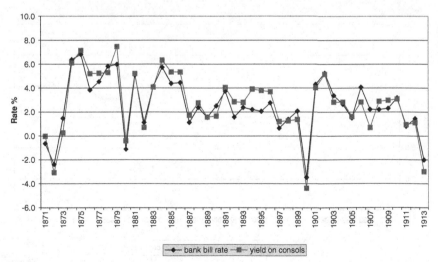

Figure 3.7b. Realized Real Rate, 1871–1913
Sources: See Appendix 1.

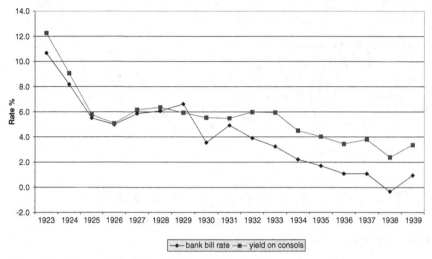

Figure 3.8a. Expected Real Rate, 1923–1939

from 1900 to 1901 is subtracted from the 1900 interest rate. That would give our 1900 "Keynes real rate." For the Fisher series, the change in the deflator between 1899 and 1900 is subtracted from the 1900 interest rate to obtain a "Fisher real rate." What was important to Fisher, however, was not so much the behaviour of that series as the behaviour of that series relative to what was expected. Consequently, we compare the Keynes and Fisher

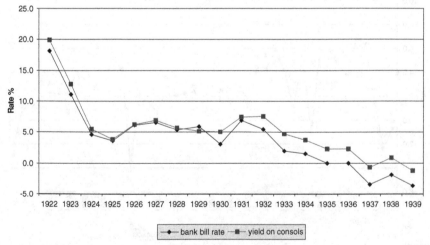

Figure 3.8b. Realized Real Rate, 1922–1939
Sources: See Appendix 1.

series and, as what is relevant are deviations of actual prices relative to price expectations, we also examine our price expectations series.

In the earlier period, the volatility year by year of the price level produces volatility in real rates by all measures. The key point is that there is no sustained rise in either version of the real rate. It is notable, though, that in the years of deflation, real rates were higher than in the later 1890s and somewhat higher than in the first decade of the twentieth century. In the interwar period, however, once the immediate postwar volatility was over, interest rates moved little, with both measures drifting gently downwards.

The Keynes and Fisher series do not display systematic differences in either period, as is to be expected, for price expectations differ little from price behaviour in either period.

A fair summary would be that there is evidence of the deflation systematically being in the United Kingdom associated with unusually high interest rates in the first deflation, but none in the second, in contrast to the U.S. experience. There is also no evidence of unexpectedly high real interest rates arising from a succession of unexpected price level falls.

EXPECTATIONS AND THE BOND MARKET

It has become common practice when investigating price expectations to examine the long-term bond market. The Fisher equation relating the real rate and expected inflation to the nominal rate is used and, in the United States and the United Kingdom, both countries with index-linked long-term government securities, there is now a well-developed set of approaches for calculating inflation expectations over various holding periods.

There were no index-linked bonds in either of the periods we examined; in view of the behaviour of prices to which people were accustomed (and which we have indicated above), it would have been hard to persuade prospective buyers that there were any benefits to be had from purchasing such securities. Nevertheless, it is possible to make some deductions about price expectations – at least those held by participants in bond markets – from the behaviour of bond yields in the two periods we examined. That task is the focus of the next section of the chapter.

We first consider the earlier period and then the interwar years. The earlier period, 1870–1913, is that for which the Gibson Paradox was first named (by Keynes 1930) and in which it was first identified by Gibson. We summarise our own and others' work on the paradox to examine what can be said about price expectations.

The paradox was that there appeared to be an association between the price level and a nominal interest rate. Various explanations have been advanced. Fisher (1930, 1907, 1896) proposed one based on the Fisher equation relating real and nominal interest rates, and this explanation was later given support by the work of Friedman and Schwartz (1982). They argued that because a move from one fully anticipated inflation rate to another would, even with the real return on physical capital unchanged, alter the nominal yield on nominal assets, the appearance of a relationship between nominal yields and the level (as opposed to the rate of change) of prices could be produced. This relationship would appear if inflation expectations adjusted to inflation with a lag, so that the longer inflation persisted (and thus the higher the price level rose), the higher the nominal would yield rise. Price expectations in this explanation of the paradox thus rise (and fall) with prices.

This is not, however, the only explanation that has been offered. Both Wicksell (1907) and Keynes (1930), suggested a real explanation – nominal rates on nominal assets were pulled down by a downward drift in the natural rate of interest, reflecting a decline in the marginal physical productivity of capital. This occurred in the first half of the period and was replaced in the second half by a rise as the American West was further developed. Price level movements were, in turn, induced because the market rate lagged behind the natural rate.

Harley (1977) supports a "Fisherian" explanation, arguing that "the money market adjusted to price expectations, and there was little effect on real interest rates." He further, argued that "the decline in the market rate of interest in the 1870s can be fully accounted for by price expectations and is fully consistent with a monetary explanation of price trends" (p. 73).

Friedman and Schwartz (1982) supported Fisher's explanation, partly by noting that the studies that rejected their explanation actually included in their data set periods when the paradox did not occur. They also rejected the Wicksell-Keynes explanation (by use of their own series for the real rate of interest), and they found shorter lags than Fisher on price expectations. Their explanation of the end of the Gibson Paradox is derived from the same analytical framework: there was a change in the monetary standard, which produced greater incentive to forecast future price movements.

After an exhaustive survey and testing of all of the available explanations of the paradox, Mills and Wood (1992) found that while decisive confirmation of Fisher was not possible, decisive rejection of all other explanations was. What is the significance of that in the present context? As noted, the Fisher explanation requires that price expectations track along with prices. Our simple time series model (inevitably simple in view of data availability) tells us that they did. Therefore, the present analysis confirms that finding and thus confirms that falling prices were expected in this nineteenth century period of deflation.

Next we come to the interwar years. As with the closing decades of the nineteenth century, in the interwar years, our (again simple) model of price expectations tracks the gentle course of the price level. Is this consistent with the behaviour of bond yields? At the time, discussion of the behaviour of yields was not at all concerned with inflationary expectations. Rather, when discussion took place at all, it was mainly in 1932 and was of the effects of the stock conversion expected in that year. We, therefore, briefly describe the details of that operation and give a flavour of the discussion surrounding it before returning to the actual behaviour of yields.

The conversion was of War Loan 1929–1947, which bore a 5 percent coupon, into "$3\frac{1}{2}$ percent 1952 or after." By March 1932, there was about £2,100 mn of the stock outstanding. (This was more than a quarter of the whole national debt, or about 50 percent of 1932 national income.)

Plans for the conversion were first discussed in 1930. By April 1931, yields had been steady for about eight months, and plans for a conversion were drawn up. These were, however, abandoned in the turbulence of first the Austro-German banking crisis and then with Britain's leaving the gold standard. In 1932, conditions changed rapidly. The bank rate fell from 6 percent to 3 percent and the treasury bill rate to just below 2 percent. Plans for a conversion into a 3 percent stock were then made. There was a massive publicity campaign; special incentives were offered to convert, and financial institutions which held the stock were lent on. The conversion was achieved.

How did interest rates behave? All the movement in the bill series is associated with the defence and subsequent abandoning of the gold standard. In the consol yield, apart from around the time of the stock conversion, there is only gentle drift downwards. Capie, Mills, and Wood (1986) confirm that to be the case. A simple time series model of the consol yield was constructed, and intervention analysis was used to see if there was any change in the series that required explanation.

There appears to have been a small but statistically significant step in the consol yield at the time of the conversion. What can be said about price expectations from this? Neither inflationary expectations nor the behaviour of the real rate would seem to fit the bill. Not only is neither of these likely to produce a step change, but the treasury was committed to monetary easing, so expectations of inflation, if affected, should have risen, and 1932 was the trough of the recession (so rising resource use should have raised the real rate). Capie, Mills, and Wood (1986) suggest the step was due to the fact that the successful conversion allowed tax reductions – one objective of the operation – and so allowed a fall in the before-tax rate of return observed in the market.

What does this say about price expectations? After the step of the stock conversion, there was a gentle drift downward – again, as was found for the earlier period – consistent with expectations of gently falling prices and, therefore, with our model of expectations. As, too, in the nineteenth century, price expectations moved sluggishly so that interest rates and the price level moved closely together. Yields and prices started to rise again in 1935. Therefore, as in the 1890s only a little more so, price movements were gentle and, so far as we can tell, were expected.

BOND RATE SPREADS

Some authors have suggested how debt-deflation might, by other routes, affect the real economy and have gone on to suggest ways by which the presence of debt-deflation might be indicated and its extent measured.

One route was outlined by Eichengreen and Grossman (1997): "By 'debt-deflation', we mean a fall in the prices of either assets or goods and services that raises the real value of net debt, thereby worsening the net wealth position of non-financial borrowers and discouraging them from consuming and investing" (p. 68). They go on to point out: "Measuring the debt burden poses difficulties for historical research" (p. 69). They therefore followed "... the procedure of Calomiris and Hubbard (1989) and Mishkin (1991) and focus on the information content of interest rate spreads" (p. 69). These spreads are, however, purged of other time-varying factors affecting the efficiency of financial intermediation (p. 71).

There are criticisms of that approach, but before turning to them, how do Eichengreen and Grossman (1997) justify it? They base their justification on adverse selection. Lenders reduce this by requiring collateral from borrowers. As the value of collateral falls (in a deflation), required interest spreads will rise as another way of compensating lenders for the risk they bear. Hence, they argue, widening spreads over a risk-free rate are produced by debt-deflation and worsen recessions by progressively restricting borrowing and investing.

For the British experience, it is well known that commercial banks lent extensively without security. It is true that, in the closing decades of the nineteenth century, the banks increasingly required some security. Yet, even by 1914, more than one-half of all loans were given on the strength of no more than a personal guarantee (Capie and Collins 1996).

What are the objections to that approach? They were cogently and forcefully set out by Schwartz (1997). The spread, she argues, reflects both liquidity and expectational forces. This yield spread usually varies procyclically. Why? It can be produced simply by the liquidity of lower quality debt falling in recessions, as default is more likely. Hence, widening spreads are a normal cyclical phenomenon, not a symptom of debt-deflation. Further, as Crafts (1997) observes, if the debt-deflation discussed works through households' balance sheets, then "...I am rather doubtful that the interest rate spread between commercial paper and the discount rate will be closely related to the relevant changes in household debt positions" (p. 97). But, as he admits, data on household balance sheets are not readily available.

We carry out a similar exercise, following several previous authors who, albeit somewhat sceptical of the value of bond spreads as an indicator of a debt-deflation process at work, have nevertheless examined them in view of the difficulties attached to testing debt-deflation theories. Eichengreen and Grossman 1997 are an example of this group. We share their scepticism, but also their willingness to see what, if anything, can be extracted from the measure.

Before doing so, though, there is another problem to be faced when studying the United Kingdom – the lack of a significant and active corporate bond market. To what can we relate the government bond yield in the absence of corporate bonds? We have chosen to use the dividend yield on the U.K. "top 100" equity index for the comparison. That comparison is, of course, open to the objection that we are comparing a nominal yield (that on consols) with an income stream that can move to compensate for inflation. In our view, however, the comparison is justifiable in this period because of the stability

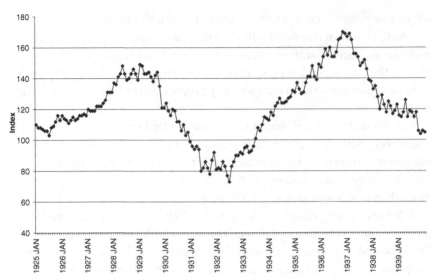

Figure 3.9. Index of Security Prices, 1925–1939 (1924 Average = 100)
Sources: See Appendix 1.

of the price level and the modesty of the year-by-year rate of change of the price level.

One further point remains to be noted. There was not a suitable index of dividend yields before 1900. Accordingly, we start the comparison at that date and run it through to 1939 (Figure 3.9). What does the comparison reveal? First, the spread was *wider* before World War I than in almost any year after it, and the years running up to 1914 were years of stability. Second, there are two big, short-lived, spikes in the series. The first occurred during the immediate postwar boom of 1919–1920 and the second during the not-much-longer-lived return to gold. Although perhaps surprising in view of the criticism the return to gold has received, we would offer essentially the same explanation for both episodes. The first period was an actual boom, the latter an expected boom, for many welcomed the return to gold as signalling the return of pre-1914 style stability (Capie, Mills, and Wood 1985). Thereafter, the spread is narrow, not even reaching pre–World War I levels in the run up to World War II.

Accordingly, we conclude that, to the extent that the spread indicates a debt-deflation process at work (and we have noted our reservations about this), it shows no evidence of such a process working during the interwar years in Britain.

Another channel is the effect of leverage on firms' investment spending. This has been proposed and tested by Calomiris, Orphanides, and Sharpe (1997), following work by Calomiris and Hubbard (1989) and Hubbard and Kashyap (1992). They argue that it is necessary to test the effects at the firm rather than the aggregate level and that the effects may be asymmetric. Their reasons are as follows. First, aggregate debt/assets may not be a good indicator of the representative debt/asset ratio of firms. Second, leverage may be important only for cyclically sensitive firms, and its effects would thus not show up in aggregate data. Third, they worked on post–World War II data, and there were too few aggregate observations, as the United States had experienced only six recessions. As for asymmetry, they argue that capital constraints do not bind as long as a firm's sales are growing, but when sales drop, debt service becomes a problem, so expenditures – particularly investment spending – are cut back. The approach is interesting, but the data to pursue it in our time periods do not exist.

INTERTEMPORAL SUBSTITUTION

There is one final channel to explore. According to Keynes, falling prices could lead to further falls in prices if some consumption and investment decisions were deferred. One, albeit casual, way of doing this is to look at house prices and equity price changes.

The 1930s saw a major house-building boom. Houses were bought not only by prosperous professionals, but by a much wider group, including skilled manual workers. Various house price series are available. None even purports to cover the whole country or to represent the entire market.

Accordingly, we report both a building cost and a house price series.[3] Before doing so, though, we should mention that there were substantial regional price divergences (these are shown subsequently) and also substantial variation within cities. This intracity variation was a systematic one; prices fell in the "inner cities" relative to the new suburbs, as not only did the new houses in the suburbs have attractions such as electric lights, but the suburbs were seen as healthier and therefore more attractive places to live. There was thus a systematic relative price change. This should be borne in mind, as the price series we report are essentially for newly built (suburban) houses. These comprised a substantial part of the stock of housing; between 1919

---

[3]   See Appendix 3.

and 1939, the stock of dwellings went up by about 30 percent. The first series is Maywald's building cost index. After a sharp rise during the war and in the postwar boom, costs fell and then drifted gently from an index level of just above 100 in 1922 to a low point of just above 80 in 1933. They climbed gently thereafter (Figure 3.10). The average cost of dwelling houses fell from £700 in 1923 to just over £500 in 1932 and was more or less stable thereafter. It must be noted, though, that houses got somewhat smaller over the period; no series that adjusts for this is available. The "Chamberlain" subsidy of £75 per house was introduced in late 1923; this seems to have produced a fall in the average house price despite a modest rise in building costs that occurred at the same time. Of course, the average price had a range of variation around it, and it showed substantial regional variation.

The intertemporal substitution effect gets essentially no support from these data. There were no prolonged periods of falling house prices coinciding with years of recession and sluggish house sales. Thus, there were few, if any, data to support the deflation story. And even if there had been, it is hard to see how intertemporal substitution could account for a prolonged recession; few items of expenditure can be postponed for many years, and if real interest rates drop, the incentive to postpone is of course reduced.

CONCLUSIONS

In this chapter we have examined, as much as the data allow, how the debt deflation theories of Keynes and Fisher contribute to an understanding of the behaviour of the British economy in either the final quarter of the nineteenth century or in the recession of the early 1930s. With Keynes's theory, the key is to see whether there was any evidence that price change was expected. With Fisher's theory, in contrast, one must see whether price shocks that occurred after nominal contracts had been set produced problems through any of the channels he or his followers listed. We also note arguments of Mundell (2000) on whether these price changes were anticipated.

After considering some qualitative views on price expectations, we use some simple time series modelling techniques to produce price expectation series. (We also draw on some earlier work we did on expectations in the bond market that provided some support for the current work.) These expectations, in turn, are used to construct a variety of short-and long-run interest rate series that accord with the views of Keynes and Fisher. On both prices

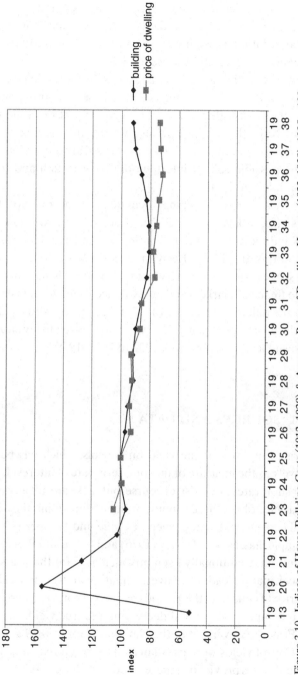

Figure 3.10. Indices of House Building Costs (1913–1938) & Average Price of Dwelling Houses (1923–1938): 1925 = 100

Sources: See Appendix 1.

and interest rates, the evidence that emerges is that there is little difference between the actual series and the predicted series. We, therefore, conclude on this basis that deflation transmitted no adverse effects to the real economy through the channels suggested by these models.

Another way of examining the issue is, at least in theory, to consider the changing behaviour of bond rate spreads. This is beset with problems, which are greater for the British than for the U.S. economy at this time because of data scarcity. Nevertheless, improvising, we did the exercise and again found little or no evidence of deflation transmitting adverse effects. Finally, we consider the possible role of intertemporal substitution and found no support for that hypothesis either.

In summary, these periods of falling prices do not appear to have brought the calamitous effects that are sometimes thought to be the consequence of deflation. Admittedly, the rate of deflation was much milder than in the United States during the 1930s. The various strands of evidence brought together here suggest also that there was in the United Kingdom little disturbance of the financial markets and no evidence of financial instability. It is true that, in the deflation of 1929 to 1932, falling prices and rigid money wages did produce unemployment. Yet, even that was relatively short-lived, and there followed a great boom from 1932 to 1937–1938.

APPENDIX 1. SOURCES AND DATA

The interest rate employed is the yield on consols, which has been used almost exclusively as the measure of the long-term rate of interest in this period. Series for short rates also exist, of course, but these are not as well suited to the examination of hypotheses about, or depending upon, the Fisher effect. The usual consol yield series, given in Capie and Webber (1985: table III.10) for example, has, as both Harley (1976) and Capie and Webber (1985: p. 316–20) point out, traditionally been miscalculated for the years 1880 to 1903. This miscalculation leads to an overestimation of the true yield for two reasons. The price of consols in this period rose above par, thus increasing the possibility of redemption at par and decreasing the true yield. In addition, the details of Fisher's conversion of the National Debt in 1889 affected the way in which Consol yields were calculated. We, therefore, employed a revised consol yield series provided in the appendix of Harley (1977), although related work reported in Capie, Mills, and Wood (1991) has used both this and the traditional series in similar exercises and found little difference in the results so obtained.

The output series used is Feinsten's (1972) compromise estimate of GDP; hence, his implicit GDP deflator is used as the price series. Although there has been some discussion recently over the reliability of this output series – see the interchange between Greasley (1986, 1989) and Feinstein (1989) and the discussion in Crafts, Leybourne, and Mills (1989) – it would still seem to be the best that is currently available.

Annual observations for all series are available from 1870 to 1913, except for M3, whose initial (1870) observation is missing. Details and descriptive discussion of the data and univariate analysis of the individual series can be found in Capie, Mills, and Wood (1991). In particular, it can be found, using a variety of methods, that the logarithms of both money series, output, and prices are all integrated processes of order one, that is, I(1), whereas the interest rate itself is I(I).

APPENDIX 2. MODELS OF THE GNP DEFLATOR AND INFLATION

Level of GNP Deflator

The GNP deflator was analysed over the two periods, 1870 – 1914 and 1919 – 39, using standard Box-Jenkins time series procedures and appropriate models for describing the trend determined. Because of the differences in the underlying trends for the two periods, there was no single model suitable for both periods. The appropriate models determined are both autoregressive processes, that is, the basic model is of the form,

$$X_t = \alpha_1 X_{t-1} + \alpha_2 X_{t-2} + \cdots + \alpha_p X_{t-p} + Z_t$$

where X_t is the observed GNP deflator in year t, α_i's are unknown parameters, and Z_t is an error term assumed to have a mean of 0. The above expression describes an autoregressive process of order p, that is, an AR(p) process. The order of the AR processes was determined by Akaike's information criterion (AIC). If k is the order of the current model, then

$$\text{AIC}(k) = -2\ln(\text{maximised likelihood}) + 2k$$

The value of k that minimises AIC(k) is chosen as the order of the AR process. The models derived are as follows,

- Period 1919–1939

$$Y_t = 0.99968(0.2408)Y_{t-1} - 0.45561(0.3233)Y_{t-2}$$
$$+ 0.11982(0.2408)Y_{t-3} + Z_t$$

where

$$Y_t = X_t - X_{t-1},$$

implying that

$$X_t = 1.99968X_{t-1} - 1.45529X_{t-2} + 0.57543X_{t-3}$$
$$- 0.11982X_{t-4} + Z_t$$

- Period 1870–1914
  Again setting: $Y_t = X_t - X_{t-1}$, the actual model fitted is

$$Y_t = 0.09046(0.3008)Y_{t-1} + 0.02707(0.3008)Y_{t-2} + Z_t$$

implying that

$$X_t = 1.09046X_{t-1} - 0.06339X_{t-2} - 0.02707X_{t-3} + Z_t$$

Hence, predictions for the period 1919 to 1939 are based on the previous four years of observations, whereas predictions for 1870 to 1914 are based on the previous three years of observations. The standard errors of the parameter estimates are given in parenthesis.

Rate of Inflation

The rate of inflation, estimated by year-by-year rates of change in the GNP deflator was similarly analysed, resulting in the following time series models,

- Period 1870–1939

$$X_t = 0.60651(0.0958)X_{t-1} + Z_t$$

- Period 1870–1913

$$X_t = 0.27316(0.1467)X_{t-1} + Z_t$$

- Period 1921–1939

$$X_t = 0.46006(0.2093)X_{t-1} + Z_t$$

Hence, for the rate of inflation, predictions are simply based on the previous year's observation.

APPENDIX 3. A NOTE ON THE COURSE OF
SOME PRICE SERIES

The main features of movements in aggregate prices have been given in the text. It is only the aggregate price level, and the annual rate of change in that, that we model. However, we describe here the course of some individual commodity prices together with some asset prices as found in residential properties and equities. These are not shown here but are available from the web page for this volume at (www.wlu.ca/~wwwsbe/faculty/psiklos/deflation.htm). These all reflect the well-known trend of falling in the first part of the period followed by some modest recovery in the second part, although it is clear there was quite a bit of difference in the extent of the fall and rise across commodities. For example, coal and metals were relatively flat throughout against the more obviously tumbling grain prices. Between the wars, the trend was generally downwards for most commodities, and they moved more closely together.

On asset prices, there are houses and equities, but the limited data allow only a description for a much shorter period. House price data are available for the interwar years but not before that. These are interesting in that they show a steady, if gentle, decline for residential housing from 1923 (approximately 105) to 1938 (approximately 75). The sharpest movement came in 1931. Deflated costs show the same pattern. There were considerable regional differences, but not always of the kind that might have been thought (see correlation table). Data on equities are also limited. An equity price index for the late nineteenth century was reported in Capie and Mills (1985). Although limited in coverage, it showed some cyclical pattern around a flat trend in the first part of the period, followed by a step up to similar fluctuation around another flat trend in the second part of the period. Data are slightly more plentiful for the period after 1920–1925. The first few years showed a strong upswing from the base of 100 to over 140 in 1929. But equity prices collapsed after that point and reached a low point in 1933 at 80. There followed a strong recovery to 1937, then a loss of these gains so that the period ended where it began. Interest rates reflect some of the course in these variables, but not entirely. It is long rates that are of particular interest for this exercise. These are given only brief comment here because they are given separate treatment in a discussion of the Gibson Paradox – a topic that has predominated in this area in the late nineteenth century. Short rates for both periods are represented by both bank rate and prime bank bill rate. Bank rate oscillated around a mean of 3.5 percent in the period 1870 to 1914. In the interwar years, it began in a higher range and fell to the fixed ("cheap money era") of 2 percent in the 1930s. A better indicator of the market rate is found in the prime bank bill rate, which was much more volatile. In the first period, it showed more of the long-term pattern of gentle "U"-shape. Between the wars, it again showed much more movement but a very similar pattern to that of bank rate. But it fell to below 1 percent for most of the 1930s.

Long rates are captured in the yield on consols. For the first period, these show clearly that U-shape, with a particularly exaggerated U in the 1890s. After the immediate postwar adjustment period (1919–1921), the yield on consols remained at about 4.5 percent without much deviation from 1922 to 1931. It then fell steeply, reaching a low of less than 3 percent in the mid-1930s before drifting up to about 3.7 percent in 1937.

4 Deflation Dynamics in Sweden: Perceptions, Expectations, and Adjustment During the Deflations of 1921–1923 and 1931–1933

Klas Fregert and Lars Jonung

INTRODUCTION

Big deflations are more like singular events than realizations of some stable stochastic process. Thus, the historical particulars, including the perceptions and expectations of central decision-makers should be assessed to understand deflations. This approach is adopted in this study of the two major twentieth-century deflations in Sweden, a big one in 1921–1923 and a small one in 1931–1933. We examine three groups of actors: (1) economists that took part in public debate, (2) policy makers, and (3) wage-setters, as well as interactions between these three groups.

The evolution of the policy recommendations of the economists, actions of the policy makers, and behavior of the labor market participants before, during, and after the two deflations is traced. We focus on how their perceptions and expectations were influenced by the experience of the past. The major reason for considering both episodes of deflations is that the two deflations were close in time. This gives an opportunity to explore how the experience during the first deflation episode in the early 1920s influenced beliefs and behavior ten years later during the second deflation.

Our general framework can be represented as follows. Prevailing perceptions and expectations held by decision-makers concerning the choice and effects of economic policies are determined by the lessons from past macroeconomic episodes. These perceptions and expectations are revised when new information is obtained from new macroeconomic episodes. The economics profession, policy makers and wage setters are involved in a never-ending process of adjusting their beliefs, in short in a learning process, where the interpretation of past events, that is, the lesson of the past, serves as the major source of information for revising perceptions and expectations.[1]

We are concerned with two sets of questions related to the above framework.

(i) *The effect of the macroeconomic outcome on perceptions and expectations.* Here we argue that it is the most recent and relevant experience that affects perceptions. Policy makers in the early 1920s looked back at the inflationary World War I period 1914–1918 and wanted a return to the pre-1914 gold standard by deflation to establish price stability anew. Wage setters may have felt the same, but did not trust the policy makers to make good on their promises. In the 1930s, policy makers wanted to avoid inflation as well as deflation in the light of the monetary turmoil of 1914–1924.

(ii) *The effect of perceptions and expectations on the macroeconomic outcome.* The actual evolution of prices and output were predicated on the perceptions and expectations of all decision-makers. We emphasize that this makes the macroeconomic process difficult to analyze. First, expectations were not unanimous across groups. For example, employees had stickier expectations than employers resulting in conflicts, strikes, and unemployment. Policy makers had more belief in wage flexibility than the contract makers themselves. Consumers had different expectations than wage makers. In short, expectations did not mesh across groups, which had real consequences. Second, perceptions and expectations were held with uncertainty. We argue that this possibly made the deflation shorter than otherwise as wage contracts were shortened and, in some cases, abandoned.

We wish to emphasize the connection through learning and memory across regimes and crises. The process described above is a temporal story, but it is not in strict calendar terms. We emphasize the linkages between periods that people use as lessons. Rare and distinct events such as deflations should be put in the context of what occurred before and after to understand what figured in the minds of decision makers at the time.

Our approach makes us go beyond standard macroeconomic data on the development of prices and quantities by exploiting more direct, albeit qualitative, data on beliefs and expectations. Three major sources of information are used here: statements by leading economists, announcements by

---

[1] We rely on the literature for lesson learning. It basically suggests that policy makers are backward-looking when framing present policies. The beliefs and perceptions of the past are thus the prime determinant of future policies. For a survey, see Jonung (1999).

policy makers, and the design and contents of collective wage agreements. As we focus on the documentation of beliefs and expectations, our method is mostly qualitative and historical. We also offer a set of stylized simulations of the Fischer contract model to illustrate the possible effects of beliefs and expectations on outcomes.

THE DEFLATION OF 1920–1922

Background

Figure 4.1 plots the evolution of major macroeconomic indicators covering the period 1913–1939. The deflation of the early 1920s should be seen in the light of the pre-1914 price stability associated with the classical gold standard introduced in Sweden in 1873 and in the light of the high and variable inflation after its suspension in August 1914. The money stock rose sharply during the war years. The Swedish cost of living index increased from 100 to 257 between 1914 and 1918. The rate of inflation was close to 40 percent in 1918. The war years were thus associated with rapid monetary expansion and a rapid rise in the price level as shown in Figure 4.1.

After the war, the major question for policy makers – that is, for the Riksbank, Parliament (the *Riksdag*), and Government – was: Which type of monetary policy should be pursued? Three options existed in public debate: (1) Should Sweden return to gold at the going rate (that is, to devalue its currency relative to its 1914 gold parity rate)? (2) Should Sweden return to gold at the prewar rate (that is, to deflate)? or (3) Should Sweden let its currency float combined with a program of price level stabilization?

Considerable confusion reigned at the end of the World War I about monetary policy. Most economists and politicians advocated a return to the gold standard, but opinion was divided on how to reach this goal. Let us give an account of the announcements and actions that led to the return to the pre–World War I gold parity de jure in 1924. The Riksbank thereby fulfilled the goal of a return to the gold standard for monetary policy first declared in September 1920.[2]

Announcements and Actions by Policy Makers

Table 4.1 gives the key monetary policy announcements and actions leading up to the return to the prewar gold parity rate of the krona. The new Social

---

[2] This section builds on Heckscher (1926) and Östlind (1945).

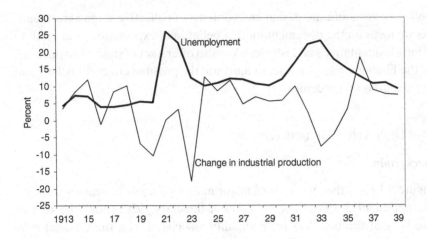

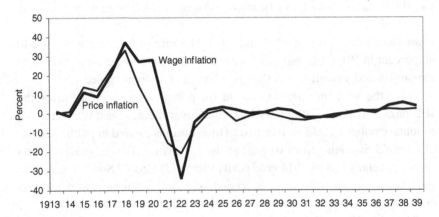

Figure 4.1. Unemployment, Change in Industrial Production, Wage Inflation, and Price Inflation, 1913–1939
Source: Statistisk årsbok.

Democratic Minister of Finance, Rickard Sandler, presented the first declaration of the restoration of the old gold parity in September 1920 as the goal of monetary policy, but with no definite date. The Riksbank was governed by a Board of Directors (*Riksbanksfullmäktige*) elected by the *Riksdag* and thus formally independent of the government. Because the government reflected the parliamentary majority, the Minister of Finance had a great influence on the Board. In turn, the Board of Directors was supervised by the banking committee of the *Riksdag*. During this period, it began to issue its own statements on the goals of monetary policy.

Table 4.1. *Monetary policy announcements and actions, 1920–1924*

Year (Day/Month)	Announcement
1920	
January	Riksbank board: Discount rate ineffective, no goal for monetary policy.[a]
February	Scandinavian central bank conference: Restoration of the gold standard can only be settled by international negotiations.
March 11	Eli Heckscher: Advice to the public to convert notes to gold.
March 13	Notes made inconvertible to gold.
March 19	Increase in discount rate from 5.5 to 7 percent.
August	Expert committee: Gradual decrease in the price level to prewar gold parity recommended.[b]
September	Increase in the discount rate from 7 to 7.5 percent Minister of Finance: Commitment to the old gold parity.[c]
December	Expert committee: Reservations about restoration of the old gold parity.[d]
1921	
January	Minister of Finance: Commitment of the Parliament to the old gold parity.[e]
April	Banking committee of the Parliament: restoration of the old gold parity is arbitrary.[f]
April	Parliament: Commitment to the old gold parity.
October 4	Decrease in discount rate from 7.5 to 5.5 percent.
1922	
October 4	Committee on duties and treatises: Speedy return to old gold parity.[g]
July 3	Decrease in discount rate from 5.5 to 4.5 percent.
November	The Riksbank pegs the krona to the old dollar parity by intervention.
1923	
September	Increase in discount rate from 4.5 to 5 percent.
1924	
April	Gold standard restored de jure. Notes convertible to gold at prewar parity.

[a] Reaction to written note by Knut Wicksell.

[b] *Finanssakkunniga* consisting of the two economists Emil Sommarin and Knut Wicksell and the *Riksbank* governor. Viktor Moll. Wicksell issued a separate statement urging the restoration of the 1914 price level and thereafter price stabilisation.

[c] Social Democratic government with Rickard Sandler as Minister of Finance and Ernst Wigforss as Assistant Secretary of the Ministry of Finance.

[d] *Ekonomiska rådet* consisting of the industrialist Wallenberg, the economist Cassel, and the Riksbank governor Moll.

[e] New government and Minister of Finance Beskow.

[f] *Riksdagens bankoutskott*. The member Ernst Wigforss issued a separate statement urging restoration of the old gold parity, which turned the Parliament's vote in favor of restoration of the old parity.

[g] *Tull-och traktatkommittén.*

In January 1921, a new government reiterated its support for the return to gold at the old parity. As the depression deepened, industrialists and business and labor leaders became skeptical. The opposition influenced the banking committee of the *Riksdag*, which issued a statement in April 1921 against the goal, although it was quickly overruled by Parliament. Ernst Wigforss, a member of the banking committee, issued a separate statement against the committee and asked for a quick gold restoration. Wigforss's statement was then voted for by parliament as its opinion. The krona reached the old dollar parity at the end of 1922, but the formal return to gold was not achieved until April 1, 1924. In the meantime, the Riksbank pegged the krona to the dollar by intervention.

To sum up, from August 1920, the announcements by policy makers were unequivocal in favor of an eventual return of the old parity. The public could therefore reasonably expect a coming deflation, but had little guidance on at what speed and how far it would go.

How Much Deflation Was Required to Restore the Old Gold Parity?

The policy of restoring the old gold parity amounted to restoring the old krona-dollar parity, as the dollar was tied to its prewar gold parity rate. Economists clearly stated that the real exchange rate must return to its prewar level, as the exceptional circumstances of the war had disappeared. To restore the prewar gold parity and the real exchange rate, the Swedish price level therefore had to decrease by the amount it had increased faster than the U.S. price level since the gold suspension in 1914.[3]

In October 1920, when deflation began in Sweden, the "required" deflation was about 40 percent. But by this time, the U.S. price level had begun to fall as well, which implied a further deflation to the extent that the U.S. deflation continued. When the deflation began, the nominal krona-dollar

---

[3] The Swedish real exchange rate had appreciated gradually from the outbreak of the war until the beginning of 1918 through a combination of faster inflation in Sweden than abroad and an appreciating krona from the end of 1915. The real exchange in 1918 stood at half the 1913 level. The driving force was a strong export demand combined with difficulties in importing goods from the belligerent countries. In 1917 the transportation cost of importing coal from England had risen thirty-five times, whereas the cost of exporting lumber to England only had risen eight times. The cost difference declined drastically with the armistice in November 1918 and disappeared by the end of 1920. Heckscher (1926: pp. 25–42) discussed in detail the real appreciation during the war as well as the general determinants of the real exchange rate. When the deflation started in the Fall of 1920, the real exchange rate had depreciated from its peak in 1918, mainly due to a depreciation of the nominal exchange rate.

exchange rate had to appreciate by about 25 percent to reach the 1914 parity. (Thus, the real exchange rate was about 15 [= 40–25] percent overvalued.) After a short period of depreciation during October and November 1920, the nominal exchange rate started to appreciate. By the end of 1922, the deflation was almost over and the krona-dollar prewar gold parity was restored. Wholesale prices had then fallen by 60 percent, and the real exchange rate had reached its long-run value for the rest of the 1920s at about 5 percent real appreciation relative to the 1914 level.

Although a return to the old gold parity was expected as the suspension of 1914 was regarded as a temporary measure, it was not until the announcement in September 1920 that the public could with any confidence believe in the restoration and, consequently, in a coming deflation. The amount of deflation was, however, highly uncertain for at least three reasons.

First, the goal of the return to gold was not a definitive one. The parliamentary situation was not stable, with changing minority governments. There was a constant majority in favor of a return to the old parity, but many policy makers and members of parliament were uncertain as opposition mounted during the subsequent deflation. Second, the speed of the return was unknown. As policy makers repeatedly stated that Sweden could not return to the gold standard as the sole country in Europe, the speed also hinged on foreign monetary policies. Finally, nobody knew how far and for how long the international deflation would go.

Beliefs and Advice of Economists

Economists can affect the public's perceptions and expectations through their interpretations and forecasts of current events. They can also affect policy makers through their direct advice as well as by that given in the media. As the Swedish economists during this period were most active in public debate while also serving as advisors to the policy makers, their potential effect on the outcome may have been large.

The rapid movements in the Swedish price level, the inflation of 1914–1920, and the subsequent deflation of 1920–1922 gave rise to some of the most lively discussions of monetary matters that has ever taken place in Sweden. The leading economists of the day participated in this exchange of opinions, including Gustav Cassel, David Davidson, Eli Heckscher, and Knut Wicksell, as well as the young Bertil Ohlin. Here, we outline the main themes of their proposals and arguments with a view to assessing their influence on actual events. In short, we argue that their almost unanimous support of the old gold parity contributed to the rapid deflation, but divisions over the timing created uncertainty as to its extent.

Eli Heckscher published a newspaper article March 13, 1920, urging the public to convert its Riksbank notes to gold. As the dollar had appreciated 44 percent above its prewar value and the dollar was back on gold at the old dollar-gold rate, the public, he claimed, could make an arbitrage profit of 44 percent on every krona were it allowed to export gold. The article started a run on the gold reserves and led the Riksbank to ask the Parliament for an immediate abrogation of its obligation to convert its notes to gold. After a heated parliamentary debate on monetary policy, the notes were made inconvertible.

The need for a policy decision was recognized. A special committee was appointed (*Finanssakkunniga*). A report was presented in August 1920 recommending a gradual return to the old gold parity, which became the basis of the September 1920 official declaration of a return to the old parity. Knut Wicksell, however, issued a separate statement pleading for a restoration of the 1914 price level and a confirmation of the paper standard with price level stabilization as the goal of monetary policy.

Prior to the end of the war, the majority of economists active in pubic debate had advocated a return to the old parity. All stuck to this view throughout the deflation, with the exception of Gustav Cassel. They all argued that in principle price stability was the paramount goal of a monetary regime, but that in practice the gold standard was the only feasible regime to achieve near price stability. All stressed the good performance of the gold standard before 1914 in comparison with the paper standard during the war. This was the proper lesson from the past. Price stabilization under a paper standard, on the other hand, required both well-intentioned and well-informed policy makers.

This majority view was opposed from two quarters. Knut Wicksell was an articulate proponent of a return to the price level of 1914 and a stabilization of prices at this level for reasons of fairness and justice.[4] Per Jacobsson, on the other hand, argued for an immediate stabilization in 1921 at the rate

---

[4] In 1919 Wicksell argued, "In my opinion we should try to return to the prewar price level. It is difficult to present any valid argument for stopping halfway. The means to do this is to maintain a high discount rate preferably combined with interest-bearing deposits with the Riksbank to reduce the stock of notes to the 1914 level. It is a very painful process, but it is probably better to do it now rather than to wait."

implied by the current exchange rate against the dollar. Neither Wicksell, nor Jacobsson had any followers among other economists or policy makers.

The near unanimity for a return to the old parity did not extend to its implementation both in terms of means and timing. To varying degrees economists were concerned about the ability to scale down nominal wages without major labor market conflicts, but on the whole they were more optimistic than representatives of business and labor. In particular, the export industries were skeptical of deflation. The industrialist Ivar Kreuger, in a 1921 debate, berated the economists for being too sanguine about the costs of bringing down nominal wages. Knut Wicksell perhaps represented the most extreme view when he declared, "The idea that the workers could not be persuaded to lower their claims, even if prices go down, is pure fancy."[5]

Gustav Cassel, who identified the reactions of wage setters as crucial, took a middle ground. He hesitated about the possibility of bringing down nominal wages, which made him waver in his support for a return to the old parity after the deflation began.

The economists' almost unanimous support for the old gold parity contributed to its implementation by influencing policy makers first to declare the goal and then stick to it. There was also general agreement on letting the deflation process be gradual. The economists differed concerning the tactics of gradualism, however. Eli Heckscher argued for immediate convertibility to gold at a depreciated rate and then a preannounced path for the conversion rate until the old parity was reached. David Davidson argued for a preset date of conversion, whereas Gustav Cassel advocated a wait-and-see tactic, which also was how the deflation was carried out.

In conclusion, the economists influenced events by their support for a return to the old gold parity. Less clear is if they also influenced events in their role as forecasters by failing to forecast the speed and the impact of the deflation.

Beliefs and Actions of Wage Setters

The response of the labor market participants is important in our account of the big deflation of the 1920s. In this section we analyze the process of wage deflation by focusing on the labor market organizations' expectations,

[5] Wicksell (1918: p. 137).

tactics, and the national collective agreements.[6] Wage setting in Sweden was dominated by the labor market organizations in the interwar period. Almost all unions belonged to the national Trade Union Federation, *Landsorganisationen* (LO), and almost all employers belonged to the Employers Federation *Svenska arbetsgivarföreningen* (SAF). Roughly half of all workers with collective agreements had national agreements through the interwar period. The coverage of collective agreements went up overall from around 60 to 80 percent during the same period. Besides making up a large part of the labor market, they probably influenced the agreements at the firm, local, and district level as well as the nonorganized part of the labor market.

The planning of the organizations for the 1921 wage bargaining round began in the summer of 1920 when the postwar boom was still being felt. On the labor side the planning took place within the individual unions, whereas the employers in SAF decided on a common policy of prolonging existing agreements. All the collective agreements had clauses that ensured prolongation for one year unless one of the parties gave notice, usually at the latest three months before the expiration of the wage contract.

The deflation, which began in October 1920, coincided with the notice deadline for a majority of the national agreements. Almost all of the unions with expiration at the end of December 1920 gave notice in the hope of higher nominal wages. Many employers reacted to the union notices by calling for a common wage reduction strategy coordinated by SAF. The idea of a common wage reduction strategy was, however, scrapped as the deflation was believed to affect industries differently. Instead, every industry had to make its own decisions, although consultations with SAF's governing board were required.

On the labor side, LO chairman Arvid Thorberg declared in January 1921 that no reductions should take place before consumer prices had decreased, "If there once is a significant reduction in consumer prices, then wages may become affected, but such a decrease has not happened, and it cannot be right that workers should pay before an expected but not actual decrease in the expense of consumption has happened."[7] One way to interpret this statement is that even if there were reasons to expect a deflation, it was

---

[6] This section builds on the history of LO by Casparsson (1947: pp. 593–601), the history of SAF by Hallendorff (1927: pp. 147–57), and SAF's annual reports. Östlind (1945: pp. 363–6) surveyed the antideflation opposition.

[7] Landsorganisationens verksamhetsberättelse 1921: p. 82.

highly uncertain and should therefore not be incorporated into the wage contracts.

In the beginning of the deflation episode, expectations and beliefs varied across the labor market. The union side appeared not to believe in any significant deflation, whereas the employers did. Apparently, the statement by the Minister of Finance in August 1920 did not have a major effect on the wage setters. Whether this was due to low credibility in the announced policy or great uncertainty about the likely consequences should the program be fulfilled is considered next.

Let us now turn to the process of changing wages. Most of the price deflation took place in 1921, whereas wage deflation took place primarily in 1922 as shown in Figure 4.1. Here we examine the process of wage deflation to consider the sources of this lagged response. The wage reductions took place under three modes: with a new agreement, within an old agreement, and without an agreement.

(1) *Wage reductions with new agreements.* The timing and size of wage reductions in the national agreements (*Riksavtal*) are reported in the government publication *Sociala meddelanden*, summarized in Table 4.2. Figure 4.2 shows the wage reductions for four groups, sawmills, pulp, textiles, and printing. The new agreements signed in the beginning of 1921 had an unchanged content, that is, they were, in practice, a prolongation. This was the case in the match, mining, and bookbinding industries. In the first quarter of 1921, four large groups – metal, sawmills, pulp, and textiles – accepted wage cuts of between 10 and 15 percent of going wages, whereas several groups prolonged their contracts. Applying the reductions of going wages was a novelty, as most previous agreements had specified absolute levels for different skill categories. Many of the agreements had a minimum wage character in normal times. The new method applied directly to going wages. The wage reductions that were negotiated in the second and third quarter of 1921 ranged from 10 to 30 percent.

Another novelty was the use of preset reductions within the agreement (*lönenedsättning i repriser*). Two small groups – the textile and printing industries – used the method in 1921, which became widespread in 1922.[8] Actual nominal wages decreased during 1921 by about 10 percent, whereas wholesale prices decreased by 40 percent and consumer prices by 20 percent.

[8] Workers in the iron ore industry went back to work without an agreement and had to accept the employers' unilateral reduction by 30 percent.

Table 4.2. Wage reductions (ordinary wage/piece rate) in national agreements by quarter in percent, 1921–1923

	Year, quarter												Total
Union	1921				1922				1923				21–23
	1	2	3	4	1	2	3	4	1	2	3	4	
Metal & mining													
Iron ores	c	c	−30 (no agreement)		−15 (no agreement)				c	c	**0**		−45
Metal	−10(p)	−10			−25(no agreement)				**0**				−45
Mines: Sweden	mid-p				−40								−40
Mines: Lapland	p				−25				**−6**				−31
Wood & forestry													
Sawmills	−10				c	−35			0				−45
Wood			−25				−10						−35
Paper & printing													
Paper	−15				c	−25			**0**				−50
Pulp		−25			−10	−10			c	**0**			−35
Litography	p				−25	−5	−5						−35
Printing			−10	−5	−5	−5	−10	−5					−40
Bookbinding	p				−25	−5	−5						−35
Textiles													
Textiles	**0**	−15	−5	−5	−5	−5	−5						−40
Chemicals													
Matches	p				**0**	−20	−10			*−2-5*			−30
Glass	c	c	−20		−25								−45
Telephone		−12	−12			−25							−49

Note: All wage reduction are percentage changes relative to the peak 1920; bold signifies new agreement, p signifies prolongation, and c signifies conflict.
Source: Sociala meddelanden, various issues.

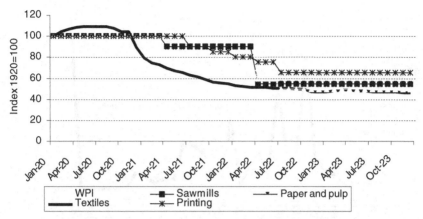

Figure 4.2. The Wholesale Price Index and the Hourly Total Wage for Males for Four Groups
Source: Statistisk årsbok.

The nominal wage cuts continued in 1922, with reductions by 20 to 35 percent. Preset wage reductions within the new agreement became the norm. Generally, the sectors with the smallest cuts in 1921 had the largest cuts in 1922. No sector prolonged, and only two went through strikes (sawmills and paper). As most of the price deflation was over by the end of 1921, real wages fell during 1922. In 1923, hardly any further wage reductions took place.

(2) *Wage reductions with old agreements.* Some agreements were not renewed for 1921, either because they did not expire or because no party gave notice. This was the case in the engineering industry (*metallavtalet*), the largest single negotiating area. The engineering industry, as a whole, reduced nominal wages by 29 percent during 1921 but with large differences.

(3) *Wage reductions without agreements.* The use of collective agreements declined during 1921–1922, from a peak in 1920 of 65 percent, to 50 percent in 1922. SAF discussed the issue in the fall of 1920 when the deflation had begun, questioning whether collective agreements were desirable during the severe deflation. The central leadership decided to recommend the continued use of collective agreements with respect to the possible detrimental effects on the future status of the collective agreement, especially as a peace treaty. As the recession deepened, SAF did not exclude that abandoning the agreements might be the only solution to save a firm or an industry. This happened with regard to mainly smaller agreements, but two large national agreements were not renewed – the iron ore industry agreement during

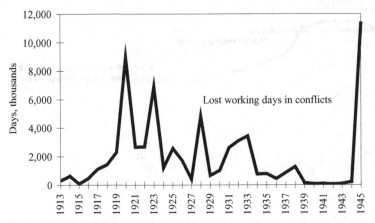

Figure 4.3. Conflict Intensity, 1913–1945
Source: Statistisk årsbok.

1921–1922 and the engineering industry agreement during 1922. Table 4.2 takes a closer look at these reductions.

To sum up, the nominal wage reductions in 1921–1922 are unique in their size and speed. By the end of 1922, the real product wage had increased by almost 60 percent relative to 1919 and by 50 percent relative to 1913. The largest reductions occurred in the forest-related industries, which were the hardest hit by the international deflation. In the wood product industry, nominal wages fell in total by 40 percent. The smallest reductions occurred in the nontraded goods industries. The increase in the average real wage became permanent, as no further decreases occurred. It is difficult not to attribute the permanently higher unemployment rate at about 10 percent, which lasted for the rest of the 1920s, to this real wage shock as displayed in Figure 4.1. This fact also points to insider forces as an additional reason for the slow wage adjustment during 1921.[9] The incidence of conflicts was high by post–World War II standards but not exceptional for the interwar period. Strike incidence was higher in 1920 – probably due to the introduction of the eight-hour week – and in 1923 than during the deflation of 1921–1922 (Figure 4.3). Possibly the low incidence was a result of the memory of the large nationwide strike in 1909 when the unions lost during a recession.

Overall, the existence of collective agreements slowed down the adjustment process, as most wage reductions did not occur until 1922 when the

---

[9] Evidence for insider wage setting during the deflation as an explanation of the permanently higher unemployment for the rest of the 1920s is given in Fregert and Magnusson (1994).

deflation was almost over. At the same time, there was an endogenous increase in wage flexibility that occurred as a consequence of the deflation. To summarize, flexibility increased through four channels:

1. Contracts changed from one wage level within an agreement to several levels.[10]
2. Synchronization increased between 1921 and 1922 as the proportion of renegotiable contracts rose from 60 percent to almost 100 percent.
3. Wage reductions occurred without a new agreement. This was possible without violating the agreement, as the reduction applied to going wages, which were higher than the stipulated minimum wage levels.
4. Two major areas abandoned contracts altogether – the metal and the iron ore sector – after the employers simply refused to sign new wage agreements and declared unilateral wage reductions.[11]

The Role of Expected Deflation

So far we have documented how deflationary expectations gradually became widespread, although uncertainty concerning the size and length of the deflation appears to have been great. In addition, expectations differed across groups. In particular, uncertainty was apparently largest among the wage setters. The labor representatives were the most skeptical of a sharp deflation. The story we outline here is that the outcome is consistent with the initial impetus being the declaration of the return to the gold standard in August 1920, leading to an expected deflation. The expected deflation, in turn, led to an actual deflation that first caught the labor market by surprise, but once established by the spring of 1921, it became expected. Thus, the story is one of inconsistent beliefs to begin with. To motivate our story, we first briefly review the discussion of expected and unexpected deflation during the Great Depression of the 1930s.

Research on the Great Depression has, since the work of Friedman and Schwartz (1963), focused on the demand side, but with shifting emphasis from the issue of the source of initial impulse (the money versus the spending hypothesis) to the relative role of expected and unexpected deflation.

---

[10] In the next section, we discuss wage adjustment with both types of contract, as they have very different implications in the context of the Fischer and Taylor wage contract models.

[11] The length of contracts had been reduced to about a year during the volatile World War I period.

The shift in emphasis is a result of the initial difficulties in reconciling the simultaneous increase in real balances and the decrease in interest rates, suggesting an expansionary monetary policy on the one hand and, on the other, the actual fall in aggregate activity, suggesting a contractionary monetary policy.

The effect of deflation on aggregate demand depends crucially on whether the deflation is expected or unexpected. Expected deflation lowers aggregate demand by increasing expected real interest rates. An expected high real interest rate lowers investment as well as consumer demand (especially for consumer durables). Hamilton (1987: p. 161) also argued that an expected high deflation lowers consumption demand by increasing the relative return of saving (hoarding) versus consuming. Thus, the increase in real money balances can be reconciled with a lower aggregate demand. Unexpected deflation works through the deterioration of debtors' net worth, in turn reducing the amount of financial intermediation.

A substantial amount of research considers the relative roles of unexpected and expected deflation, although no definite conclusions have yet emerged.[12] Here, we look at the issue from both the demand and the supply side by examining wage behavior. Was the actual evolution consistent with the major part of the deflation being expected? And, if that is the case, when during the deflation process did this phenomenon take place?

As a starting point, we first consider the demand side through the evolution of money, prices, and interest rates, as shown in Figure 4.4. The wholesale price index peaked in August 1920 and consumer price index a month later, whereas the money stock was roughly constant until April 1921, when it began to decline. The result was an increase in the real money stock beginning during Fall 1920. We propose that this pattern is consistent with an expected deflation leading to an increase in savings through the hoarding of money and thus that the announcement of a return to the old gold parity of the krona in August 1920 indeed had some credibility. The credibility may have been boosted by the discount rate increase by the Riksbank in September 1920, from 7 percent to 7.5 percent.

The first piece of evidence is the lead of prices over money through the deflation process, as shown in Figure 4.4. Our second piece of evidence is the scatter plot of real balances versus the actual rate of deflation in Figure 4.4, which suggests a tight negative relation between the real money stock and

---

[12] See, for example, Calomiris (1993).

(A) Money Supply and Wholesale Prices

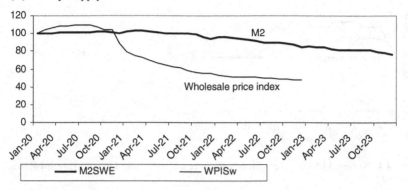

(B) Real Balances and In(De)flation

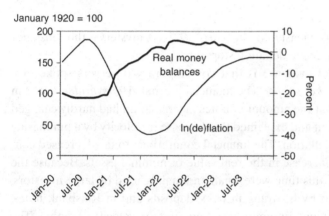

(C) In(de)flation

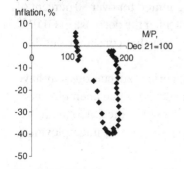

Figure 4.4. (Cont.)

(D) Interest Rates

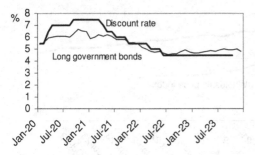

Figure 4.4. Nominal Money, Real Money Balances, Prices, Inflation, and Interest Rates, 1920–1923
Note: The vertical axes in both figures are index values with January 1920 = 100. M2SWE is M2 and WPISW is the wholesale price index.
Sources: Riksbankens årsbok (Yearbook of the Riksbank; various issues) and *Statistisk årsbok* (various issues).

expected deflation, at least until the end of 1921. (A mystery is the constancy of real balances after the deflation stopped.)

A third piece of evidence is that contemporary observers spoke of a purchasing strike (*köpstrejk*). The financial journal *Affärsvärlden* noted in December 1920 that the amount of notes in circulation had hardly changed despite the deflation and explained the decrease in velocity by a purchasing strike due to the deflation. The financial counterpart to the decreased consumption was an increase in the real value of nominal assets. Because the capital markets at this time were small and mainly used by large investors, most people saved by hoarding in bank deposits and in Riksbank notes. Thus, increased savings automatically decreased the velocity of money. The interpretation is buttressed by the fact that consumption decreased most of all GDP components (by 30 percent). As it accounted for over 80 percent of GDP, the consumption decline explains almost all of the decrease in GDP.[13] Consistent with the hoarding story is also the fact that consumer durables were also the hardest hit.[14]

We now turn to the supply side. We ask: What price expectations may have been consistent with the actual wage deflation and the actual unemployment rate? Before turning to the simulations, let us examine the outcome. It was a deep and quick recession. Figure 4.5 shows the rise in unemployment

---

[13] The change in consumption is from Krantz and Nilsson (1975).
[14] See Östlind (1945, p. 418–9).

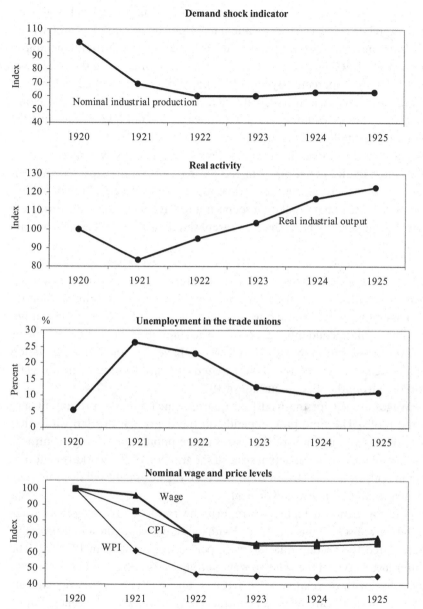

Figure 4.5. Shocks and Outcome in the Industrial Sector, 1920–1925, Relative to 1920 = 100, Yearly Averages
Sources: See Figure 4.7

coincident with the precipitous fall in the wholesale price level beginning in September 1920. The mean annual unemployment rate registered by the trade unions soared from 5 percent in 1920 to 26 percent in 1921. Unemployment peaked at 35 percent in December 1921 by which time the price level had fallen by 45 percent. By mid-1923, unemployment reached its long-run value at 10 percent, as it stayed at that level for the rest of the decade. Nominal wages lagged behind prices, with most of the fall taking place in 1922 with only a small decrease in 1923.

Was the development of wages, prices, and unemployment consistent with most of the deflation from the Spring 1921 being expected? We already argued that before the start of the deflation process in September–October 1920, a sharp deflation seems not to have been generally expected. To get some sense of numbers, we present simulations of the Fischer contract model.[15]

We use Fischer's (1986) model with relative wage setting. The key assumptions are that wages are preset at different levels within the contract period and that the contracts are overlapping. Wages are simulated under two assumptions: (1) static price expectations, and (2) perfect foresight beginning in the second quarter of 1921. The simulation can be interpreted as answering the question: How would wages have developed if the deflation at all stages was completely unanticipated compared with it being perfectly foreseen from the second quarter of 1921?

Wages are set for the next four quarters, including the present, at separate levels. The time path depends on the degree of overlap with other groups as given by their relative sizes in the population of wage contracts. The simulation uses the actual sizes of the fraction of the workers negotiating in a given quarter taken from the yearly government publication *SOS: Arbetsinställelser och kollektivavtal.*

The top panel in Figure 4.6 reports the result for the aggregate wage (quarterly observations) compared with the actual wage (the annual average, here dated the second quarter) with perfect foresight from 1921:Q2. The difference between the relative wage setting cases – the bracketed curves – and those with no relative wage setting – the solid curves – occurs entirely during the first year. When all contracts have a chance to be renegotiated, relative wage setting no longer binds and wages fall drastically. This is also shown in the bottom panel in which each series represents the wages within

---

[15] The set-up of the model is presented in detail in an appendix available from the second author upon request.

Aggregate wages: perfect foresight form 1921:Q2

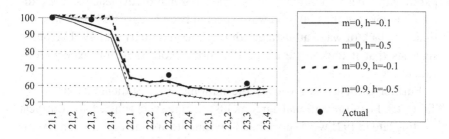

Aggregate wage: static price expectations

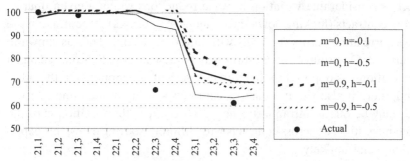

Figure 4.6.[a] Simulated Aggregate Wage Under Four Sets of Parameter Assumptions and the Actual Wage, 1921–1923.

[a] The vertical axis is in index form 1921 quarter 1 (21,1) = 100. M is defined as the weight of the relative wage concern relative to the unemployment and price effect; h is the sensitivity of wages to unemployment. More details are available at (www. nek.lu.se/nekkfr/defappendix). The horizontal axis is the year, quarter.

one contract, starting in the quarter when they were concluded. There is a drastic fall in the first quarter of 1922 for all contracts under relative wage setting (also see Figure 4.2), including those concluded before 1922:Q1. This is the first quarter when there is no contract left from the predeflation period. All contracts reduce wages for the first quarter of 1922 knowing that they will not suffer a relative wage decline. The first old contract to reopen in the first quarter of 1922 will reduce its wage to include the deflation fully, taking into account that the contracts concluded before had done so.

How do these simulations compare with the outcome? The actual aggregate wage observations, shown as points in Figure 4.6, lie slightly above those simulated under perfect foresight during 1921. In particular, two features are captured, the predicted much larger fall in 1922 than in 1921 and the subsequent stabilization in 1923. In contrast, static expectations (lower panel in Figure 4.6), the wage deflation is delayed for another year, compared with the actual outcome. Thus, the labor market evidence would indicate that most of the deflation was expected from Spring 1921. At the same time, the lack of wage adjustment during the first quarter of 1921 strongly suggests that it took some actual deflation before deflation expectations caught on.

Further evidence is given by the national wage settlements shown in Table 4.3. First, the national agreements became synchronized, as contracts starting late in 1921 were shortened to terminate around the end of the year. Unfortunately, we cannot therefore see if there was a preset large reduction in the first quarter of 1922 in contracts negotiated before 1922:Q1. Second, there is considerable variation in wage reductions within a given quarter across contracts (looking down the columns in Table 4.2), in contrast to the close correlation across contracts with different starting dates as shown in Figure 4.2. One source of variation may be new information that changed expectations, as opposed to the perfect foresight assumption. On the other hand, there is also variation across contracts starting in the same quarter. This may be due to intraquarter news, but because the variation is of the same magnitude as across contracts with different starting dates, this explanation seems unlikely.

The overall impression of these simulations is one of relative wage smoothing speeded up by presetting wage reductions within the contracts, although not quite in the even manner predicted by the Fischer model. Still, the overall picture of a delayed but then rapid wage deflation is what would be predicted by the knowledge that the wage setters switched to preset by the nonconstant wage contracts of the Fischer (1986) type as opposed to the Taylor (1979) type.

Let us summarize our view of the deflation of 1920–1922. It was driven strongly by expectations that first pushed prices downwards and later – but not completely – pushed nominal wages down. Rigidities in the form of wage contracts limited nominal wage adjustment.

THE DEFLATION OF 1931–1933

Background

Initially, the international depression that started in the end of the 1920s had little impact on the Swedish economy, although Swedish wholesale prices began to fall in 1928. In early 1931, there was hope that Sweden would not be dragged into a deep recession. In the spring of 1931, however, sentiment turned pessimistic as continental Europe was hit by banking crises and the international financial system began to crumble.

When the Bank of England was forced off gold in September 1931, the Riksbank followed a week later. At the same time, the Minister of Finance made a public announcement that the goal of Swedish monetary policy was to stabilize the internal purchasing power of the krona. Apparently, the statement was drafted by Gustav Cassel at the request of the Minister of Finance when it became clear that the Riksbank could no longer defend the fixed krona rate.[16]

After the paper standard was introduced, the krona was permitted to fluctuate freely. The free floating was interrupted after only two months, when the Riksbank attempted to peg the pound rate. This experiment lasted for only three days, long enough to exhaust the foreign reserves of the Riksbank. After this episode, the krona returned to a flexible exchange rate system. In June 1933, the krona was again pegged to the pound at a rate that was 7 percent above the gold parity. This return to a fixed exchange rate may be considered as a part of the price stabilization policy. The fixed krona-pound rate resulted in a growing inflow of gold and foreign reserves. During the Kreuger crises in March 1932, the Riksbank accepted the role of lender of last resort to the commercial banking system, thereby contributing to financial stability.

The depreciation that accompanied the decision to leave the gold standard in September 1931 had favorable effects on the performance of the Swedish economy by partially isolating it from the ongoing world deflation. As shown in Figure 4.1, the fall in consumer prices and wholesale prices stopped in 1931–1932. Thereafter, consumer prices remained almost constant until the end of 1939 with the exception of a small jump in 1937. The monetary policy program based on price level stabilization was successful in the sense that the Swedish consumer price index remained stable during the 1930s (during several years, the index varied less than one percent). Sweden avoided the international deflation that occurred in countries that remained on gold early in the decade due to the depreciation of the krona. However, this depreciation could not prevent industrial production from falling when the demand for Swedish exports was reduced. Real national income was reduced

---

[16] According to Cassel's autobiography; see Jonung (1979).

by 12 percent between 1930–1932 and exports were 30 percent lower in 1932 than in 1929. Unemployment rose from 12 percent in 1930 to 16 percent in 1931, and to 23 percent in 1932 and 1933, as shown in Figure 4.1.

The new Social Democratic government, which came to power after the election of 1932, adopted an active fiscal policy to revive the domestic economy. However, the relative size of those fiscal measures was small compared with the expansion of the foreign trade that started in 1933.[17] Changes in exports clearly dominated changes in public expenditures. Thus, both the depression and the recovery are mainly explained by the behavior of Swedish exports. The policy measure that most significantly influenced the rapid expansion of the Swedish economy during the 1930s compared with countries that remained on gold was the depreciation of the krona.

Why Was Price Stabilization Adopted in 1931?

In September 1931 the Riksbank became the first and so far the only central bank to have adopted price stabilization or price level targeting as the guideline for its activities. Why was price stabilization adopted as the guide, for Swedish monetary policy in 1931? Two major forces were at work, the influence of the economics profession on policy makers and the experience of high inflation and sharp deflation of World War I and the 1920s.

The academic economists provided the major source of inspiration. In 1898 Knut Wicksell addressed a meeting of the Swedish Economic Association, presenting for the first time his view that price level stabilization should be the aim of central bank policy. Wicksell's rule for the conduct of monetary policy was a simple one: The central bank should raise its discount rate as long as prices were rising, lower it as long as prices were falling, and keep it constant when the price level was stable. In addition, Wicksell's scheme required a "free standard," that is, a monetary system based on an inconvertible paper standard.

Initially, Wicksell's ideas did not spread. However, as a consequence of the monetary disorder during and following World War I, price level stabilization became perceived as a serious alternative to the gold standard. As economists were influential in public debate, were highly respected, and successful in a way difficult to comprehend today, they eventually paved the way for the adoption of the monetary program of 1931.

The second major force accounting for the price stabilization program was the experience of the past. As demonstrated above, Swedish policy makers

[17] See Jonung (1979).

and economists were in favor of a return to the gold standard at the prewar parity in the early 1920s. They simply could not envisage the deep depression, output losses and rise of unemployment associated with the deflation process. In addition, unemployment remained at a high and persistent level throughout the 1920s, most likely due to the real wage shock caused by the deflation of 1921–1922. These events undermined the legitimacy of the gold standard and led to discussion of alternative monetary arrangements and policy norms.

Notably, Gustav Cassel, once a supporter of the gold standard, became critical of the workings of the interwar gold standard. He published several articles prior to September 1931, in which he strongly opposed the deflation process in the world economy. He blamed it on the "scarcity of gold" created by central banks that did not follow the rules of the gold standard. According to Cassel, countries with gold inflows, like France and the United States, should allow their money supplies to expand accordingly. Instead they hoarded the gold, sterilizing the inflow and causing a worldwide deflation. The deflation process was a damaging one, as it created expectations of a continuous fall in prices. Cassel made his views known internationally through his frequent travels and through his many articles in the international press.[18] At that time, Cassel was probably the most well-known international expert on monetary matters.

In summary, the worldwide depression starting in 1928–1929 and manifested in falling prices and rising unemployment undermined the standing of the gold standard within policy and academic circles in Sweden. When Sweden was forced off the gold standard in 1931, the ground was laid for the acceptance of price stabilization as the norm for the Riksbank. The fall of the krona became a window of opportunity for the proponents of price stabilization and a method to escape from deflation as well as from inflation.

Announcements and Actions by Policy Makers[19]

The introduction of the price level target in 1931 was initially viewed as a temporary step by the Swedish policy authorities. When the Minister of Finance announced the new monetary policy goal, he declared that the divorce from gold was to be a temporary one. A return to gold should be aimed for as soon as the conditions for this were at hand. As the international gold standard

---

[18] See Cassel (1941), in which he paints a gloomy picture of the passivity of central bankers and politicians in Europe during the run-up to the breakdown of the gold standard in the 1930s.

[19] This section builds upon Jonung (1979), and Berg and Jonung (1999).

gradually dissolved in the 1930s, a return to gold became no longer a viable alternative for Sweden. Instead, the monetary program was maintained and gradually amended in various ways.

After the announcement of price stabilization in the autumn of 1931, the Riksbank started to calculate a consumer price index on a weekly basis. The aim of the Riksbank index was to register the development of the internal purchasing power of the krona at short intervals and to convey this information both to the directors of the Bank of Sweden and to the Swedish public.

Uncertainty was great in September 1931 about the future of monetary policy and the new price norm. Judging from the official documents on monetary policy during the subsequent years, price stabilization was eventually defined as price level targeting. In April 1932, the Governing Board of the Riksbank stated that the departure from the gold standard in September 1931 was expected to start a process of inflation. The monetary policy program was "intended to calm such fears." The Board also stated that the program was intended "to prevent the price level in Sweden from following the downward international price trend."[20]

The credibility of the price level norm was dependent on how strongly it was backed up by policy makers. Subsequent actions and announcements revealed, as the depression deepened, that the commitment to price stability was not absolute (Table 4.3). The goal of price stabilization was, however, not severely compromised. The Riksbank appears to have given priority to exchange rate stabilization over price stabilization, as revealed by the failed attempt to peg the krona in November 1931 and the subsequent pegging to the British pound in 1933 at a depreciated level, which lasted until the outbreak of World War II. The Riksbank raised the discount rate in September 1931 from 4 percent to 6 percent before the suspension and then to the record level of 8 percent the day after the suspension. The discount rate was lowered to 6 percent in October 1931 and then gradually during 1932 and 1933 to 2.5 percent by the end of 1933 (see Table 4.3). The initial contractionary stance was conditioned by a fear of inflation, which disappeared as Swedish prices stabilized and the international deflation continued.

If the Riksbank had a deflationary bent, their principal – the *Riksdag* and, in practice, the Minister of Finance – had an inflationary bent. The Minister of Finance, Felix Hamrin, declared in January 1932 that the wholesale price level should be raised. The parliament banking committee declared

[20] The Board of Directors in a document dated April 14, 1932, cited in Banking Committee, Submission no. 40, May 1932: p. 13.

Table 4.3. *Monetary policy announcements and actions, 1931–1933*

Year (Month/Day)	Announcement
1931	
September 7	Increase in discount rate from 3 to 6 percent.
September 27	Suspension of gold standard. Minister of Finance: Price stabilization norm was announced.
September 28	Discount rate increased from 6 to 8 percent.
October	Discount rate decreased from 8 to 6 percent.
November	The krona pegged for three days at the old parity of 18.15 kronor per British pound.
1932	
January	Minister of Finance: Price stabilization does not preclude a rise in wholesale prices.
February	Riksbank Board: Price and employment stabilization.
April	Riksbank Board: Price stabilization and low interest rates.
May	Banking committee of the Parliament: Price stabilization, increase of wholesale prices, and the needs of business.
September 2	Discount rate decreased from 6 to 3.5 percent.
1933	
April	Expert committee: Moderate rise in wholesale prices.[a] Minister of Finance: Price stabilisation and the needs of business.
June	The krona pegged to the British pound at 19.40 kronor per pound.
December 6	The discount rate decreased from 3.5 to 2.5 percent.
1937	
May	Riksbank Board: Exchange rate stabilization. Banking committee of the Parliament: Price stabilization and low interest rates. Minister of Finance: Primary goal is price stabilization, secondary goal is exchange rate stabilization.

[a] *Valutasakkunniga.* Committee appointed by the Minister of Finance Ernst Wigforss under his chairmanship consisting of representatives of the Riksbank, Riksgäldskontoret, the banking sector, and the economics profession.
Note: Source of announcement in italics in the notes.
Sources: Kock (1961) and *Riksbankens Årsbok (annual report; various issues)*.

in February 1932 that the goal of price stabilization should not be absolute and employment should also be taken into account. Similar statements were issued subsequently (Table 4.3). The deflation in wholesale prices was arrested. Prices started to rise from the end of 1933 when the recovery began.

In 1936 prices started to rise following an increase in prices in Great Britain. The policy of price level stabilization was put to its first severe test. Several economists demanded an appreciation to insulate Sweden from the foreign inflation, but the Minister of Finance Ernst Wigforss refused, arguing that the price increase had been moderate. His opinion also became the opinion of the Board of Directors of the Riksbank.

Beliefs and Advice of Economists

The Riksbank was faced with a new task after the gold suspension in September 1931, that of implementing a program of price stabilization. It had no prior experience nor any foreign examples to use as guidance. It simply lacked knowledge about the proper conduct of monetary policy under a "free standard" – as Swedish commentators described the new monetary regime. At the suggestion of Ivar Rooth, the Governor of the Riksbank, the Board of Directors decided on October 8, 1931, to turn to three renowned economists for advice, Gustav Cassel, David Davidson, and Eli Heckscher. Each was sent a questionnaire concerning the monetary policy choices facing Sweden.

About a month later, in their replies to the questionnaire of the Riksbank, the economists were roughly of the same opinion. Heckscher stated for the moment that there was general agreement that a stable purchasing power of money was the best goal for monetary policy as outlined in the monetary declaration made at the adoption of the paper standard, although there were conflicting views concerning which prices ought to be stabilized. In his report, Cassel argued that Sweden must have an independently managed paper standard and that there could hardly be any other norm for this standard than the stabilization of the domestic purchasing power of the krona. The great advantage of the paper standard was that Sweden became isolated from the "destructive" deflation that was taking place in countries still on gold. This ability of the paper standard to prevent the world deflation from spreading to Sweden should be regarded as the main reason Sweden left the gold standard. Davidson declared that the reestablishment of a well-functioning gold standard system would be most desirable. However, Davidson could not say if and when such a return would be desirable, doubting that a gold standard system would ever function in a normal way again after the recent international disturbances, and he suggested that the krona should be founded on "a completely free standard."

To sum up, the three economists recommended that Sweden should maintain a free standard based on price stabilization as long as the world monetary system remained disorganized. They did not consider any other goals, for the Riksbank, such as output or employment stabilization although their reports were written when Swedish industrial production was declining and unemployment was rising dramatically.

The policy of the Riksbank was closely followed, commented on, and criticized by the economics profession. Initially in the fall of 1931, they were all in favor of the monetary program of September 1931, although they did not share exactly the same view. Eventually, the economists split up into two groups, some favorable toward price stabilization and others critical of the monetary program, viewing it as an inadequate response to the depression.

The first group consisted of the older generation of economists, influenced by the monetary events of World War I. They were liberal in their general outlook and critical of government intervention. Throughout the 1930s, they remained staunch proponents of price stabilization.

The second group was made up of the new generation of economists that was making its way in the 1930s. They were influenced by the high and persistent unemployment of the 1920s and 1930s. To them the challenge was to develop theories and policies to reduce unemployment and the fluctuations of the business cycle. They became early proponents of government intervention and "active" counter-cyclical policies.[21]

They viewed the monetary program as arresting the deflationary process but not as adequate to raise production and employment. Instead, monetary policy should be coordinated with fiscal policy to stabilize the economy. This view eventually became the majority view in the post–World War II period.

Beliefs and Actions of Wage Setters

When the depression began to affect Sweden in the fall of 1930, a deep depression was not expected, although uncertainty was great.[22] Both employer

---

[21] This group was later termed the Stockholm School. Gunnar Myrdal and Bertil Ohlin were the most prominent members of the Stockholm School.

Table 4.4. *Wage reductions (ordinary wage/piece rate) in major national agreements by quarter in percent, 1931–1934*

Sector/union	Previous agreement year (length)	1931				1932				1933				1934			
		1	2	3	4	1	2	3	4	1	2	3	4	1	2	3	4
Metal & mining																	
Iron ores	1930 (2)					**−4/−6**								p			
Metal	1928 (3)					**−4/−6**								p			
Mines: mid-Sweden	1928 (2,5)		p							**−5/−8**						p	
Mines: Lapland	1930 (2)							p			**−12/−17**						
Earth & stone																	
Stone industry	1930 (2)							n									
Building materials		**0**								**0/−10**							
Wood & forestry																	
Sawmills	1929 (3)			p		**−6/−9**											
Paper & printing																	
Paper	1930 (2)					**−4**								p			
Pulp	1928 (1)		p			c		**−7**						p			
Litography	1930 (1)					p								**−5**			
Printing	1929 (3)							p				**−5**					
Bookbinding	1930 (3)													**−5/−5**			
Food																	
Mills											**−4**						
Textiles		c **0**				p								p			
Chemicals																	
Matches	1930 (2)					p				**0/−10**							
Glass	1929 (3)					c		c	**0/−7**							p	

Note: All wage reductions are percentage changes relative to the peak 1930. Changes are given for hourly wages and piece rates before and after slash. Bold signifies new agreement, p signifies prolongation, and c signifies conflict.
Source: Sociala meddelanden, various issues.

and worker organizations that had agreements to expire at the end of 1930 were expectant. SAF recommended that its members not conclude agreements for periods exceeding one year. The majority of contract makers did not give notice and, hence, most contracts were prolonged for a year. Of the larger unions, only the textile workers' gave notice in September 1930, with the expectation of higher wages. When the negotiations started at the end of 1930, the textile employers demanded wage reductions, which eventually happened, following major conflict. In spite of the few agreements being renegotiated for 1931, nominal wages fell between 3 percent and 4 percent in most industries (Table 4.4). These reductions were due to lowered piece rate compensations, as straight hourly wages were practically unchanged. The prolongations decided in Autumn 1930 thereby delayed the reactions by at least a year.

The next large round of wage negotiations occurred in the Fall 1931 for those areas in which one of the parties had given notice. As the gold suspension occurred in September 1931, just before the time of notice for most agreements, a couple of days remained in which to react. As it turned out, about 50 percent of the agreements were up for renegotiation after one of the parties had given notice; in most cases it was the employer. Because most new agreements did not have to be finished before the end of December 1931, the parties had Fall 1931 to plan their actions and interpret the impact of the new price stabilization norm.

It is clear that the price stabilization norm did not meet with instant credibility. A critical testimony is given by Sigfrid Hansson in *Fackföreningsrörelsen* in 1931 the week after the gold suspension. He wrote "Now the promises are that the krona should uphold its internal value ... it is obvious that the workers have reason, at the conclusion of new agreements, to doubt the basis of proud promises of the fate of the krona, which so far have had very little substance."

This uncertainty is also evident in the contract makers' actions, to which we now turn. Under the influence of the deepened recession during 1931, SAF's leadership planned a concerted wage reduction offensive for the 1932 agreements. A binding agreement between the major employers to give notice and reduce wages under SAF's leadership was concluded in August 1931. The decision to reduce wages took on a new meaning when Sweden left the gold standard on September 27, and the krona immediately depreciated by 15 percent (against the dollar). The SAF journal *Industria* (1931: nr 23, p. 648) described the situation as follows,

Should the industrial sector take the risk of giving notice and there by not only liberate themselves from the agreements but also the workers under an exchange rate situation that could lead to a reduction of nominal wages as well as demands for compensations against the depreciation? It was difficult to solve such a problem in three days, before the effects of the exchange rate changes could be seen .... Theoretically there were three ways to choose from: 1) prolongation which binds the parties for the coming year; 2) giving notice with the wish to conclude a new agreement with longer or shorter duration; 3) to give notice with the purpose of not concluding a new agreement.

On September 29, the day before the last chance to give notice to the agreements that expired at the end of the year, SAF decided that the decision to give notice was no longer binding, although it was still recommended. Most employers also gave notice, but the common wage reduction offensive was broken. The third alternative – abandoning collective agreements – only occurred for some smaller agreements (see the dip in Figure 4.8). *Industria's* author ruled it out on account of the strength of the Swedish union movement, as such a strategy would risk major conflict.

The labor side did not decide on a common strategy for the unions. At the national trade union conference in October 1931, the LO chairman expressed uncertainty and thought that employers, too, would "find the situation in the money market confusing."[22] Some employers argued for a common strategy of prolongations, but others were opposed, fearing inflation. No common policy was decided, as it was felt the situation was too uncertain. Regarding prolongations, most employers had already given notice anyway. A common statement released by the conference expressed regret that the employers had given notice and also called for measures to stabilize the exchange rate. In general, the unions favored constant wages, as evidenced by an article in the LO journal *Fackföreningsrörelsen*. One argument against wage reductions was the fear that it could induce a depression spiral triggered by an expected deflation as a result of wage cuts,

In the quest for a stabilization of the value of money ... a stabilization of wages should contribute favorably. A reduction of wages precipitates the expectation of also a reduction of prices and thereby procrastinates purchases and the start of new employment. Just as constant talk of inflation can contribute to panic buying, an expected reduction of prices can lead to speculation in lower prices and thereby cause an actual price reduction. It is difficult to assume that the Riksbank with a possible increase in the discount rate could stop the recession

---

[22] This section builds on the history of LO by Casparsson (1948: pp. 257–304), De Geer (1986: ch. 6), and the annual reports of SAF.

caused by notices of existing agreements with associated wage reductions . . . . It would be best to give the public inside and outside the country the idea that the wage level would be kept. This stabilization would hinder the public as well as the entrepreneurs from speculating in changed exchange rates. Thereby another uncertainty element would be reduced. (*Fackföreningsrörelsen* 1931: p. 368.)

The combination of the breakdown of the SAF wage reduction strategy and the unwillingness to reduce wages on the labor side, both conditioned on the suspension of the gold standard, resulted in small actual wage reductions. About 70 percent of all contracts were renegotiable for 1932 but only about half of them were renegotiated. The actual wage reductions for 1932 were between 3 percent and 4 percent, as in 1931, whereas the contractual reductions were larger, between 5 percent and 10 percent (Table 4.4). The largest reductions occurred in the sawmill industry, which had been the first to feel the depression and was also hurt most. Some sectors, such as the sawmill industry, reduced wages within existing agreements.

The large metal agreement was the first to be concluded after a short conflict when the employers unilaterally reduced wages after the old agreement had expired. The same happened in the large pulp industry, but the strike lasted until August 1931, when wages were reduced. Small wage reductions of between 1 percent and 3 percent took place in 1933.

SAF's leadership had planned for a new wage reduction offensive for 1933, but most members opposed it this time. New agreements with wage reductions primarily occurred in areas, that had not previously had their wages changed. The largest reductions occurred in the Lapland mines, where wages were reduced by 12 percent and piece rates by 17 percent. The mining sector was also among the worst hit. During 1933, the economy began to recover, although unemployment did not return to the 1929 level until 1937.

Impact of Beliefs and Actions on the Outcome

In this section, we briefly look at the effect of the wage setters' decisions on shock propagation. Figure 4.7 shows how nominal industrial output – a possible indicator of nominal demand – decreased temporarily by 20 percent, in contrast to the permanent negative shock in 1921. The difference between the two episodes can clearly be attributed to the different policies: a return to the old gold parity in the 1920s and the abandoning of the gold standard in 1931. The 1930s depression was about as deep as in the 1920s, but it lasted longer. Real industrial output and unemployment reached the predepression

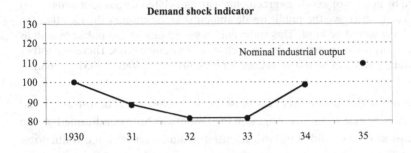

Demand shock indicator

Nominal industrial output

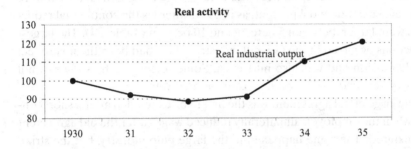

Real activity

Real industrial output

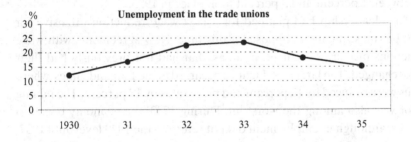

Unemployment in the trade unions

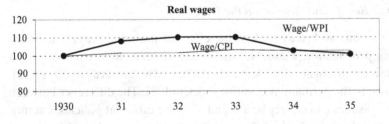

Real wages

Wage/WPI

Wage/CPI

Figure 4.7. (Cont.)

124

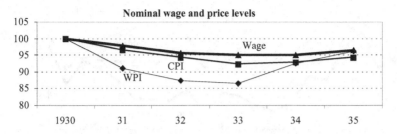

Figure 4.7. Shocks and Outcome in the Industrial Sector, 1930–1935, Relative to 1930 = 100, Yearly Averages

level in 1934, two years after aggregate demand bottomed in 1932. Wages decreased very little during the crises and then only gradually began to grow.

Is the outcome consistent with broadly correct expectations? The stipulations in the collective agreements, given in Table 4.4, are consistent with the Taylor contract model in that there were no preset reductions within the contract period. The shock and the real outcome appear consistent with the Taylor model: a temporary shock leading to a long recession. Wages adjusted slowly in a protracted manner and were also slow to rise during the upturn, which is broadly consistent with the Taylor model.

Table 4.4, however, also reveals features that do not seem consistent with the Taylor model. The groups took turns in reducing wages, but there is no gradual adjustment for the individual agreements. Each national agreement reduced wages only once. In effect, the most common response for those whose contracts were up for renegotiation was no change in the wage at all through prolongations of the existing agreement. Figure 4.8 shows how a large number of the contracts up for renegotiation did not use the opportunity to change the wage. Contracts thus appear not to have been the only source of inertia. Fregert (2000) argues that the evidence favors the so-called coordination failure explanation over the Taylor model. As shown by Ball and Romer (1991), small fixed costs of changing wages in combination with relative wage concerns (as also posited by Taylor) may result in unchanged wages if shocks are not too large, as was the case after the gold suspension.

CONCLUSIONS

We have attempted to analyze the process of deflation by exploiting qualitative data on beliefs and expectations, in addition to quantitative data on the

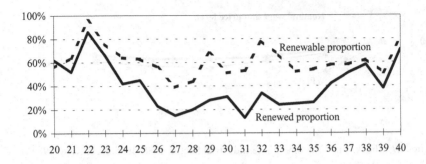

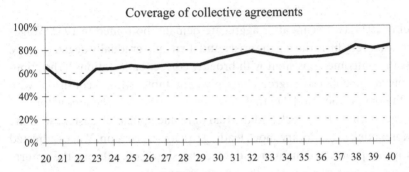

Coverage of collective agreements

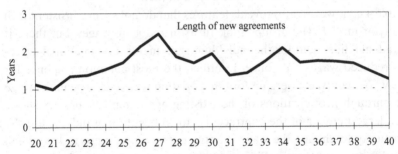

Length of new agreements

Figure 4.8. Collective Agreements, 1920–1940 in the Industrial Sector
Sources: SOS: Kollektivavtal och arbetsinställelser, various issues, and own calculations of renewable proportion of collective agreements from Fregert (1994: ch 6).

actual outcome of prices and quantities. Our major sources of information have been various policy documents and statements by policy makers and leading economists, as well as the design and contents of collective agreements. Using this information, we have dissected and compared the anatomy of the two major twentieth-century deflations that occurred in Sweden in the early 1920s and 1930s. We suggested two sets of questions to examine: What were the effects of expectations on outcomes? and How did outcomes influence expectations?

Regarding the effect of expectations on outcomes, a primary issue is whether the expectations were consistent across groups. We found that economists influenced and lent credibility to the policy goals during both deflations by displaying an almost united front. Thus, there was broad agreement between policy makers and economists. Employers pushed for larger wage cuts than the labor unions once the deflation had begun in earnest. A combination of differing expectations and genuine dislike of wage cuts on the labor side were behind the differences between labor unions and employers. This caused large conflicts and high unemployment in the 1920s.

Given the lack of unanimity across groups and the unique features of these episodes, uncertainty was substantial. During the 1920s, the ultimate size of the deflation implied by the return to gold parity, as well as the speed of deflation, was uncertain, even after the decision to go back to the old parity was almost certain. During the 1930s, it took time to establish credibility for the new price stabilization norm. Uncertainty had real effects through its influence on contract design. An increase in uncertainty may lead to more flexible contracts, which may result in faster adjustment than would be predicted from earlier time series evidence. The effect was clear in the 1920s, when wage flexibility increased by a change to Fischer-type contracts from previous Taylor-type contracts, as well as by the phrasing of wage reductions as percentages of going wages and by the rise of spot contracts. During the 1931–1933 deflation, contracts were shortened to one year, but the opportunity to revise wage rates was often not used. Thus, we find large differences in the propagation mechanism across the two deflations, which cautions against using models estimated for longer periods to analyze more extreme episodes.

Regarding the effect of outcomes on beliefs and expectations, we found that all participants looked at the most immediate experience that appeared relevant. Policy makers and economists were willing to engineer a deflation in the 1920s to return to the gold standard at the prewar parity. The deflation induced by the gold standard in the 1930s was enough to abandon it as an ultimate goal. The change in goals reflects a change in beliefs about the functioning of the gold standard as the guarantor of economic stability. The cost of deflation had also turned out to be greater than anticipated. Hesitations about the ability of the labor market to adjust had been strengthened by the rise and persistence in unemployment in the 1920s. All decision makers were involved in a learning process, using the "lessons from the past" when considering proper future measures.

None of these events represent clean regime breaks as, for example, Sargent (1982) argued was the case with the end of the big hyperinflations in the 1920s in countries like Germany. This means that standard methods of economists for studying deflation are lacking. In particular, if expectations are important, there may be no straightforward way to model them. Expectations and actions (behavior) are predicated on the strength of beliefs about how the economy works and beliefs held by economic agents about each other's beliefs.

In conclusion, we suggest that it is fruitful to study episodes of deflation and deflation dynamics by bringing in evidence that is commonly not used in studies of deflation. Sweden provides us with a wealth of data in the form of statements by policy makers, analyses by the economics profession, and the changing design of collective wage agreements.

PART TWO

DEFLATION AND ASSET PRICES

5   Boom–Busts in Asset Prices, Economic Instability, and Monetary Policy

Michael D. Bordo and Olivier Jeanne

INTRODUCTION

The link between monetary policy and asset price movements has been of perennial interest to policy makers. The 1920s stock market boom and 1929 crash and the 1980s Japanese asset bubble are two salient examples in which asset price reversals were followed by protracted recessions and deflation.[1] The key questions that arise from these episodes is whether the monetary authorities could have been more successful in preventing the consequences of an asset market bust or whether it was appropriate for the authorities only to react to these events ex post.

In this chapter we consider the potential cases for proactive versus reactive monetary policy based on the situation in which asset price reversals can have serious effects on real output.

Our analysis is based on a stylized model of the dilemma with which the monetary authorities are faced in asset price booms. On the one hand, letting the boom go unchecked entails the risk that it will be followed by a bust accompanied by a collateral-induced credit crunch. Restricting monetary policy can be thought of as insurance against the risk of a credit crunch. On the other hand, this insurance does not come free: Restricting monetary policy implies immediate costs in terms of lower output and inflation. The optimal monetary policy depends on the relative cost and benefits of the insurance.[2]

---

[1] Other recent episodes of asset price booms and collapses include experiences in the 1980s and 1990s in the Nordic countries, Spain, Latin America, and East Asia (see e.g. Schinasi and Hargreaves 1993; Drees and Pazarbasioglu 1998; International Money Fund 2000; and Collyns and Senhadji 2002).

[2] It is important to note that we do not address the case where asset price movements act as predictors of future inflation. The evidence on this issue is mixed (see Filardo 2000).

Although the model is quite stylized, we find that the optimal monetary policy depends on the economic conditions – including the private sector's beliefs – in a rather complex way. Broadly speaking, a proactive monetary restriction is the optimal policy when the risk of a bust is large *and* the monetary authorities can defuse it at a relatively low cost. One source of difficulty is that, in general, there is a tension between these two conditions. As investors become more exuberant, the risks associated with a reversal in market sentiment increase. At the same time, leaning against the wind of investors' optimism requires more radical and costly monetary actions. To be optimal, a proactive monetary policy must come into play at a time when the risk is perceived as sufficiently large but the authorities' ability to act is not too diminished.

Another, more difficult question is whether (and when) the conditions for a proactive monetary policy are met in the real world. We view this question as very much open and deserving further empirical research. In the meantime, we present in this chapter some stylized facts on asset booms and busts that have some bearing on the issue. We find that, historically, there have been many booms and busts in asset prices, but they had different features, depending on the countries and whether one looks at stock or property prices. Boom–bust episodes seem to be more frequent in real property prices than in stock prices and in small countries than in large countries. However, two dramatic episodes (the United States in the Great Depression and Japan in the 1990s) have involved large countries and the stock market. We also present evidence that busts are associated with disruption in financial and real activity (banking crises, slowdown in output, and decreasing inflation).

This chapter is related to growing policy and academic literature on monetary policy and asset prices. On the policy side, the dominant view among central bankers is that in response to movements in asset prices, monetary policy should be reactive, not proactive, e.g." ... the general view nowadays is that central banks should not try to use interest rate policy to control asset price trends by seeking to burst any bubbles that may form. The normal strategy is rather to seek, firmly and with the help of a great variety of instruments, to restore stability on the few occasions when asset markets collapse" (Ms Hessius, Deputy Governor of the Sveriges Risksbank, BIS Review 128/1999).

This view is vindicated, on the academic side, by the recent work of Bernanke and Gertler (2001). These authors argue that a central bank dedicated to price stability should pay no attention to asset prices per se, except insofar as they signal changes in expected inflation. These results stem from the simulation of different variants of the Taylor rule in the context of a new Keynesian model with sticky wages and a financial accelerator. Bernanke and Gertler also argue that trying to stabilize asset prices per se is problematic because it is nearly impossible to know for sure whether a given change in asset values results from fundamental factors, nonfundamental factors, or both.

In another study, Cecchetti et al (2000) argued in favor of a more proactive response of monetary policy to asset prices. They agree with Bernanke and Gertler that the monetary authorities would have to make an assessment of the bubble component in asset prices, but take a more optimistic view of the feasibility of this task.[3] They also argue, on the basis of simulations of the Bernanke-Gertler model, that including an asset price variable (e.g. stock prices) in the Taylor rule would be desirable. Bernanke and Gertler (2001) attribute such a finding to the use of a misleading metric in the comparison between policy rules.

Our approach differs from these in several respects. First, we view the emphasis on bubbles in this debate as excessive. In our model, the monetary authority needs to ascertain the risk of an asset price reversal but it is not essential to ascertain whether the reversal reflects a bursting bubble or fundamentals. Nonfundamental influences may exacerbate the volatility of asset prices and thus complicate the monetary authorities' task, but they are not the essence of the question. Even if asset markets were completely efficient, abrupt price reversals could occur and pose the same problem for monetary authorities as bursting bubbles.

Second, we find that the optimal policy rule is unlikely to take the form of a Taylor rule, even if it is augmented by a linear term in asset prices. If there is scope for proactive monetary policy, it is highly contingent on a number of factors for which output, inflation, and the current level of asset prices do not provide appropriate summary statistics. It depends on the risks in the balance sheets of private agents assessed by reference to the risks in asset markets. The balance of these risks cannot be summarized in two or three macroeconomic variables, and it shifts over time.

---

[3] Assessing the bubble component in asset prices should not be qualitatively more difficult, they argue, than measuring the output gap, an unobservable variable that many central banks use as an input into policy making.

More generally, our analysis points to the risks of using simple monetary policy rules as the guide for monetary policy. These rules are blind to the fact that financial instability is endogenous – to some extent and in a complex way – to monetary policy. The linkages between asset prices, financial instability, and monetary policy are complex because they are inherently nonlinear and involve extreme (tail probability) events. The complexity of these linkages does not imply, however, that they can be safely ignored. Whether they like it or not, the monetary authorities need to take a stance that involves some judgment over the probability of extreme events. As our model illustrates, the optimal stance cannot be characterized by a simple rule. If anything, our analysis emphasizes the need for some discretionary judgment in monetary policy.

The chapter is structured as follows: As background to the analysis, some of the salient features of two famous episodes of asset price deflation associated with extreme economic distress – the interwar Great Depression experience of the United States and the Japanese asset price boom and bust in the 1980s and 1990s – are discussed. In the next section, we present stylized facts on boom and bust cycles in asset prices in the post-1970 experience of fifteen countries in the Organisation for Economic Cooperation and Development (OECD). Then, we present the model and discuss policy implications, followed by the conclusions.

HISTORICAL PERSPECTIVES: TWO DRAMATIC EPISODES

Asset price reversals have been an important phenomenon since the dawn of capitalism. Classic examples of a boom–bust cycle were the tulip mania in the early seventeenth century (Garber 2000) and the South Sea bubble in England in the early eighteenth century (Kindleberger 1989). In this section, as historical background to our analysis, we document the two most dramatic episodes of asset price reversals of the twentieth century: the 1929 U.S. stock market crash and the Japanese "asset price bubble" of the late 1980s and early 1990s. In both of these episodes, asset price reversals played a major role in precipitating severe recessions.

The United States, 1929–1933

The Great Contraction in the United States from 1929 to 1933 is often associated with a classic boom and bust episode in the stock market (Figure 5.1).

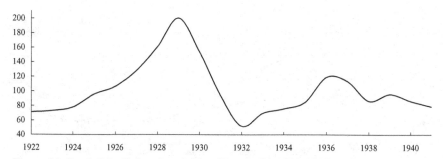

Figure 5.1. Stock Price Index: Standard and Poor's 500, 1922–1941
Source: Historical Statistics of the United States: Millenial Edition (2003).

According to legend, the boom, focused on the "new economy" stocks such as GE and RCA, began in 1926 and turned into a bubble in March 1928, which burst on October 24, 1929 (Galbraith 1958; Kindleberger 1978). The bottom was not reached until 1932. The boom, which some argue was fueled by expansionary Federal Reserve policy in the spring of 1927, was financed by easy bank credit (Figure 5.2) and brokers loans (White 1990). The bust, it is sometimes argued, was triggered by tight Federal Reserve policy in 1929 to prick what they perceived as a stock market bubble (Friedman and Schwartz 1963).

Beginning in late 1927, the Federal Reserve Board favored a policy of moral suasion to discourage member banks from financing stock market speculation, an activity viewed as anathema to the prevailing "real bills" doctrine. This policy was opposed by Benjamin Strong, President of the New York Fed and head of the influential Open Market Investment Committee,

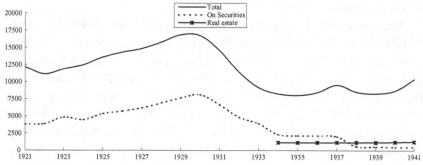

Figure 5.2. Bank Loans: Total, Secured by Securities, and Secured by Real Estate 1921–1941
Source: Bordo, Ito, and Iwaisako (1997).

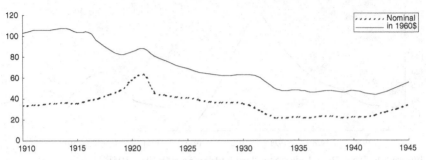

Figure 5.3. Agricultural Land Prices Per Acre, 1910–1945
Source: Lindert (1988).

and, after he became seriously ill and died in October 1928, by his successor George Harrison. They advocated a rise in the discount rate as the method to stem speculation. The stalemate, which it is argued allowed the stock market boom to continue unchecked, lasted until August 1929, the cyclical peak, when the discount rate was raised from 5 percent to 6 percent (Meltzer 2003).

The ensuing stock market crash in October 1929 in which stock prices declined by 40 percent in two months (Figure 5.1) is not generally viewed as the key cause of the severity of the contraction that followed but as having some impact on household wealth, expenditures on consumer durables, and expectations (Romer 1992). The source of the subsequent depression in 1930–1933 was a series of banking panics, which led to a collapse in money supply, financial intermediation, and aggregate demand (Bernanke 1983; Friedman and Schwartz 1963).

Asset price deflation, however, was an important ingredient in the propagation of the Great Contraction (Bernanke and Gertler 1989) because declining asset prices (both stock prices and land prices; see Figures 5.1 and 5.3) reduced the value of bank loans and collateral (Figure 5.2); weakened banks in turn dumped their loans and securities in fire sales leading to further asset price deflation. In this environment of massive bank failures, greatly reduced collateral, and negligible bank lending, financial intermediation seized up, significantly exacerbating the distress of the real economy. Especially hard hit by the plunge in asset prices were savings and loan associations whose assets were pummeled by the decline in real estate prices and delinquent mortgage payments. Life insurance companies were also hard hit. If their

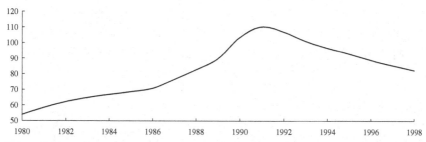

Figure 5.4. Nominal Land Prices, Japan: 1980–1998
Source: Bordo, Ito, and Iwaisako (1997).

mortgages and bonds had been marked to market, most companies would have been insolvent (White 2000).[4]

The recovery began on March 1933 after the Banking Holiday and massive reflation following the devaluation of the dollar and treasury gold and silver purchase programs (Romer 1990). The real economy, however, took close to a decade to recover to its predepression level of activity and may have taken longer in the absence of World War II. Asset prices took two decades to recover, as did the value of collateral and private financial intermediation.

Japan, 1986–1995

The Japanese boom–bust cycle began in the mid 1980s with a run-up of real estate prices (Figure 5.4) fueled by an increase in bank lending (Figure 5.5) and easy monetary policy. The property price boom in turn led to a stock market boom (Figure 5.6) as the increased value of property owned by firms raised future profits and hence stock prices (Iwaisako and Ito 1996). Both rising land prices and stock prices, in turn, increased firms' collateral, encouraging further bank loans and more fuel for the boom. The bust may have been triggered, like the U.S. example sixty years earlier, by the Bank of Japan's pursuit of a tight monetary policy in 1989 to stem the asset market boom.

---

[4] Deflation was also an important ingredient in the Great Depression. Its role is well described by Irving Fisher's debt-deflation story (Fisher 1933), in which collapsing prices led to a rise in debt burdens in an environment where contracts were not fully indexed. Deflation reduced the value of firms' net worth and the collateral for bank loans. This produced widespread insolvency for both firms and banks. Declining real activity also reduced collateral by weakening the performance of assets.

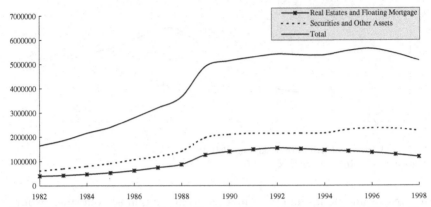

Figure 5.5. Bank Loans: Total, Secured by Securities and Other Assets, and Secured by
Real Estate, 1982–1998
Source: Bordo, Ito, and Iwaisako (1997).

The subsequent asset price collapse in the next five years led to a collapse in bank lending with a decline in the collateral backing corporate
loans (Figure 5.6). The decline in asset prices further impinged on the banking system's capital, making many banks insolvent. This occurred largely
because the collapse in asset prices reduced the value of their capital
(in Japan, commercial banks could hold their capital in the form of stock
market equity, see Bayoumi and Collyns 2000).

Lender of last resort policy prevented a classic banking panic as had
occurred in the United States in the 1930s, but regulatory forbearance has
propped up insolvent banks. The banking crisis has yet to be resolved, bank
lending remains moribund, and Japan thirteen years after the bust is still
mired in stagnation and deflation in the face of tight monetary policy and the
slow resolution of bank insolvencies. Thus, in the Japanese case, because of
tight connections between asset prices, collateral, bank lending, and banking

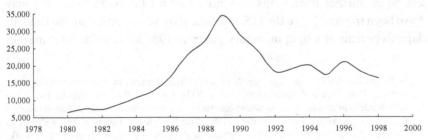

Figure 5.6. Stock Price Index: Nikkei, 1980–1998
Source: Bordo, Ito, and Iwaisako (1997).

capital, the boom–bust episode has been crucially intertwined with serious macroeconomic instability.

IDENTIFYING BOOMS AND BUSTS IN ASSET PRICES: THE POSTWAR OECD

Many countries have experienced asset price booms and busts since 1973. Although none were as dramatic as the U.S. and Japanese cases, a number were followed by serious recessions. In this section, we present a criterion to delineate boom and bust cycles in asset prices. We apply this criterion to real annual stock and residential property price indexes for fifteen countries: Australia, Canada, Denmark, Finland, France, Germany, Ireland, Italy, Japan, the Netherlands, Norway, Spain, Sweden, the United Kingdom, and the United States over the period 1970–2001 for stocks and 1970–1998 for property prices.[5]

Criterion

This section presents a criterion to ascertain whether movements in an asset price represent a boom or bust. A good criterion should be simple, be objective, and yield plausible results. In particular, it should select the notorious boom–bust episodes, such as the Great Depression in the United States or Japan in 1986–1995, without producing (too many) spurious episodes. We found that the following criterion broadly satisfied these conditions.

Our criterion compares a moving average of the growth rate in asset prices with the long-run historical average. Let $g_{i,t} = \frac{100}{3} \log(P_{i,t}/P_{i,t-3})$ be the growth rate in the *real* price of the asset (stock prices or property prices) between year $t - 3$ and year t and in country i, expressed in annual percentage points. Let $\bar{g}$ be the average growth rate over all countries. Let v be the arithmetic average of the volatility (standard deviation) in the growth rate g over all countries.

Then, if the average growth rate between year $t - 3$ and year t is larger than a threshold,

$$g_{i,t} > \bar{g} + xv$$

---

[5] Some data points are missing for some countries. The source for the stock price data is International Financial Statistics (IFS) and for property prices is the Bank for International Settlements.

we identify a *boom* in years $t - 2, t - 1$ and t.

Conversely, we identify a *bust* in years $t - 2, t - 1$ and t if

$$g_{i,t} < \bar{g} - xv.$$

Our method detects a boom or a bust when the three-year moving average of the growth rate in the asset price falls outside a confidence interval defined by reference to the historical first and second moments of the series. Variable x is a parameter that we calibrate so as to select the notorious boom–bust episodes without selecting (too many) spurious events. (We implement some sensitivity analysis with respect to this parameter.) We use the three-year moving average so as to eliminate the high-frequency variations in the series. (This is particularly a problem with stock prices, which are more volatile than property prices.)

For real property prices, the average growth rate across the fifteen countries is 1.0 percent, with an average volatility of 5.8 percent. For real stock prices, the growth rate and the volatility are both higher, 3.8 percent and 13.4 percent, respectively. For both prices, we take $x = 1.3$.[6]

Boom–Busts in the OECD, 1970–2001

Figures 5.7 and 5.8 show the log of the real prices of residential property and stocks[7], with the boom and bust periods marked with shaded and clear bars, respectively. We define a boom–bust episode as a boom followed by a bust that starts no later than one-year after the end of the boom. For example, Sweden (1987–1994) exhibits a boom–bust in real property prices but Ireland (1977–1984) does not, because the boom and the bust are separated by a two-year interval (Figure 5.7). We also show banking crises marked by an asterisk country by country.[8] A few facts stand out.

First, boom–bust episodes are much more prevalent in property prices than in stock prices. Of twenty-four boom episodes in stock prices, only four are followed by busts: Finland (1989), Italy (1982), Japan (1990), and

---

[6] We experimented with different values of x to see how the number of boom–bust episodes declines as x increases. Thus, for property prices at $x = 1.0$, there are fourteen boom–bust and for stock prices there are eight. We settled on $x = 1.3$ because lowering the threshold below that level produces an excessively large number of booms and busts.

[7] Nominal prices were deflated using the gross domestic product deflator, and a constant was added to the logs to show only positive values.

[8] The data on banking crises come from Eichengreen and Bordo (2002).

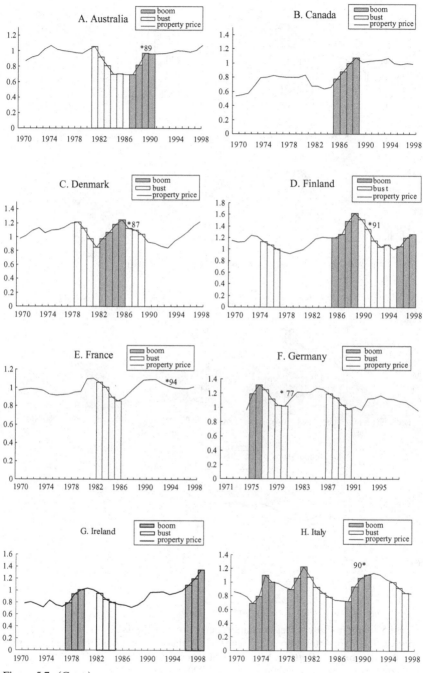

Figure 5.7. (Cont.)

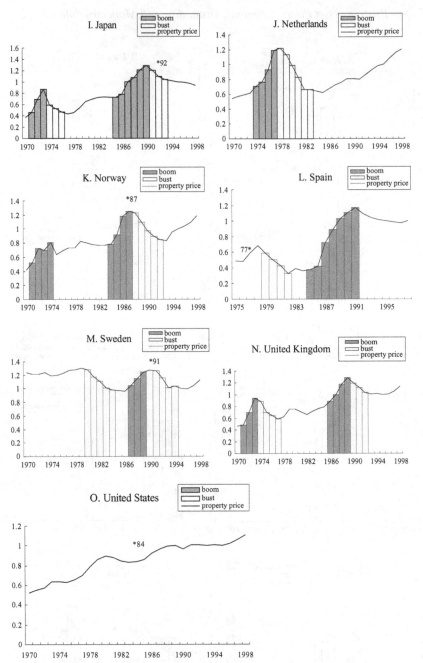

Figure 5.7. Boom–Bust in Residential Property Prices, 1970–1998[†]
Sources: Bank for International Settlements database *International Financial Statistics*
and *World Economic Outlook*, International Monetary Fund.
[†]Banking crisis. See Eichengreen and Bordo (2002), Appendix A.
[†]Booms and busts are calculated by a three-year moving average.

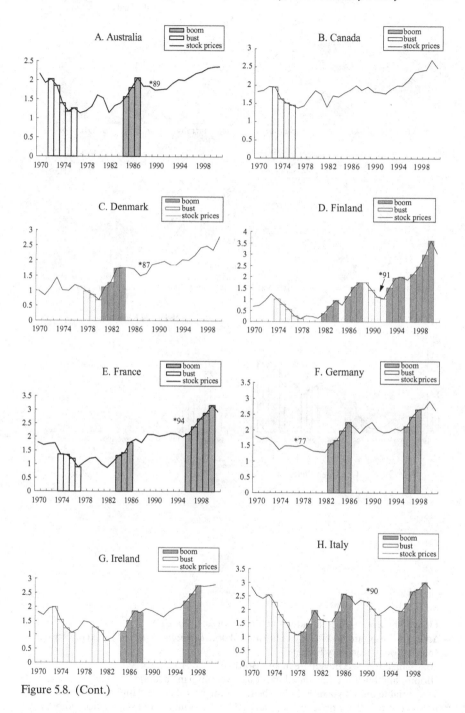

Figure 5.8. (Cont.)

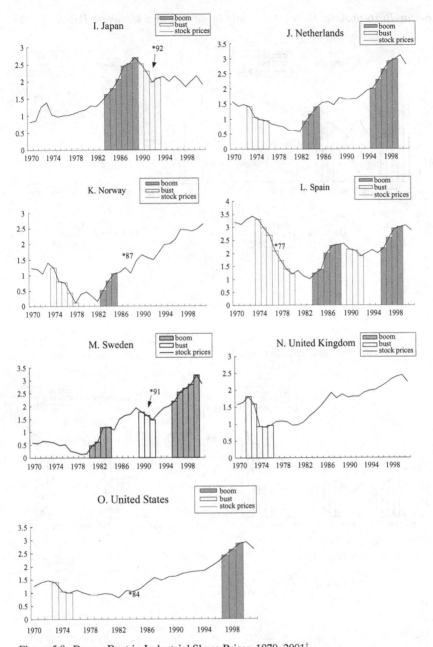

Figure 5.8. Boom–Bust in Industrial Share Prices, 1970–2001[†]
Sources: International Financial Statistics, *World Economic Outlook*, and country desks, International Monetary Fund.
*Banking crisis. See Eichengreen and Bordo (2002), Appendix A.
[†]Booms and busts are calculated by a three-year moving average.
The variable on the y-axis is 2 plus the log of the real share deflating the IPS share price index. The real share price index is derived by deflating the IFS share price index by the GDP deflator. It is normalized to 1995=1.

Spain (1990).[9] (We give the first year of the bust in parentheses.) Hence, the sample probability of a boom ending up in a bust is 16.7 percent. Of course, the boom–bust episode in Japan is very significant. Also, there might be more boom–bust episodes in the making because it is too early to tell whether the recent slides in stock markets in all countries are busts according to our criterion.[10]

Of twenty booms in property prices, eleven were followed by busts: Denmark (1987), Finland (1990), Germany (1974), Italy (1982), Japan (1974, 1991), the Netherlands (1978), Norway (1988), Sweden (1991), and the United Kingdom (1974, 1990).[11] The probability of a boom in property prices ending up in a bust is 55 percent. That is, more than one in two property booms end up in a bust, against one in six for stock market booms. Only three countries had boom–busts in both stock prices and property prices, Finland, Italy, and Japan. In all three cases, the peaks virtually coincided.

One explanation for the larger number of boom–bust episodes in property prices than in stock prices may be that property price episodes are often local phenomena occurring in the capital or major cities of a country. This would explain their high incidence in small countries like Finland or even in countries with relatively large populations like the United Kingdom, where the episode occurred in London and environs. The fact that no such episodes are found in the United States may reflect the fact that boom–busts in property prices that occurred in New York, California, and New England in the 1990s washed out in a national average index.[12]

Second, in a number of cases, banking crises occurred either at the peak of the boom or after the bust. This is most prominent in the cases of Japan and the Nordic countries.

Finally, to provide historical perspective to our methodology, we do the same calculations for two U.S. stock price indexes for the last century: the S and P 500 from 1874 to 1999 and the Dow Jones Industrial Average from 1900 to 1999. As can be seen in Figures 5.9 and 5.10, there are very few

[9] If we were to take a lower threshold, such as $x = 1.0$, then two more countries would be listed as having boom–busts: Australia and Sweden.

[10] Note that the incidence of a boom–bust episode by our criterion is very different from what is usually referred to as a stock market crash. For the United States, for example, Mishkin and White (2002) document 15 crashes from 1900 to 2000 and 4 from 1970 to 2000. They define a crash as a 20 percent decline in stock prices in a 12-month window.

[11] Again, a lower threshold of $x = 1.0$ would add in two countries: Ireland and Spain.

[12] This fact has an interesting implication for the theory of Optimum Currency Areas and the euro zone. One important source of asymmetric shocks could be boom–busts in real estate prices.

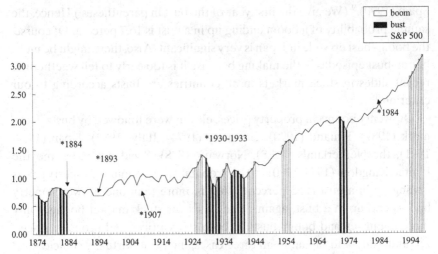

Figure 5.9. U.S. Stock Prices S and P 500, 1874–1994[†]
Source: Historical Statistics of the United States: Millennial Edition (2003)
[*]Banking crisis. See Eichengreen and Bordo (2002), Appendix A.
[†]Booms and busts are calculated by a three-year moving average.

boom–bust episodes. The crash of 1929 stands out in both figures. In the S and P, we also identify a boom–bust in 1884, the year of a famous Wall Street crash associated with speculation in railroad stocks and political corruption, and one in 1937, the start of the third most serious recession of the twentieth century.[13] As is well known, the bust of 1929 is followed by banking crises in each of the years from 1930 to 1933.

Ancillary Variables

Associated with the boom–bust episodes for property and stock prices that we have previously isolated, we provide figures for three macrovariables directly related to the asset price reversals: Consumer price index (CPI) inflation, the real output gap, and domestic private credit.[14] The figures are averages of each variable across all the boom–bust episodes demarcated above. The seven-year time window shown is centered on the first year of the bust.

[13] Using a lower threshold of $x = 1.0$ does not change the outcome.
[14] Private Credit, line 22 of IFS is defined as "claims on the private sector of Deposit Money Banks (which comprise commercial banks and other financial institutions that accept transferable deposits, such as demand deposits)."

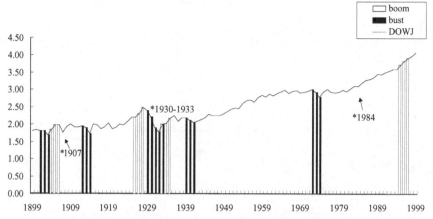

Figure 5.10. U.S. Stock Prices: Dow Jones Industrial Average (DOWJ), 1899–1999[†]
Source: Historical Statistics of the United States: Millennial Edition (2003)
*Banking crisis. See Eichengreen and Bordo (2002), Appendix A.
[†]Booms and busts are calculated by a three-year moving average.

In Figure 5.11 for property price boom–busts, we observe inflation (panel A) rising until the first year of the bust and then falling, whereas the output gap plateaus the year before the bust starts and then declines with the bust (panel B). Domestic private credit (panel C) rises in the boom and then plateaus in the bust.[15] This pattern is remarkably consistent with the scenario relating asset price reversals to the incidence of collateral, to the credit available, to liquidity-constrained firms, and to economic activity, which we develop in the next section.

Figure 5.12 shows the behavior of inflation, the output gap, and domestic private credit averaged across the four boom–bust episodes in stock prices demarcated in Figure 5.8. Inflation rises to a peak in the year preceding the bust and then declines, although not as precipitously as with the property price episodes (panel A). The output gap plateaus the year the bust starts and then declines (panel B). Domestic credit plateaus the year after the bust starts (panel C). Although the pattern displayed for the three ancillary variables for stock price boom–busts is quite similar to that seen in Figure 5.11, we attach more weight to the property price pattern

---

[15] The figure shows the nominal level of private domestic credit. Real private domestic credit declines in the bust.

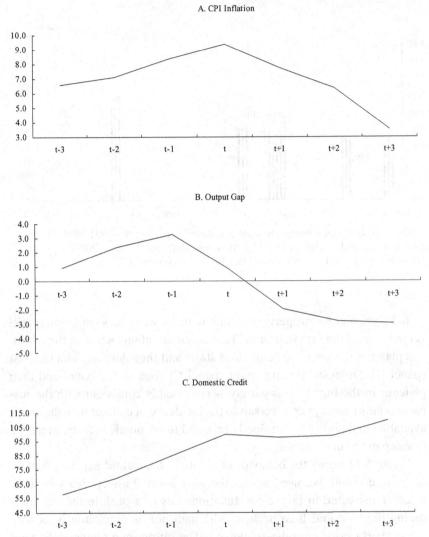

Figure 5.11. Ancillary Variables: Boom–Bust in Stock Prices
Sources: International Financial Statistics and *World Economic Outlook*, International
Monetary Fund.

because it is based on a much larger number of episodes (eleven versus
four).

   With this descriptive evidence as background, in the next section we develop a model to help us understand the relationship between boom–busts,
the real economy, and monetary policy.

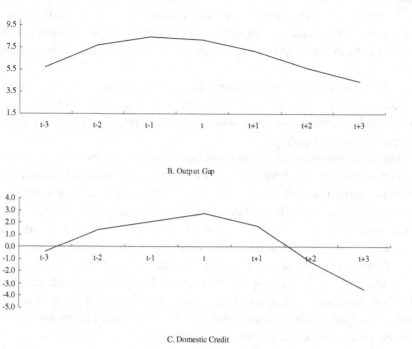

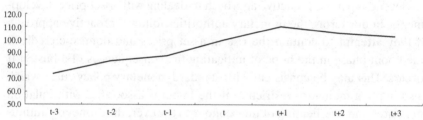

Figure 5.12. Ancillary Variables: Boom–Bust in Property Prices
Sources: *International Financial Statistics* and *World Economic Outlook*, International Monetary Fund.

THEORY

A regular feature of boom–bust episodes is that the fall in asset prices is associated with a slowdown in economic activity (sometimes negative growth), as well as financial and banking problems. There may be a number of explanations for this pattern, and they do not all give a causal role to asset

prices.[16] However, there is evidence that the bust in asset prices contributes
to the fall in output by generating a credit crunch. The domestic private sector accumulates a high level of debt in the boom period; when asset prices
fall, the collateral base shrinks and so do firms' ability to finance their operations.[17]

This section addresses the following question. Assuming that asset market
booms involve the risk of a reversal in which the economy falls prey to a
collateral-induced credit crunch, what is the consequence of this risk for the
design of monetary policy?

There are two ways in which monetary policy can respond. First is the
reactive approach. We define the reactive approach as the case in which the
monetary authorities wait and see whether the asset collapse occurs and, if it
does, respond accordingly. This is consistent with standard monetary policy
rules, such as the Taylor rule, which imply an accommodating response ex
post. If need be, this monetary relaxation can be complemented by a lending-
in-last-resort injection of liquidity to stabilize the financial system (Bernanke
and Gertler 2001). In this respect, the Federal Reserve's quick actions after
the 1987 crash and September 11, 2001, contrast with the absence of large-
scale injections of liquidity after the 1929 crash or after the plunge in the
Japanese stock market at the end of the 1980s.

Second is a more proactive approach to dealing with asset price developments. In our terms, the monetary authorities follow a proactive approach
if they attempt to contain the rise in asset prices and domestic credit in
the boom phase in the hope of mitigating the consequences of a bust, if it
occurs. This may be consistent with standard monetary policy rules, which
also imply a monetary restriction if the boom is associated with inflation
pressures and overheating of the economy. However, the monetary authorities may want to restrict monetary policy above and beyond what standard
rules prescribe. The question, then, is in which circumstances the authorities should deviate from standard rules and on which indicators should they
base monetary policy in these cases. In other words, should central banks
worry about "irrational exuberance" in the stock market, as Alan Greenspan

---

[16] For example, bad news about future productivity could cause financial and banking problems
at the same time as a slowdown in economic activity, without causality from the former to
the latter.

[17] This meaning of a collateral-induced credit crunch differs from an earlier meaning, which
viewed a credit crunch as a restriction on bank lending induced by tightening monetary
policy.

famously suggested several years before the 1990s market run-up came to an end?

This section presents a stylized model that clarifies the difference between the two views and draws some implications for monetary policy. Unlike a number of related papers (Batini and Nelson 2000; Bernanke and Gertler 2001; Cecchetti et al. 2000), the aim is not to compare the performance of different monetary policy rules in the context of a realistic, calibrated model of the economy. Rather, it is to highlight the difference between a proactive monetary policy and a reactive monetary policy in the context of a simple and transparent framework. It turns out that, although the model is quite simple, the optimal monetary policy is not trivial and depends on the exogenous economic conditions in a nonlinear way. Although this nonlinearity complicates the analysis, we think it is an essential feature of the question we study in this chapter because financial crises are inherently nonlinear events. We hope that in a second step, the approach can be transposed to more realistic models of the economy.

Our analysis is based on a reduced-form model that is very close to the standard undergraduate textbook macroeconomic model. In the Appendix we provide microfoundations in the spirit of the "Dynamic New Keynesian" literature. Private agents have utility functions and optimize intertemporally. The government prints and distributes money, which is used because of a cash-in-advance constraint. Nominal wages are predetermined, giving rise to a short-run Phillips Curve. Monetary policy has a credit channel, based on collateral. The collateral is productive capital; its price is driven by the expected level of productivity in the long run.

The reduced-form model has two periods, $t = 0, 1$. Period 0 is the period in which the problem "builds up" (debt is accumulated). In period 1, the long-run level of productivity is revealed. An asset market crash may or not occur, depending on the nature of the news. If the long-run level of productivity is lower than expected, the price of the asset falls, reducing the collateral basis for new borrowing. If the price of collateral is excessively low relative to firms' debt burden, the asset market crash provokes a credit crunch and a fall in real activity.

Note that these market dynamics are completely driven by the arrival of news on long-run productivity. The asset market boom is not caused by a monetary expansion or a bubble. Nor is the crash caused by a monetary restriction or a self-fulfilling liquidity crisis. Irrational expectations or multiple equilibria can be introduced into the model, but keeping in line with our desire to stay close to the textbook framework, we prefer to abstract from these considerations in the benchmark model. At the end of this section, we briefly discuss a variant of the model in which investors are irrationally exuberant. The Appendix presents a variant of the model in which investors are rational but asset market crashes are self-fulfilling.

The Model

The equations of the reduced-form model are as follows,

$$
\begin{cases}
y_t = m_t - p_t & (5.1) \\
y_t = \alpha p_t + \varepsilon_t & (5.2) \\
y_0 = -\sigma r & (5.3)
\end{cases}
$$

where y_t is output at time t, m_t is money supply, p_t is the price level and r is the real interest rate between period 0 and period 1. All variables, except the real interest rate, are in logs.

The first two equations characterize aggregate demand and aggregate supply. Aggregate supply is increasing with the nominal price level because the nominal wage is sticky. The third equation says that the first-period output is decreasing with the real interest rate. It is based, in the microfounded model, on the Euler equation for consumption.

The key difference between our model and the standard macromodel is the "supply shock," ε. In the standard model, the supply shock is an exogenous technological shock or, more generally, any exogenous event that affects the productivity of firms (e.g., an earthquake). Here, the supply shock is instead a "financial" shock and it is not entirely exogenous because its distribution depends on firms' debt and the price of assets, two variables that monetary policy may influence. That monetary policy can influence debt accumulation ex ante (in period 0) plays a central role in our analysis of proactive monetary policy.

The supply shock ε results from the occurrence of a credit crunch in the corporate sector. For simplicity, we assume that the credit crunch can occur only in period 1,

$$
\varepsilon_0 = 0
$$

$$
\begin{cases}
\varepsilon_1 = 0 & \text{if no credit crunch} \\
 = -\nu & \text{if credit crunch.}
\end{cases}
$$

In the microfounded model, the occurrence of a credit crunch depends on two variables, the debt burden of the corporate sector and the price of collateral. Firms issue a quantity of debt D in period 0 and must repay $(1 + r)D$ in period 1. (Debt is in real terms.) In addition, some firms must obtain new credit in period 1 to finance working capital. The firms that need but do not obtain this intraperiod credit simply do not produce, which reduces aggregate supply.

In period 1, the firms' access to new credit depends on the value of their collateral. Because of a debt renegotiation problem a la Hart and Moore (1994), firms' total debt cannot exceed the value of their collateral. Denoting by Q_1 the real value of collateral in period 1, and by γ the required level of intraperiod credit, the firms that require intraperiod credit can operate if and only if $(1 + r)D + \gamma \leq Q_1$. There is a credit crunch if and only if this condition is not satisfied,

$$Q_1 < (1 + r)D + \gamma. \tag{5.4}$$

That is, there is a credit crunch if the value of firms' collateral is low relative to their debt burden.

Monetary Policy and Financial Fragility

Monetary policy influences the two key variables that determine the occurrence of a credit crunch in period 1. First, a monetary expansion ex post (in period 1) should increase the price of collateral and may, if it is large enough, relax the collateral constraint. This is the ex post credit channel of monetary policy.[18] Second, and more interestingly, a monetary restriction ex ante (in period 0) can reduce the accumulation of corporate debt D. This is the ex ante credit channel of monetary policy. Indeed, containing firms' debt burden is the purpose of a proactive monetary policy in our framework. For simplicity, we abstract from the ex post channel by assuming that the ex post real price of collateral is exogenous to monetary policy.[19]

The probability that the economy falls in a credit crunch is a measure of its financial fragility. We denote this probability by μ. It is equal to the probability that the price of collateral falls below the threshold defined in

[18] Note that if corporate debt were nominal, the ex post credit channel would involve another effect. A monetary expansion would contribute to relax the collateral constraint by inflating away a fraction of the debt.

[19] This result is obtained, in the microfounded model, by assuming that households' utility is linear in period 1.

equation (5.4),

$$\mu = \Pr[Q_1 < \gamma + (1+r)D]. \tag{5.5}$$

The probability of a credit crunch is increasing with the ex post debt burden, $(1+r)D$. In turn, the level of firms' borrowing in period 0, D, is a decreasing function of r. For a monetary restriction in period 0 (a rise in r) to reduce the probability of a credit crunch, the debt burden $(1+r)D$ must be *decreasing* with r. That is, the semielasticity of firms' borrowing with respect to the real interest rate should be lower than -1. The model in the Appendix satisfies this property, because it yields the expression,

$$(1+r)D = E_0(Q_1) - (1+r)K \tag{5.6}$$

where K is the level of firms' equity. The debt burden is linearly increasing with the expected price of collateral and linearly decreasing with the real interest rate. Hence, the probability of a credit crunch is decreasing with the ex ante real interest rate,

$$\frac{\partial \mu}{\partial r} < 0. \tag{5.7}$$

This result is central to our analysis: *A preemptive monetary restriction at period 0 reduces the risk of a credit crunch at period 1.* The monetary restriction reduces the debt accumulated by firms and so makes them more resilient to negative shocks in the price of collateral.

Reactive and Proactive Monetary Policies

As noted earlier, the difference between our model and the standard textbook model is that the distribution of supply shocks at period 1 is endogenous to monetary policy at period 0. We call a proactive monetary policy a policy that is geared toward avoiding a credit crunch in period 1. This is in contrast to a reactive policy, which simply responds to a credit crunch if it occurs – making no difference between a credit crunch and a standard supply shock.

A proactive monetary policy involves a trade-off between the level of output in period 0 and the risk of a credit crunch in period 1. The risk of a credit crunch can be reduced by a monetary restriction, but this restriction also depresses output and prices in period 0, because

$$y_0 = -\sigma r \tag{5.8}$$

$$p_0 = -\sigma r / \alpha. \tag{5.9}$$

By contrast, with a reactive monetary policy, a proactive monetary policy is determined in the context of a trade-off between period 0 policy objectives in terms of output and prices and the risk of a credit crunch in period 1.

To investigate this trade-off, one has to endow the monetary authorities with an intertemporal objective function. We assume that the government minimizes the following quadratic loss function,

$$L = \sum_{t=0,1} \left(p_t^2 + \omega \gamma_t^2 \right). \tag{5.10}$$

Variable ω is the weight of output stabilization in the authorities' objective function, and there is no discount factor.

A Nonconventional, Nonlinear Taylor Rule

We now illustrate the difference between proactive and reactive monetary policies with a specification of the model that draws on the recent debates on the "New Economy" and the stock market. Assume that in the second period, the price of collateral can take two values, a high level, Q_H, corresponding to the New Economy scenario, and a low level, Q_L, corresponding to the "Old Economy" scenario. Viewed from period 0, the probability of the New Economy scenario is a measure of the optimism of economic agents. We denote it by P_{NE} and by $P_{OE} = 1 - P_{NE}$, the probability of the Old Economy scenario.

The realization of the Old Economy scenario is associated with a fall in asset prices and, possibly, a credit crunch. By equation (5.4), a credit crunch occurs in the event of the realization of the Old Economy scenario if $Q_L < (1+r)D + \gamma$. Substituting out D with equation (5.6) and noting that $E_0(Q_1) = P_{NE}Q_H + (1 - P_{NE})Q_L$, the condition for a credit crunch can be written

$$K(1+r) < \gamma + P_{NE} \cdot (Q_H - Q_L). \tag{5.11}$$

A credit crunch is more likely to occur ex post if private agents are more confident in the New Economy ex ante (P_{NE} is large) because firms borrow more. It is also more likely if the asset price differential between the New Economy and the Old Economy is large.

The authorities can maintain the probability of a credit crunch at its minimum level of 0 by setting the first period real interest rate at the following level,

$$1 + r = \frac{\gamma + P_{NE} \cdot (Q_H - Q_L)}{K}. \tag{5.12}$$

This rule implies that *the monetary authorities should respond to rising confidence in the New Economy (an increase in P_{NE}) by restricting monetary policy (raising r).*

Note the difference with standard rules, such as the Taylor rule. Standard rules make the monetary authorities respond to the current or expected levels of macroeconomic variables, such as the output gap or the inflation rate. The rule above suggests that the monetary policy maker should respond to prospective developments in asset markets, for which macroeconomic aggregates do not provide appropriate summary statistics.

It is not clear, however, that the authorities always wish to reduce the probability of a credit crunch to zero. The required level of the real interest rate may be excessively high. There is a threshold $\bar{r}$ above which the authorities prefer to take the risk of a credit crunch and respond ex post if need be – that is, to be reactive rather than proactive.

By adopting a reactive approach, the government can set its loss to zero in the first period, but takes the risk of incurring a strictly positive loss in the second period if a credit crunch occurs. In the latter case, the authorities minimize the loss function $p_2^2 + \omega y_2^2$ under the constraint $y_2 = \alpha p_2 - v$. The solution is $p_2 = \omega \alpha v/(1 + \omega \alpha^2)$, $y_2 = -v/(1 + \omega \alpha^2)$, and the loss is equal to $\omega v^2/(1 + \omega \alpha^2)$.[20] The intertemporal loss is equal to the probability of a credit crunch, P_{OE}, times the loss conditional on a credit crunch

$$L_{reactive} = P_{OE} \frac{\omega v^2}{1 + \omega \alpha^2}. \tag{5.13}$$

---

[20] The credit crunch increases the price level because it reduces supply without changing demand. If firms used variable production inputs other than labor – or if households were credit-constrained – the credit crunch would also reduce demand (making the model more consistent with the evidence that busts are deflationary; see Figures 5.11 and 5.12).

By contrast, if the government raises the real interest rate to the level implied by equation (5.12) to avoid a credit crunch, ouput and prices are depressed below the target levels in period 1. One has $y_1 = -\sigma r$, $p_1 = -\sigma r/\alpha$, so that the authorities have to suffer a loss of

$$L_{proactive} = (1 + \omega\alpha^2)\left(\frac{\sigma r}{\alpha}\right)^2. \tag{5.14}$$

The government adopts a proactive policy if $L_{proactive} < L_{reactive}$. Simple computations show that this is the case if the real interest rate required by a proactive policy is not too high,

$$r \leq \bar{r} \equiv \frac{\alpha}{\sigma}\frac{\nu}{1 + \omega\alpha^2}\sqrt{\omega P_{OE}}. \tag{5.15}$$

The maximum real interest rate that the government is ready to bear to forestall a credit crunch is increasing with the probability of a credit crunch, P_{OE}, and with the output cost of a credit crunch, ν. It is decreasing with the sensitivity of output to the real interest rate, σ.

Figure 5.13 illustrates how the optimal monetary policy depends on the optimism of the private sector. It shows how the real interest rate r, the first-period level of output and prices, y_0 and p_0, and the level of domestic credit D depend on the probability of realization of the New Economy scenario. The figure was constructed for the following values of the parameters,

$$Q_H = 100, Q_L = 75, K = 75, \gamma = 200/3, \alpha = 1/2, \sigma = 1/4, \omega = 1/2, \nu = 10\%.$$

The price of collateral is 25 percent lower in the Old Economy scenario than in the New Economy one. A credit crunch is associated with a 10 percent drop in output. The elasticity of first-period output with respect to the real interest rate is 0.25 (i.e., a 1 percent rise in the real interest rate depresses first-period output by 0.25 percent).

As the private sector's optimism increases, the economy goes through three different phases. First, if P_{NE} is low (lower than 33 percent in the figure), firms' borrowing is sufficiently low that the realization of the Old Economy scenario is not associated with a credit crunch. In this case, the government adopts a reactive policy because there is no reason to be proactive. If P_{NE} takes intermediate values (between 33 percent and 60 percent in the figure), the government restricts monetary policy in a proactive way. Finally, if P_{NE} is high, the government reverts to a reactive stance, even though there is a risk that the economy falls in a credit crunch. The reason is that, given the

private sector's high level of optimism, the government would have to raise
the real interest rate to an excessive level to insure the economy against
a credit crunch. At the same time, the benefit of the proactive policy is
lower because the credit crunch is less likely to occur. Leaning against the
market has higher costs and lower benefits. *The proactive policy dominates
for intermediate levels of "market exuberance."*

The model highlights both the potential benefits and the limits of a proactive monetary policy. It may be optimal, in some circumstances, to sacrifice
some output to reduce the risk of a collateral-induced credit crunch. However, there are also circumstances in which the domestic authorities are better off accepting the risk of a credit crunch (i.e., a reactive policy). Whether
the authorities should in practice engage in a proactive policy at a particular time is contingent on many factors and is a matter of judgment. In our
model, the optimal monetary policy depends on the observable macroeconomic variables and on the private sector's expectations in a highly nonlinear
way. This suggests to us that the optimal monetary policy probably does not
take the form of a simple mechanical rule, such as the Taylor rule, even if it
is augmented by a linear term in asset prices. Which form it should take in
practice is difficult to assess on the basis of our very stylized model. Further
theoretical and empirical work is needed before we can assess with some
confidence the scope for proactive monetary policies.

Irrational Exuberance

To conclude this section, let us reemphasize that our analysis of proactive
monetary policy is not premised on the assumption that asset prices deviate
from their fundamental values. The essential variable, from the point of view
of policy making is the risk of a credit crunch induced by an asset market
reversal. This assessment can be made based on the historical record (as
illustrated earlier in this chapter), as well as information specific to each
episode. In particular, the suspicion that an asset market boom is a bubble
that will have to burst, at some point, is an important input in this assessment.
However, bubbles are not of the essence of the question because, as our
model shows, the question would arise even in a world without bubbles.
Hence, the debate about proactive versus reactive monetary policies should
not be reduced to a debate over the central bank's ability to recognize a
bubble when it sees one.

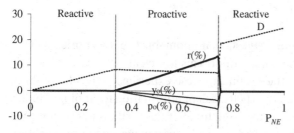

Figure 5.13. The Irrational Exuberance Case
Note: In Figures 5.13 and 5.14 the vertical axis is in percent. Both figures plot the impact of rising optimism (i.e., rising probability of the New Economy (NE) scenario). In Figure 5.13 that rising public optimism is not shared by The Central Bank and is, therefore, termed the irrational exuberance case.

Going back to our model, the notion of irrational expectations can be captured by assuming that private agents base their decisions, in period 0, on an excessively optimistic assessment of the probability of the New Economy scenario. Let us assume that firms borrow in period 0 on the basis of a probability P_{NE}, which is larger than the true probability P_{NE}. The monetary authorities base instead their policy on the true probability.

Figure 5.13 shows the optimal monetary policy as a function of the private sector's optimism (measured by P_{NE}), assuming that the monetary authorities keep their own estimate at $P_{NE} = 0.1$. Otherwise, the calibration is the same as in Figure 5.14. The real interest rate required by the proactive monetary policy is exactly the same as before because it is dictated by the expectations of the market, not those of the central bank. However, the proactive monetary policy is maintained for higher levels of market optimism than before because this optimism is not shared by the monetary authorities. Hence, irrational exuberance broadens the scope for proactive monetary policy.

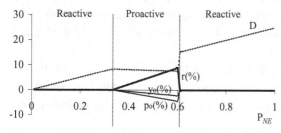

Figure 5.14. The Role of Private Sector Optimism

CONCLUSIONS AND POLICY IMPLICATIONS

The analysis in this chapter suggests that boom–busts in asset prices can be very costly in terms of declining output. This was clearly the case in the U.S. Great Depression and in the recent Japanese experience. Thus far in 2003, the recession that followed the 2000 crash of information technology studies has been relatively mild. It is too soon to tell if this result is permanent. We also argue that there is a case under certain circumstances to use monetary policy in a proactive way to restrict private domestic credit and diffuse an asset price boom to prevent a credit crunch.

The consensus view among policy makers today, however, is not to pursue such a course but rather to follow a reactive policy and deal with the consequences of an asset price bust after it happens. We believe our chapter suggests that the case for a proactive policy is a real issue – that the current strategy of following a Taylor rule that focuses the policy instrument exclusively on deviations from inflation forecasts and the output gap – and then injecting liquidity ex post in the event of a credit crunch – may, in certain circumstances, be more costly in terms of lost output than a proactive policy incorporating asset prices directly into the central bank's objective function. In a sense, had the Federal Reserve followed the views of Strong and later Harrison and successfully defused the stock market boom in 1928 rather than following the policies that it did, the outcome would have been very different.[21] A similar conjecture could be made about the Bank of Japan's policy in the late 1980s. What would have been the optimal policy, given the conditions of each episode and the information that policy makers had available to them, remains to be examined.

Our analysis in this chapter should be interpreted as being mainly suggestive because we do not provide empirical estimates of the magnitude of the output losses under the alternative policy strategies. To do this would require either simulating the effects of alternative policy rules in an econometric model or in a calibrated dynamic general equilibrium model that would involve the kind of nonlinearity we have emphasized in this chapter. These are topics for future research.

Finally, the descriptive evidence that we present shows that stock market boom–busts are rare events, whereas property boom–busts are quite frequent. This suggests prima facie that the case for a proactive policy may

[21] For a contrarian view, see Bernanke (2002a).

be more telling to deal with property price credit crunches. Because these events occur quite regularly in the smaller countries of Europe, this issue may pose a challenge for the European Central Bank, which sets its policy based primarily on Europe-wide objectives.

APPENDIX

The model has three periods, $t = 0, 1, 2$ (one period more than the reduced-form model). The last period is added so as to endogenize the price of the asset. There are two types of private agents, households and entrepreneurs. There is a continuum of mass 1 of each type. Households supply labor and funds to entrepreneurs, who produce a homogeneous consumption good. We assume that there is a fixed quantity of productive capital in the economy. Capital does not depreciate, and it cannot be reproduced. Productive capital can be though of as "land," and the consumption good as "fruit."

Households are identical and live for three periods. Their intertemporal utility is given by,

$$U^h = u(C_0) + C_1 + C_2 \qquad (A1)$$

where $C_\tau (t = 1, 2)$, denotes the representative household's consumption of fruit, and $u(\cdot)$ is increasing and concave.

Entrepreneurs live in the first two periods, $t = 0, 1$. They have a native ability to combine land with labor to produce fruit. We assume that each entrepreneur operates exactly one unit of land. When combined with L_t units of labor, one unit of land yields,

$$y_t = L_t^{1-\eta}, \qquad t = 0, 1, \qquad (A2)$$

units of good ($\eta \in (0, 1)$).

We assume that in the last period, entrepreneurs are no longer required in the production process. The production process in period 2 is the same as in Lucas's "tree economy": Each unit of land yields an exogenous quantity of good, denoted by R. This assumption captures the idea that, in the long run, the economy reaches a state of equilibrium in which the type of financial disruption that we focus on no longer matters. Variable R may be interpreted as the long-run productivity of capital. Its value is unknown at time 0, and is revealed at time 1.

At time 0, the productive asset (land) is owned by households. The entrepreneurs must take possession of the asset to produce, but they do not have enough cash. We assume that the entrepreneurs finance the purchase of the asset by issuing debt. Let Q_0 be the real price of the asset in period 0. At the beginning of period 0, each entrepreneur is endowed with K and borrows $D = Q_0 - K$.

Entrepreneurs produce in periods 0 and 1. We assume that in period 1, entrepreneurs must borrow "inside the period" to finance working capital. This can be justified by the fact that inside the period, production takes time, and some production inputs that are immobilized in the production process must be financed by credit. The entrepreneurs that do not manage to obtain the intraperiod credit are inactive – they do not produce. In general, the intraperiod credit requirement could differ across entrepreneurs, for example, because of idiosyncratic shocks in the production process. The real value of the credit required by entrepreneur j is denoted by $\gamma(j)$.

We further assume that entrepreneurs' debt is subject to a renegotiation problem a la Hart and Moore (1994) and Kiyotaki and Moore (1997). An entrepreneur has the option to walk away with the output after production has taken place, leaving the asset for his creditors to seize. The entrepreneur walks away after production has taken place in period 1 if and only if his total debt (the repayment of the period 0 loan contracted to purchase the productive asset, plus the intraperiod credit) exceeds the value of collateral. If creditors anticipate that the entrepreneur will default, they do not provide the intraperiod credit and the entrepreneur cannot operate. Hence, the entrepreneur can operate if and only if the required intraperiod credit is lower than the net value of the firm, that is, if

$$\gamma(j) < Q_1 - (1+r)D. \qquad (A3)$$

At the level of the entrepreneur, this constraint is of the "all-or-nothing" type. If it is not satisfied, the entrepreneur is simply inactive and the asset is sold at the end of the period. If it is satisfied, the entrepreneur operates free of credit constraint. We assume that the proceeds of the sale are always sufficient to repay the period 0 lenders (i.e., $Q_1 \geq (1+r)D$), so that there is no default risk in equilibrium.

One has to make an assumption on the distribution of the intraperiod credit requirement across entrepreneurs. For simplicity, we assume that there are two types of entrepreneurs: Some need a level γ of intraperiod credit, and the others do not need intraperiod credit at all. Denoting by ϕ the fraction of entrepreneurs of the first type, the number of active entrepreneurs at period 1, N_1, is given by,

$$\begin{cases} N_1 = 1 & \text{if } Q_1 - (1+r)D \geq \gamma \\ = 1 - \phi & \text{if } Q_1 - (1+r)D < \gamma. \end{cases} \qquad (A4)$$

In periods 0 and 1, after production has taken place, there is a financial market in which households exchange consumption good, money, IOUs, and the productive asset. For the sake of simplicity, we assume that entrepreneurs do not participate in the financial market. (This is necessarily true in period 1 because entrepreneurs consume their end-of-life wealth.) Hence, in period 0 the real price of the asset results from the first-order conditions of the intertemporal optimization problem of households

$$Q_0 u'(C_0) = E_0(Q_1) \qquad (A5)$$
$$u'(C_0) = 1 + r. \qquad (A6)$$

The utility function being linear in periods 1 and 2, the price of the asset at period 1 is simply equal to its final return,

$$Q_1 = R \qquad (A7)$$

Money is used by households in periods 0 and 1. Money demand results from a cash-in-advance constraint,

$$C_t = \frac{M_t}{P_t} \qquad t = 0, 1. \qquad (A8)$$

The domestic government prints and transfers money to households in a lump-sum way. For simplicity, we assume that the government makes the consumption of households equal to that of entrepreneurs by lump-sum transfers, so that the consumption of the representative households is proportional to aggregate output,

$$C_t = \lambda Y_t \qquad (A9)$$

(where λ is equal to $\frac{1}{2}$ because there is the same number of entrepreneurs and households).

We assume that the nominal wage levels of periods 0 and 1, W_0 and W_1, are preset at the beginning of period 0, before M_0 and M_1 are known. For simplicity, we take the nominal wages as exogenous to the analysis.

The labor market is perfectly competitive. Aggregate supply at time t is equal to the number of active entrepreneurs times the supply per active entrepreneur. An active entrepreneur produces $(W/(1-\eta)P)^{-(1-\eta)/\eta}$, whereas inactive entrepreneurs produce nothing. Hence, aggregate supply can be written

$$Y_t = N_t \cdot \left(\frac{1}{1-\eta} \frac{W_t}{P_t} \right)^{-\alpha} \tag{A10}$$

where $\alpha \equiv (1-\eta)/\eta$ is the elasticity of aggregate supply with respect to the real wage.

Leaving aside unimportant constants, the model can be written in log form like in the text (equation (5.2)), with $\varepsilon_t = \log N_t$. We have $\varepsilon_t = 0$, except in period 1 if there is a credit crunch, in which case $\varepsilon_1 = -\nu \equiv \log(1-\phi)$.

It results from $D = Q_0 - K$ and the first-order conditions (A5)–(AA6) that the debt burden in period 1 is,

$$(1+r)D = E_0(Q_1) - K(1+r) \tag{A11}$$

(equation (5.6) in the text).

We conclude by presenting a variant of the model in which credit crunches can be self-fulfilling, which gives scope for a form of lending-in-last-resort policy. Assume now that households' utility is concave in period 1 consumption, that is, equation (AA1) is replaced by

$$U^h = u(C_0) + u(C_1) + C_2. \tag{A12}$$

The period 1 price of the asset must now satisfy

$$Q_1 u'(C_1) = R. \tag{A13}$$

Substituting out P_1 from (A8) and (A10) and using $C_1 = \lambda y_1$, aggregate supply can be written as a function of the number of active firms

$$Y_1 = \kappa N_1^{1/(1+\alpha)} \tag{A14}$$

where $\kappa \equiv \lambda^{1/(1+\alpha)} \left(\frac{(1-\eta)M_1}{W_1} \right)^{\alpha/(1+\alpha)}$.

An equilibrium without a credit crunch can coexist with an equilibrium with a credit crunch. To see this, let us denote by Y^H and Q^H the levels of output and asset price in the equilibrium without a credit crunch and by Y^L and Q^L the analogs in the equilibrium with a credit crunch. One has $Y^H = \kappa >$

$Y^L = \kappa(1 - \phi)^{1/(1+\alpha)}$ and $Q^H = R/u'(\lambda Y^H) > Q^L = R/u'(\lambda Y^L)$. Output and the price of the asset are both lower in the equilibrium with a credit crunch. For both equilibria to exist, one must have $Q^H \geq \gamma + (1+r)D > Q^L$. The price of collateral in the credit-crunch equilibrium must be sufficiently low so as to provoke a credit crunch and sufficiently high in the no-credit-crunch equilibrium so as to avoid a credit crunch. The intuition behind the multiplicity involves the following vicious circle. A fall in the price of collateral reduces aggregate supply and consumption; households' attempt to sell the asset (to smooth consumption intertemporally) then depresses the price of the asset in equilibrium. The bad equilibrium is removed if the monetary authorities peg the price of the asset at the good equilibrium level Q_1^H. This requires a promise by the monetary authorities to inject money into the economy would it threaten to switch to the bad equilibrium, a policy that can be interpreted as a form of lending-in-last-resort.

6   Deflation, Credit, and Asset Prices

Charles Goodhart and Boris Hofmann

INTRODUCTION

Over the last two decades, most industrialised and developing countries have experienced episodes of boom and bust in credit markets. These credit cycles often coincided with cycles in economic activity and asset prices. The unwinding of the imbalances built up in the boom has, in some cases, led to severe problems in the financial sector, sometimes culminating in an outright banking crisis. In Japan, the second biggest economy of the world, asset price deflations, both in equity and property, were followed by a decade of financial fragility and deflationary developments in goods prices, with consumer prices falling continuously after 1999. With short-term interest rates having reached the zero lower bound, the country appears to be trapped in a deflationary spiral out of which it finds itself unable to escape. Other South-east Asian countries, such as Hong Kong and Singapore, have also experienced asset price deflations followed by a marked drop in credit creation and goods price deflation in recent years. Some commentators argue that the United States and other industrialised countries are also now, in the wake of the worldwide slump in share prices, on the brink of deflation.[1]

Both the experience from historical episodes of financial crisis in the late nineteenth and early twentieth centuries and from recent boom–bust cycles in credit markets, suggest that consumer prices respond with a lag to developments in credit markets. Consumer price inflation is often low or falling during credit booms and peaks after the onset of the bust. Asset prices, especially property prices, on the other hand, appear to follow closely behind or even to lead bank lending.

---

[1]   See, for example, *The Economist* (October 2002b) "Of debt, deflation and denial."

The recurrence of boom and bust cycles in asset and credit markets, followed by financial sector distress and deflationary pressures on goods prices has led to a resurgence of both academic and policy interest in the interlinkages between asset, credit, and goods markets. As a result, Fisher's (1933) theory of debt-deflation, which was motivated by the deflationary spirals evolving in the United States and other countries during the Great Depression of 1929 to 1932, has gained new topicality. Fisher developed a chain of interlinkages between asset prices, goods prices, economic activity, and the financial sector, which may set in motion a deflationary spiral once a negative shock occurs.[2] After a wave of optimism and confidence, leading to overinvestment, excess indebtedness, and inflated asset prices, households' and firms' balance sheets are highly exposed to asset price, and interest rate movements. A sudden drop in confidence triggers a desire to reduce debts, followed by asset liquidation, a fall in asset prices, and rising real interest rates.[3] The resulting reduction of borrowers' net worth triggers a surge in bankruptcies, contraction of bank lending, and a fall in output. These developments lead to a further weakening of confidence, further falls in asset prices, and falling consumer prices leading to a further reduction of borrowers' net worth, so that a deflationary spiral gradually evolves. The process is reinforced by negative repercussions on the balance sheets of financial institutions due to falling asset values and rising rates of default and nonperforming loans.[4]

At the heart of the debt-deflation theory is the effect of falling asset and goods prices on the borrowing capacity of investors. Falling asset prices reduce the value of borrowers' assets, whereas falling goods prices increase the real value of their debts, eroding their net worth. Recent theoretical advances in understanding the interlinkages between asset prices, the financial system, and the real economy, such as the business cycle models developed by Bernanke and Gertler (1989) and Kiyotaki and Moore (1997), are all more or less rooted in Fisher's theory of debt-deflation. In these models, a financial accelerator, working via the effect of asset prices on the borrowing capacity of households and firms, amplifies the macroeconomic effects of productivity shocks. However, the financial accelerator could also be an

---

[2] King (1994) provides an overview and a contemporaneous interpretation of Fisher's debt-deflation theory. See also Bernanke (1983).

[3] Real interest rates increase because a negative shock to asset prices raises the conditional volatility of returns so that lenders demand a higher risk premium.

[4] The negative effect of collapsing asset and goods prices on banks' balance sheets was already stressed by Keynes (1931).

independent source of business cycle fluctuations, transmitting shocks to asset prices, reflecting a wave of justified or unjustified optimism about future economic prospects, or shocks to credit, reflecting financial liberalisation or a credit demand disturbance to the real economy.

In any case, the existence of a financial accelerator or debt-deflation mechanism implies a close empirical correlation between bank lending and asset prices. Such a close correlation, especially between bank lending and property prices, has in fact been widely documented in the policy-oriented literature (e.g. International Monetary Fund (IMF) 2000; Bank for International Settlements (BIS) 2001). But whether this correlation is merely driven by the business cycle as a common factor or whether credit or asset price shocks also play an independent role remains an open empirical question.

In this chapter, we will assess the effect of independent movements in credit and asset prices for a sample of twelve countries. The sample of countries comprises the G7 (United States, Canada, Japan, France, Germany, Italy, and United Kingdom), three Nordic countries (Sweden, Norway, and Finland), which have experienced financial sector distress from the late 1980s to the early 1990s, and two Asian countries (Hong Kong and Singapore), which have recently experienced deflationary pressures in the wake of boom–bust cycles in credit and asset markets. A simple impulse response exercise suggests that property price innovations have a significant effect on bank lending, whereas credit shocks appear to affect property prices in only a few countries. Shocks to equity prices do not appear to have a significant effect on bank lending, nor do credit shocks have a significant effect on equity prices in the majority of countries.

Because price stability is defined in terms of the consumer or retail price index, a policy conflict between the goals of financial stability and price stability may arise in times of a credit boom because of the lagged response of consumer prices to the build up of financial imbalances. Developments in the financial sector may call for a monetary tightening, whereas consumer price inflation may not give any signal of overheating.[5] Rather, signals of overheating may be evident in asset markets. Goodhart (1995) argues that this is one reason why a definition of price stability in terms of a

---

[5]   An example of this dilemma is the recent development in the United Kingdom, where sharply rising house prices raise concerns about financial fragility whereas consumer price inflation stays at moderate levels.

broader-based price index also including asset prices, especially housing prices, might be preferable.[6]

The role of asset prices in the conduct of monetary policy has turned out to be a highly controversial issue. Cecchetti et al. (2000) argue in favour of a direct response of monetary policy to asset price movements that are not in line with perceived fundamentals, whereas Bernanke and Gertler (1999) and Gertler et al. (1998) argue against it. Bordo and Jeanne (this volume) show that whether an active response of monetary policy to asset prices is beneficial or not depends in a highly nonlinear way on private sector sentiment and confidence.

A rather neglected issue is the question how monetary policy can actually influence asset prices and bank lending to contain financial cycles. There is only scarce empirical evidence on the effect of interest rate movements on asset prices in general. Based on a simple impulse response exercise, we investigate the effect of interest rate shocks on economic activity, asset prices, and bank lending. The results suggest that interest rate innovations have a significantly negative effect on asset prices, whereas bank lending is found to be rather unresponsive to interest rate shocks. These findings lend only weak support to the view that interest rate policy is a useful instrument to smooth cycles in asset and credit markets. Moreover, the effect of interest rate movements on asset prices and bank lending is most likely a highly nonlinear function of market sentiment, being rather ineffective in times of boom and bust and highly effective at the time market sentiment changes. A successful smoothing of cycles in asset and credit markets, therefore, may only be possible if monetary policy acts *before* an upswing has turned into a boom. But when exactly this is the case is almost impossible to tell ex ante. Such a policy may also involve interest rate hikes in times of low or falling headline inflation rates, which will prove to be difficult for a central bank to justify either to the public or to politicians.

In the next section, we investigate the historical record of financial crises and deflation and the co-movements of consumer prices, asset prices, and bank lending in recent times. The next section discusses the theoretical background for the co-movements between asset prices and bank lending and

---

[6] The general case for a broader-based price index is made by Alchian and Klein (1973). They argue that assets represent claims on future consumption, so that a correct measure of inflation would also need to include asset prices to account for the expected price of future consumption. An early reference of this line of thought is, again, Fisher (1911), who states that: "To base our index number [of purchasing power] for time contracts solely on services and immediately consumable goods would be illogical" (p. 174).

presents evidence from a simple impulse response exercise. Then, we discuss the potential role of interest rate policy as an instrument to smooth financial cycles, followed by our conclusions.

DEFLATION AND FINANCIAL FRAGILITY: THE HISTORICAL RECORD

In this section, we will explore the behaviour of consumer prices during historical episodes of financial crises of the late nineteenth and early twentieth centuries, and the correlation between credit growth and consumer and asset prices more recently, since the mid-1980s.

First, we look at nine pre-1914 episodes of financial crisis analysed in Delargy and Goodhart (1999) and the Great Depression in the United States in 1929–1932. The crisis episodes analysed by Delargy and Goodhart comprise the 1873 crises in the United States and Austria; the 1890 crises in the United States and Australia; the 1893 crises in the United States, Australia, and Italy; and the 1907 crises in the United States and Italy.[7] Delargy and Goodhart describe the period prior to these crisis episodes as being characterised by credit booms and unsustainable rates of output growth. The Great Depression, preceded by the U.S. stock market crash of October 1929, also followed a boom in bank lending and the stock market. Average growth rates of bank lending and the Standard and Poor's Composite Index between 1925 and 1928 were 5.5 percent and 20 percent, respectively.

Figure 6.1 shows the development of the change in consumer prices (wholesale prices for Austria) in the two years before and after the crisis. The graphs reveal that, in all cases, consumer prices were falling for at least one year after the onset of the crisis. In the nineteenth-century crises, goods prices did not show any sign of overheating prior to the crisis. Inflation rates were either falling or even negative. In the two 1907 crises, inflation picked up just in the year of the crisis. Likewise, in the two years before the onset of the Great Depression, consumer prices were stable or even falling. Thus, in no case did consumer prices give an early warning signal of overheating in the financial sector.

Long runs of historical data on credit aggregates and asset prices are unavailable for most countries, so that we cannot provide an assessment of

---

[7] In addition to the nine crises referred to here, Delargy and Goodhart (1999) also analyse the 1890 financial crisis in Argentina. We could not analyse this crisis episode here because we were not able to find consumer or wholesale price data for Argentina for this period.

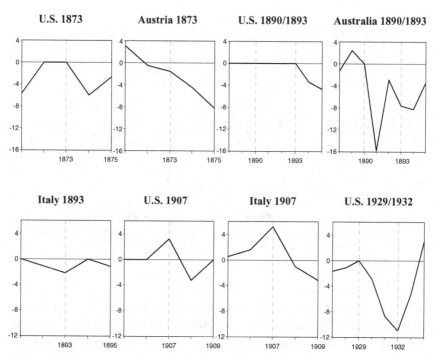

Figure 6.1. Early Episodes of Consumer Price Deflation and Financial Fragility
Source: Mitchell (1998).

the behaviour of asset prices around the crisis episodes. The exception is
the United States, where we were able to find data for total bank lending,
the Standard and Poor's index of common stocks, and the price index for
single-family houses in the *Historical Abstract of the United States* published
by the U.S. Bureau of the Census (1960). Figure 6.2 shows the co-movement
of the percent change in total bank lending (dotted line, right-hand scale)
and, respectively, the percent change in the consumer price index, the share
price index, and the house price index (solid line, left-hand scale). The graphs
reveal that contractions in bank lending in the wake of the financial crises
in 1893, 1907, 1929, and also 1921 were accompanied by consumer price
deflations. Prior to the 1893 and 1907 crises, bank lending was growing at
a brisk pace, whereas consumer price inflation was flat. The same holds for
the mid-1920s, where lending was growing at high rates and consumer price
inflation was low or negative.

The second graph in Figure 6.2 suggests that, except for the period 1910–
1920, credit booms were associated with high rates of share price inflation.

Credit growth and   Credit growth and   Credit growth and
CPI inflation   equity price inflation   property price inflation

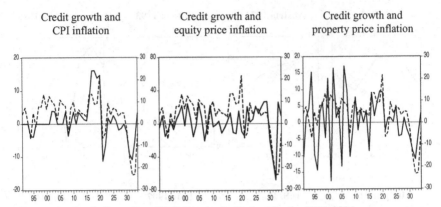

Figure 6.2. Credit Growth and Inflation in the United States, 1891–1934
Note: The dotted line represents credit growth (right-hand scale), and the solid line represents the rate of change in the respective price index (left-hand scale).
Source: Bureau of the Census (1960).

This holds in particular for the periods prior to the 1907 crisis and prior to the Great Depression. House prices were highly volatile before 1918, so that no clear correlation between house price inflation and credit growth emerges. After 1918, the correlation appears to be somewhat closer; However, although the sharp drops in credit growth in 1921 and 1929 were accompanied by falling house prices, the credit boom prior to the Great Depression was not reflected in high rates of house price inflation. Like consumer prices, house prices were basically falling since 1925.

Historical U.S. data, therefore, suggest that credit is closely correlated with equity prices rather than consumer or property prices, especially in times of a credit boom. A somewhat different picture emerges when we look at more recent data. Figures 6.3, 6.4, and 6.5 display the co-movement of credit growth (dotted line, right hand scale), defined as the year-on-year percent change in bank lending to the private nonbank sector and, respectively, the year-on-year percent change in the consumer price index (CPI), equity price index, and residential property price index (solid line, left-hand scale). The sample of countries comprises the G7, three Nordic countries (Sweden, Norway, and Finland) and two Southeast Asian countries (Hong Kong and Singapore). The sample period is first quarter 1985 to fourth quarter 2001.

Figure 6.3 suggests that credit growth is generally leading consumer price inflation. The credit boom experienced by most industrialised countries in the late 1980s was often accompanied by low or falling rates of consumer

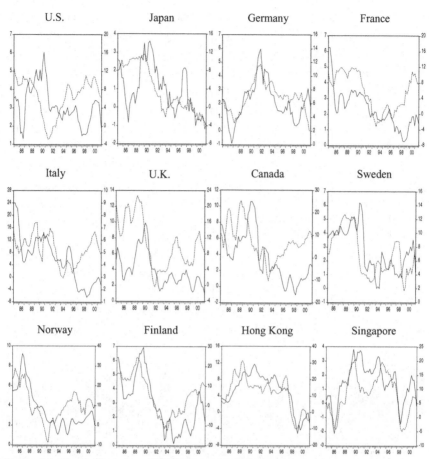

Figure 6.3. Credit Growth and CPI Inflation, 1985–2001
Note: The dotted line represents credit growth (right-hand scale), and the solid line represents the rate of change in the consumer price index (left-hand scale).
Sources: See appendix, and Bank for International Settlements data base.

price inflation. When the boom turned into a bust in the early 1990s, consumer prices often continued to rise and peaked several quarters after credit growth. In the late 1990s, again, many countries experienced high rates of credit growth together with low or falling rates of CPI inflation. In Hong Kong, credit growth also leads CPI inflation by several quarters, whereas in Singapore, the correlation appears to be rather coincident. Figures 6.4 and 6.5 show that credit and property prices follow the same cycle swings, with house price inflation leading credit growth, rather than conversely. On the

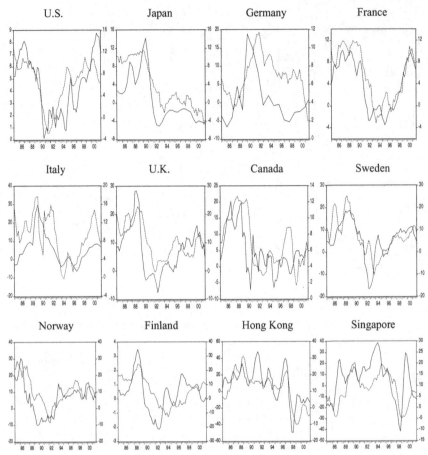

Figure 6.4. Credit Growth and House Price Inflation, 1985–2001.
Note: The dotted line represents credit growth (right-hand scale), and the solid line represents the rate of change in the consumer price index (left-hand scale).
Sources: See appendix, and Bank for International Settlements data base.

other hand, the movements in credit and share prices appear to be largely uncorrelated due to the high volatility of share price movements.

CREDIT AND ASSET PRICES: THEORY AND EVIDENCE

Theory

In the previous section, we showed that bank lending has, in recent decades, been closely correlated with property prices. There are various theoretical

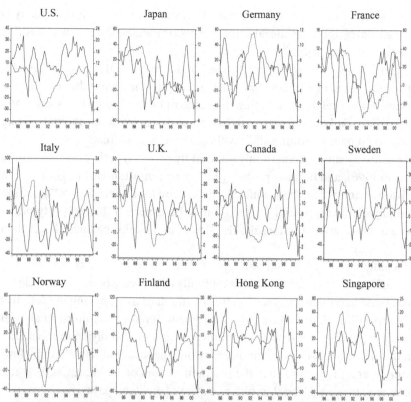

Figure 6.5. Credit Growth and Equity Price Inflation, 1985–2001.
Note: The dotted line represents credit growth (right-hand scale), and the solid line represents the rate of change in the consumer price index (left-hand scale).
Sources: See appendix, and Bank for International Settlements data base.

explanations for such a close empirical correlation. First, asset prices may have a direct wealth effect on credit demand. Asset prices affect consumers' perceived lifetime wealth, inducing them to change their spending and borrowing plans to smooth consumption over the life cycle.[8] A change in asset prices may, therefore, induce a change in credit demand in the same direction.

Second, households and firms may be borrowing constrained due to asymmetric information in the credit market, which gives rise to adverse selection and moral hazard problems. As a result, households and firms can only

---

[8] The life cycle model of household consumption was originally developed by Ando and Modigliani (1963). A formal exposition of the life cycle model can be found in Deaton (1992) and Muellbauer (1994).

borrow when they can offer collateral, so that their borrowing capacity is a function of their collateralisable net worth, which is in turn a positive function of asset prices.[9]

Third, as has already been stressed by Keynes (1931), asset prices also affect the value of bank capital, both directly to the extent that banks own assets and indirectly by affecting the value of loans secured by assets.[10] Via their effect on banks' balance sheets, asset prices influence the risk-taking capacity of banks and thus their willingness to extend loans.

Because loans are commonly secured by property rather than by equity (Borio 1996), and because property makes up a substantially larger share of private sector wealth than equity (Organisation for Economic Co-Operation and Development [OECD] 2000), it may be expected that property prices have a larger effect on households', firms', and banks' balance sheets than equity prices.

Kindleberger (1978) and Minsky (1982) argued that credit conditions may also affect asset valuations, so that mutually reinforcing boom–bust cycles in credit and asset markets may evolve. In standard asset pricing models, it is of course difficult to make a case for a role for credit conditions. Real asset prices depend on the discounted future stream of real dividend payments. In this framework, higher liquidity may only have an indirect effect by lowering interest rates and thus the discount factors or by indicating brighter economic prospects and thus higher expected dividend payments. However, asset prices may not always obey asset pricing formulae, and it may simply be that additionally available liquidity increases the demand for a (temporarily) fixed supply of assets, which results in higher real asset prices.

Empirical Evidence

Little empirical research has been done on the relationship between credit and asset prices. Most studies rely on a single equation set up, either relating indicators of financial distress or credit aggregates to asset prices or relating asset price developments to credit conditions. Goodhart (1995) investigates the determinants of credit growth in the United States and the

[9] Basic references of this literature are Bernanke and Gertler (1989) and Kiyotaki and Moore (1997). For a survey, see Bernanke, Gertler, and Gilchrist (1998).

[10] Chen (2001) develops an extension of the Kiyotaki and Moore (1997) model, in which an additional amplification of business cycles results from the effect of asset price movements on banks' balance sheets.

United Kingdom over a long sample period (1919–1991 and 1939–1991, respectively) using annual data, regressing the change in bank lending on the change in house prices, the change in equity prices, and several other explanatory variables. For the United States, he finds a significant coefficient for the change in stock prices, but not for the change in house prices, a finding that is consistent with our descriptive analysis of the historical U.S. data in the previous section. For the United Kingdom, he finds that the change in house prices had a strong and highly significant effect on credit growth, whereas the change in stock prices came out insignificantly and even wrongly signed. Rolling regression estimates suggest that for the United Kingdom, the relationship between credit and house price has strengthened over the postwar period, whereas the relationship between credit and share prices has weakened.

Hutchison and McDill (1999) and Hilbers, Lei, and Zacho (2001) find that the change in share prices and the change in residential property prices significantly enter multivariate probit-logit models to explain the outbreak of financial distress in industrialised and developing countries. Borio and Lowe (2002) show that a measure of the aggregate asset price gap,[11] measured as the deviation of aggregate asset prices from their long-run trend, combined with a similarly defined credit gap measure, is a useful indicator of financial distress in industrialised countries.

Borio, Kennedy, and Prowse (1994) investigate the relationship between credit to GDP ratios and aggregate asset prices for a large sample of industrialised countries over the period 1970–1992 using annual data. They focus on the determinants of aggregate asset price fluctuations, hypothesising that the development of credit conditions as measured by the credit to GDP ratio can help to explain the evolution of aggregate asset prices. They find that adding the credit to gross domestic product (GDP) ratio to an asset pricing equation helps to improve the fit of this equation in most countries. Based on simulations, they demonstrate that the boom–bust cycle in asset markets of the late 1980s and early 1990s would have been much less pronounced or would not have occurred at all had credit ratios remained constant. For a panel of four East Asian countries (Hong Kong, Korea, Singapore, and Thailand), Collyns and Senhadji (2002) find that credit growth has a significant

[11] Aggregate asset price indices are calculated as a weighted average of residential property prices, commercial property prices, and equity prices. The weights are based on the share of each asset in national private sector balance sheets, which are derived based on national flow-of-funds data or UN standardised national accounts.

contemporaneous effect on residential property prices. They conclude that bank lending contributed significantly to the real estate bubble in Asia prior to the 1997 East Asian crisis.

None of these studies, however, control for potential simultaneity, which is strongly suggested by our prior theoretical considerations. The findings, therefore, do not tell us anything about the direction of causality between credit and asset prices. Gerlach and Peng (2002) and Hofmann (2001) analyse the relationship between bank lending and property prices respectively for Hong Kong and for a set of industrialised countries, based on a multivariate empirical framework. Both studies find that both long-run and short-run causality goes from property prices to credit.

A Simple Impulse Response Exercise

In the following exercise, we also use a multivariate modelling approach to analyse the relationship between bank lending and equity and property prices. We estimate a vector autoregression (VAR) comprising real bank lending, real GDP, real equity prices, real property prices, and a short-term real interest rate. The analysis covers twelve countries – the G7, Sweden, Norway, Finland, Hong Kong, and Singapore. The sample period is first quarter 1985 to fourth quarter 2001. We do not perform an explicit analysis of any potential long-run relationships because of the relatively short sample period and large number of endogenous variables. By doing the analysis in levels, we allow for implicit cointegrating relationships in the data.

Nominal bank lending, share prices, and property prices were transformed into real terms by deflating with the CPI. The (ex post) short-term real interest rate is measured as the three months interbank money market rate less annual CPI inflation. All data except for the share price index and the money market rate are seasonally adjusted. With the exception of the real interest rate, all data were transformed into natural logs. All data were taken from the BIS or the IMF database. Detailed information about the original source of the residential property price series can be found in the data in the Appendix.

The VAR model estimated for each of the twelve countries under investigation is given by,

$$x_t = A_1 x_{t-1} + \cdots + A_n x_{t-n} + \mu + \delta t + \varepsilon_t.$$

Table 6.1. *Summary of impulse response analysis*

Significant effect of equity on credit	Significant effect of property on credit	Significant effect of credit on equity	Significant effect of credit on property
4	10	4	2

x is a vector containing the log of the real GDP, the log of real domestic credit, the log of real property prices, the log of real equity prices, and the short-term real interest rate. t is a deterministic time trend. The lag order n was in each case based on sequential Likelihood Ratio tests.

To recover the structural shocks from the reduced form system, we use a standard Cholesky decomposition. The ordering adopted here is real GDP, real property prices, real bank lending, real interest rate, and real share prices. We, therefore, assume that real GDP does not respond contemporaneously to innovations to any of the other variables, but may affect all other variables within quarter. This assumption is fairly standard in the monetary policy transmission literature. We further assume that real property prices are rather sticky, so that they are not affected contemporaneously by credit, interest rates, and share prices. Share prices are rather flexible and are allowed to respond within quarter to innovations to all other variables. Money market interest rates are also rather flexible, so that they are allowed to respond within quarter to innovations to economic activity, property prices, and credit. The chosen ordering also reflects the common assumption that interest rate changes are transmitted to the economy with a lag. The chosen ordering of the variables has, in our view, the most intuitive appeal and also yields plausible impulse responses. The results are generally not sensitive to a reordering of the variables. The exception is the ordering of the real interest rate and bank lending. Allowing for an immediate effect of interest rates on lending often yields an implausible positive response of bank lending to a positive interest rate shock.

Figure 6.6. displays standardised impulse responses of credit to asset price shocks and of asset prices to credit shocks in a two standard error confidence band. The results of the impulse response analysis are summarised in Table 6.1, where we report the number of significant impulse responses of each variable.[12] The findings suggest that property prices have a significant

---

[12] Here, we do not count the significantly negative response of property prices to credit shocks in Germany and the significantly negative response of share prices to credit shocks in Canada.

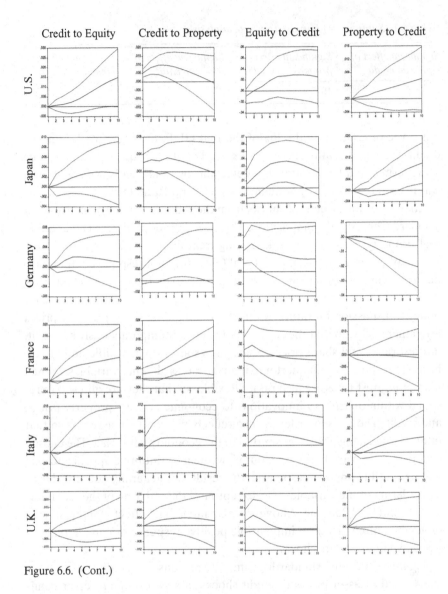

Figure 6.6. (Cont.)

effect on bank lending, whereas the evidence of significant dynamic effects of credit shocks on asset prices or of equity price shocks on credit is rather weak. In ten of twelve countries, bank lending responds very positively to a property price shock. Only in Italy and the United Kingdom is the dynamic effect of property price shocks on lending not significantly larger than zero.

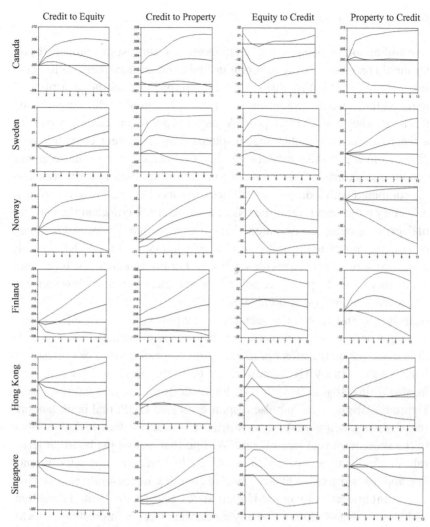

Figure 6.6. Dynamic Interaction Between Credit and Asset Prices
Note: The figures display impulse responses to a one standard deviation shock in a two standard error confidence bank.

Credit shocks have a significant effect on equity prices only in one third of the countries and on property prices only in two countries. Share prices shocks are found to affect bank lending significantly only in four of twelve countries.

A ROLE FOR MONETARY POLICY?

The findings of the two previous sections seem to suggest that monetary policy should respond actively to booms in credit and asset markets, both for the sake of financial stability and long-run price stability. In another contribution to this volume, Bordo and Jeanne set up a small stylised model to investigate this issue. They consider two possible ways of conducting monetary policy – a reactive monetary policy that responds only to current economic conditions and a proactive monetary policy that trades off current economic conditions against the future risk of a credit crunch caused by overborrowing combined with a drop in asset prices. Via its effect on firms' borrowing, monetary policy can reduce the risk of a future credit crunch at the expense of depressing current economic activity. It appears that the optimal response of monetary policy to the build up of financial imbalances depends in a highly nonlinear way on private sector sentiment. For intermediate levels of "market exuberance" the proactive policy is preferable, whereas for low and high levels, the reactive policy dominates.

In Bordo and Jeanne's model, monetary policy operates via firms' borrowing, whereas asset prices are assumed to be exogenous. There is only little evidence on the effect of interest rate movements on asset prices and bank lending. The VAR framework set up in the previous section enables us also to investigate the effect of innovations on the real interest rate.[13] Figure 6.7 displays the impulse responses of real GDP, real bank lending, real share prices, and real property prices to a one standard deviation shock to the short-term real interest rate. We find that, across the board, interest rate shocks have, as expected, a negative effect on economic activity, lending, and asset prices. In eight of twelve counties, interest rate shocks have significant effects. Only in the United States, France, the United Kingdom, and Hong Kong we do not find any significant effect of interest rate shocks. The results of the impulse response analysis are summarised in Table 6.1 by reporting for each variable the number of significant impulse responses to the real interest rate shock. It appears that interest rate shocks have a significant effect on real output and real asset prices in about half of the countries under investigation. A significant effect on lending is found only in Canada.

[13] The real interest rate shocks should, of course, not be interpreted as monetary policy shocks as such because there are variables missing from our simple empirical model that may affect interest rate policy, such as oil prices or the exchange rate.

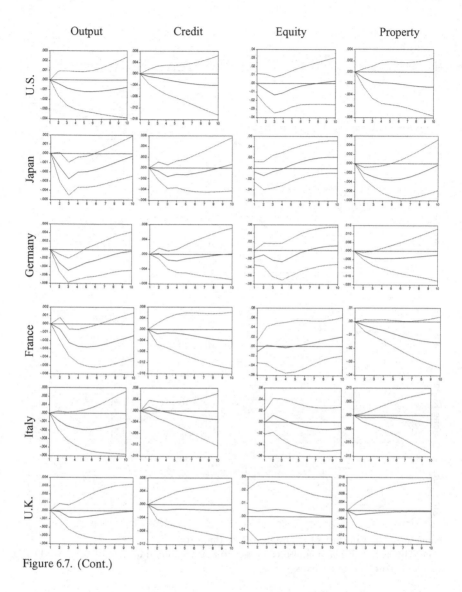

Figure 6.7. (Cont.)

These results suggest that, if anything, interest rate policy may contain the build up of financial imbalances via its effect on asset prices, whereas bank lending in general appears to be unresponsive to interest rate movements. On the whole, the results lend only weak support to the view that interest rate policy is a powerful tool to smooth cycles in credit and asset markets. Moreover, the effects of interest rate movements on asset prices and bank

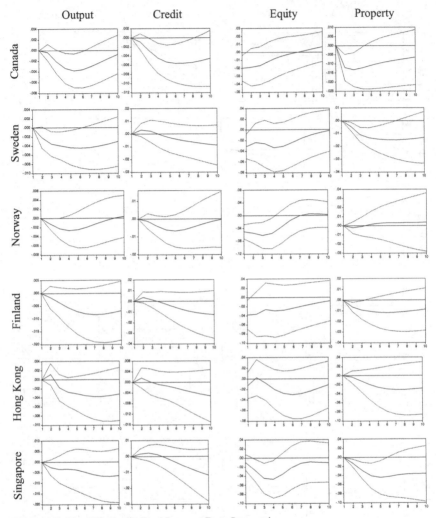

Figure 6.7. The Effect of a Real Interest Rate Innovation
Note: The figures display impulse responses to a one standard deviation shock in a two standard error confidence bank.

lending are most likely highly nonlinear. During the boom, general euphoria will most likely lower the sensitivity of asset valuations and lending to interest rate hikes. Once market sentiment changes, investors realise how high interest rates have gone and asset prices start to tumble. Spreading pessimism may then again render interest rate cuts ineffective. A successful smoothing of cycles in asset and credit markets, therefore, seems to be only

The U.S. Discount Rate and the U.S. Stock Market, 1925-1934

The Bank of Japan Discount Rate and the Japanese Housing Market, 1985-2001

The U.S. Federal Funds Rate and the U.S. Stock Market, 1995-2001

Figure 6.8. Monetary Policy and Asset Price Bubbles
Source: NBER Macro History Database at (www.nber.org), see Appendix, and Bank for International Settlements data base.

possible if monetary policy acts *before* an upswing has turned into a boom. But getting this timing right is an extremely difficult task, especially in times of low or falling headline inflation rates when public opposition to such a policy is most likely to be immense.

The two most (in)famous attempts of central banks to influence excesses in credit and asset markets have gone horribly wrong. Both the Fed's attempt to prick the U.S. stock market bubble in 1929 and the Bank of Japan's attempt to prick the Japanese real estate market bubble in 1989–1990 triggered disastrous asset market crashes, followed by financial crises and deflations.

These two cases provide compelling anecdotal evidence of the highly nonlinear effect of interest rates on asset prices. In Figure 6.8, we display the co-movement of the New York Fed Discount Rate and the Standard and Poor's Composite Index over the period 1925–1934 and of the Bank of Japan Discount Rate and the countrywide residential land price index over the period 1985–2001. The New York Fed increased its discount rate between January 1928 and October 1929 from 3.5 percent to 6 percent without any effect on the stock market until the crash on October 24. Within one year after the crash, the discount rate fell to 2.5 percent, again without any effect on the sliding stock market. The Bank of Japan increased its discount rate from 2.5 percent in April 1989 to 6 percent in August 1990. Although the Japanese stock market bubble burst in early 1990, land prices continued to increase until mid-1991. During the 1990s, successive rate cuts by the Bank of Japan proved to be ineffective to stop the economy from sliding into a deflationary spiral. In 2001, interest rates reached the zero lower bound, whereas asset and consumer prices continued to fall.[14]

The recent experience of the Fed tells a similar story. Figure 6.8 shows that the second half of the 1990s was characterised by sharply rising stock prices and little variation in the Federal Funds rate. From 1995 to 1998, the Funds rate fell from about 6 percent to less than 5 percent. From early 1999 until early 2000, the Fed raised rates modestly by 1.5 percentage points, partly in an attempt to curtail "irrational exuberance" in the stock market. These modest rate hikes did not have any noticeable effect of share prices until the end of 2000, when a sharp reversal in stock set in and continued through the end of 2001, despite a drop in the Federal Funds rate by more than 4 percentage points, to 2 percent.

In all three cases, the central bank might have been successful in preventing asset price bubbles to evolve, had monetary policy been tightened early enough. Instead of lowering the discount rate in 1927, the Fed would probably have done better to tighten monetary policy, the Bank of Japan may have done better to start raising interest rates already in 1987–1988, and the Fed should probably have raised rates rather than lowering them in 1998. But such statements are easy to make with hindsight, and how different policies would have changed events is highly hypothetical.

CONCLUSIONS

Boom–bust cycles in credit markets, often followed by financial distress, depressed economic activity, and deflation, have been a recurring phenomenon since the late nineteenth century. The experience of both historical episodes of financial crises in the late nineteenth and early twentieth centuries and recent episodes of boom and bust cycles in credit markets suggest that consumer prices often do not show any sign of overheating during the credit boom prior to the crisis. Rather, the build up of financial imbalances appears to be reflected in asset prices, especially property prices.

Based on a simple VAR impulse response exercise for a sample of twelve countries, we assess the nature of the close empirical correlation between bank lending and asset prices. The results suggest that innovations to property prices have significant effects on bank lending in the large majority of

[14] For a discussion of the Bank of Japan's policy record in the 1990s, see Burdekin and Siklos (this volume) and Hutchison (this volume).

countries, whereas shocks to bank lending are found to have a significant effect on property prices in only a few countries. For most countries, we do not find evidence of significant dynamic interaction between share prices and credit in either direction.

The same empirical framework enables us to investigate the effect of interest rate innovations on economic activity, bank lending, and asset prices. We find some evidence of a significantly negative effect of interest rate shocks on asset prices, whereas bank lending is found to be rather unresponsive to interest rate innovations across countries. This finding provides only weak support for the view that interest rate policy is a useful instrument to smooth boom–bust cycles in asset and credit markets.

Moreover, the effects of interest rate movements on asset prices and bank lending are almost certainly highly nonlinear. During the boom, general euphoria will most likely lower the sensitivity of asset valuations and lending to interest rate hikes. Once market sentiment changes, investors realise how high interest rates have gone, triggering a sharp reversal in asset prices. Spreading pessimism may then again render interest rate cuts ineffective. The two most (in)famous attempts of central banks to influence asset prices, the U.S. Fed's attempt to prick the U.S. stock market bubble in 1929 and the Bank of Japan's attempt to prick the bubble in the Japanese real estate market in 1989–1990, as well as the recent experience of the U.S. Fed, provide compelling evidence of the highly nonlinear effect of interest rates on asset prices. Although the danger of boom and bust cycles in asset prices ushering in deflation seems clear, the usefulness of monetary policy as an instrument to effectively safeguard financial stability remains in doubt. The key problem is that the driver of the nonlinear relationship, market sentiment, remains unobservable to policy makers (and likely everyone else).

APPENDIX. DEFINITIONS AND SOURCES OF PROPERTY PRICES DATA

Residential Property Prices

Canada	Average house price index Source: Bank of Canada
Finland	National house price index Source: Bank of Finland

(continued)

Residential Property Prices

France	Residential house price index Source: Banque de France
Germany	Average sales price of owner-occupied dwellings in Frankfurt, Munich, Hamburg, and Berlin Source: Ring Deutscher Makler <www.rdm-Gundesverband.de> Note: Annual observations from the first quarter of each year converted to quarterly frequency by linear interpolation
Hong Kong	Residential property price index Source: CEIC Data Company Ltd <www.ceicdata.com>
Italy	National house price index Source: Bank of Italy Note: Semiannual observations converted to quarterly frequency by linear interpolation
Japan	Nationwide residential land price index Source: Japan Real Estate Institute <www.reinet.or.jp/e/> Note: Semiannual observations converted to quarterly frequency by linear interpolation
Norway	Sales price index for one family houses Source: Bank of Norway
Singapore	Residential property price index Source: CEIC Data Company Ltd. (www.ceicdata.com)
Sweden	Single-family house price index Source: Riksbank
United Kingdom	All dwellings price index Source: Department of the Environment, UK Government
United States	Single-family house price index Source: office of Federal Housing Enterprise Overtight, <www.ofheo.go/HPI.asp> (OFHEO) and National Association of Realtors

INTERNATIONAL PERSPECTIVES ON DEFLATION

PART THREE

INTERNATIONAL PERSPECTIVES
ON DEFLATION

7 Is Deflation Depressing? Evidence From the Classical Gold Standard

Michael D. Bordo and Angela Redish

INTRODUCTION

In the four decades before World War I, most of the countries in the world adhered to the classical gold standard. The period was characterized by two decades of secular deflation, followed by two decades of secular inflation. This early price level experience should be of great contemporary interest because most advanced countries have returned to an environment of price stability not terribly dissimilar to that of the classical gold standard era.[1]

Deflation has had a "bad rap." Possibly as a consequence of the combination of deflation and depression in the 1930s, deflation is associated with (for some, connotes) depression. On the face of it, the evidence from the late nineteenth century was mixed. On one hand, the mild deflation in the period 1870–1896 was accompanied by positive growth in many countries; however, growth accelerated during the period of inflation after 1896. We distinguish between good and bad deflations. In the former case, falling prices may be caused by aggregate supply (possibly driven by technology advances) increasing more rapidly than aggregate demand. In the latter case, declines in aggregate demand outpace any expansion in aggregate supply. This was the experience in the Great Depression (1929–1933) and the recession of 1919–1921, and may be the case in Japan today.

In this chapter, we focus on the price level and growth experience of the United States and Canada, 1870–1913. Both countries adhered to the international gold standard, under which the world price level was determined by the demand and supply of monetary gold, and each member followed the rule of maintaining convertibility of its national currency into a fixed

[1] This is not to say that monetary authorities adhere to the principle of gold convertibility but that they are dedicated to low inflation or price stability.

weight of gold.[2] This meant that the domestic price level was largely determined by international (exogenous) forces. In addition, neither country had a central bank that could intervene in the gold market to shield the domestic economy from external conditions.[3] Although both countries had relatively similar resource endowments, the United States was much more developed than Canada and, hence, was more exposed to the business cycle. In addition, the United States unit banking system was more prone to panics than its Canadian branch banking counterpart.[4] The experiences of the two countries, with their similar base money arrangements yet different economic structures and institutions, add two more data points to the slim quantitative history of deflation and further evidence of the significance of the distinction between good and bad deflation.

Table 7.1 and Figures 7.1 and 7.2 illustrate the macroeconomic performance of the U.S. and Canadian economies over the period 1870–1914. Table 7.1 splits the period 1870 to 1896 in 1880 because of the distinct difference in the U.S. growth experience before and after 1880. The 1870s, saw rapid growth accompanied by fairly significant deflation. In the remainder of the period to 1896, growth slowed as did deflation – although price levels continued to fall. In the period after 1896, prices rose at roughly 2 percent, and the growth rate of gross domestic product (GDP) and per capita GDP rose above that of the 1880s–early 1990s, although it remained off the blistering pace of the 1870s.

In Canada, prices fell by about 0.4 percent per annum (p.a.) to 1896 and subsequently rose secularly by about 2 percent. Real GDP grew by 2.4 percent during the deflationary period and rose by 6.5 percent from 1896 to 1913. A considerable part of the economic growth in the latter period was extensive growth coming from immigration, but the change in the growth rate of real per capita GDP between the two periods was still stark – 1 percent in the first period, 4.3 percent in the latter.

For both historians and macroeconomists, this period is a teaser. For macroeconomists, the period provides a rare opportunity to study a secular deflation. For historians, the causes of both the underperformance of the economy in the early years and the boom in the second half of the period are somewhat puzzling. For both groups, the fundamental question

---

[2]   This is a slight simplification. The United States suspended the gold standard during the Civil War and only returned to convertibility in January 1879.

[3]   The central banks of the core countries of Western Europe did have some limited flexibility to provide some insulation (Bordo and MacDonald 1997).

[4]   See Bordo, Redish, and Rockoff (1994).

Table 7.1. *Income, money, and prices: levels and growth rates*

	Real GNP (m$1971)		Real GNP pc ($1971)		Prices ($1971)	
	U.S.	*Canada*	*U.S.*	*Canada*	*U.S.*	*Canada*
1870	33,540	2,071	865	573	22.7	18.5
1880	64,070	2,573	1275	606	18.2	18.5
1896	94,490	3,810	1332	753	14.6	16.7
1913	195,260	11,114	2008	1454.6	20.25	23.9

Income Growth Rates and Inflation

	Real GNP (m$1971)		Real GNP pc ($1971)		Prices ($1971)	
	U.S.	*Canada*	*U.S.*	*Canada*	*U.S.*	*Canada*
1870–80	6.7%	2.2%	3.9%	.5%	−1.8%	0
1880–96	2.5%	2.5%	.2%	1.3%	−1.1%	−0.5%
1870–96	4.1%	2.4%	1.6%	1%	−1.2%	−.36%
1896–13	4.4%	6.5%	2.4%	4.3%	1.9%	2.1%

Money Stock Growth Rates

	Growth of Money Stock		Mpc		Growth of M pc	
	U.S.	*Canada*	*U.S.*	*Canada*	*U.S.*	*Canada*
1870–80	4.2%	2.9%	$45.86	$20.72	1.8%	1.2%
1880–96	4.9%	5.3%	$54.87	$23.43	2.6%	4.1%
1870–96	4.6%	4.4%	$83.22	$44.70	2.3%	3.0%
1996–13	7.8%	9.7%	$219.55	$143.55	5.9%	7.1%

Sources: U.S. data (except population) are all from Balke and Gordon, (1989); Canadian nominal Gross Domestic Product (GDP) and population are from Urquhart (1993); Canadian prices are from Dick and Floyd (1992); Canadian money stock data are from Metcalf, Redish, and Shearer (1998).

concerns the relationship between the real and the nominal performance of the economy. Was there causation or merely correlation? In this chapter, we use time-series statistical methods to try to determine – albeit at a very aggregate level – the answer to this question.

We proceed by identifying separate "supply" shocks, money supply shocks, and demand shocks using a Blanchard-Quah methodology. We model the economy as a small open economy on the gold standard and identify the shocks by imposing long run restrictions on the impact of the shocks on output and prices. We then do a historical decomposition to examine the impact of each shock on output. The results for the United States are clear: The different rates of change in price levels before and after 1896 are attributed to different monetary shocks, but these shocks explain very

(a)

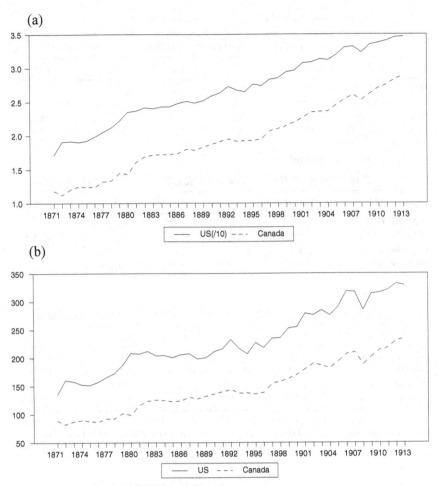

Figure 7.1a. Log Real GDP, U.S. and Canada
Figure 7.1b. Per Capita Real GDP ($1900), U.S. and Canada

little of output growth or volatility, which is almost entirely a response to supply shocks. For Canada, the results are murkier. As in the United States, the money supply shocks before 1896 are predominantly negative and after that are largely positive. However, they are non-neutral, and relative to the United States, money supply shocks play a larger role in determining output behaviour in Canada. We discuss possible explanations for this.

We begin by providing a brief historical context for the analysis and then discuss the underlying theoretical model and empirical strategy that we follow. We then discuss the estimation results for the United States and Canada.

(a)

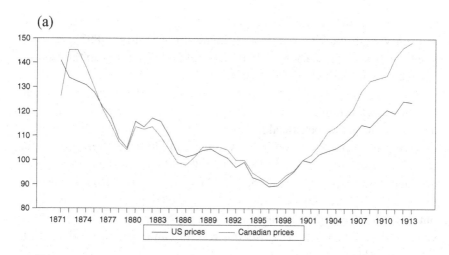

(b)

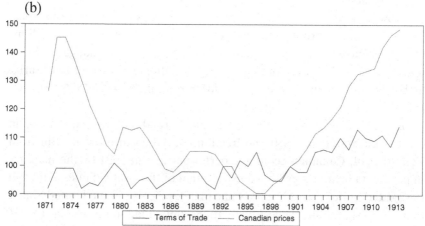

Figure 7.2a. Price Levels (1900 = 100), U.S. and Canada
Figure 7.2b. Canadian Terms of Trade and Price Level

We conclude by integrating the somewhat contrasting results for the two countries.

Historical Context

The U.S. economy expanded rapidly in the early years after the Civil War, and the 1880s saw both the development of heavy industry in the East and rapid settlement of the West. It was the period of massive expansion of a transcontinental railroad network. Yet, this growth was accompanied by severe cyclical downturns in the post–Civil War era, most of which were associated with banking panics and financial crises, 1873, 1893, and 1907 being the most severe. The net effect was that real GNP per capita was only 5 percent higher in 1896 than in 1880.

Williamson (1974) provides a detailed analysis of this period. He argues that the deceleration in economic growth until the mid-1890s, primarily reflected traditional neoclassical forces: A high savings rate put the economy on a transition path to a new steady state, and along the transition path, capital accumulated, the return to capital fell, and the growth rate of income declined. His is a purely real model, and he concludes (p. 116) that because the quantitative predictions of his model capture the behaviour of the economy, monetary factors were not important in the growth slowdown.[5] One view of our chapter is that it tests this result in an empirical model with a monetary side.

Growth accelerated after 1896. There were dramatic technological changes in goods production and equally so in the organization of firms and the economy. Industrialization and urbanization both changed the face of the economy. Yet, even in these good years, there were major downturns, and real per capita income fell in five different years between 1896 and 1914, 1903, 1907–1908, and, 1913–1914.

In 1870, incomes per capita in Canada were about two thirds those in the United States. By 1880, the fraction had fallen to one half. But from 1880 to 1914, Canadian economic performance – at least by the measure of per capita income growth – outshone that of the United States, although the United States was still starkly ahead in levels.[6] As in the United States, there were significant cyclical fluctuations embedded in the secular trends. In eleven of the twenty years from 1875 to 1895, per capita real incomes fell despite the overall increase across the subperiod.

Canada experienced a short-lived boom after Confederation, which ended in 1873. The stark contrast with U.S. economic performance in the mid-1870s led to a migration of Canadians into the northern states (Inwood and Irwin 2000) and the imposition of the National Policy tariff in an attempt to protect potential infant industries. The impact of that tariff is debated: Certainly per capita incomes rose, but it was not until the mid-1890s that

---

[5] He does not explain the pick up in growth after 1896 and suggests that it remains a puzzle.

[6] In 1880, Canada and the United States had the same gold parity and, therefore, an exchange rate of 1 between the two currencies. In 1870, the U.S. dollar was valued at approximately C$ 0.75 as a result of the suspension of gold convertibility during and after the Civil War.

the economy flourished. Data on wages and unemployment are notoriously sparse; what little we have suggests that unemployment rose in the mid-1870s and, after relatively better performance in the end of that decade, it was again high in the late 1880s. Nominal wages fell from 1888 to 1890 and remained flat in the 1890s.[7]

From 1896 to 1913, a period known to Canadians as the Wheat Boom, there was massive migration into Canada (primarily from Europe), rapid settlement of the Canadian West, and, especially after 1907, very large foreign capital inflows. The relationship between the acceleration of intensive growth (rising per capita incomes) and that of extensive growth (increasing population) has been hotly debated among Canadian economic historians. In particular, research has focused on whether or not there was a mechanism that explains how the increasing population (assumed to be driven by the new availability of land) can explain the rising per capita income, given that the rise in the value of farms seems insufficient to explain the gains.[8]

Both Canada and the United States (after the resumption of convertibility in 1879) were on the gold standard and so were similarly affected by the world monetary market. In the 1870s, Germany and France (effectively) joined the gold standard, and by 1879, the United States had resumed convertibility of the Greenback. Gold stocks, however, were largely stagnant in the face of this increase in demand for gold, requiring that prices fall. Figure 7.3 shows that annual gold production averaged about six million ounces from 1870 to 1893. Gold discoveries in South Africa, and to a lesser extent in Australia and the Klondike, led to dramatically higher levels of gold production after 1893.

Figure 7.2a shows the behaviour of price indices for the United States and Canada. Deflation averaged only 1.2 percent p.a. in the United States and less than 1 percent in Canada between 1870 and 1896, but the cumulative effect over more than two decades was a fall in the price level of 37 percent in the United States and 21 percent in Canada. This situation was reversed after 1896, when gold discoveries increased the global stock of gold and, therefore, national money stocks, and prices rose worldwide. Secular deflation was replaced by secular inflation in both Canada and the United States.

Although both Canada and the United States had monetary systems based on gold, the "inside" money component of the money supply was produced

[7] Olley (n.d.), Tables 27 and 10.
[8] The seminal article is Chambers and Gordon (1966). For a summary of the debate, see Norrie and Owram (1996).

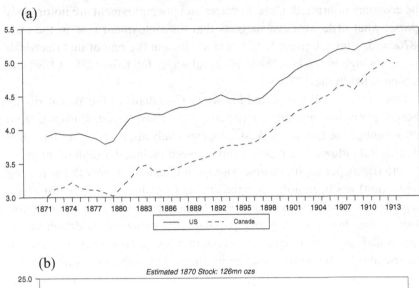

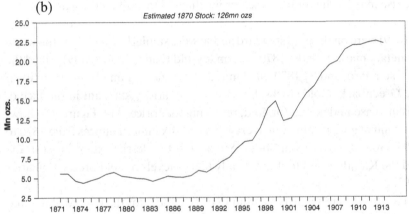

Figure 7.3a. (log) Per Capita Money Stocks, U.S. and Canada
Figure 7.3b. Annual Gold Production
Note: Mn: OZS = Millions of ounces.

under very different arrangements in the two countries. In Canada, a branch banking system was permitted to issue bank notes secured by the general assets of the bank, subject only to the limit that the quantity of notes not exceed the paid-in capital. As a matter of practice, the banks often held significant money at call in New York, which they looked on as "secondary reserves." In the United States, the national banking system established in 1864 mandated that bank notes be (111 percent) secured by Federal government bonds and created a tiering of reserves.[9] Thus the U.S. banking system had difficulty dealing with the seasonal fluctuations in the demand for money, and the New York money market acted as the central reserve for both countries.

Theoretical Perspective

The fundamental question we are trying to resolve is the role of aggregate demand relative to aggregate supply shocks in output behaviour over the period. In the context of a simple supply-demand model, if the short run aggregate supply curve is vertical, then demand shocks will have no impact even in the short run, and the pattern of output growth would have been entirely driven by supply shocks. If the aggregate supply curve is upward sloping (for some time horizon), demand shocks would have an impact on output, and the deflation/stagnation followed by inflation/growth may reflect demand shocks.

Earlier studies have applied a bivariate Blanchard-Quah methodology to gold standard economies, typically in contrasting gold standard and Bretton Woods regimes (e.g., Bayoumi and Eichengreen 1995; Bordo 1993; Keating and Nye 1998). These studies used data on prices and output and identified a supply shock as the innovation that has a permanent impact on output. An aggregate supply/aggregate demand model would predict that a positive supply shock would lower prices; however, in all three studies, the estimated supply shocks had a permanent positive effect on prices, the opposite of the theoretically predicted effect.[10] One explanation proposed for this – but not explicitly tested – is that the dominant supply shock is a terms of trade effect, which raises both output and prices. Figure 7.2b graphs the price level and the terms of trade for Canada and provides casual evidence that the price level and terms of trade are uncorrelated.[11] Furthermore, the terms of trade are improving during the 1871–1896 period when prices and output in Canada are falling and then stagnate while prices and output rise rapidly at the beginning of the twentieth century. When we included a terms of trade

9   Country banks had to hold 15 percent of the value of their deposits on reserve (of which 60 percent could be a deposit at a reserve city bank); reserve city banks had to hold 25 percent reserves (of which 50 percent could be a deposit at a central reserve city bank); central reserve cities – New York, Chicago, and St. Louis – had to hold 25 percent reserves. Goodhart (1969: 16).

10 The positive effect is also found on impact.

11 The contemporaneous correlation is −0.24, and the correlation is smaller at 1 or 2 leads or lags. Terms of trade data are from Dick and Floyd (1992: Table B.3).

variable in the estimation of the traditional model, it was insignificant and did not eliminate the perverse price effect of the estimated supply shock. The supply shock estimated in the bivariate model must confound a demand shock that has permanent positive effects on prices and output with a true supply shock.[12]

We propose an alternative identification scheme that is consistent with a standard monetary model for a small open economy on the gold standard.[13] We model the behaviour of output, prices, and the money stock and identify three stochastic disturbances by assuming that the demand disturbance has no long run impact on either prices or output and the domestic supply shock has no long run impact on the price level. Implicitly, we are assuming that, in the long run, the domestic price level was tied down by the world price level (through monetary flows). Let Y represent real GDP, P the price level, and M the money stock, and let ε_s be the supply shock, ε_{ms} the money supply shock, and ε_d a demand (i.e., demand other than money supply) shock. Then, if the matrix $A(1)$ represents the long run multiplier matrix where each element $a_{ij}(1)$ captures the long run effect of shock j on variable i, we can write,

$$
\begin{bmatrix} \Delta P \\ \Delta Y \\ \Delta M \end{bmatrix} = \begin{bmatrix} a_{11}(1) & 0 & 0 \\ a_{21}(1) & a_{22}(1) & 0 \\ a_{31}(1) & a_{32}(1) & a_{33}(1) \end{bmatrix} \begin{bmatrix} \varepsilon_{ms} \\ \varepsilon_s \\ \varepsilon_d \end{bmatrix}
$$

The identification of the demand shock is uncontroversial, but the critical assumption here is that supply shocks do not affect the price level in the long run. Here, we rely on the small open economy assumption under which the domestic economy takes the price level as exogenous. We assume that the supply shock captures supply shocks that were specific to the domestic economy – and did not have an effect on the world price level *in the long run*. (Importantly, we find the restriction is not a binding one for the U.S. economy – a result consistent with Bayoumi and Eichengreen who find a horizontal aggregate demand curve.) Because the major determinant of world

---

12 See Calomiris and Hanes (1994) for an extended discussion of the sources of persistence from demand shocks.

13 Our identification strategy is similar to that of Dupasquier, Lalonde, and St. Amant (1997). They use a trivariate Blanchard and Quah (1989) decomposition with the same ordering to identify monetary, supply, and nonmonetary demand shocks for the post–Bretton Woods period, but use interest rates rather than the money stock (and assume that the price level is I [2]).

prices over our period was the changing world production of gold, we refer to the shock that has a long run impact on prices as the money supply shock.[14] Using this identification of supply and money supply shocks, we can measure separately the effect of each on output.

The third shock captures impulses that have no permanent effect on prices or output. In the context of a small open economy on the gold standard, these are essentially shocks to the IS curve (aggregate demand), or money demand shocks, and they cannot be disentangled in this empirical specification. If IS shocks dominate, the impact effect of the shock on all three variables will be positive, and it will have no long run effect on the money stock. If money demand shocks dominate, then prices and output will fall on impact and there will be a permanent increase in the money stock.

The restrictions imply that $A(1)$ is lower triangular and, by imposing the restrictions and the assumption that the three shocks are orthogonal, we can estimate the parameters of $A(L)$ – the impulse response functions – and identify the structural innovations.[15] The key to the validity of this methodology is that the identifying restrictions indeed identify objects consistent with the theoretical model. The usual way to test this is to look at the over-identifying restrictions. That is, theory has implications for the long run and short run impacts of each shock on each variable. Our basic framework is the Cambridge money demand equation with stochastic money demand shocks, applied to a small open economy on a gold standard. A positive money supply shock is defined as one that raises the money stock in the long run, and it is predicted to increase each of the three variables on impact. If money were neutral, the money shock would cause equal (proportionate) increases in the money stock and prices in the long run with no effect on output. A positive supply shock is one that raises output in the long run and would lead to an endogenous, long run increase in the money stock. The model predicts that, in the short run, prices would fall and the money stock would rise. Finally, the demand shock is defined as one that causes an increase in the money stock, and its short run impact is indeterminate as discussed previously.

There are eighteen combined impact and long run responses to the shocks. Table 7.2 summarizes the predicted effects and indicates whether the restriction was imposed, used as a normalization, or can be used as an

---

[14] The money supply shock could equally be viewed as a world price level shock.
[15] See Clarida and Gali (1994). The method is briefly described in the Appendix.

Table 7.2. *Predicted effects of each innovation*

	On output		On prices		On money stock	
	Impact	*Long run*	*Impact*	*Long run*	*Impact*	*Long run*
Money supply	+	=	+	+	+	+(N)
Supply	+	+(N)	−	0(I)	+	+
Demand	?	0(I)	?	0(I)	+(N)	?

Note: I indicates an identifying restriction; N represents a normalization i.e., not an overidentifying restriction.

overidentifying restriction. If the estimated impulse response functions are consistent with these overidentifying restrictions, then we can be relatively confident that the estimated shocks are consistent with the innovations in the model.

Having estimated the matrices $A(L)$ and the innovations ε_t, we can examine the behaviour of each of the shocks (the variance of each shock is normalized to 1). The impact of the various shocks can be measured by a forecast error variable decomposition, which measures the contribution of each type of shock to forecast errors at various horizons, and, most importantly for our purposes, we can measure the effect at each point of historical time of each kind of shock. For example, we can decompose the growth rate of output in 1880 say into (1) the effect of shocks that occurred before 1873 – the start of the sample – and are having continued effects, and (2) the effect of each of the shocks since 1873. For example, the effects of supply shocks are computed by taking the supply shock for each period from 1873 to 1880 and multiplying it by the impulse response parameter for the number of periods between the occurrence of the shock and 1880.

We use this method of historical decompositions to identify the role of supply shocks, money supply shocks, and money demand shocks on the levels of output, prices, and money in the United States and Canada from 1873 to 1914.

There are, of course, other approaches that could and have been taken to determine the role of monetary factors in this period. An approach that is similar would involve estimating a VAR that incorporated a co-integrated money demand function. The advantage of this approach is that by imposing the structure of a money demand function, one can get tighter parameter estimates. However, there are major disadvantages. Essentially, it requires the existence of a stable money demand function, for which the evidence is weak at best.[16] For Canada, this may be because of the absence of interest rate data or because of more fundamental money demand instability.

EMPIRICAL ANALYSIS – UNITED STATES

Figure 7.4 presents the impulse responses for the United States.[17] The graphs show the cumulative effect, at every point in time, on each variable, of an isolated shock at time 0. Thus, the upper graphs show that an average positive money supply shock caused prices to rise on impact, to rise somewhat further in the next year or two, and to stay at that higher level. The bottom graph shows that the money stock itself behaved similarly, whereas the middle graph shows that the money supply shock caused output to rise on impact, but that after the first two years, output was back at its initial level. These results show money to be non-neutral in the short run and (roughly) neutral in the long run. Importantly, this long run neutrality is not imposed.[18]

The supply shock causes a positive and permanent increase in the level of output and, after the first year, to the quantity of money. That is, the quantity of money responds endogenously to the increases in output, with an elasticity of approximately one half. The supply shock causes a fall in the price level – although probably insignificantly – and after the first period, the price level returns to its previous level.

The demand shock leads to a permanent increase in the money stock and a (very) temporary decrease in prices. These results are consistent with the interpretation of the demand shock as a money demand innovation, but the demand shock also causes an increase in output that is not consistent with such an interpretation. As noted previously, the model does not have sufficient restrictions to enable us to identify the demand shock, other than as a compound of the temporary disturbances to output.

[16] *Johansen and Juselius* estimation methods reject a co-integration relationship between money, prices, and income for Canada, although *Engle and Granger* (1987) single equation methods do not. The former is, however, the more powerful technique and the one that is appropriate for the multivariate context – that is, one in which money, prices, and output may all respond to deviations from the long run relationship.

[17] The money supply data and output data are found to be unambigously $I(1)$ in pretesting. The characteristics of the price level are more ambiguous with the order of integration (0 vs. 1) depending on the lag length selection criterion and unit root test used. The unrestricted VAR is estimated with two lags.

[18] The *imposed* restrictions are that the supply shock does not affect prices in the long run and that the demand shock only affects the stock of money in the long run.

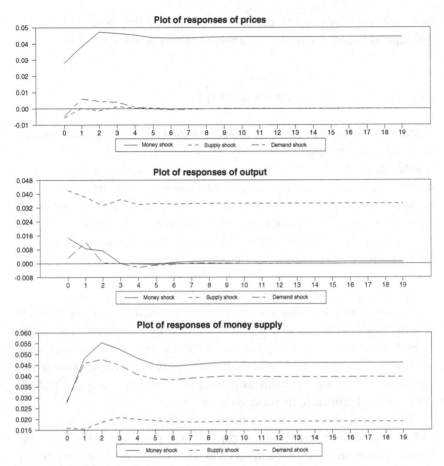

Figure 7.4. U.S. Impulse Responses

Although impulse response functions indicate the impact of an isolated shock over time on each variable because their variance is normalized to unity, they do not measure the relative importance of the shocks. A forecast error variance decomposition (FEVD) combines the information in the variances of the shocks and the impulse responses, and so describes their relative contributions. The FEVDs are presented in Table 7.3 and can be interpreted as follows: take the two-year ahead decomposition of the forecast error for output. If one were trying to forecast output two years ahead, one would, on average, make an error that depends on the size of the three (by definition, unobservable) shocks in each future year, their usual impact on the variable and their persistence. In an extreme case, supply shocks

Table 7.3. *Forecast error variance decomposition(FEVD): United States*

Horizon	Money Supply	Supply	Demand
Impact on FEVD for output of			
1	10.85	88.66	0.49
2	11.93	83.84	4.23
3	11.14	78.86	10.05
4	13.08	77.19	9.73
5	13.01	77.12	9.86
10	13.06	77.00	9.94
Impact on FEVD for prices of			
1	93.53	3.80	2.67
2	81.14	6.25	12.61
3	82.08	6.02	11.91
4	81.65	6.49	11.86
5	81.03	6.50	12.47
10	80.95	6.50	12.56
Impact on FEVD for money of			
1	42.06	14.00	43.94
2	46.41	9.94	43.65
3	47.27	10.08	42.65
4	47.25	10.19	42.57
5	47.23	10.08	42.69
10	47.33	10.04	42.63

might have a permanent impact whereas money supply shocks have only a one-year influence. Thus, the two-year ahead forecast would reflect two years worth of supply shocks but only one year of money supply shocks.

Largely by assumption, at the five-year horizon, forecast errors for the price level primarily arise from money supply shocks. However, output is mostly driven by supply shocks. The money stock is driven by shocks to both demand and the money supply. The estimated structural innovations themselves are illustrated in Figure 7.5. Again, because they are normalized to have a variance of unity, their absolute size has no interpretation. There was a run of negative money supply shocks in the early 1890s followed by a run of positive shocks after 1896. In the last decade of the sample, there was a string of negative demand shocks.

The historical decompositions are illustrated in Figures 7.6 through 7.8. We are particularly interested in output, shown in the three panels of Figure 7.7. In each of the three panels, two curves are reproduced – the actual growth rate of income and the base case, which comprises trend growth plus the lingering effects of shocks that occur before the start date. The third

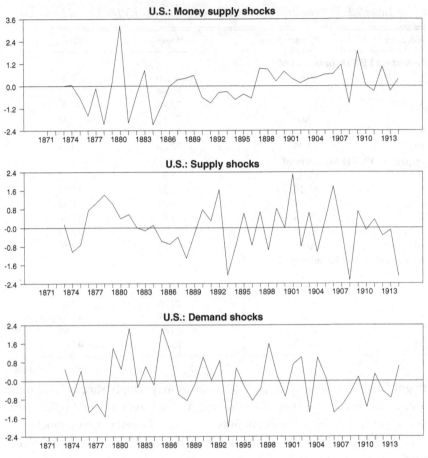

Figure 7.5. U.S. Shocks

curve shows the sum of the base case plus the effect of one particular shock. For example, in the top graph in Figure 7.7, the third curve shows how (according to the model) output growth would have evolved if there had been no supply or demand shock, isolating the impact of the money supply shock on output growth. The fact that this curve is, particularly after 1890, not very different from the base case, shows that the money supply shock did not drive output growth. Similarly, the fact that, in the middle panel, the third line is very close to the "actual" line implies that the supply shock explains most of output growth. In the lowest panel, (nonmonetary) demand shocks were nontrivial, but much less important than the supply shocks.

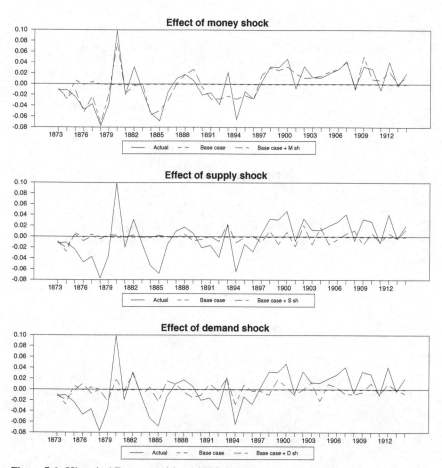

Figure 7.6. Historical Decomposition of U.S. Prices

The historical decomposition of the price level (Figure 7.6) tells a parallel story. The price level was largely determined by the money supply shocks, whereas supply shocks (and again to a lesser extent nonmonetary demand shocks) were not important drivers of prices. The money stock reflected both money supply and money demand shocks, but not supply shocks. This latter effect is a reflection of the low income elasticity of money demand seen in the impulse responses (compare the impact of supply shocks on output and the money stock in the bottom two panels of Figure 7.4).

The interpretation of behaviour in the United States over the period is fairly straightforward: Positive (negative) money supply shocks explain the behaviour of the price level and did have temporary positive (negative)

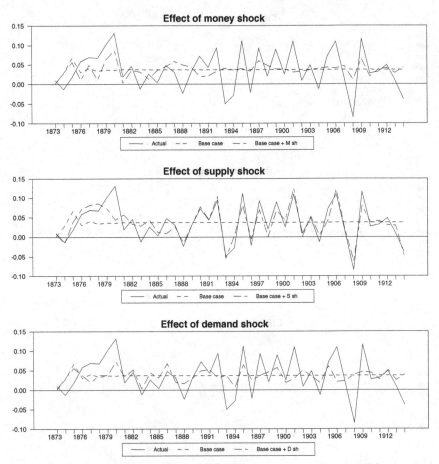

Figure 7.7. Historical Decomposition of U.S. Output

effects on output. However, apart from the volatility between 1877 and 1887, money supply shocks had only a small impact on output and do not explain the trends in output growth.

EMPIRICAL ANALYSIS – CANADA

Figure 7.9 shows the estimated impulse response functions for Canada.[19] As in the United States case, the money supply shock is estimated to cause

[19] As for the United States, the money stock and output series were found to be $I(1)$ and the price data either $I(1)$ or $I(0)$ depending on the test. We estimate the model in first differences to be sure the data are stationary. For Canada, lag length tests led us to use only first-order terms in the unrestricted VAR.

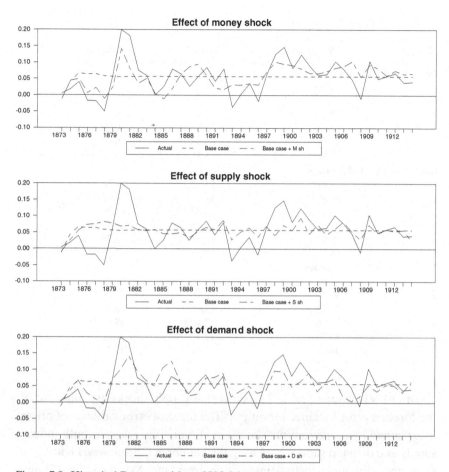

Figure 7.8. Historical Decomposition of U.S. Money

an increase in prices and the level of the money stock but, unlike in the United States, money is not neutral in the long run. We find a persistent positive effect on output from a positive money supply shock. We return to this surprising result later.[20] The supply shock has the expected positive effect on the level of output and the stock of money, and, again, the elasticity of money demand is approximately one half. The price level falls on impact of the supply shock and quickly returns to its initial level. The demand shock has its major impact on the money stock, with a small temporary positive impact on output and prices.

[20] The result is robust to changes in specification, such as lag length and use of alternative monetary aggregates.

Table 7.4. *Forecast error variance decomposition: Canada*

Horizon	Money Supply	Supply	Demand
Impact on FEVD for output of			
1	16.20	81.86	1.93
2	16.01	77.98	6.00
3	17.45	75.98	6.57
4	17.66	75.71	6.62
5	17.81	75.57	6.62
10	17.87	75.51	6.62
Impact on FEVD for prices of			
1	83.97	13.25	2.78
2	84.30	11.68	4.02
3	85.23	10.88	3.89
4	85.52	10.66	3.82
5	85.65	10.58	3.78
10	85.71	10.53	3.75
Impact on FEVD for money of			
1	16.96	21.76	61.23
2	30.79	18.18	51.02
3	33.78	17.45	48.77
4	34.96	17.19	47.85
5	35.35	17.10	47.55
10	35.58	17.04	47.37

The FEVD results (Table 7.4) show that supply shocks explain most of the forecast error variance for output. The forecast error variance of prices is explained by money supply shocks at all horizons, whereas both money supply and demand shocks have a significant impact the money. Figure 7.10 shows the estimated structural innovations over time. As in the United States, money supply shocks were predominantly negative in the pre-1896 period and then positive in the post-1896 period. Perhaps surprisingly, supply shocks were positive from 1876 to 1883, with the exception of 1880. The decade from 1884 to 1895, however, saw a run on negative supply shocks.

The historical decompositions for Canada are in Figures 7.11 through 7.13. Again, for each variable, we present three panels. In each panel, the behaviour of the growth rate of the variable over time and the "base case" (trend growth) are depicted, as well as a line illustrating the base case plus the effect (contemporaneous plus lagged) of one of the shocks. Again, beginning with the decomposition of output in Figure 7.12, the similarity between the dashed line and the actual behaviour in the middle panel indicates that the behaviour of output was driven very much by the supply shocks. The upper

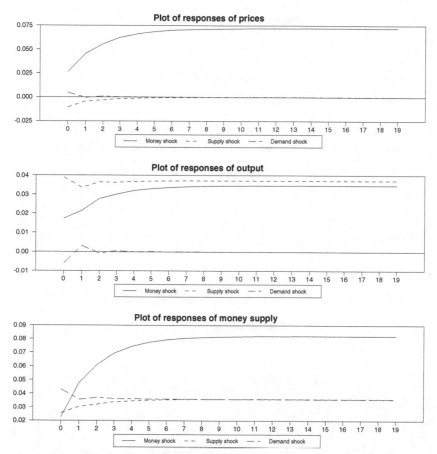

Figure 7.9. Canadian Impulse Responses

and lower panels show that both money supply shocks and demand shocks affected output (their dashed lines deviate from the almost horizontal base case), but do not play as major a role as the supply shocks. In Figure 7.11, we see that the money supply shocks do explain price behaviour.[21] Finally, Figure 7.13 suggests that money supply shocks and demand shocks were the major forces driving the evolution of the Canadian money stock. The supply shock did cause some of the variation in the growth rate of the money stock, as that stock responded to changes in money demand coming from changing income, but the other factors were larger influences.

[21]   In Figure 7.11, the base case and actual are very similar because the trend rate of inflation over the entire period was virtually zero.

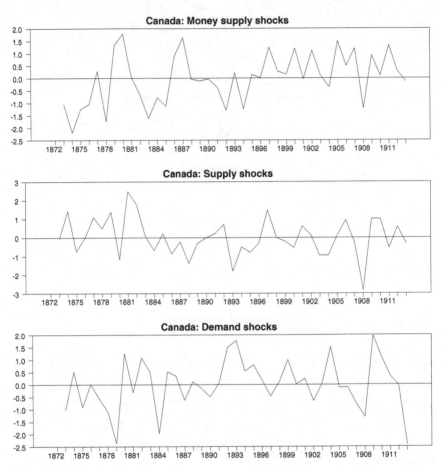

Figure 7.10. Canada Shocks

Overall, in Canada as in the United States, we find that the economy evolved in a relatively classical way. Exogenous changes in the money stock drove the behaviour of the price level, and supply shocks drove the behaviour of output.

DISCUSSION OF RESULTS AND CONCLUSION

In the 1870s, the gold standard became virtually universal, raising monetary gold demand with no significant increases in supply. Unsurprisingly, the

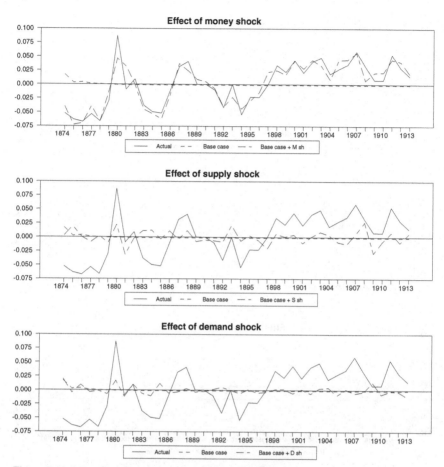

Figure 7.11. Historical Decomposition of Canadian Prices

world price level fell. Gold discoveries in the 1890s caused the world gold stock to rise, and so did prices. In the United States, and more so in Canada, the deflation was contemporaneous with slow economic growth and the inflation with a booming economy. Was there a direct connection? Did monetary forces generate the bust and boom? We find that the connection was more coincidence than causation. The money supply shocks were large and explain most of the variation in the price level. Yet, in both the United States and Canada, they do not explain the behaviour of output. That behaviour was driven primarily by supply shocks.

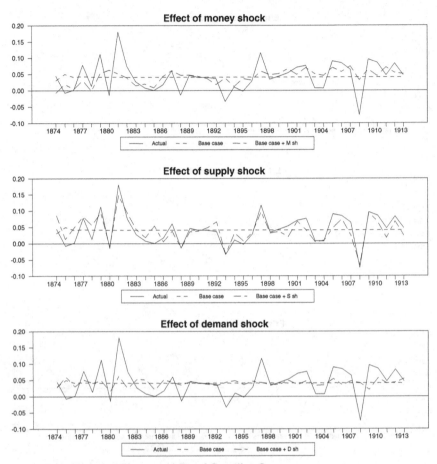

Figure 7.12. Historical Decomposition of Canadian Output

An open question that our analysis has raised is the apparent non-neutrality of the money supply shocks in Canada and why the Canadian responses are so different from those in the United States. One possible answer would be that there were greater nominal rigidities in Canada, although it is difficult to ascertain what those would have been. An alternative resolution relates to the differences between the banking systems in the two countries and their possible consequences for the transmission of monetary shocks to the real economy. For example, the Canadian banking system had lower reserve ratios than that of the United States and proportionately more loans in their portfolios, implying that the credit channel may have

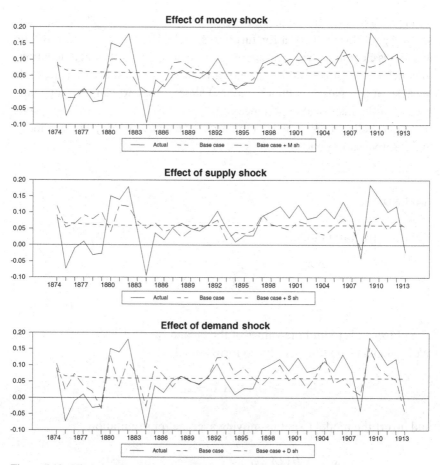

Figure 7.13. Historical Decomposition of Canadian Money

been more significant leading to greater persistence of monetary shocks in Canada. This is obviously an area for future work, and, in particular, we plan to expand the data set by including other gold standard countries and use a panel approach that will give us more power to identify global monetary and technology shocks.

Finally, the fact that growth was lower in both countries during the deflation era, 1870 to 1996, than during the subsequent period of inflation may be due to a different real environment. However, it could also be due to another set of issues that we do not explore in this chapter, namely, the relationship of deflation/inflation to growth via channels such as expectations formation and incomplete contracts, as in, for example, Irving Fisher's debt-deflation story. Again this is an area for future research. The key conclusion of our analysis is clear, however. The simple demarcation of good vs. bad deflation, in which either prices fall because of a positive supply shock or prices fall because of a negative demand (money) shock, does not capture the complexity of the historical experience of the pre-1896 period. Indeed, we find that prices fell as a result of a combination of negative money supply shocks and positive supply shocks.

APPENDIX

Define a structural model,

$$\Delta X_t = A(L)\varepsilon_t$$
$$= A_0\varepsilon_t + A_1\varepsilon_{t-1} + A_2\varepsilon_{t-2} + \cdots$$
$$i = 0, 1, 2, \cdots$$

The objective is to find the values of the A_i and ε_t.
We begin by estimating a reduced form model

$$B(L)\Delta X_t = e_t$$

and invert the model to get its moving average representation

$$\Delta X_t = B(L)^{-1}e_t$$
$$= C(L)e_t = e_t + C_1 e_{t-1} + C_2 e_{t-2} + \cdots$$

where by definition, $C_0 = 1$.

Let $E(e_t e_t') = \sum$ be the estimated reduced form variance covariance matrix, and note that $e_t = A_0\varepsilon_t$ and $C_1 e_{t-1} = A_1\varepsilon_{t-1}$, which together imply $A_1 = C_1 A_0$ and more generally $A_i = C_i A_0$. Thus, knowledge of A_0 combined with the estimated C_i and e_t will identify all A_i and ε_t.

Assume that the structural innovations are orthogonal to each other and normalize them to have unit variance. Then, $E(\varepsilon_t \varepsilon_t') = I$. But because $E(e_t e_t') = \sum$, $E(A_0\varepsilon_t \varepsilon_t' A_0') = \sum$ and therefore $A_0 A_0' = \sum$. Because there are only six independent variables in $\sum$ and nine elements in A_0, this relationship does not uniquely identify the elements of A_0. To do so, we impose the restriction that $A(1)$, the matrix of long run multipliers, is lower triangular, as described in the text.

Define $C(1) = C_0 + C_1 + C_2 + \cdots$, where $C_0 = I$, and rewrite this as

$$C(1) = A_0 A_0^{-1} + A_1 A_0^{-1} + A_2 A_0^{-1} +$$
$$= A(1) A_0^{-1}.$$

Form $C(1) \sum C(1)'$ and find the Choleski decomposition of this, which yields the unique lower triangular matrix H such that $C(1') \sum C(1)' = HH'$. Note that $C(1) \sum C(1)' = A(1)A(1)'$, so that $H = A(1)$. Now we can find A_0 from $C(1) = A(1)A_0^{-1}$.

8 The Strong Lira Policy and Deflation in Italy's Interwar Period

Michele Fratianni and Franco Spinelli

INTRODUCTION

In 1927, the Italian general price level fell by almost 15 percent; deflation continued for six more years, that is, until 1933 (Figure 8.1). This deflation was sharper but briefer than U.S. deflation, which had started in 1920, had an interlude of price stability from 1922 to 1929, and resumed from 1929 to 1933. Italian deflation extended also to asset prices and nominal wages. Share prices fell by 40 percent from January 1927 to December 1933. Prices of existing dwellings declined in the range of 37 percent to 40 percent from 1927 to 1934; those of new constructions declined from 33 percent to 35 percent.[1] Nominal wages had started to decline in 1926, after Mussolini announced the fixing of the exchange rate, and lasted through the end of 1935, for a cumulative drop of 42 percent; real wages fell by a third of nominal wages (14 percent) over the same period.[2] Price and asset deflation was accompanied by a severe economic contraction, however, not of the same order of magnitude experienced by the United States during the same period. Real gross national product fell by approximately 4 percent from the peak of 1929 to the trough of 1934; per-capita real gross national product (GNP) fell by approximately 8 percent.[3] Industrial production declined by approximately 9 percent in the 1929–1933 period and 12 percent in the 1929–1934 period, a decline that was considerably less than in France and much less than in Germany and the United States.[4] Services, on the other hand, held

---

[1] Share prices are from Cotula and Garofalo (1993: Table A.13); construction prices are from Ferri and Garofalo (1994: p. 116).

[2] Nominal wages are money monthly wages; see Zamagni (1994: Tables 5 and 8).

[3] See Rey (1931: Tables 5.02 and 6.01).

[4] The decline in France was 19.5 percent, in Germany and the United States 31.6 percent; see Cotula and Spaventa (1993: Table 21).

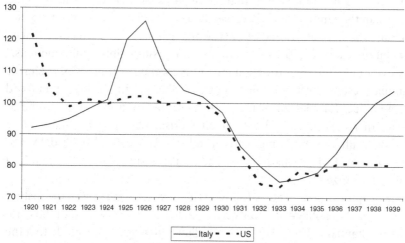

' Figure 8.1. Price Level, 1920–1939
Sources: For Italy, Fratianni and Spinelli (2001: data Appendix to ch. 2) and for the United States, Friedman and Schwartz (1982: Table 4.8).

well and partially cushioned the impact of industrial production on national output.

The seven-year deflation and its impact on Italian economic activity is the main focus of this chapter. Methodologically, we analyze Italian events in the context of the international gold-exchange standard and compare the Italian deflation with the deflation in the United States in the same period.[5] We also compare the 1930s with the late 1980s and the 1990s, when Italy undertook two disinflationary programs, one under the auspices of the European Monetary System (EMS) and the other under the prospect of joining the European Monetary Union (EMU). The first came to a halt with the EMS crisis of September 1992; the second was very successful and made it possible for Italy to join the final phase of EMU.

The main lesson we draw from the chapter is that fixed exchange rates, often adopted to signal the country's determination to a course of deflation or disinflation, create unsustainable conflicts with other goals of economic policy and, hence, are not a credible precommitment device for deflation or

[5] See Jonung (1978) for another historical comparison of a European country (Sweden) with the United States in the Great Depression.

disinflation. In the gold-exchange standard, the fixed exchange rate system had a deflationary bias; those countries that stuck to it fared worse, in terms of output and unemployment, than countries that abandoned it. Italy did better than the United States because it loosened the constraint of the gold-exchange standard at the end of 1931, while formally remaining on it. Faced between the exchange rate commitment and incompatible "fundamentals," Italy eventually let go of the exchange rate commitment in 1936. A similar dilemma presented itself during the "hard" phase of the EMS. Again faced with a choice, Italy let go of the exchange rate commitment, this time as a result of the September 1992 currency crisis. On the other hand, clear objectives, inflation targeting, and an independent central bank delivered entry into the EMU. This time, disinflation was successful in a regime of flexible exchange rates.

The chapter is organized as follows. The next section reviews the history of the strong lira policy – also known as Quota 90 – in the context of the gold-exchange standard. Then, we analyze Italian deflation and conclude that the Italian policy failure was smaller than the U.S. policy failure. The reason was that Italian monetary and fiscal authorities, unlike their U.S. counterparts, were not reluctant to act as lenders of last resort, albeit in an unorthodox way; this issue is explored in the next section. After that, we consider the link between deflation and economic depression; the main conclusion there is that Italian nominal wage rigidities were less severe than in the United States. We then compare the deflation in the 1930s with the two disinflations in the late 1980s and the 1990s and conclusions are drawn in the last section.

THE STRONG LIRA POLICY

The Mussolini government came to power on October 31, 1922. This date marked not only the end of an era of political and social instability, but also the beginning of a new economic regime. Several commentators note the positive reaction of markets to the new government; read, for example, Alberti (1931). At the time, the dollar exchange rate (number of lire per U.S. dollar) was slightly above 23. It fell to the low 20s by year's end and stayed at this level through May 1923; then it rose again to 23 where it stabilized from July 1923 to July 1924 (Figure 8.2). Similar movements took place in the pound exchange rate (Figure 8.3).[6] The beneficial impact of the

---

[6] The pound exchange rate was approximately 106 in October 1992, fell to 94 in April 1923, and rose to 109 in December 1924.

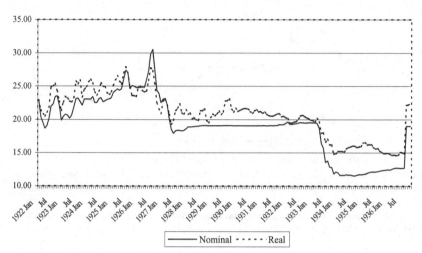

Figure 8.2. Lira-Dollar Exchange Rate
Note: The real exchange rate = (Nominal exchange rate) (U.S. wholesale price index)/(Italian wholesale price index). Wholesale price indices were rescaled with January 1922 = 100.
Source: For monthly nominal exchange rates and wholesale prices, Cotula and Garofalo (1993: Tables A.14 and A.15).

new government on economic expectations showed up also on prices, which continued to decrease until June 1924 (Figure 8.3).

Then, the economic situation degenerated in the autumn of 1924. The inflation rate rose by more than ten percentage points from 1924 to 1925. In sympathy, the external value of the lira declined. This prompted the authorities to intervene massively in the foreign exchange markets. These interventions managed to stabilize the dollar and pound rates at 25 and 120 lire, respectively. But tranquility was of brief duration; on May 13, 1926, under increasing market pressure, the authorities halted their interventions. The dollar and pound rates climbed, and on July 28, they peaked at 31.6 and 153.7 lire, respectively (Fratianni and Spinelli 2001: p. 278).

On August 18, 1926, Mussolini delivered a widely publicized speech in Pesaro, announcing that his government would defend the lira. The impact was immediate and spectacular: The lira appreciated immediately after the speech. By the end of the year, the lira-pound rate had already dropped to 107 lire; at the beginning of May 1927, it was around 90 lire; in June, the authorities had to intervene to prevent a further lira appreciation. Between

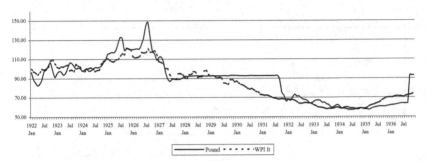

Figure 8.3. Lira-Pound Rate and Italian Wholesale Price Index
Note: The real exchange rate = (Nominal exchange rate) (U.S. wholesale price index)/(Italian wholesale price index). Wholesale price indices were rescaled with January 1922 = 100.
Sources: For monthly nominal exchange rates and wholesale prices, Cotula and Garofalo (1993: Tables A.14 and A.15).

August and December 1926, the lira-dollar rate fell to 22.5; in the following June, it was down to 18.

In the second half of 1927, exchange rates remained stable. At the end of the same year, the authorities fixed the new gold parity of the lira and sanctioned the end of flexible rates, which had prevailed officially since 1894 but de facto since 1866 (Fratianni and Spinelli 1997: ch. 3). The commitment was to stabilize the lira-dollar rate at 19 and the lira-pound rate at the so-called Quota 90, literally (but only approximately) the 90-lire mark.[7]

Between 1927 and 1930, the lira's real exchange rates remained relatively stable and close to the 1922 values (Figure 8.2). By 1930, the lira was slightly undervalued against the dollar, but overvalued against the pound. Later, the strong lira policy became increasingly unsustainable in the light of economic depression in much of the world and a wave of competitive devaluations.

The pound abandoned the gold standard on September 21, 1931, leading to a lira appreciation both in nominal and real terms (Figure 8.3). The U.S. dollar depreciated against gold on April 19, 1933, again leading to another lira appreciation (Figure 8.2). Pressure on the exchange rate rose in 1934. The authorities were strongly opposed to a depreciation, even at the cost of introducing protectionist measures. But the Ethiopian war placed the government in a difficult situation. On the one hand, the increase in monetary

[7] In fact, the parity with the pound was set at 92.46. Quota 90, as Cohen (1988: p. 97) puts it, had the "intrinsic appeal" of being the rate that prevailed when the fascists came to power in 1922.

base and domestic prices argued for a devaluation. On the otherhand, the need to purchase large quantities of military equipment abroad and the existing international sanctions argued for maintaining the exchange rate parity. In the short run, the latter considerations prevailed and the authorities postponed the devaluation.

The devaluation took place in October 1936, after raw materials had been replenished. Various countries, such as Belgium, France, Switzerland, and the Netherlands, had devalued their currencies with respect to gold from 10 percent to 40 percent. International sanctions against Italy had been removed, and international trade again started to grow.

The decree passed on October 5, 1936, reduced the metal content of 100 Italian lire from 7.919 to 4.677 grams of fine gold. This implied a devaluation of 40.9 percent, which matched the 1934 official dollar devaluation, thus restoring the gold parity lira-dollar to 19 lire and setting the lira-pound parity at 93 lire. Following the devaluation, the real value of the lira vis-à-vis both the dollar and the pound quickly returned to its 1922 values (Figure 8.2). Thus, the strong lira policy came to an end.

Why Quota 90?

Far from being an isolated event, Quota 90 was part of a broader and structural economic policy design. Two reasons stood out. The first was the strong intellectual appeal of the gold standard, including the practice of reestablishing a par value against sterling that prevailed at an earlier time (Eichengreen 1992a: ch. 2; Fratianni and Spinelli 2001: pp. 279–80). It was Mussolini himself who decided that the new lira-pound parity had to be set at its 1922 value.[8] The second was the belief that an appreciated currency would act as a catalyst to rejuvenate the country's industrial structure.[9] Traditionally,

---

[8] During the Council of Ministers of February 8, 1927, Mussolini argues as follows (Fratianni and Spinelli 2001: p. 305), "Sterling was 90 in October, 1922 ... when: a) the government budget was in deficit; b) foreign debt a problem; c) internal debt not yet consolidated; d) foreign capital did not flow into the country; e) uncertainty reigned on the new political regime; f) circulation was 22 billion lire and rising; g) agriculture and industry had suffered a series of economic and political strikes; h) the balance of payments was unfavorable. It is obvious that sterling must go back to 90...."

[9] A controversy exists in the literature on whether Quota 90 should be interpreted as part of a growth-oriented industrial policy or simply an ad-hoc measure in response to the intellectual climate and political circumstances of the times. In the English-language literature, Gregor (1979) is a proponent of the first view and Cohen (1988) of the second (we thank Joel Mokyr for making us aware of these references). The Italian literature on the subject, quite naturally, is much bigger and has been reviewed by Fratianni and Spinelli (1997: ch. 5; 2001: ch. 7).

Italian imports had been very sensitive to domestic income and insensitive to own prices. Exports, on the other hand, had been much less sensitive to foreign income but quite sensitive to own prices. The consequences were persistent trade deficits (Fratianni and Spinelli 2001: Figure 7.6). Furthermore, rising protectionism further eroded the size of the market for Italian exports (Gualerni 1982: p. 28; Paradisi 1976: p. 274–5; Tattara and Toniolo 1976: p. 115). What could deflation do to help restructuring the economy?

To begin with, a monetary deflation would attract foreign capital by delivering a stable if not an appreciating currency (Migone 1971: p. 46; Ciocca 1976: p. 33; Rey 1978: p. 286). Furthermore, price deflation would be accompanied by wage deflation, which the fascist regime could implement through its control of labor unions. This, too, was attractive to foreign capital. The U.S. financial community monitored the Italian theatre with keen interest and encouraged Italian authorities to proceed with a stabilization program. Benjamin Strong, Governor of the Federal Reserve Bank of New York, was a close observer of the Italian scene and did not refrain from "advising" the Mussolini government on how to proceed. Strong was not only pushing for fiscal and monetary discipline and central bank independence, but was encouraging the Italian authorities to cooperate with the French and Belgian governments to minimize the amount of foreign currencies required to run a strong currency policy and reduce chances of failure (De Cecco 1993: p. 211–19; Meyer 1970: p. 45–6). Mussolini, for his part, paid close attention to Strong, fully realizing that an official "imprimatur" by the Federal Reserve Bank President would be a necessary condition for Italy to tap the rich U.S. capital market.[10] In sum, both sides understood that, should the Mussolini government follow Strong's advice, financial assistance and capital inflows would be forthcoming.

In fact, foreign capital played a critical role before, during, and after stabilization. The investment house of J. P. Morgan extended two loans to Banca d'Italia (BI) before the Pesaro speech; after the speech, the central bank obtained a large credit from fourteen central banks and from Morgan, Hambros, Baring, and Rothschild (Asso 1993: Table 3). The Italian government obtained loans from the Netherlands, Sweden, Brazil, and most of all from the United States (Asso 1993: Table 1). J. P. Morgan also took the lead in the issue of several dollar bonds, by both the Italian government and Italian corporations, in the U.S. capital markets (Asso 1993: Table 13).

[10] In fact, Mussolini welcomes Governor Strong in Rome at the end of May (when the letter was sent to Harrison) with the pomp of a head of state (De Cecco 1993: p. 64).

Table 8.1. *Italian balance of payments, 1928–1933 (millions of lire)*

Balance	1928	1929	1930	1931	1932	1933
Current account	−2,590	−1,860	−900	1,510	660	−680
Changes in international reserves with Banca d'Italia	−1,040	−730	−720	−1,830	−870	−370
Net capital flows	1,550	1,130	180	−3,340	−1,530	310

Source: Storaci (1993: Table 5, p. 485).

There were significant net inflows of capital during the period (see Table 8.1). In 1928, net inflows amounted to 1.2 percent of national income; in 1929 to 0.9 percent of national income (Storaci 1993: Table 1).

The final reason for an appreciating lira was to reduce the cost of importing raw materials and machinery necessary to carry out the industrial restructuring program. Manufacturing, which depended on foreign imports, was very much behind Quota 90 (Grifone 1971). Finance Minister Volpi (1928: p. 259) reflected those interests when he stated that "... there is no doubt that for Italy, largely a nation importing raw materials absolutely necessary for its very existence and work force, it is beneficial that its currency has a higher purchasing power abroad."

Why the Collapse of Quota 90?

But the strong lira policy had two weaknesses. The first was that it penalized the exporting sector. Roselli (2000: pp. 12–13) cites evidence of the opposition of Italian "light" industry – food and textiles – to Quota 90. The failure of Banca Agricola Italiana in 1931 reflected the difficulty of the textile industry, whose fortunes were not helped by Quota 90. More generally, we can compare the effects of Quota 90 with those of the strong lira policy of the 1980s, when Italy as a member of the EMS was devaluing its currency by much less than its inflation differential with respect to Germany. In both the 1920s and the 1980s, the strong lira sparked a substitution of nontraded goods for traded goods, current account deficits, and net capital inflows. In reaction, in the 1920s, the Italian export sector resorted to dumping (Filosa, Rey, and Sitzia 1976: p. 62; Rey 1978: p. 291); in the 1980s, it sought subsidies from government (Minford 1994). The second and more fundamental weakness was that it could not cope with the deflationary bias of the gold-exchange standard. A big set of concomitant negative factors was militating against Quota 90.

First, with the Great Depression came a sudden collapse in world trade, which amplified the inherent difficulties of the strong lira policy. Second, capital flows – in particular, those from the United States to Europe – petered out. And with it, one of the pillars sustaining the strong lira policy had collapsed. Third, the international monetary order was under severe strain. The United Kingdom went off the gold standard in 1931, an action that was followed by several other countries, including Canada, Denmark, India, Sweden, and Norway. The United States suspended the gold convertibility of the dollar in 1933 and devalued against the metal in 1934. Restrictions on capital movements and exchange rates became widespread. Fourth, protectionism became endemic; coupled with competitive devaluations, it penalized mainly small countries like Italy, whose exports were relatively elastic with respect to prices.[11]

In sum, the fundamentals were inconsistent with a strong lira. In the short run, the strong lira could be defended only through a continuous hemorrhaging of international reserves. The measures adopted by the authorities and business, aimed at mitigating the negative effects of the exchange policy, proved to be inadequate in relation to the gravity of the situation and, often, were even in conflict with each other. The action most widely utilized by business was dumping.

The authorities revised their commercial policy, but not adequately enough to match the extent of the lira appreciation and the ongoing trade war (Gualerni 1982; Guarnieri 1953: p. 256; Mochi 1982: p. 131). Instead, they aimed at containing production costs by favoring a strategy of industrial and financial concentration. Despite these measures, Italian exports became less competitive; their international market share dropped from 2.8 percent to 2.3 percent between 1931 and 1934.

In fact, the constraints of the gold-exchange standard had been weakened as early as September 29, 1931, with the introduction of exchange controls. The controls were applied a week after the United Kingdom abandoned

---

[11] The Italian Statistical Office (Istat) is the primary source of the income deflator for Italy. For the United States, the time series is the wholesale price index up to 1868, the income deflator in Friedman and Schwartz (1982: Tables 4.8 and 4.9) up to 1975, and the deflator of gross domestic product for the rest of the period; for more details, see Fratianni and Spinelli (2001: Appendix to ch. 2).

the gold-exchange standard and were tightened over the years; in 1935, the backing of gold and convertible currencies against currency in circulation and sight liabilities issued by BI was abolished.

THE DEFLATION YEARS

To put Italian deflation in an international context, we continue comparing Italy with the United States. We begin with the persistence properties of the rate of inflation in the two countries, using the same AR(1) model of Burdekin and Siklos (this volume),

$$\pi_t = \alpha_0 + \alpha_1 \pi_{t-1} + \epsilon_t, \tag{8.1}$$

where π_t is the annual rate of inflation, α_0 is the drift, and α_1 is the coefficient of inflation persistence. The inflation rate is measured in terms of the income deflator. We consider two separate sample periods, 1865–1914 and 1915–1939; the first period is identified with the classical gold standard and the second has at its core the gold exchange standard. Estimates of (1) are presented in Table 8.2. In the first period, the sample means were 0.67 for Italy and −0.76 for the United States; the standard deviations were 5.59 for Italy and 3.72 for the United States. Thus, Italian inflation, on average, exceeded U.S. inflation by 150 basis points a year; Italian inflation was also more volatile than U.S. inflation. Neither series showed any degree of persistence: The rates of inflation have the typical zig-zag pattern of the classical gold standard. The two series were uncorrelated. In the second period, the sample means were 6.4 for Italy and 0.92 for the United States; the standard deviations were 13.08 for Italy and 8.3 for the United States. Thus, Italian inflation, on average, exceeded U.S. inflation by 550 basis points a year; relative variability did not change. The two series showed sizeable, significant, and similar degrees of persistence. The two series were also positively correlated. In sum, in both the classical gold standard and the gold exchange standard, Italian inflation differed from U.S. inflation more in the trend than in its dynamic structure.

Because trend is what differentiates Italy from the United States, we now turn to a discussion of it. Recall that Italy went back to the gold standard on December 21, 1927, with a sterling exchange rate of 92.46. Fixed exchange rates lasted until October 5, 1936, when Italy devalued the gold content of

Table 8.2. *AR(1) Models of the rate of inflation for Italy and the United States*

Sample period	A_0	α_1	$\bar{R}^2$	LM: $\chi^2(4)$
1865–1914	0.73 (.80)	−.09 (.14)	−0.01	11.16[†]
Italy				
U.S.	−.76 (.53)*	0.25 (0.21)	−0.01	12.26[‡]
1915–1939 Italy	2.29 (2.22)	.66[‡](.16)	0.41	3.32
U.S.	0.5 (1.56)	0.41[†](0.19)	0.13	2.53

Note: Estimates are based on equation (1). Standard errors are in parenthesis. LM is the Lagrange test for serial correlation with $\chi^2(4)$. *indicates significance at 10 percent level, [†] at 5 percent, and [‡] at 1 percent.

the lira by 40.9 percent. In fact, as we have already noted, the constraints of the gold-exchange standard had been weakened as early as September 29, 1931, with the introduction of exchange controls. We sandwich the deflation period of 1927–1933 between two adjacent periods, one preceding it (1921–1926) and another following it (1934–1937). The first subperiod coincides with the lira's domestic and international depreciation; the second with the stabilization program, the return to the gold-exchange standard, and the world great depression; and the third with the resumption of higher money growth and inflation.

In Italy, the growth of the money stock was high in the first period, low in the second, and again high in the third (Table 8.3). Velocity growth was positively correlated with money growth, thus exacerbating the swings in the

Table 8.3. *The exchange equation for Italy and the United States from 1921 to 1937 (annual percentage changes)*

	Money	Velocity	Price level	Output
Italy				
Avg. 1921–26	6.7	1.9	5.2	3.4
Avg. 1927–33	0.9	−7.9	−7.4	0.4
Avg. 1934–37	2.2	6.8	5.4	3.6
US				
Avg. 1921–26	3.8	−1.9	−2.9	4.8
Avg. 1927–33	−4.3	−5.4	−4.7	−5.0
Avg. 1934–37	8.7	5.4	2.5	11.6

Money is defined in a broad sense, that is inclusive of time deposits; output is real national income; price level is the national income deflator; and velocity is computed using the equation of exchange MV = Py, where M = money, V = velocity, P = price level, and y = output. For more details, see Fratianni and Spinelli (1997: ch. 5) for Italy and Friedman and Schwartz (1982: Tables 4.8 and 4.9) for the United States.

price level changes: 5.2 percent in the first subperiod, −7.4 percent in the second, and then back again to 5.4 percent in the third. The dynamics of real income did not differ qualitatively from those of the money stock, but the correlation between money and prices was much stronger than that between money and output. Italian deflation lagged behind U.S. deflation: although the Italian price level grew at 5 percent in the first subperiod, the U.S. price level declined in absolute terms. In the third subperiod, inflation resumed in both countries, but more vigorously in Italy. With regard to output, the depression was deeper and longer in the United States than in Italy.

Money Growth Determinants

Both Italy and the United States restrained their monetary base in the first subperiod, relaxed it in the second, and expanded it in the third. All of this is in accord with the restraint that the gold-exchange standard placed on monetary authorities. The system had a deflationary bias because of the asymmetric response of surplus and deficit countries with respect to flows of gold and foreign exchange. Surplus countries sterilized foreign reserves inflows, whereas deficit countries did not, leading to a general monetary contraction (Bernanke and James 1991; Eichengreen 1992a; Bernanke 1995). The monetary contraction in the deficit countries followed automatically from the fact that there was a minimum ratio of foreign reserves to the monetary base.

Both the monetary base and the money multiplier declined much more sharply in the United States than in Italy. Table 8.4 decomposes money growth in terms of the growth of the monetary base and the two determinants of the money multiplier, the ratio of monetary base held by the public to total bank deposits (k), and the ratio of total bank reserves to total bank deposits (r).[12] In the United States, k and r contributed to an annual destruction of 7.4 percentage points of money growth from 1927 to 1929 (Friedman and Schwartz 1963: p. 332–33). The Fed failure was in letting the monetary base compensate less than a third of this destruction (Friedman and Schwartz 1963: ch. 7). Another Fed failure was in not preventing or dampening banking panics.

In Italy, the policy failure was small compared with that in the United States. To begin with, the negative impact of k on money growth was

---

[12]   The money multiplier is defined as $(1 + k)/(k + r)$. The decomposition includes an interaction term as well.

Table 8.4. *Decomposition of money growth in Italy and the United States,*
1921–1937 (percentage points)

Period	Money growth	Contribution k	Contribution r	Interaction	Contribution monetary base
Italy					
Avg. 1921–26	6.71	5.66	−0.05	0.05	1.05
Avg. 1927–33	0.93	−0.65	0.32	0.01	1.25
Avg. 1934–37	2.22	−5.09	0.26	−0.01	7.05
US					
Avg. 1921–26	3.67	3.02	0.81	0.03	−0.19
Avg. 1927–33	−4.77	−4.14	−3.26	0.38	2.25
Avg. 1934–37	8.89	2.67	−5.88	−0.33	12.43

Sources: Fratianni and Spinelli (1997: ch. 5) for Italy and Friedman and Schwartz (1982: Tables 4.8 and 4.9) for the United States.

negligible. As we document extensively in the next section, Italian authorities were quite keen in preventing bank failures. BI acted often and massively as the lender of last resort (LOLR) under the tutelage and the fiscal backing of the Italian government, which kept some of the rescue operations in total secrecy. The public, although clearly aware of the high-risk environment of the times, felt on the whole that its bank deposits were safe and never produced a serious run on banks. The behavior of the Italian k reflected this state of relative calm of the public. In addition, the actual decline in the money multiplier was more than offset by changes in the monetary base. Government budget deficits were a potent source of monetary base creation. On average, from 1927 to 1933, 84 percent of budget deficits was monetized (Fratianni and Spinelli 2001: Table 7.4). The policy failure in Italy was in restraining BI bank lending, which in turned buffered the growth of the Treasury component of the monetary base. This evidence is consistent with the hypothesis that the authorities were committed to the gold-exchange standard. The net outcome, however, was that, although Italian money growth declined drastically in this period relative to the previous period, its decline was a small fraction of the U.S. money stock decline.

Was the smaller Italian policy failure the result of luck or of a conscious policy? What would the authorities have done if they had faced rising k and r of the magnitude experienced in the United States? A look at the subsequent subperiod sheds some insights on this question.

The subperiod 1934–1937 is distinct from the seven deflation years in several respects. First, the k ratio rose sharply in response to concerns about the banking system and the economy and caused a destruction of five percentage points of money growth; the size of the event is comparable with what had happened in the United States from 1927 to 1933. Second, there were significant losses of foreign reserves, such to produce a destruction of 2.4 percentage points of money growth.[13] Finally, the treasury component of the monetary base swung from a positive to a negative source of monetary base creation (Fratianni and Spinelli 2001: Table 7.4). Confronted with this scenario, the monetary authorities opened widely the spigot of bank lending and more than offset the depressing effect of the money multiplier on money growth.[14] The evidence on bank lending is consistent with the willingness of the monetary authorities to act as LOLRs.

BI bank lending was obviously tied to the official discount rate policy. Between the spring of 1932 and the autumn of 1934, this rate was lowered from 7 percent to 3 percent also to facilitate the conversion of the "Consolidated Debt 5 percent" into redeemable securities at 3.5 percent. Subsequently, the rate was raised, but never above 5 percent. From 1932 onward, the domestic real interest rate declined on a continuous basis, and so did its differential relative to the U.S. rate, which became zero by 1934 (Fratianni and Spinelli 2001: Figure 3.4). As a result, monetary policy became fully dependent on purely domestic political considerations. BI adapted to the political reality, as transpires from the following excerpt (Banca d'Italia 1935: p. 63).

Credit and monetary policies are no longer governed by a numerical ratio related to the value of metal reserves held, a ratio that often imposes hardship on the country's economy.

[13] The authorities reacted in two different ways to the depletion of foreign reserves. First, between May 1934 and December 1935, they restricted commercial and financial dealings with the rest of the world (Banca d'Italia 1934: p. 34–5 and Banca d'Italia 1935, p. 37–9). For the first time, therefore, the government introduced a protectionist policy in international trade and foreign exchange activities. The second reaction was to remove the 40 percent reserve requirement against paper currency. This historic decision was embodied in a decree passed on July 21, 1935, and enabled the authorities to monetize a larger portion of the 1935 and 1936 budget deficits.

[14] The interaction term complicates the interpretation of the data in Table 8.5. If the entire interaction is attributed to treasury, we obtain a significant amount of BI lending to government; if we attribute it to the foreign component, we obtain that this makes a positive contribution to money growth; and if we attribute it to BI bank lending, our thesis is reenforced.

In a fascist political regime, credit is more closely tied to the nation's resources and economic needs, while the currency's purchasing power is also protected by an adequate control over price levels.

In sum, Italian monetary authorities finally understood the implications of the gold-exchange standards and opted for reflation. Despite a rising ratio of currency to deposits and falling foreign reserves, they were able to create enough monetary base, through the bank lending channel, to raise money growth above the level of the 1927–1933 period. In several ways, the 1934–1937 years resemble the earlier seven years in the United States.

LENDING OF LAST RESORT

In the period under consideration, large Italian banks were called *banche miste*, that is, financial institutions that mixed commercial with investment banking activities; today, we would call them universal banks. For the very largest – Banca Commerciale Italiana, Credito Italiano, Banca Italiana di Sconto, and Banco di Roma – investment banking prevailed over commercial banking. These banks had a heavy exposure in long-term credits and equity participations. At the root of the problem was a permissive legislation, as well as an undeveloped capital market that opened opportunities for banks to move into long-term financing. When economic crises erupted in the 1920s and early 1930s, the authorities came to the rescue of industrial enterprises and their respective bankers. Italian monetary and fiscal authorities, unlike their counterparts in the United States, acted as LOLR to prevent significant industrial and bank failures. This activity was particularly vigorous in the 1920–1924 and 1931–1933 periods (Toniolo 1993: p. 13).

The first wave of industrial and banking rescues took place when, in the early 1920s, the Italian manufacturing sector had to grapple with a transition to a peace economy and with structural changes in international trade. In 1922, the government established the Division of the Consortium for Financing Industrial Enterprises (*Sezione autonoma del Consorzio per sovvenzioni su valori industriali*, or simply, Sezione). The Sezione was no more than an office located in BI (Gigliobianco 1993: p. 177), which was set up to manage industrial crises. The funding of the Sezione came from the banks of issue,[15]

---

[15] There were several banks of issue in Italy until 1926. For details, see Fratianni and Spinelli (1997: chs. 3 and 5).

which made an initial commitment of 1 billion lire that was raised several times. The Sezione lent to (or liquidated) firms and banks in precarious conditions, such as Ansaldo, Banca Italiana di Sconto, Ilva, and Banco di Roma.[16] In 1926, the Sezione was closed and was replaced with the Liquidation Institute (*Istituto di Liquidazione*), an organization formally separate from BI. The objectives of the Liquidation Institute, however, were not different from Sezione's. The second wave of rescues came after the deflationary measures to reach Quota 90. These caused a collapse in capital goods prices as well as in equity prices and, consequently, led to the failure of a large number of firms. In this period, the banks in difficulty were Banco di Roma again, in 1928, the so-called catholic banks, in 1928 and 1929, and Banca Agricola Italiana, in 1929 (Toniolo 1993: pp. 58–69). The final and biggest wave of rescue operations occurred with the crisis of 1931. These included the two largest "mixed" Italian banks, Banca Commerciale Italiana and Credito Italiano.

LOLR activity was organized in an unorthodox manner to preserve the fiction that BI (and the other two banks of issue up to 1926) adhered to classic Bagehot principles. The problem was that the "mixed" banks were insolvent. Their assets would have not qualified as eligible for rediscounts with BI because of both their long maturity and the deep discounts to book values. To get around this difficulty, the Sezione and later the Liquidation Institute acted as buffer between BI and the rescued banks. Thus, the Sezione or the Liquidation Institute financed the banks and rediscounted their claims with BI.[17] In other instances, BI lent against the collateral of securities. BI, keenly aware that the loans to the buffer institutions were not self-liquidating and that the collateral received was inadequate to cover the entire value of the transaction, sought and obtained coverage of the losses by the government. The government obliged in virtually all instances by reducing the tax rate

[16] The Sezione issued notes that grew from 898 million lire at the end of 1922 to 3,306 at the end of 1923 and reached a maximum of 4,081 million lire at the end of 1924. At that particular point, the value of the Sezione's notes, which were not guaranteed by collaterals and were not subject to reserve requirements, represented more than 20 percent of total currency outstanding. In principle, there should not necessarily have been a close relationship between the Sezione's notes and the overall stock of paper money. In fact, the authorities could have reacted to the creation of new notes by the Sezione by eliminating some other component of the monetary base. In practice, however, in view of the nature and urgency of the Sezione's activities, such a close relationship could not but exist. This was also later admitted by BI's Governor, Menichella (1956). Supino (1929: p. 240) speaks of a "deterioration of currency quality" and Alberti (1931: p. 188) of "currency dilution."

[17] The transaction was further complicated by buffer institutions that acted as intermediaries between the Sezione or the Liquidation Institute and the rescued banks (Roselli 2000: p. 49; Toniolo 1993: p. 36–7).

on the new flow of currency issued by BI. Thus, the central bank was the LOLR, but treasury acted as the deep pockets in the system. Without the government assumption of the losses, BI would have not acted as LOLR.

The banking crisis was finally resolved in 1933 with the creation of the government-owned Istituto Ricostruzione Industriale (IRI), which assumed assets and liabilities of Banca Commerciale Italiana, Credito Italiano, Banco di Roma, and several other banking and industrial enterprises. At the end of 1933, IRI posted budget losses for the staggering sum of 11.4 billion lire, representing 85 percent of currency in circulation, of which 6.5 billion were due to the losses of the three banks (Guarino and Toniolo 1993: p. 855). IRI was an effective reorganizer and privatized several ongoing concerns. In the restructuring process, banks were restricted only to commercial banking even before the deep reforms of the Banking Law of 1936.[18]

Estimates of LOLR from 1928 to 1935 are shown in Table 8.5. The first part of the table identifies the three channels of BI lending to all banks and "buffer" institutions; the second part estimates LOLR as the sum of lending to large banks and to buffer institutions. Our estimates of LOLR are biased downward because they assume that lending to "other banks" falls outside the domain of LOLR. Yet, BI for the end of 1932 reports an exposure to troubled banks and buffer institutions of Lit. 7,353 million, considerably more than the estimate of Lit. 6,427 of Table 8.5.[19] Because we have no comparable data for other years, we opted for the biased estimates to underscore the evolution of LOLR from 1929 to 1935. Two observations emerge from the table. The first is the sheer magnitude of the interventions. At the peak of 1932, LOLR accounted for 47 percent of currency in circulation; at the end of the sample period, LOLR petered down to 29 percent of currency in circulation. IRI's debt to BI stayed on the books for years as a reminder of the depth of those interventions (Toniolo 1993: p. 92). The second is that

---

[18] The main features of this legislation were as follows. First, deposit-taking and credit activities were officially recognized as public services, even though provided by the private sector. Second, longer-term financing was sharply separated from short-term financing. The Italian banking system was divided between institutions that were lending for eighteen months and longer ("credito mobiliare") and commercial banks that were limited to lending eighteen months and shorter ("credito ordinario"). Third, the supervisory role over banking activities was delegated to the "Ispettorato per la Difesa del Risparmio e per l'Esercizio del Credito" (Office of the Inspector for the Protection of Savings and the Business of Banking), which had the critical task of ensuring that the banking system would fulfill the economic objectives set by political authorities. Finally, BI was transformed into a public interest, functioning as bank of banks.

[19] The source of BI exposure for Lit. 7,353 is reported in Toniolo (1993: p. 73, footnote 158).

Table 8.5. *Lending of last resort (LOLR) estimates, 1928–1935 (millions of lire)*

Years	1928	1929	1930	1931	1932	1933	1934	1935
BI discounts and rediscounts	3720	4318	3946	4598	5249	3683	4005	4897
BI lending against collateral	1761	1802	1661	1066	1289	1009	2449	4090
Sezione, Liqui, Inst., IRI	1160	851	626	1540	1888	1137	1091	802
TOTAL	8569	8900	8163	9135	10358	7762	9479	11724
LOLR	2062	2333	2448	4345	6427	3848	4413	4678
Large banks	902	1482	1822	2805	4539	2711	3322	3876
CSVI, Liqui, Inst., IRI	1160	851	626	1540	1888	1137	1091	802
Other banks	6507	6567	5715	4790	3931	3914	5066	7046
Δ LOLR		271	115	1897	2082	−2579	565	265
Δ Other banks		60	−852	−925	−859	−17	1152	1980

Sources: Gelsomino (1994, pp. 90–91) for the first three lines and Cotula and Spaventa (1993: p. 178) for LOLR to large banks. CSVI is Consorzio per Sorenzioni per Valori Industriali.

changes in LOLR were more than offset by contraction in lending to other banks in 1930, were imperfectly offset in 1931 and 1932, and were not offset in later years.[20] This evidence is consistent with qualitative accounts of BI being very sensitive to meet the government's objective of a strong lira up to 1931 and then shifting to an output-employment target (Toniolo 1933: p. 13). Thus, by refusing to let the burden of LOLR fall on smaller private banks, BI was signaling a more expansionary policy and an implicit abandonment of the strong lira policy.

In sum, Italian monetary and fiscal authorities used the LOLR instrument extensively. The rescue of industrial and banking firms prevented significant bank failures and bank panics. This stood in sharp contrast with the position of the U.S. monetary authorities who failed to act as LOLR (Cecchetti 1998). The consequence of the extensive LOLR activity meant that the Italian banking system fell under direct government control. Although this outcome meant a significant efficiency loss for the industry (that would last all the way through the nineties), it had the salutary effect of reassuring bank depositors, thus stabilizing the behavior of the money multiplier.[21]

[20] Ferri and Garofalo (1994) believe that the credit crunch forced on small private banks through the compensatory policy of LOLR was an important contributor to the economic crisis.

[21] Jonung (1978), in his analysis of the depression in Sweden and the United States, comes to a similar conclusion.

THE LINK BETWEEN DEFLATION AND DEPRESSION

We have already indicated that the loss of output during the seven-year deflation period from 1927 to 1933 was much smaller in Italy than in the United States (Table 8.3). We have argued that the behavior of the Italian monetary authorities had a great deal to do with this outcome. But money growth is not the entire story. The collapse of world trade was another reason for the depression in Italy (Mattesini and Quintieri 1997: Table 2a). Italy was a small open economy and extremely sensitive to external shocks. International trade collapsed during the period under study. The extent of this collapse can be measured by the dramatic drop in the ratio of exports to GNP – from eighteen in 1924 to six in 1936 (Fratianni and Spinelli 2001: ch. 2; Rey 1991: Table 5.01). In sum, money deceleration and the collapse of international trade explain a great deal of the Italian depression.

The next question is how did price deflation affect real economic activity? The literature underscores three separate channels: the real interest rate (Cecchetti 1998), real wages, and financial crises (Bernanke 1995). The first channel impacts negatively on aggregate demand through the interest rate sensitive sectors and on the long run aggregate supply through a decline in the stock of capital. The second channel impacts negatively on the short run aggregate supply of output. The third channel affects the real sector by redistributing funds from borrowers to creditors; this redistribution is not neutral because borrowers have a comparative advantage in selecting good investment projects and are effectively constrained by internally generated funds.

Neither real interest rates nor financial system variables appear to have played a role in the Italian depression (Mattesini and Quintieri: 1997 Tables 3a and 4). The finding that financial system variables exerted no significant impact on the real sector is consistent with our assessment of LOLR by Italian authorities. The lack of evidence on the real interest rate channel may well result from money growth deceleration being a mirror image of the real interest rate: money growth effects swamp real interest rate effects in the econometrics. More research is needed on this topic.

The final issue concerns the behavior of wages. There is a significant difference between Italy and the United States concerning the relationship between price deflation and output growth. During the 1927–1933 period, the two variables are highly and positively correlated for the United States and uncorrelated for Italy.[22] These patterns suggest that nominal rigidities were more of a force in the United States than in Italy. Regardless of the nature of the aggregate demand shocks, the evidence is consistent with the Italian aggregate supply schedule being more flexible than the U.S. supply. Part of the explanation lies with the policy of the Fascist government to exert strong influence on money wages and labor bargaining. The right to strike was suppressed in 1926 and money wages were cut, by decree, in 1927 by 10 percent and in 1930 between 8 and 12 percent. The nominal wage adjustment in the American economy was not present to the same extent. It is true that real wages rose in Italy in 1933 and 1934. But real wages had declined from 1927 to 1930 and had been stable in 1931 and 1932 (Zamagni 1994: Table 8), periods when nominal wages had been cut. The point is that nominal wage flexibility – to be sure, imposed from above – had an impact on real wages and made aggregate output supply more responsive to market conditions.

THE THIRTIES VS. THE NINETIES

The 1927–1933 deflation invites a comparison with two recent periods of Italian disinflation: the hard phase of the EMS (1987–1992) and the qualification to the final stage of the EMU (1993–98). In the first period, Italy operated under a strict fixed exchange rate regime with respect to the currencies of the EMS, an experience that ended with the currency crisis of September 1992. The second disinflation began soon after the currency crisis and lasted until the end of 1998. In those years, Italy operated under flexible exchange rates, with an increasingly independent central bank.

The strong similarity between the 1927–1933 deflation and the hard phase of the EMS is that, in both instances, the fixed exchange rate became unsustainable in light of external shocks and deteriorating domestic fundamentals. Global depression, protectionism and competitive devaluations were the external shocks of the thirties. Italian monetary and fiscal policies at first tried to align with the strong lira but later shifted to domestic objectives. After a period of real appreciation of the lira, the fixed exchange rate was abandoned. An output growth decline – much more moderate than the decline

[22] The correlation coefficient for the United States is 0.82 and for Italy is 0.03. For output data, we have used real national income in Fratianni and Spinelli (2001: ch. 2) for Italy and the output series in Friedman and Schwartz (1982: Table 4.8) for the United States.

in the 1930s, for sure – was the external shock of the 1987–1992 disinflation. As was true in the 1930s, the lira appreciated in real terms in the 1987–1992 period, as Italian inflation exceeded the inflation rate in the rest of the EMS (Fratianni and Spinelli 2001: Figure 11.1). Finally, as was true in the 1930s, fiscal and monetary policies did not align with the maintenance of the exchange rate regime (Fratianni and Artis 1996). The inconsistency between fundamentals and the fixed rate was resolved in September 1992 with Italy exiting the EMS.

There are also differences between the deflation of the 1930s and the 1987–1992 disinflation. We mention two. The first concerns the direction of causality between the inflation rate and the exchange rate. In the 1930s, the authorities were convinced that the direction of causality went from domestic inflation to the exchange rate and consequently adjusted policies, at least during the phase in which the strong lira policy prevailed. In the 1980s, the direction of causality was seen as going the other way, with monetary policy partially adjusting to the exchange rate target. Real exchange rate appreciation was used deliberately to force a downward cost readjustment in Italian industry (Fratianni and von Hagen 1992: p. 28). The second difference involves the institutional structure. The deflation of the 1930s ended with a purely nationalistic solution, with the Fascist government becoming increasingly intrusive in economic management. The disinflation of the 1980s ended with the prospect that Italy, having signed the Maastricht treaty, would eventually qualify for the European monetary union.

The disinflation of the 1990s, instead, was successful and was accompanied by stable output growth. Antonio Fazio, the BI Governor, adopted inflation targeting, at least since 1995, and pursued diligently the elimination of the Italian inflation differential with respect to Germany. Monetary policy, to be sure, was helped by an extremely restrictive fiscal policy. Jointly, the monetary and fiscal "fundamentals" were responsible for the Italian qualification in the third and final stage of EMU.

The obvious parallel with respect to the deflation of the 1930s is that inflation was seen as the causal factor of long-term exchange rate changes. Fazio targeted the rate of inflation without making any explicit reference to EMU and the obligations of the Maastricht treaty. In fact, the press often depicted him as unfriendly towards EMU. Yet, the Governor, who did not perceive a fixed exchange rate as a binding constraint, brought Italy into EMU.

The main lesson we draw from these comparisons is that tying one's hands with the fixed exchange rate is not a robust strategy for disinflation and even less so for deflation.

CONCLUSIONS

The main conclusions of the chapter are as follows. Mussolini signaled the strong lira policy in August 1926, sixteen months before adopting the gold parity. The authorities used the lira policy not only to achieve price deflation but also to restructure the country's industrial system.

The gold-exchange standard had a deflationary bias. Part of the problem stemmed from the asymmetric response of surplus and deficit countries with respect to flows of gold and foreign exchange. Surplus countries sterilized foreign reserves inflows, whereas deficit countries did not, leading to a general monetary contraction.

The strong lira policy, undoubtedly supported by the international economic doctrine of the time, became difficult to sustain. The Italian authorities watered down the rigor of the gold-exchange standard. In addition to controls on capital flows and foreign exchange transactions, the Italian authorities implemented an income policy, introduced new tariffs, and progressively embarked on the road of trade and financial protectionism.

The decision to loosen the straight jacket of the gold-exchange standard saved the Italian authorities from a large policy failure that instead took place in the United States. Money growth deceleration in Italy was considerably less than in the United States.

Unlike their U.S. counterparts, Italian monetary and fiscal authorities were very active as LOLRs and set up an institutional structure designed to bail out large industrial and banking firms. Although the efficiency implications of this strategy were quite negative for years to come, the rescue operations prevented banking panics and stabilized the money multiplier.

As a result, the Great Depression was less severe in Italy than in the United States. It would have been even less severe if Italy had not been swept by the sharp decline in international trade.

Nominal wage flexibility – imposed by fiat by the Fascist regime – had an impact on real wages and made aggregate output supply more responsive to market conditions. Nominal rigidities had less of an impact on the Italian real sector than on the U.S. real sector.

The 1927–1933 deflation and the disinflation that took place during the hard phase of the EMS, 1987–1992, have one important element in common: In both instances, the fixed exchange rate became unsustainable in light of external shocks and deteriorating domestic fundamentals, and it was abandoned. In contrast, the post-EMS disinflation of 1993–1998 was set in an environment of flexible exchange rates and central bank independence. Aided by a conservative fiscal policy, the central bank targeted the inflation rate without any material regard to the exchange rate. The outcome was the elimination of the inflation differential with respect to Germany, which permitted Italy to qualify (with some fudging on the fiscal requirement) to the final phase of the EMU.

9 Deflation and Stagnation in Japan: Collapse of the Monetary Transmission Mechanism and Echo From the 1930s

Michael M. Hutchison

INTRODUCTION

On February 13, 2002, Japanese Prime Minister Koizumi directed ministries to formulate *emergency countermeasures to deflation*, stating, in a press release that "while deflation has a varied background, the resolution of the immediate financial problems is indispensable to overcoming deflation" (italics added). Koizumi linked deflation, shown in Figure 9.1,[1] to banking problems and a credit crunch, and called on the Bank of Japan to take action. The same press release goes on to state, "In particular, with regard to the disposal of non-performing loans which presently stands as a top-priority issue, actions shall be taken to achieve concrete progress in line with the ongoing process of special inspections, thereby solidifying the prospects for an early resolution of the so-called 'non-performing loans problem.' Meanwhile, the government shall stand ready to take any and all necessary measures to prevent a financial crisis. Overcoming deflation will require the government and the Bank of Japan to act in unison. Therefore, we turn to the Bank of Japan with the request that it act with due *audacity* in implementing monetary policy" (italics added; Japan Ministry of Foreign Affairs 2002).

The call by the Prime Minister for the government to take emergency action reflects the concern that the deflation in Japan, if allowed to persist, would gradually erode the foundation of the economy and eventually lead to a much deeper and dramatic decline reminiscent of the Great Depression in the 1930s. Initially viewed by policy makers as a "good deflation," price declines were now seen as a harbinger of economic collapse.

---

[1] GDP (nominal and real values) and unemployment numbers are from the International Financial Statistics (IFS) data base. All other data used to construct the charts and employed in the regression analysis are from the Bank of Japan.

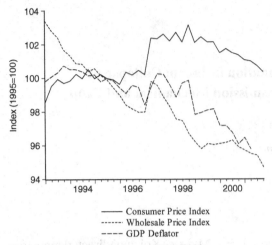

Figure 9.1. Deflation in Japan, 1993–2002

Japan experienced slow growth, recession, and sustained deflation over the course of the 1990s, and the period is sometimes characterized as the "lost decade" (Cargill, Hutchison, and Ito 2000) or the "Great Recession" (Kuttner and Posen 2001). The slowdown in real gross domestic product (GDP) growth and the rise in unemployment, shown in Figure 9.2, are evident. And the loss in "potential output" is even greater, judging by the very high rate of output growth seen in Japan in previous decades. But as Fischer (2001) points out, Japanese economic performance during the 1990s was unimpressive but

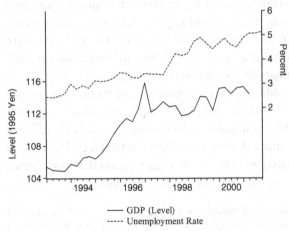

Figure 9.2. Unemployment Rate and Real GDP Growth in Japan

not disastrous and that policy would probably have been forced to be more decisive had there been a full-blown crisis. Nonetheless, Japan's economic weakness is worrying, and many commentators have voiced the same concerns as the Prime Minister and called for decisive action against recession, deflation, and banking problems (e.g. Cargill, Hutchison, and Ito 2000).

This chapter reviews the deflation episode in Japan – its causes and the seemingly ineffectiveness of policy in alleviating it – and discusses the similarities and differences between the Japanese case and the Great Depression of the 1930s. There are a number of similarities between Japan and the Great Depression. The words Irving Fisher (1933: p. 341) wrote in his classic article on "the debt-deflation theory of great depressions" in 1933 seem to apply to Japan today: "Disturbances in these two factors – debt and the purchasing power of the monetary unit – will set up serious disturbances in all, or nearly all, other economic variables."

The most significant facts about Japan are that prices are falling and the burden of debt is slowing the economy. The experience to date, of course, is less startling than that of most countries during the Great Depression in the 1930s. But Japanese consumer prices have been declining since 1998, and both wholesale prices and the GDP deflator have trended downward since the early 1990s. Asset prices have also declined at an alarming rate, with the Nikkei stock price index (average) declining by 63 percent from its peak in the fourth quarter of 1989 to the first quarter of 2002 (Figure 9.3). Moreover, we present statistical evidence suggesting that asset price declines are a dominant factor behind the continued slump in the Japanese economy – at the very time that monetary policy is ineffective. In addition to the zero

Figure 9.3. Equity Prices in Japan (Index), 1970Q1–2001Q4

interest rate floor, monetary policy is constrained by two other factors: (i) a structural break has occurred in the money multiplier so that rapid base money growth is not translating into substantial broad money growth, and (ii) a structural break has occurred in the monetary transmission mechanism so that a policy "innovation" in the broad monetary aggregate (M2 + CDs) has almost no effect on output in the current environment.

Nonetheless, the Japanese experience over the 1990s differs markedly from the deflation episode seen in the 1930s. These differences are especially noteworthy with respect to fiscal policy, the external environment, the exchange rate regime, and banking problems. And the resulting outcome, of course, is that Japan has experienced more modest declines in prices and output than those seen in the 1930s.

The following section provides a brief overview of the deflation-recession cycle in Japan. Then, I present new empirical evidence on the causes of the continuing malaise, attempting to distinguish between the "credit crunch" and the "liquidity trap" hypotheses. This section describes the timing of the structural break in the money multiplier and, using a vector autoregression (VAR) model, investigates the role of monetary policy and asset prices in the continuing Japanese recession. A separate section compares the main reasons Japan has fared better, relatively speaking, than would have been the case had the contractionary effects of deflation been allowed to fully impact the economy. Next, I discuss the limits to monetary policy and the zero interest rate policy, and compare Japan with countries that faced these same dilemmas in the 1930s. The merits of an inflation-targeting proposal to end deflation in Japan are also analyzed, followed by conclusions.

RECESSION AND DEFLATION IN JAPAN

Background: Recession, Deflation, and Banking Problems

Japan had experienced decades of strong growth in the 1950–1989 period. At the end of the 1980s, the economy was characterized by inflationary pressure, labor shortages, and unprecedented increases in equity and land prices ("asset price bubble"). This changed dramatically in the early 1990s with the burst of the bubble economy – asset prices fell dramatically, in turn, leading to serious banking problems that were exacerbated by recession and deflation. Cargill, Hutchison, and Ito (1997, 2000) discuss in detail the causes of the shock to Japan's economy. They argue that not one but several factors were responsible for the recession and price deflation in Japan. An asset price bubble was not sustainable, and a collapse was inevitable at some point. The asset price collapse was initially preceded by a gradual but eventually very large and sustained rise in the Bank of Japan's call money rate (from 3.2 percent in May 1988 to 8.2 percent in March 1991). Banking problems in Japan were also likely to emerge, partly as the result of the asset price collapse and partly due to underlying structural changes in the financial system. However, regardless of the underlying asset price, monetary, or banking shock, the unanswered question is why Japanese slow growth/recession and deflation persisted for more than a decade and what policy measures should be taken.[2]

Three main features characterize the Japanese economy in the 1990s and beyond. First, Japan began a low growth/recession and deflation cycle in 1993 that continued into the new millennium. The economy experienced a series of recessions and stagnation periods in the decade since the burst of the bubble economy in the early 1990s, with the most recent being three consecutive quarters of GDP decline at the end of 2001. Overall, real GDP stood only 8 percent higher in 2001Q4 compared with 1993Q1 – an annual growth rate of less than 1 percent per annum over almost a decade. Slow growth, in turn, was accompanied by the rise in unemployment to the highest levels recorded in modern Japan, climbing to the 5.5 percent level by late 2001.

Price deflation, the second feature of the economy during this period, accompanied the weakness in the Japanese economy. Japanese consumer prices fell 1.2 percent in December 2001 year on year; extending a deflationary spiral that has been continuous since the end of 1998. Wholesale prices have trended downward throughout the 1990s, and by year-end 2001, were more than 10 percent below the level reached at the end of 1991. Moreover, the broadest measure of the price level, the deflator for GDP, fell by 5 percent since its peak in 1993. Finally, asset prices – especially land and equities – declined throughout the 1990s. Japanese share prices, for example,

---

[2] Hetzel (1999), and Burdekin and Siklos (this volume), argue that the cause for the deflation was a negative monetary shock. It is likely that the rise in interest rates, ending in March 1991, led to the decline in monetary growth in the early 1990s. Deflation became most pronounced, however, in the late 1990s in tandem with the banking crisis, continued declines in asset prices (especially land prices), and short-term interest rates at zero. The rapid rise in base money in the late 1990s also argues against a continuous policy contraction, and the transmission lags would be very long if the rise in interest rates and initial fall in monetary growth were still depressing the economy more than a decade later.

lost two-thirds of their value between December 1989 and February 2002. Land prices have fallen continuously since the early 1990s and in some locations, such as central Tokyo, have fallen by more than half.

The third key characteristic of the Japanese economy in the 1990s is the acute banking and nonperforming loan problem referred to in the quote from Prime Minister Koizumi in the introduction to this chapter. The collapse of equity and land prices, recession, and deflation may be seen as the proximate cause of the banking problems in Japan. But the structural transformation in Japanese finance from a bank-dominated system to more open markets also is applying long-term pressure on the financial system (Cargill, Hutchison, and Ito 1997; Hoshi and Kashyap 2000). The problem became acute in November 1997 when the accumulation of nonperforming loans pushed many financial institutions toward bankruptcy and took Japan to the edge of a financial panic (Cargill, Hutchison, and Ito 2000).

Despite substantial efforts and infusion of public monies since 1997 to resolve the banking problem, concerns continue to center around credit assessment standards, the quality of bank capital, and exposure to equity price risk, as well as lack of progress in improving core profitability in banks. As of September 2000, major and regional banks reported gross nonperforming loans according to the Financial Reconstruction Law standard (loans to borrowers in or near bankruptcy and loans that have been restructured) of thirty-two trillion yen, compared with eleven to twelve trillion yen in general and specific reserves. This underestimates the problem, however. The total amount of loans covered by ordinary collateral to potentially impaired borrowers (companies whose financial condition requires attention) or borrowers close to bankruptcy amounts to sixty-four trillion yen. In addition, there are forty-eight trillion yen in loans covered by "superior" collateral amount or guarantees, but the quality of such enhancements is open to question. A slow recovery would also put additional pressure on banks. By many accounts, the banking sector in Japan is insolvent.

Interest Rates and Credit in a Deflationary Environment

With the decline in economic performance, short-term interest rates were reduced gradually and, by early 1999, money market (call money) rates reached the zero minimum point. Lending rates and government bond yields also declined to unprecedented low levels (Figure 9.4). Despite zero interest rates since 1999, the economy moved further into recession. The low interest rates

Figure 9.4. Interest Rates in Japan, 1985–2002

seen in Japan at the end of the 1990s are unprecedented for any industrial country since the 1930s.

Injections of liquidity by the central bank have also not been very effective in raising the growth rate of the broader money aggregates. Figure 9.5 shows base money growth averaging about 10 percent per annum from 1996 to midyear 2002 and a huge 35 percent rise for the year ending in March 2002 (right-hand-side scale). The key broad money aggregate in Japan, M2+CDs (also shown in Figure 9.5) has fluctuated between 2 percent and 5 percent and has averaged less than 3 percent growth in 2000–2001 (left-hand-side scale). The upshot is that the money multiplier – the ratio of broad money to the monetary base – has declined from about thirteen in 1993 to about eight in 2002 (see Figure 9.6).

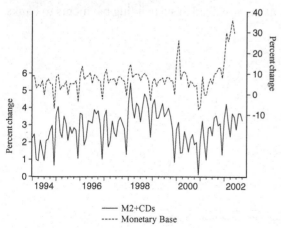

Figure 9.5. Monetary Base and Broad Monetary Growth

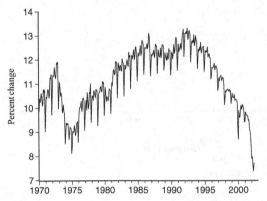

Figure 9.6. Money Multiplier in Japan (Ratio of M2 + CDs to Base Money)

Bank lending has also declined markedly in recent years, as shown in Figure 9.7, indicating that either the demand for funds has collapsed or that the banks are not willing to provide new loans. The 5 percent drop in lending by domestic commercial banks in the year ending March 2002 is the fourth successive year of declines. The sharp decline in lending may also be attributable to a more cautious lending attitude by Japanese banks, given their recent experience with the buildup of nonperforming loans and, with the deepening recession, weakening of firm balance sheets and rise in bankruptcies.

Weakness in business conditions is also reflected in the liabilities associated with bankruptcies in Japan in the late 1990s. Although the actual number of firm bankruptcies was higher in the mid-1980s, now large firms with large outstanding loans are involved in suspending payments to banks.

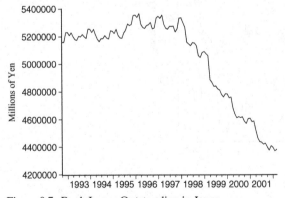

Figure 9.7. Bank Loans Outstanding in Japan

These circumstances make firms less desirable potential borrowers than had previously been the case from the banks' point of view. But it also has the self-reinforcing effect of tightening credit conditions and worsening the recession.

The Tankan-Short-Term Economic Survey of Enterprises in Japan – a monthly survey complied by the Bank of Japan – indicates that credit conditions are tight in Japan.[3] Despite the low interest rate environment, the Tankan survey indicates a sharp tightening of credit conditions facing small enterprises in Japan since mid-1997. The "lending attitudes" of financial institutions, at least from the perspective of borrowers, has become much more stringent.

Beyond these quantifiable factors, business and consumer confidence also appears to have been adversely affected by the general malaise hanging over the banking system. Several identifiable factors have contributed to this malaise. The emergence of the so-called "Japan premium" (the additional interest rate charged on international loans to Japanese banks that are viewed as risky) played a role. The Japan premium is the extra expense Japanese banks must pay for raising funds in overseas markets. The downgrading of the investment-grade ratings (by international debt-rating agencies such as Moody's) on debt issued by Japanese financial institutions, and later by the Japanese government, was also a contributing factor. More generally, the widespread negative publicity over the Japanese financial system and economy clearly contributed to a very pessimistic atmosphere in Japan from the late 1990s through 2003.

CREDIT CRUNCH OR LIQUIDITY TRAP?

With interest rates at historic lows, why is the Japanese economy still in a slump? One explanation, put forward by Krugman (1998) and others, is that traditional monetary policy instruments are powerless to provide effective stimulus to the economy because Japan is in a "liquidity trap." A liquidity trap is characterized by a situation – similar to that in Japan today – where interest rates are at or near zero and people expect deflation. Monetary policy is seemingly impotent to stimulate demand and increase

---

[3] The Tankan "Diffusion Index" reports the number of firms stating that favorable borrowing conditions are prevalent less the number of firms stating that unfavorable borrowing conditions are prevalent.

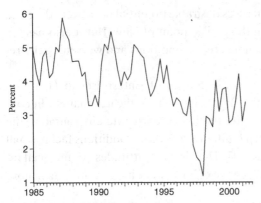

Figure 9.8. Real Lending Rate in Japan
Note: Banking lending rate less four-quarter average of GDP deflator percentage change.

spending because interest rates are already at the lowest point possible. The main alternative explanation for the ineffectiveness of monetary policy to stimulate the economy is the "credit crunch" view. This explanation focuses on the contraction of the supply of bank credit (credit crunch) caused by massive nonperforming loans accumulating in the financial system.

Summary Evidence: Observational Equivalence?

Beyond zero interest rates and price deflation, at least two additional statistical facts are consistent with the liquidity trap argument – but may also be consistent with other explanations. Short-term interest rates have reached a minimum point, and real interest rates appear high by international standards.[4] Figure 9.8 shows the real lending rate in Japan (nominal lending rate less the four-quarter average of the GDP deflator). Despite the move to zero money market rates, lending rates remain above 3 percent and real lending rates around 5 percent to 6 percent over 1997–2001.

Secondly, injections of liquidity by the central bank have raised base money but have not been very effective in raising the growth rate of the broader money aggregate (M2 + CDs). The charts on monetary aggregate growth and bank lending highlight this problem (Figures 9.5 and 9.7). Indeed, bank lending has seen substantial declines in recent years. Figure 9.6 shows

---

[4] High real interest rates are also consistent with the credit crunch theory.

that the money multiplier (ratio of M2 + CDs to base money) declined dramatically, falling from 13.3 in June 1992 to 7.7 in May 2002. Base money growth is not translating into the growth of the broader monetary aggregates or spending.

On the other hand, several recent developments in the economy are also consistent with the credit crunch argument. The decline in bank capital due to the accumulation of bad loans held by Japanese banks is one factor. The sharp decline in the market value of equities held by banks has also decreased bank capital. (Japanese banks maintain large equity holdings as part of their close relationship banking ties with affiliated firms; see Kashyap and Hoshi 2001). As a consequence, the capital asset ratios of financial institutions in Japan have fallen significantly since 1994. Less-than-candid reporting by both banks and the ministry of finance about the magnitude of the nonperforming loan problem in the early years and new information that the problem is much larger than originally envisaged have made it difficult for banks to raise capital in domestic and international financial markets. They therefore have responded by reducing the amount of loans. Japanese financial institutions have attempted to raise capital-asset ratios, in part in response to recently tightened international capital standards (Bank for International Settlements capital ratios), as well as in response to pressure from the markets and the government. But building capital-asset ratios by restraining lending takes a long time. It induces a credit squeeze in the process – the origins of the credit crunch in Japan.

The cautious lending attitude of Japanese banks following their recent experience with bankruptcies, nonperforming loans, and recession is also consistent with the credit crunch explanation. Liabilities associated with bankruptcies jumped to 2.7 trillion yen in October 1997, and a trend line shows a sustained rise. These circumstances make firms less desirable potential borrowers than they used to be from the banks' point of view. They also have the self-reinforcing effect of tightening credit conditions and worsening the recession.

Evidence of a credit crunch also is suggested by the Bank of Japan's Tankan survey. Despite the low interest rate environment, the survey indicates a sharp tightening of credit conditions in Japan since mid-1997 facing both large and small enterprises. These lending attitudes, at least from the borrower's perspective, have become much more stringent. A credit crunch implies injections of liquidity (base and narrow money expansion)

do not increase credit and aggregate lending. This is exactly what has occurred in Japan. Base and narrow money have increased at a robust pace in
1997–1999, but the broader money aggregates most directly related to spending in the economy grew modestly. Aggregate lending by banks has decreased sharply, the flip side of which is the tightening of credit conditions
faced by enterprises in Japan.

The difficulty with casual empiricism provided in support of the two explanations is that they are in large part observationally equivalent. Low
interest rates, slow broad money growth, falling commercial loans, and robust narrow money growth are consistent with either a liquidity trap or a
credit crunch explanation for the sustained malaise in the Japanese economy.
Moreover, elements of a liquidity trap and a credit crunch/nonperforming
loan explanation probably lie behind the extremely weak economic performance of Japan in recent years. Prime Minister Koizumi expressed this view
(in the press release quoted in the introduction to this chapter) when he
emphasized the need to resolve problems in the financial sector as well as
an accommodative stance by the Bank of Japan to restore growth to the
economy.

Statistical Evidence

Although the drop in the money multiplier during the 1990s is consistent
with both the liquidity trap and credit crunch explanations of the Japanese
recession, the timing of the break in the link between broad money (M2 +
CDs) and base money may provide some indication of which factor is pre-
dominant. In particular, the liquidity trap presumably would only be operative after late 1995 when the Bank of Japan call money rate fell below
0.5 percent (dropping from 2.2 percent in March to 0.5 percent in September). The timing of a credit crunch associated with banking problems is more
difficult to pinpoint, however, but should show up by November 1997 when
large-scale bankruptcies in the financial sector emerged.

The point estimate from regressing the log of M2 + CDs on a constant
and the log of base money over the January 1970 to May 2002 sample is 1.03
(standard error equal to 0.008). This is the average value of the "money multiplier" (interpreted in growth rate terms) over the full sample. To address
the timing of the break point, a simple recursive least squares equation is estimated and used at each point to give a one-step-ahead prediction of broad

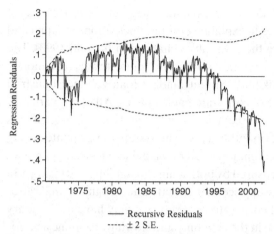

Figure 9.9. Recursive Residual Test for Structural Break in Money Multiplier
Note: Recursive residuals generated from a regression of the log of M2 + CDs on a constant and the log of base money over the period January 1970–May 2002.

money.[5] The one-step-ahead forecast error resulting from this prediction is the recursive residual. Residuals outside the standard error bands suggest instability in the parameters of the equation.

The recursive residual results, shown in Figure 9.9, indicate a break point in the money multiplier in late 1997 – matching precisely the pinnacle of the banking crisis in Japan (November 1997). This evidence supports the credit crunch explanation. However, regardless of the validity for the credit crunch view, it is apparent that the main transmission mechanism of monetary policy – short-term interest rates – has been severely restricted since late 1995 when interested rates fell below 0.5 percent for the first time. Moreover, the direct channel linking base money growth to income growth – the only channel (other than an expectational channel) available to the Bank of Japan – appears weak and is probably not able to fully supplant the interest rate channel as an effective transmission mechanism for monetary policy.

This conjecture is supported by the casual empirical evidence presented in the previous section and also by a simple vector autoregression model

---

[5] The equation is estimated repeatedly, using ever-larger subsets of the sample data. There are two coefficients to be estimated, and the first two observations are used to form the first estimates. The next observation is then added to the data set, and three observations are used to compute the second set of estimates. This process is repeated until all the T sample points have been used, yielding T-2 + 1 estimates of the coefficient vector. At each step, the last estimate of the coefficient vector is used to predict the next value of the M2 + CDs.

(VAR).[6] We use the VAR model to examine the relative importance of monetary and other variables in explaining output fluctuations in Japan and whether the linkages among these variables changed in the mid-1990s. The VAR model consists of five variables: short-term interest rates (call money rate), stock price index (Nikkei 225), outstanding loan volume, industrial production, and the number of corporate bankruptcies. All of the variables are in natural logarithm form except for interest rates. The data sample is January 1990 to March 2002 (monthly data). The system was estimated using a lag length of two.[7] The call money interest rate is a direct measure of monetary policy, bank credit is measured by both loans outstanding and changes in the stock price index (the asset price that directly affects bank capital ratios and lending behavior), and corporate bankruptcies may have a secondary effect in lowering confidence in the economy and slowing economic activity. The focus is on how these variables influence industrial production and the business cycle in Japan.

Table 9.1 shows the variance decompositions from the model with the focus on industrial production for the 1990:1 to 1995:8 period (panel A) and the 1995:9 to 2002:3 period (panel B). The objective is to measure how the influence of monetary policy has changed since late 1995, at least via the transmission mechanism of short-term interest rates. The variance decomposition breaks down the variance in industrial production into the percentage that is explained by each variable of the model (including an unexplained component represented by industrial production itself).

The results indicate that call money interest rates explain about 19 percent of the variation in industrial production (ten-step-ahead variance) during the 1990–1995 period, but less than 1 percent over the 1995–2002 period. Not surprisingly, short-term interest rates have not been an effective instrument

---

[6] There are many possible VAR models that could be specified and many possible identification procedures that could be used in this exercise. The model employed here is quite simple but appears to capture the main stochastic properties in the data. Miyao (2002) also uses a simple recursive VAR model, with interest rates, stock prices, money, and output (industrial production) in first difference form. He considers monthly observations from January 1975 to April 1998. Surprisingly, Miyao finds that nominal interest rate (call money) changes have a permanent effect on the level of output. He finds, using a historical decomposition of output developments, that call money rate changes play a large role in the run-up in the bubble economy in the later 1980s, and weakness in the economy in the early 1990s, but have a negligible effect on output since 1993. This is consistent with the interpretation of these episodes by Cargill, Hutchison, and Ito (1997, 2000).

[7] A lag length of two is indicated by the final prediction error, Schwartz information criterion, and the Hannan-Quinn information criterion.

Table 9.1. *Variance decomposition of industrial production: short-term interest rates as the monetary policy variable*

Period	Call money rate	Nikkei	Loans	Industrial Production	Bankrupt
Panel A Sample: January 1990 to August 1995					
1	1.790433	2.963127	0.075208	95.17123	0.000000
2	9.175898	4.156791	2.461433	82.54578	1.660098
3	8.389627	9.346877	1.980100	78.60600	1.677402
4	12.30405	10.50264	1.671330	69.72088	5.801105
5	13.29781	10.04316	2.355432	64.11594	10.18766
6	12.90296	9.756404	2.571049	64.02554	10.74404
7	14.02605	9.343260	2.489974	63.93645	10.20427
8	16.09290	9.219507	3.068353	62.18512	9.434124
9	17.84613	9.491448	4.926449	59.14007	8.595896
10	**19.00765**	**10.02713**	**7.850553**	**55.35432**	**7.760339**
Panel B Sample: September 1995 to March 2002					
1	1.095502	7.820407	7.525021	83.55907	0.000000
2	0.933401	6.665591	7.711791	80.84705	3.842171
3	0.856913	12.84654	7.300930	74.70822	4.287394
4	0.706719	18.75199	6.493790	69.64691	4.400586
5	0.583177	25.36344	5.665509	63.70663	4.681250
6	0.516623	31.46097	4.985273	57.77851	5.258625
7	0.505131	36.68994	4.450474	52.04319	6.311268
8	0.529361	40.93776	4.052335	46.68312	7.797419
9	0.563677	44.22590	3.772370	41.81449	9.623560
10	**0.590516**	**46.66938**	**3.594319**	**37.50453**	**11.64125**

Note: CALL MONEY RATE is a short-term interest rate, NIKKEI is the stock price index (Nikkei 225), LOANS is the volume of outstanding loans, and BANKRUPT is the number of corporate bankruptcies. Data are monthly. Based on a VAR with lag length of two months. All variables are in log levels except CALL MONEY RATE.

of monetary policy in the post-1995 period. Asset prices (Nikkei 225 average) were also important in the first half of the 1990s, but account for only about 10 percent of the variance of industrial production. However although short-term interest rates were ineffective in the latter period, asset price fluctuations were dominant – explaining 47 percent of the variance in industrial production.

Table 9.2 shows the results from estimating the same system but with the broad monetary aggregate as an indicator of monetary policy (M2 + CDs). A secondary transmission mechanism of monetary policy works through the broad monetary aggregates, and in principle this could have played an increasingly important role during the period when interest rates were at

Table 9.2. *Variance decomposition of industrial production: broad money*
(M2 + CDs) as the monetary policy variable

Period	M2 + CDs	Nikkei	Loans	Industrial Production	Bankrupt
Panel A	**Sample: January 1990 to August 1995**				
1	37.36166	0.371532	14.61908	47.64773	0.000000
2	38.99882	3.580312	14.55498	40.80970	2.056187
3	51.18009	5.190141	10.83283	30.94526	1.851674
4	55.31429	4.383150	10.13230	25.53267	4.637584
5	56.74922	3.858434	11.00156	22.58294	5.807850
6	59.32749	3.524033	11.28096	20.59767	5.269851
7	61.58372	3.286832	10.90235	19.14117	5.085928
8	63.29714	3.127262	10.56475	18.19562	4.815218
9	64.53921	2.981191	10.29423	17.36049	4.824882
10	**65.59098**	**2.868686**	**10.14300**	**16.65905**	**4.738287**
Panel B	**Sample: September 1995 to March 2002**				
1	0.972293	8.615026	6.748269	83.66441	0.000000
2	0.798035	7.517032	7.029938	81.64657	3.008425
3	1.403313	13.73142	6.250504	75.21475	3.400015
4	1.345669	20.73102	5.216389	69.36558	3.341348
5	1.205653	28.03273	4.329603	63.06945	3.362569
6	1.113968	34.72846	3.637718	56.79125	3.728605
7	1.105383	40.63845	3.090498	50.73475	4.430918
8	1.168000	45.56861	2.660621	45.20819	5.394578
9	1.273644	49.48148	2.324692	40.37384	6.546345
10	**1.396192**	**52.45074**	**2.062287**	**36.26595**	**7.824840**

Note: See Note to Table 9.1.

or near-zero. The VAR model does not support this point, however. Similar to call money rates, broad money fluctuations played a dominant role in industrial production movements during the early 1990s (explaining fully 65 percent of the variance for horizons extending beyond ten months). This dropped to less than 2 percent in the 1995:8–2002:3 sample, however, indicating that *both* short term interest rates and broad money were apparently ineffective as instruments of monetary policy in stimulating industrial production. The mirror image is again seen with asset prices. In the recent period, asset prices played a dominant role in explaining fluctuations in industrial production, especially as the horizon is extended to six months and longer.

The key role of asset prices, and ineffectiveness of monetary policy, in recent years is also indicated by the impulse response functions, shown in Table 9.3. The impulse response function indicates how much industrial production responds to a one-standard-deviation innovation to each of the

Table 9.3. *Response of industrial production to one standard deviation shock (standard errors in parentheses)**

	Shock to M2CDs		Shock to asset prices	
Steps ahead	*1990:1–1995:8*	*1995:9–2002:3*	*1990:1–1995:8*	*1995:9–2002:3*
1	**0.006495**	0.001199	0.000648	**0.003570**
	(0.00213)	(0.00149)	(0.00183)	(0.00144)
2	**0.004040**	0.000364	0.002225	0.001432
	(0.00275)	(0.00170)	(0.00202)	(0.00175)
3	**0.007342**	0.001511	0.002455	**0.004786**
	(0.00320)	(0.00163)	(0.00229)	(0.00158)
4	**0.006145**	0.000881	0.000707	**0.005797**
	(0.00357)	(0.00175)	(0.00261)	(0.00172)
5	0.004985	0.000652	7.93E-06	**0.006797**
	(0.00399)	(0.00185)	(0.00313)	(0.00189)
6	0.005174	0.000717	0.000294	**0.007489**
	(0.00431)	(0.00202)	(0.00359)	(0.00212)
7	0.005085	0.000967	0.000404	**0.008095**
	(0.00496)	(0.00217)	(0.00417)	(0.00235)
8	0.004440	0.001217	0.000267	**0.008512**
	(0.00577)	(0.00234)	(0.00495)	(0.00261)
9	0.004156	0.001413	5.29E-05	**0.008730**
	(0.00669)	(0.00250)	(0.00614)	(0.00286)
10	0.003974	0.001543	−0.000202	**0.008755**
	(0.00786)	(0.00266)	(0.00768)	(0.00311)

Note: *Significance at the 5 percent level or better indicated in bold; based on the VAR as described in the text and in Tables 9.1 and 9.2.

variables of interest. We report the response of industrial production to shocks in M2 + CDs for the early and latter periods, comparing these results with shocks in asset prices (Nikkei 225 index). Standard errors, shown in parentheses below the impulse coefficients, are calculated by Monte Carlo methods (1000 repetitions). The coefficients in bold indicate statistical significance at the 5 percent level or better.

In the early 1990s, innovations in broad money had large and significant effects on industrial production. In the latter period, however, a positive but statistically insignificant effect of a monetary impulse on industrial production is indicated. The reverse case is again seen with asset prices. A shock to the Nikkei 225 does not seem to affect industrial production in the early period, but persistently large and significant positive effects on industrial production are found for the latter period. In particular, a one-standard-deviation rise in the Nikkei 225 index is estimated to increase industrial production (in log terms) by 0.004 after one month and a further 0.009 after 10 months (equivalent to a 1 unit rise in the index of industrial production).

In sum, the break in the money multiplier seems to have occurred in late 1997 at the time of the banking crisis in Japan. Rapid base money in recent years is not translating into similarly high rates of growth in the broad monetary aggregates, and the growth that is evident is not seemingly effective in stimulating output (unlike the early 1990s). The interest rate channel is cut off due to the zero rate floor, and the transmission mechanism working through the broad monetary aggregates also seems to have failed. Asset price fluctuations appear to be the dominating factor behind the business cycle in Japan since the mid-1990s, and weakness in the Nikkei has depressed the economy. The balance of evidence supports the credit crunch view of the weakness in the Japanese economy.

WHAT HAS HELD UP THE JAPANESE ECONOMY?

Japan is the first major industrial economy to experience a sustained deflation since the 1930s, and the broad outline of deflation, sustained recession, and serious banking problems seems eerily reminiscent of the conditions characterizing the Great Depression. Why hasn't Japan experienced the complete collapse in economic activity seen in many countries in the 1930s?

Japan's economic malaise exhibits most of the general characteristics of the Great Depression, but in a much milder form. The ongoing deflation and recession in Japan have not been nearly as severe as that experienced in the United States, Japan, or Europe in the early 1930s. Wholesale prices in Japan fell 30 percent during 1930–1931, in large part due to the move back to the gold standard in January 1930. (Japan again left the gold standard in late 1931, and prices subsequently rose.) The GDP deflator and consumer prices in the United States declined by 24 percent during 1930–1933. Stock prices in the United States also fell much more sharply in the Great Depression than Japanese stocks in the 1990s. The Dow Jones Industrial Average index in the United States peaked at 381 on September 29, 1929, and fell below 50 by mid-1932 – only 13 percent of the peak value.

The output losses have also been comparatively modest in Japan compared with the depression of the 1930s. Between the time Japan entered recession in 1993 and the end of 2001, real GDP climbed about 8 percent. This rate of growth is not impressive (averaging less than 1 percent per annum), especially by Japan's historical standard, but not a disaster. By contrast, real GDP declined almost 30 percent in the United States in the four-year period ending in 1933, and many economies in Europe also severely contracted in the early 1930s. (Japan was an exception, with net domestic product climbing about 25 percent between 1931–1933.)

There are number of factors in Japan that were more favorable in the economic environment of the 1990s than had been the case during the Great Depression. First, fiscal policy was expansionary in Japan through much of the 1990s. Second, the sustained banking problems in Japan did not evolve into a full-blown crisis (and only reached the crisis point briefly in 1997) due to policy and both public and private institutional structures affecting the banking system. Third, monetary policy attempted to be expansionary – albeit not very successfully – and the fact that the banking system did not experience systemic failure probably allowed Japan to avoid the huge contraction in money growth associated with the Great Depression in the United States and elsewhere. Fourth, the external environment was favorable over much of the 1990s, without a rise in world trade barriers and generally strong growth abroad. The Asian Currency Crisis was the closest counterpart to the external crisis facing the world in the 1930s, but this was concentrated on relatively small economies and was fairly short-lived. The currency regime has been flexible, with a weak yen in the latter part of the 1990s supporting external demand. This is contrary to the deflationary impulses to the economy associated with the gold standard in the early 1930s.

Fiscal Policy

Fiscal policy was expansionary in Japan in the 1990s, although perhaps not as expansionary or effective as could have been desired (Posen 1998). The general government fiscal deficit in Japan (excluding social security) averaged about 8 percent of GDP over the 1998–2001 period, and numerous supplementary budgets since 1993 were passed by the Diet to try to stimulate the economy. The International Monetary Fund estimates the "structural" deficit in Japan at over 5 percent of GDP during 1998–2001.

The downside to a continuously expansive fiscal policy, however, is a rapid rise in government debt that, by mid-2001, had reached the highest level among the industrial countries at 140 percent of GDP. Nonetheless, long-term government bond yields declined after mid-2000 despite surging government borrowing and debt, as well as sovereign credit rating downgrades.

(Banks appear willing to absorb new Japanese government bond [JGB] issues, given the dearth of profitable lending opportunities under stagnant
economic conditions, whereas another condition is the continued support to
the JGB market from the social security and postal savings systems.) Reflecting these trends and the lack of a credible strategy to put public finances
on to a sustainable footing, Moody's Investors Service in May 2002 downgraded the Japanese local currency debt rating to A2 from Aa3 – the same
level as Poland and Latvia.

Fiscal policy was also expansionary in many countries during the Great
Depression, but stimulus was typically late in coming, automatic stabilizers
were much less operative, and the conscious attempt to stabilize the economy
through fiscal measures was a relatively new and untried concept in policy
circles. In the United States, for example, the expansionary policies followed
by the Roosevelt Administration resulted in the unprecedented (peacetime)
federal budget deficit of 5.9 percent of GDP in 1934. Gross federal debt
at the end of the Great Depression in the United States (1939) peaked at
54 percent of GDP. This stimulus is noteworthy and significant, but in today's
context, appears small considering the magnitude of the output collapse in
the Great Depression.

BANKING CRISIS

Banking problems in Japan, though severe, have not stopped the normal
workings of the financial system. The system was threatened with systemic
failure in November 1997, but this was averted by short-term policy measures
and the promise of substantial reform. Indeed, the banking problem in Japan
is frequently termed the "nonperforming loan" problem, reflecting the large
and growing fraction of loans on banks' balance sheets that are not repaying
on schedule. Many of these loans will never be repaid. Disposal of these loans,
and the underlying collateral, is an ongoing task that includes sizable public
monies and bank management restructuring (see Cargill, Hutchison, and Ito
2000; Kashyap and Hoshi 2001). Public funds totaling sixty trillion yen (12
percent of GDP) finally were set aside in 1998–1999 to recapitalize banks.

By contrast, the banking crisis of the Great Depression in the United
States was a clear systemic failure. There were some 9000 bank failures
in the United States during the worst depression years, 1930–1933, before
legislation was passed creating deposit insurance and taking other action to

restore stability and confidence in the financial system. During this time, the money supply (M1) in the US declined by over 25 percent – the largest decline in U.S. history – despite a 20-percent rise in the monetary base (Mishkin 1991).

Monetary Policy

The Bank of Japan tried to follow a more expansionary policy in the 1990s by successively lowering the call money (interbank) interest rates from the peak of 8.2 percent in March 1991 to virtually zero in March 1999. As discussed previously, base money has grown quickly, but the broader money aggregate of M2 + CDs (the key policy indicator) has stagnated. The empirical evidence in the previous section suggests both a structural (downward) shift in the money multiplier in the late 1990s, as well as a structural break in the monetary transmission mechanism. The monetary transmission mechanism works through the banking system, and this channel has been stymied since 1995 – our estimates indicate that a rise in the level of M2 + CDs in the present environment only has a small effect on output. (Asset prices, by contrast, are seemingly much more important in recent years, and their continued weakness is a key reason why sluggishness in the economy has been so prolonged.) Nonetheless, there was not a collapse in either the narrower or broader monetary aggregates. The most disturbing factor, however, is the sharp decline in bank credit.

In many way, the ineffectiveness of monetary policy in Japan at the end of the 1990s reflects that in the United States in the early 1930s.[8] The discount rate of the Federal Reserve Bank of New York declined from 5.16 in 1929 to 2.56 in 1933 and 1.00 in 1939. The rate on U.S. three-month securities (new issues) declined to .5 percent by 1933 and virtually zero by 1939. The monetary base also increased in the United States, as it has in Japan, but the broader money aggregates did not increase proportionately. The similarities stop at this point, however.

Money growth (M2 + CDs) slowed in Japan in the late 1990s (fluctuating between 2 percent and 5 percent between 1997 and 2002), but M1 growth was always more than 5 percent per annum and peaked at more than 30 percent in the year ending March 2002. By contrast, M1 collapsed by 25 percent in the United States in the 1930–1933 period. This difference reflects, in

[8] See Cargill (2001) for a discussion of Federal Reserve monetary policy in the 1930s and some policy implications for Japan.

part, the fact that the banking problem in Japan to date has been much less severe than that in the United States in the 1930s. In particular, Japan has not faced a wholesale run on deposits in the banking system and systemic failure. Again, it is a matter of degree – the Japanese situation is disturbing, but not comparable with the financial panic and collapse in the economy seen in the United States in the early 1930s.

External Environment and Exchange Rate Policy

Japan has maintained a managed floating exchange rate over the 1990s, allowing some flexibility in *pursuing stimulative* monetary and fiscal policies.[9] For example, the yen depreciated more than 20 percent against the dollar in the year following the November 1997 financial panic in Japan. Since the downturn started in 1993, the Japanese exchange rate has fluctuated widely, ranging from 83 to 145 yen/dollar, and has not imposed an overriding constraint on Japanese monetary policy (Cargill, Hutchison, and Ito 1997).[10]

By contrast, the attachment to the gold standard in the 1930s is well known to have played a very deflationary role in the economies at the time (Eichengreen 1992a). Japan, for example, reestablished the gold standard in January 1930, and wholesale prices dropped 30 percent in 1930–1931. (On its abandonment of the gold standard in December 1931, only two years later, prices rose substantially and economic growth resumed.)

Sweden was similarly adversely affected by maintaining the gold standard, and recovery was enhanced when it was abandoned. Swedish consumer prices had been falling gradually and wholesale prices sharply since late 1928, as the workings of the interwar gold standard transmitted deflationary pressures to Sweden. The consumer price index (CPI) declined between 1928 and 1932–1933 and then turned upward. The wholesale price index (WPI) fell sharply from January 1928 to September 1931 and then

---

[9] The International Monetary Fund classification scheme officially identifies the Japanese exchange rate regime as independently floating. The regime in Japan is better characterized as "independent managed floating", however, because the Japanese government is very active in the foreign exchange market (with the most active intervention policy among the industrial nations), has massive foreign exchange reserves, usually intervenes in a predictable fashion following exchange rate changes (leaning against the wind), and frequently attempts to maintain the exchange rate around a particular target range. See Cargill, Hutchison, and Ito (1997), Ito (2002), and Fatum and Hutchison (2002).

[10] McKinnon and Ohno (2000), however, argue that exchange rate management has induced the deflation in Japan.

remained roughly constant, with minor decline, until spring 1933. The WPI then began a gradual rise until 1937.

Japan has also faced a generally strong external environment in the 1990s, providing strong export markets and a large net stimulus to aggregate demand, and little rise in protectionism. The external sector has provided Japan with much of their final demand, helping to stem but not fully offset weakness in consumption and investment. Although the Asian Crisis may have slowed growth somewhat in late 1997 and 1998, strong U.S. and European economies provided a strong net stimulus to Japan. This development, of course, contrasts sharply with the world economy in the 1930s, in which trade was stymied by a wave of protectionism, world recession, and moves toward isolationism through much of the world (Kindleberger 1995).

Is the Economic Environment Changing for the Worse?

Some the factors supporting the Japanese economy in the 1990s are no longer operative, giving rise to concern about the future development in the economy. Fiscal policy has little room for future expansion, and high levels of government debt have already brought about a downgrading of the government's credit ratings internationally. The banking crisis remains unresolved, and some observers point to even greater problems in other financial sectors (e.g., insurance companies) in Japan (Fukao 2000). Finally, world economic growth has also slowed, and recessions in many countries, such as the United States, emerged in 2000–2002.

EFFORTS BY THE BANK OF JAPAN TO STOP DEFLATION
AND INFLATION TARGETING

Despite maintaining zero interest rates, the Bank of Japan has come under intense pressure for the failure of policy to move the economy out of recession and deflation. Faced with growing signs of a faltering recovery, the Bank of Japan took a number of steps to ease the policy stance in February and March 2001, including establishing a Lombard-type facility to provide loans to financial institutions on demand at the official discount rate (ODR), lowering the ODR from 0.5 percent to 0.25 percent, and noting that it would increase outright purchases of long-term government bonds if the reserves target was not met. Perhaps most important, the Bank of Japan made clear that deflation was a serious problem and that its more aggressive policy stance would remain in place until year-on-year changes in the CPI rise stably to zero or above.

An Inflation Target for the Bank of Japan?[11]

In this context, a number of economists and policy makers have called for an inflation target by the Bank of Japan with the intent of ending deflation. However, the focus of almost all the literature on central bank independence and inflation targeting is to establish an institutional framework designed to maintain low and stable rates of inflation against the upward bias created by the myriad of political and economic pressures. Of course, the situation in Japan is the opposite – deflation, bank failures, and recession. Even in Europe, some argue that the "conservative" design of the new European System of Central Banks (i.e., institutionally independent with the primary objective of price stability) may be out of step with the low inflation, high unemployment, and Asian difficulties in the second half of the 1990s.

Deflationary experiences are not common, but there is some evidence from the United States in the 1930s that, had the Federal Reserve pursued an inflation target, policy would have been much more simulative. As it turned out, the tight monetary contraction in the United States at the time exacerbated the initial downturn and banking problems.

By contrast, Sweden left the gold standard in the fall of 1931 and adopted an explicit price level target (Berg and Jonung 1999). These moves were taken at the onset of the Great Depression with the objective of stopping price deflation. However, price-level targeting also mitigated widespread concerns that abandonment of the gold standard would eventually lead to rising prices. Hence, the Swedish case may be the best example to date of how an explicit price- or inflation-targeting regime might work in a deflationary environment such as that faced by Japan in the late 1990s. A coherent inflation-targeting (or price-level-) targeting regime, of course, presupposes that an exchange rate target be abandoned.

Swedish consumer prices had been falling gradually, and wholesale prices sharply, since late 1928, as the workings of the interwar gold standard transmitted deflationary pressures to Sweden. Industrial production declined by 21 percent during 1929–1931 (compared with a fall of 46 percent in the

[11] This section draws on Cargill, Hutchison, and Ito (2000).

United States during this period), and unemployment rose sharply. Against this background, the Swedish Minister of Finance announced in September 1931 that the central bank (Riksbank) was relieved of its legal obligation to convert domestic currency notes into gold on demand. The new objective for Riksbank policy should "now be aimed at, using all means available, preserving the domestic purchasing power of the Swedish krona" (Berg and Jonung 1999: p. 3).

By most measures, price-level targeting in Sweden in the 1930s was an effective way to stop price deflation and help mitigate the depression. CPI and WPI movements followed similar patterns, but the WPI was much more extreme. The CPI declined between 1928 and 1932–1933 and then turned upward. The WPI fell sharply from January 1928 to September 1931 and then remained roughly constant, with minor decline, until spring 1933. The WPI then began a gradual rise until 1937.

The depression in Sweden did not abruptly stop with the introduction of price-level targeting, but the output declines appear to have been mitigated and recovery enhanced by the monetary program. Swedish unemployment rose sharply in 1930–1931 and then drifted upward slightly until peaking at more than 30 percent in spring 1933. Unemployment then began to fall, reaching a 15-percent level by 1937. Industrial production reached a low point in mid-1932, declining roughly 20 percent from the 1928 level. By the end of 1933, however, Swedish industrial production had recovered to the 1928 level and climbed an additional 28 percent by the end of 1934. Industrial production in the United States, by contrast, fell by almost 50 percent at its trough in 1932 and did not reach the 1928 production level again until the end of 1936.

Would Inflation Targeting Have Stopped Japan's Deflation?

The numerous calls for some form of an inflation-targeting regime in Japan (Cargill, Hutchison, and Ito 2000) stem in part from the Bank of Japan's reluctance to "think outside the box" (i.e., going beyond interest rates) in designing ways to pursue a more expansionary monetary policy and in part from the view that a concrete and transparent operating goal is the best way to conduct monetary policy. The nature of this proposal, however, stands in sharp contrast to recent reforms in other countries that have been directed toward inflation control. The concern in the late 1990s in Japan, and an objective of the inflationary targeting proposal, would be to counter price deflation, stagnation, and a potential liquidity trap situation. As with Sweden in the early 1930s, the objective would be to provide a credible and transparent nominal anchor so that the private sector could expect either price stability or a low positive rate of inflation.

There is a strong theoretical argument for some form of inflation targeting, but in practice it appears that a strong commitment to low inflation such as that epitomized by the German Bundesbank may work as well as the more formal legal and institutional approach followed, for example, by New Zealand. Germany, however, has strong public and political support for low inflation rooted in its prewar history. An inflation-targeting regime may well help other central banks maintain price stability in the face of adverse shocks and political pressures.

We have much less experience with inflation-targeting regimes in times of price deflation. The Swedish case is instructive, however, and suggests that inflation-targeting may be an important institutional mechanism to help stabilize expectations in a period of recession and falling prices (also see Fregert and Jonung, in this volume). Although the Japanese economy in the late 1990s was not in a severe depression and facing a worldwide collapse in production and trade, some insights from the Swedish case in the 1930s may be drawn as well as from Japan's own history in the 1930s. In particular, the counterfactual policy stance, if the Bank of Japan had been following inflation-targeting, would presumably have been an even more aggressive attempt at monetary stimulus than that actually followed.

The question, of course, is how would an inflation-targeting regime be implemented, that is, what effective measures could be taken by the Bank of Japan to achieve the target? This is not obvious, but more aggressive purchases of government debt, foreign exchange, and other assets is one avenue to pursue. Indeed, the Bank of Japan announced in fall 2002 that it would purchase equities from banks in the hopes of both providing liquidity to the system and supporting bank balance sheets. Although the money multiplier declined in the late 1990s, it is not zero. And although the transmission mechanism from broad money to real output appears to be weaker, a sufficiently large rise in money would – by all historical precedent – increase the price level. Cargill, Hutchison, and Ito (2000) weigh all the costs and benefits of an inflation-targeting regime, including the political dimension. They argue that the benefits of an inflation-targeting regime would greatly outweigh the risks and that the inflation target should be achieved by much aggressive asset purchases by the Bank of Japan. Inflation targets are a mechanism to keep inflationary expectations within bounds, as long as the policy is both credible and backed with action by both the government and the central bank.

CONCLUSIONS

Japan's modern deflation episode is the first in a major industrial economy since the Great Depression. This chapter considers the background behind the deflation and compares the experience in modern Japan with that of several countries, especially the United States, in the 1930s. A number of features have distinguished the Japanese episode from earlier, more disastrous, experiences with deflation. These include a simulative fiscal policy, a less severe banking crisis, and a more supportive external environment.

Despite Japan's resiliency to date in avoiding a collapse in economic activity, the rise in unemployment and especially the loss of output relative to potential is still very large. Perhaps most disturbing is how long the deflation and recessionary conditions have continued and the possibility that a confluence of negative shocks combined with underlying structural weaknesses could push Japan into much greater problems. It is not clear that the external environment will continue to provide a strong positive stimulus to the Japanese economy or that the banking problems will soon be resolved. Moreover, the fiscal stimulus that has supported the Japanese economy is now approaching its limit – fiscal sustainability has recently been questioned by the financial market and Japanese government debt has been downgraded by credit rating agencies.

The statistical evidence presented in this chapter also indicates a structural downward shift in the money multiplier – the link between base money and the broader monetary aggregates (that are more closely related to spending in the economy) is weaker now than in the early 1990s. The VAR model also suggests that a given monetary stimulus (rise in broad monetary growth) is a less effective instrument in stimulating the economy than had been the case before the mid-1990s. Both of these phenomena are probably related to the continued banking crisis that has made a large part of the Japanese financial system and monetary transmission mechanism dysfunctional. The results of the VAR model also suggest that asset price fluctuations are increasingly important and that continued weakness in equity and land prices have been a factor in depressing the economy.

There is a great deal of uncertainty over the ability of monetary policy alone to pull the Japanese economy out of stagnation and deflation under these circumstances. However, a move by the Bank of Japan to adopt an inflation-targeting regime would provide the zero-interest-rate policy with stronger institutional support. The focus on an inflation target rather than interest rates would also be a welcome change, necessitating that the Bank undertake larger purchases (and a wider variety) of assets to achieve the target. An inflation target and larger asset purchases by the Bank of Japan would be even more effective if the banking problems were resolved, thereby helping to increase the money multiplier and support the monetary transmission mechanism working through the banking system. Adopting an inflation target has few risks and would likely stop deflation much faster than the present course of policy.

PART FOUR

STOCK MARKET ADJUSTMENTS
TO DEFLATION

10 Deflation, the Financial Crises of the 1890s, and Stock Exchange Responses in London, New York, Paris, and Berlin

Lance Davis, Larry Neal, and Eugene White

INTRODUCTION

Since the August 1971 collapse of the Bretton Woods system, financial historians have concluded that there is something almost uncanny about the evolution of the global financial system. They are increasingly struck by the similarities of its origins, the system's continuing stresses, and its occasional setbacks with the origins, stresses, and setbacks that characterized the first global financial system over the years between 1880 and 1914. Both eras arose after a prolonged period of inflation that had disrupted the previous structures of international finance – the outpouring of California gold soon to be followed by the $431 billion (U.S.) in "greenbacks" that were issued to help finance the American Civil War in the earlier period (Dewey 1903: p. 288) and the creation of fiat money to help finance the import of high-priced oil in the later period. Both eras were touched off by a sustained reversal of the previous inflationary experience – deflation in the period 1879 to 1897 and disinflation between 1980 to 1999. Both were, therefore, ultimately the result of a widespread change in monetary regimes – a nearly universal gold standard among the world's richest countries in the first period and a set of monetary rules that restricted the growth of the money supply in the second.

In the two periods, the changes in financial returns – the result of falling bond yields and rising financial asset prices – were both unexpected and significant; and, in each case, they eventually led to a series of financial crises – crises that threatened to become systemic. The decade of the 1990s was beset by exchange rate crises in Asia and the meltdowns of emerging markets in the former centrally planned economies in Eastern Europe. Similarly, a century earlier, the decade of the 1890s witnessed a number of financial crises

271

that ranged from Argentina to Australia and from London to New York. Even the striking convergence of government bond yields leading up to the introduction of the European common currency in 1998 had a precedent in the nineteenth century.[1] In the 1870s, when the major European countries either adopted the gold standard or limited their silver coinage, the yields on their long-term bonds converged more closely than ever before.

The effect of the fall in bond yields in the first decades of the gold standard period was, however, not limited to government finance. Railroads the world over, as well as canals, ports, and steamship lines, had all issued bonds. Such issues were the preferred mode of financing the unprecedented sums that were required to produce the steel rails, rolling stock, ships, and cranes that were used to build the transportation infrastructure that created the then-unprecedented near-merging of the world's commodity markets. As deflationary forces affected the value of the huge inventory of bonds – bonds that were traded on the stock markets of the world – those forces triggered major and irreversible transfers of wealth. Those transfers disrupted existing methods of doing business. Snowden (1990), for example, has documented how this process affected railroad finance in the United States and, then, how the new demands for railroad finance shaped the structure and performance of the New York Stock Exchange over the next two decades.

Similar economic processes were at work in the other major industrial, capitalist economies of the time; but, because of different political and legal arrangements, the effects of deflation were different. We have, therefore, a possible laboratory for a natural experiment in the effect of institutions on economic growth and development. In this case, we can compare and contrast the responses of differently organized capital markets with an ongoing process of deflation. A comparison of the responses of the stock markets in these four countries during the global deflation that terminated in the 1890s allows us to evaluate the effects of, first, different institutional arrangements (focusing on the responses in the organizations most sensitive to systemic financial shocks) and, second, the macro results of the different institutional responses to a common shock (global deflation in this case, at least among the core industrial countries of the nineteenth century Atlantic economy, all of whom were committed to the gold standard). The stock exchanges in each country were well-developed organizations at the time, each providing a well-functioning market for widely held financial assets that were sensitive

---

[1]   Government bond yields for the period can be found in Homer and Sylla (1991).

to monetary conditions and general price development. As detailed in this chapter, they did respond in each case, but in quite distinct ways that were conditioned by their separate institutional environments. These included the political structure, the legal framework, and the economic microstructure for each stock exchange.

Comparing the core industrial countries of the time – Great Britain, France, Germany, and the United States – one finds that each differed from the others in at least one important political or legal respect. Great Britain and France were centralized political systems, with the financial power and the major capital market located in each country's capital city, London and Paris, respectively. But they differed dramatically in their legal systems: Britain functioned on the basis of precedent-driven, judge-decided common law, and France operated with statutory civil codes that were interpreted by civil servants. Thus, in Great Britain, there were a number of securities exchanges (although the numbers fluctuated, between nineteen and twenty two provincial exchanges operated in each year between 1840 and 1914); and, although the exchanges outside London tended to specialize in local issues, until 1912, shunting was common. Moreover, because of the rules of the London Stock Exchange, firms were limited in size; and, as a result, there were no branches of London brokers or jobbers operating in Manchester, in Bristol, or in any of the other "twenty" provincial markets.[2] In France, because of government rules, there was little overlap in the securities traded on the Paris and the regional exchanges; moreover, security broking firms that operated on the Paris bourse were not allowed to engage in any other business.

Germany and the United States were fragmented, federal political systems with financial power dispersed and with regional capital markets that competed with each other. Moreover, Germany had its own version, or versions, of statutory civil law and the United States had its own set of judges who interpreted common law in ways that increasingly diverged from the British cases that were originally taken as the binding legal precedents. In the United States, over the years 1800 to 1970, there were about 200 "local" exchanges that operated at one time or another. That list included such places

---

[2] On the London Stock Exchange, the number of partners in a firm was limited; every partner in a London firm had to be a member of the London Stock exchange, and no member of the London Stock Exchange was allowed to have any business other than broking and jobbing. For a list of the provincial exchanges whose records have survived, see Thomas (1973: p. 327).

as Spokane, Washington, hardly a major financial center. However, there were no constraints on the size of firms operating on the New York Stock Exchange (NYSE), and, although there were local stock broking firms operating in the "regional" markets, they faced direct competition from branches of firms with seats on the NYSE. The result of that competition can be seen in the distribution of business among the NYSE, other New York exchanges, and the major exchanges located outside of New York. In 1910, the NYSE handled 68.5 percent of the total number of all stocks traded, other New York exchanges handled 21.2 percent, and the "regional" exchanges in Boston, Philadelphia, and Chicago handled 10.4 percent. In terms of the value of bonds traded, the NSYE handled 90.6 percent, other New York exchanges handled 1.5 percent, and the three "regional" exchanges handled 7.9 percent (Michie 1987: p. 170). In Germany, the unification of the Reich in 1871 under Prussian domination meant that the great universal banks concentrated their stock market activities in Berlin, at the expense of the Frankfurt exchange, which had been the leading stock exchange in Germany previously. The various regional exchanges in Germany soon lapsed into their respective niche markets, leaving the major market for government, railroad, mining, and industrial securities to the Berlin exchange (Gömmel 1992).

To set the background conditions for this experiment with the effects of deflation on stock exchanges, the next section reprises Snowden's argument for the U.S. case. It emphasizes the forces that were specific to the United States and those that were not. Next, the arguments that are developed are applied to the cases of Great Britain, Germany, and France. Finally, the evidence developed in the previous section is shown to support the conclusion that the financial innovations in each of the four cases was a significant factor in determining the future economic performance of the respective countries. In particular, the evidence indicates that the competitive forces were strongest in the U.S. case – a consequence of the combination of a federal political structure and of the diversity of the judges that "wrote" the common law. As a result, among the four countries considered, the set of U.S. financial innovations appears to have been the most productive in underwriting the future performance of its economy. The British innovations seem to have been less productive for the real economy, as they discouraged competition within the London Stock Exchange. The German regulations were even less productive as they tended to drive trading business by the great banks toward the Amsterdam and London exchanges. The French regulations were the most stifling, as they curbed the innovative impulses of the informal stock exchange that had been the driving source of capital market developments in France previously.

THE EFFECT OF DEFLATION ON THE U.S. FINANCIAL MARKETS

According to Snowden, (1987; 1990), in the United States, it was the continued effect of the deflation on the values of that nation's huge stock of railroad bonds that motivated the innovative responses of the NYSE in the 1890s. Snowden points out that the market response to persistent deflation in the United States – deflation that raised the real price of railroad bonds – increased the wealth of existing bondholders, but then decreased the interest rate on bonds purchased by new investors. Because the U.S. railroad companies were private enterprises that lacked financial backing from the federal or state governments, they had originally offered very favorable terms to bondholders – terms that included not only high nominal interest rates but also a guarantee that the bonds would not be called or redeemed if their market price rose above par. As the price of more and more bonds did rise above par, railroads found themselves in the unpleasant position of having to continue to lay out high fixed nominal interest payments while, at the same time, they faced falling prices for their freight and passenger services. Moreover, they could not take advantage of the falling market yields to replace high-interest debt with new low-interest bonds because they would have to buy the existing bonds at market prices, and they could not turn to the money markets to cover those costs because the value of the collateral available to back new bonds was declining due to the general deflation.[3]

The management of the railroads responded in a variety of ways to this financial dilemma. Their strategies included attempts to maintain high prices through monopolistic cartel arrangements and financing further construction by selling stocks and bonds of newly incorporated railroad companies, rather than carrying out those operations through the established firms. Ultimately, however, their best recourse was to declare bankruptcy and to throw themselves at the mercy of a judge's decision about the appropriate method for settling creditors' claims. At the time, there was no federal bankruptcy law; therefore, railroads declaring bankruptcy not only had the advantage

---

[3]   As an aside, it might be noted that the noncallable provisions in corporate bonds helps to explain why the dramatic concurrent reduction in government debt did not elicit a "crowding-in" effect on private investment (see James 1984).

of suspending interest payments while continuing normal operations during the time that they were in the hands of a receiver, but they also had some discretion in picking the judge, or at a minimum, the state that had jurisdiction over the legal proceedings and that would decide the terms of reorganization (Campbell 1938). In the early 1890s, the series of competitive bankruptcies, had, by the end of 1895, put 25 percent of the total U.S. railroad mileage into the hands of receivers.

The suspension of interest payments to bondholders brought investment houses into the center of the reorganization schemes that were proposed in the series of attempts that were made to restore the long-run viability of American railroads. Three interrelated courses of action were developed and deployed: first, to replace the outstanding bonds with new bonds bearing a lower coupon rate; second, to write down the principal of outstanding bonds at the same coupon rate (essentially a partial default); and third, to substitute contingent income claims, usually in the form of preferred stock, for the existing bonds (Snowden 1990: p. 403). The Union Pacific Railroad, a firm that was not only the largest of the bankrupt roads but a railroad that was also the leading innovator in designing new financial assets, issued stock warrants – warrants that could be converted to bonds if the market price recovered. Across the board, the net result was to restore the profitability of American railroads; and profitability led to a new surge of investment in the period 1897–1907 – investment that was focused on double-tracking, rail yards, and stations rather than on new routes (Neal 1969).

It has been argued that investors – investors confronted with the uncertainty of the future yields on their holdings of railroad bonds – turned to other possibilities for maintaining their rentier incomes. Snowden (1990: p. 405), for example, concludes:

Had deflation and a reduction in yields not appeared in the late 19th century, as market participants expected, there would have been far less incentive for the stockholders of railroads to default. . . . In the absence of the delays created by the reorganizations, the rapid growth of rail capitalization that manifested itself between 1900 and 1913 would have continued to focus the attention of the investment houses and the bulk of investors primarily on the rails. The industrials, on the other hand would not have benefited from the change in investor attitudes that resulted from widespread rail bankruptcy. As a result, the market for industrial shares would have developed more slowly and been shaped to a larger extent by the individual promoters who began the process in the early 1890s.

This scenario, however, although perhaps containing an element of truth, badly distorts the importance of the financial shenanigans of railroads in the evolution of the market for commercial and industrial securities. The sources for railroad finance were not severely limited after the 1890s moreover, investment banks, which had previously focused on railroad finance, were no longer leaders in developing finance for commercial and industrial corporations thereafter (Davis and Gallman 2001). The effects of the railroad reorganizations, however, were reflected in some of the changes that occurred in the NYSE during the 1890s, as Snowden suggests. Although it would be another two decades before industrial and commercial securities became the center of activity on the NYSE, it is certainly true that the market for that sector's securities, especially preferred stock, became both formalized and important in the 1890s (Navin and Sears 1955). Moreover, Snowden is correct when he shows that the returns on these new securities were highly variable and provided investors with a high risk, but a high-return alternative to their traditional railroad holdings.

Although the stock market panics of 1890 and 1893, which demonstrated to investors the risks now confronting them, produced government investigations of the stock market's operations in New York, only the state legislature was involved, and the legislators in Albany were easily and frequently bribed into rescinding threatened regulations. The regulations of the NYSE were, however, revised, but the revisions were made by the operators of the Exchange. The revisions came partly in response to the threat of competition from other exchanges, the Consolidated in New York and the regional exchanges elsewhere in the country. Over time, however, in large part they were revised because the competitive threat of other exchanges was reduced. As competition weakened, the threat of members deserting to other exchanges was reduced. As a result, the NYSE was able to impose more constraints on its members.

In the last decade of the nineteenth century, the Exchange was able to institute two rule changes that strengthened its imprimatur of quality. In 1892, after three failed attempts, the Governors finally established a clearing mechanism – a mechanism that was expanded until, by the end of the century, it included almost all listed securities (Sobel 1965; Wilson 1969). Again, in 1895, the Governing Committee voted to require that listed companies file annual reports, although it is clear that their word was still not law; they received no reports in either 1895 or 1896. By 1900, however, annual reports, including both audited balance sheets and profit and loss statements, became

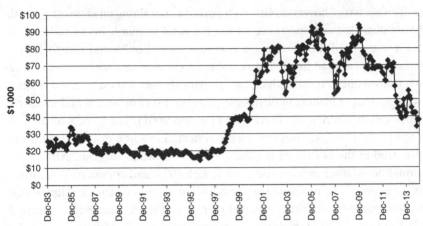

Figure 10.1. Seat Prices: New York Stock Exchange, 1883–1914
Source: New York Stock Exchange archives.

a prerequisite both for initial listing and for retaining that listing (Sobel 1965: pp. 123, 127). Both changes had been long considered by the members to be in their interests, but the competitive threats from other exchanges had previously prevented the Governing Committee from implementing them.

The NYSE's listing requirement had the desired effect of establishing the Exchange as the "blue chip" market, creating an imprimatur of quality that has lasted to this day. The imprimatur greatly advanced the education of the unsophisticated American investors of the late nineteenth century, and, in so doing, it went a long way toward solving the nation's capital accumulation and mobilization problems. It also produced excellent profits for the members holding seats on the Exchange, which showed up in the sharp rise in their prices after 1898 (see Figure 10.1). The new requirements also greatly aided the Exchange in its battle with its chief New York rival, the Consolidated Exchange. At the turn of the century, in terms of volume, about two-thirds as many shares were traded on the Consolidated as on the NYSE. Although competition continued through World War I, the NYSE's policies – policies designed to discourage members of exchanges located outside of New York from dealing with the Consolidated and to deny the Consolidated easy access to the NYSE's prices – appear to have blunted, if not halted, the competitive threat.[4]

[4]   Although on average the shares traded on the Consolidated were lower valued, between 1886 and 1913, the volume traded on the Consolidated averaged 64 percent of the volume of shares traded on the NYSE; and between 1888 and 1896 the figure was 95 percent, and it exceeded 100 percent in four of those years (Davis and Gallman 2001: pp. 321–22).

The improvement in the NYSE's imprimatur of quality also made it possible to alter – although much less violently – its relationship with the New York "Curb" market. Previously, the Curb had existed somewhat uneasily alongside the NYSE. Between 80 percent and 90 percent of its business was carried out on behalf of members of the formal exchange. Gradually, as the Curb became a recognized part of the evolving securities market, its relations with the NYSE became better defined. In 1909, the representatives of the NYSE argued, "the curb market represents, first, securities that cannot be listed; second, securities in the process of evolution from reorganization certificates to a more solid status; and third, securities of corporations which have been unwilling to submit their figures and statistics to proper committees of the Stock Exchange" (New York State 1909: p. 44). By 1900, a listing on the NYSE provided a substantial guarantee of stability, and the Curb provided a market for riskier and more uncertain securities within the U.S. financial infrastructure. The two had become complementary, rather than competitive, organizations.

To sum up, the long-term effects of deflation on the secondary market for securities in the United States did lead to a series of innovative initiatives by businessmen engaged in stockbroking, especially those fortunate enough to be members of the club called the NYSE. Driven primarily by the goal of restoring their incomes – incomes that had declined because of the loss of business as their wealthiest customers abandoned the stock market, the brokers took steps both to retain their traditional customers and to attract a wider customer base. To compensate for the disappointing returns now available in the dominant securities – railroad stocks and bonds – they widened the range of products available. Not only industrial stocks, but also new forms of railroad securities – securities such as warrants, preferred stocks, and bond issues backed by specific forms of new capital – were promoted by the NYSE. To reassure their clients, they imposed listing requirements that, over time, steadily became more detailed and demanding. To reduce the costs of operating the exchange, they finally created a clearinghouse. To limit the threat of competition from competing exchanges, both within and without New York, they tightened their control over access to the ticker tape providing up-to-date price information.

The beneficial effects – beneficial at least to the members of the exchange – are seen in the turnaround in seat prices. From the lowest prices of fourteen thousand dollars and fourteen thousand five hundred dollars obtained on September 24, 1896, seat prices began a steady upward movement at the beginning of September 1898 and rose steadily until leveling off in 1906, before falling again after the crash of 1907. A similar sequence of events was traced out in the three overseas stock markets. However, in France, Germany, and the United Kingdom, because of the differences in political and economic institutions, the outcomes were different.

THE EFFECT OF DEFLATION ON THE OTHER CORE FINANCIAL MARKETS

London

The effects of continued deflation on bond prices and market returns affected the London Stock Exchange largely through the repercussions that the economic difficulties in the United States, South America, and Australia posed for British investors – investors who had increasingly diversified their holdings of securities in the global capital market that British merchant bankers had created in the middle of the nineteenth century. The decade of the 1890s began with a near escape from disaster brought about by the failure of the House of Baring. That failure, in turn, can be traced to Argentina's default on bonds underwritten by what had been Britain's leading merchant bank. The story is well known: The Bank of England organized a bail-out financed by an ad hoc consortium of leading London bankers. Perhaps less well known is the reaction of the members of the London Stock Exchange to the episode. At their meeting on December 22, 1890, the Committee for General Purposes of the London Stock Exchange formally addressed the Governor of the Bank of England, William Lidderdale, Esq., praising him for his actions in the Baring Crisis. The Chair of the Committee, Mr. Rokeby-Price stated,

Being from their position necessarily well acquainted with the unexampled character of this crisis, the Committee are fully able to estimate the magnitude of the disaster which at one time threatened to disorganize, if not to overwhelm, the vast financial and commercial interests of this and other countries, and they are convinced that it was almost entirely owing to the masterly ability with which the measures of yourself and the Court of Directors were carried out in the negotiations in this country and abroad, and more especially to the firm and decisive manner in which your great influence, as governor, was so wisely and courageously exercised, that a panic of unparalleled dimensions was averted.[5]

---

[5] Guildhall Library, MS 14600/63, f.232.

Governor Lidderdale was very pleased to receive these plaudits from the Members of the London Stock Exchange and responded by stating that he appreciated their opinion all the more,

. . . as coming from a body peculiarly well able to judge of the magnitude of the crisis, and of the consequences that would have followed the suspension of Messrs. Baring Brothers & Co., with liabilities to the extent of £21,000,000. What these consequences might have been I hardly dare to think. What security would have been saleable: What bills could have been discounted, if so great a disaster had really come to pass. . . . When you thank the Bank of England it is very important to bear in mind the willing and cheerful assistance that we have received from others. In the first place, from Lord Rothschild, whose influence with the Bank of France was of such assistance to us in obtaining those means, without which we could not have rendered the aid we were enabled to give. Secondly, the help of Her Majesty's Government in the assurance of support if required, a support which it has happily not been necessary to claim. Equally valuable was the prompt assistance of those who subscribed to the Guarantee Fund, without which it would have been impossible even for the Bank of England to have undertaken so enormous a responsibility.[6]

Lidderdale's response to the gentlemen of the stock exchange demonstrates the government's commitment to maintaining a regulatory and monetary environment within which the securities business could continue to flourish. There followed a continued expansion of both the business of the London Stock Exchange and the size of its membership (see Tables 10.1a and 10.1b, and Figure 10.1). As in the United States, between 1893 and 1913, commercial and industrial shares were the largest gainers. The impetus to their innovation came first in the form of so-called debenture shares that permitted breweries to pledge the incomes they received from tied public houses toward payment of the dividends on new capital – new capital that had been issued precisely to purchase the exclusive vending rights to beverages sold in previously independent, free pubs. Watson (1996) has documented the stock market boom in brewery shares that ensued. By the late 1890s, the current rage among investors was mining shares in the new claims created in South Africa. The "kaffir" shares led to such an increase in trading business that special settlement days and procedures had to be created to cope with the ticket claims – claims that often had changed hands many times before the completion of the sale. Meanwhile, after-hours trading in American shares

[6]   Guildhall Library, MS 14600/63, f.233.

Table 10.1a. *Value of shares quoted in the London stock exchange official list,*
1853–1913 (millions of pounds)

Class of security	1853	1873	1893	1913
British Government and U.K. Public Bodies	853.6	858.9	901.6	1290.1
Colonial & Foreign Governments & Public Bodies	69.7	486.5	1031.5	2034.4
Railways	225.0	727.7	2419.0	4147.1
Banks and Financial Institutions	13.1	113.2	199.5	609.1
Public Utilities	24.5	32.9	140.3	435.8
Commercial and Industrial	21.9	32.6	172.6	917.6
Mines, Nitrate, Oil, Tea, and Coffee	7.4	8.8	34.6	116.4
TOTAL	1215.2	2260.6	4899.1	9550.5

expanded to meet the competition that arose as New York brokerage houses
established branches in London to serve their British clients (Michie 1999:
ch. 3).

These new activities, however, clearly bore higher risks for the members undertaking them. Brutal evidence of the costs of risk-taking for the
small, numerous firms making up the memberships in the London Stock
Exchange comes from the accounts of the Exchange's Official Assignees.
These individuals were charged with administering the estates of defaulting

Table 10.1b. *Percentage of the value of shares quoted in the London stock exchange*
official list, 1853–1913

Class of security	1853	1873	1893	1913
British Government and U.K. Public Bodies	70.2	37.8	18.4	13.5
Colonial & Foreign Governments & Public Bodies	5.7	21.4	21.1	21.3
Railways	18.5	32.0	49.4	43.4
Banks and Financial Institutions	1.1	5.0	4.0	6.4
Public Utilities	2.0	1.4	2.9	4.6
Commercial and Industrial	1.8	1.4	3.5	9.6
Mines, Nitrate, Oil, Tea, and Coffee	0.6	0.4	0.7	1.2
TOTAL	99.9	99.4	100.0	100.0

Note: Foreign government bonds payable abroad but quoted in London are not included.
Source: Michie, R. C. (1999), *The London Stock Exchange: A History* (Oxford: Oxford University), p. 89.

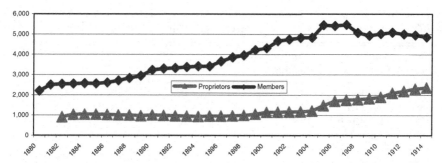

Figure 10.2. Members and Proprietors of the London Stock Exchange, 1880–1914
Source: London Stock Exchange archives.

members of the Exchange until their creditors were paid off, at which time the defaulters could be readmitted to membership on approval of the Committee for General Purposes. By the end of the 1890s, the burdens of the Official Assignees had grown so onerous that their salaries were frequently raised and the size of their office staff enlarged. Table 10.2 shows that there was an exceptionally large number of defaults in the 1890s with an unusually high level of outstanding debts to be discharged by the defaulters.

To confront the problems raised by the increasing number and severity of failures among the members despite the absence of banking or financial crises, a series of protective measures were taken by the rules making body of the London Stock Exchange. All were designed to reduce risks for the majority of the members. The ultimate shape of these innovations in the financial products that were traded on the London Stock Exchange came from the relative increase in the number of members devoted to the brokerage, as opposed to those members who specialized in the jobbing, or market-making, business on the exchange. The turning point in the balance of power between proprietors, concerned mainly with increasing the volume of business and the number of subscribing members on the exchange, and the members, concerned mainly in maintaining their incomes from brokerage fees, came as early as 1875 and 1882 (see Figure 10.2). Changes in the Deed of Settlement – changes that were required to underwrite the finance needed to pay for the construction of larger facilities – increased the original 400 shares to 20,000 shares, and those changes stipulated that all new shareholders had to be members (Morgan and Thomas 1962: p. 144). As the membership continued to increase over the following years, the interests of the proprietors and members tended to converge.

Table 10.2. *Size and number of failed members of the London stock exchange,
1879–1899 (commissions are a fixed percentage of the payouts to creditors)*

Years	Total Commissions	Number of Failures	
1879	£693:16:5	30	
1880	£692:11:10	23	
1881	£1,304:10:0	19	
1882	£2,604: 1:11	27	
1883	£3,180:19:9	31	
1884	£2,038:15:8	32	
1885	£1,990:9:11	33	
1886	£1,038:2:10	12	
1887	£1,554:5:3	20	
1888	£1,680:1:9	25	
1889	£987:5:2	17	
1890	£1,247:15:6	19	
1891	£3,164:6:8	37	
1892	£1,105:1:11	22	
1893	£504:15:3	14	
1894	£4,298:7:10	49	(£151,000 paid in dividends at cost of £2:16:6 p.c.)
1895	£763:7:8	10	
1896	£4,416:12:8	23	(£208,000 paid in dividends at cost of £2:2:6 p.c.)
1897	£1,592:16:6	10	
1898	£1,354:1:5	19	
1899 (ending March)	£3,193:18:3	18	

Source: Guildhall Library, Ms. 14600/65, Minutes of the Committee for General Purpose, October 1896 to 14 July 1899.

Convergence, however, was by no means instantaneous, and it was not until 1945 that the two Committees, Trustees and Managers and the Committee of General Purposes, were finally merged.

By 1912, the members, now largely brokers, voted to enforce minimum commissions and to outlaw the practice of the jobbers shunting trades to outside brokers (Morgan and Thomas 1962: p. 154). Even then, however, the vote was very close (1670 to 1551). The new system did not work as well as its supporters had argued. The regional exchanges proved much more resilient than anyone had expected. As a result, a system that, for almost half a century had underwritten a very efficient national market, was no longer effective. The national market was splintered into a number of only loosely connected regional markets. If World War I had not broken out, it is very likely that the minimum commission rule would have been repealed in 1914. As it was, between the problems engineered by the rule change and the Great War, the London Stock Exchange never fully recovered the international position that it had previously held.

Earlier, in 1904, the members had voted to require that a new member purchase a nomination from a retiring member, therefore providing something close to a property right to a seat. Although initially the costs were not high – between 1905 and 1914 prices ranged between £15 ($73) and £150 ($731) – this change, for the first time, began to place some limits on the number of members – a number that peaked at 5,481 in 1905 (Michie 1999: pp. 85–6). Compare that restriction with the rules that limited membership on the NYSE. On the NYSE, a property right to seat had been established after the merger with the "Open Board" in 1869. The number of members admitted was set at 1,060. Only once, in the years before the World War I, was this figure increased – by 40 in 1879 (Michie 1987: p. 194). Again, in contrast to London, between 1879 and 1914, the prices of those seats ranged from $13,000 to $95,000. The trustees and members of the London Stock Exchange passed other rules that also mimicked, but most often did not duplicate, key features of the regulations that governed the NYSE. These new rules included listing requirements that were intended to assure customers of the quality of the securities available for purchase. The key differences that remained were the much larger membership, the greater number of securities listed, and the greater importance of foreign securities on the London Stock Exchange, as opposed to that of New York.

In Britain, unlike in the United States, the threat of financial crises caused by continued deflation and defaulting debtors was circumvented by the concerted efforts of the central bank and the central government. Nevertheless, the difficulties of sustaining incomes for the members of the London Stock Exchange increased throughout the 1890s, as seen by the increasing number and severity of defaults. For different reasons than in the U.S., then, the problem created for capital markets by continued deflation was left to the London Stock Exchange itself to work out, as was the case for the NYSE. The solutions generated internally within each exchange were similar in that listing requirements were increased substantially for both exchanges and clearing arrangements were enlarged to reduce costs of trading among the members. Gradual limitations on the number of members and moves toward enforcing minimum commissions were initiated in London in the 1890s, in belated imitation of the success of New York, but these could not take effect until well into the new century.

Paris

In France, the government's regulatory role varied with changes in the political regime; but even these rules affected the role of the *Coulisse*, the
informal or bankers' exchange dominated by dealers and speculators, more
than that of the *Parquet*, the formal exchange under government protection
and regulation and inhabited exclusively by bonded brokers. The relative
stability of the *Parquet*'s microstructure, in turn, can be attributed to the
organizational strength of its *Compagnie*, composed as it was of a small
number of individuals with life tenure. Its internal cohesion was further
strengthened when, in 1816, the government asked the remaining individual agents (their number had dwindled to 50 by the end of Napoleon's
reign) to pay an additional twenty-five thousand francs for their offices.
In return, the government allowed each *agent de change* to name his successor. Thus, although the government continued to formally control the
nomination and the disposition of the title, the current titleholder now had
a property right that could be sold. The *agents de change* were no longer
civil servants named for life, but public-private officers possessing specific
powers. The act of 1816 also strengthened the self-governance of the *Compagnie* by restoring the *Chambre Syndical* – an organization that enjoyed
the triple powers of recruitment, discipline, and regulation. The corporate
solidarity that naturally arose within the *Compagnie des Agents de Change*
enabled them to effectively influence the government's policies, and, thus,
to maintain the *agents'* privileged position within France. For the remainder
of the long nineteenth century, the power that the Minister of Finance had
exercised over the operation of the bourse was effectively conceded to the
Compagnie.

In Paris, the *Coulisse* originally served a complementary function to the
official *Parquet*. It provided counter parties to agents of the *Parquet* who
were seeking matching buy or sell orders, but who were unable to serve
as dealers themselves. During the Second Empire, the *coulissiers* expanded
their business rapidly. They organized two separate markets: one for dealing
in government *rentes* and the other for trading in securities that were not yet
listed on the official exchange. The *coulissiers* were mainly bankers who were
dealing on behalf of the large joint-stock banks and the customers of those
banks. The *coulissiers* occupied the outer hallways and colonnades of the
bourse before and after official trading hours. In the evening, they regrouped
in the lobby of the *Credit Lyonnais*. However, when their competition with

the *Parquet's* brokerage business raised the anger of the *Compagnie*, as in 1823 and in 1850, the police were called in to remove them (Boissière 1908: p. 142).

By the 1890s, the volume of business on the *Coulisse* was more than 50 percent greater than that done in the official market. That fact was only discovered when, in 1888, the French government, in response to the crash of the *Union Générale*, imposed a transactions tax on sales in both the *Parquet* and the *Coulisse*. Business on both was slow to recover after the shock to investors of the losses incurred in 1888. As the number of *agents de change* was fixed at sixty since 1815, and the size of the bond required by the government changed only rarely, it is difficult to find a measure of the changing fortunes of stockbrokers in Paris comparable with the price of seats in New York or the number of members and proprietors and the size and number of their failures in London. The only quantitative measure available for Paris is the "filiation" information – the number of cessations of seats for whatever cause and the number of nominations of new members. Cessations could be for any cause – retirement, death, expulsion, or failure – and vacated places were soon taken up on whatever terms might be arranged between the vacating member (or the *Chambre Syndical* in the cases of failures or expulsion) and the incoming member.

Table 10.3, nevertheless, picks up an increase in cessations in 1881, 1882, 1888 (the *Union Générale* crash), and 1894. These were quickly made up the same or following year, however. The jump in 1898 in nominations is the effect of the legislation of that year, which raised the number of *agents de change* from sixty to seventy, and allowed each *agent* to employ a larger staff, especially *remisiers* or shunters. These individuals directed business from the *Coulisse* or foreign or provincial exchanges to the *agent de change* who employed them. The majority of the *remisiers* were traders on the *Coulisse* who were put back in their place as subordinates of the *agents de change* by the legislation of 1898. Thus, like the Curb market in New York, the *Coulisse* ended as a complement, rather than as a competitor, to the official exchange (Boissière 1908: pp. 142–49).

Émile Vidal (1910), author of the National Monetary Commission's 1910 study of the Paris bourse, was also editor of the weekly price listing for the *Coulisse*. It is, therefore, not surprising that he argued strongly in favor of replacing the official *Parquet* with an organization very similar to the *Coulisse*, as it had existed before the regulations of 1898. He felt that the *Coulisse* had been much more efficient and innovative than the *Parquet*.

Table 10.3. *Nominations and Cessations, annually: Paris Bourse, 1880–1914*

Year	Nominations	Cessations
1880	2	2
1881	7	7
1882	8	8
1883	4	4
1884	2	2
1885	3	3
1886	2	3
1887	7	4
1888	3	6
1889	2	1
1890	2	2
1891	1	3
1892	3	2
1893	3	1
1894	2	5
1895	5	4
1896	2	3
1897	2	1
1898	9	1
1899	2	0
1900	1	1
1901	3	3
1902	0	1
1903	0	0
1904	1	2
1905	6	5
1906	3	3
1907	2	2
1908	2	1
1909	3	3
1910	2	3
1911	5	6
1912	2	1
1913	4	4
1914	3	4

Source: Euronext archives.

Unfortunately, his advice was rejected. Not only did the *Parquet* remain the official market, but the redesigned *Coulisse* was reorganized as rigidly as the *Parquet* – with a limited membership and similar internal rules of conduct. Further, it was limited in scope to the forward business of stock trading and to the same, mostly government, government-backed, or government-sanctioned securities that were listed on the *Parquet*. The *agents de change* of the Parquet, however, were compensated in two ways. The number of securities permitted by the government to be listed on the Parquet was enlarged regularly, at the request of the *Chambre Syndical*, and the size of each agent's office staff was allowed to increase. Formal recognition was given to the *remisiers* – intermediaries employed by the more aggressive *agents de change* to bring outside business into the Parquet.

Both markets, then, became effectively arms of the government – arms that helped enforce the government's political policies. For example, after 1895, in an attempt to thwart the rising power of Germany, France developed strategic ties with Russia. As a part of those ties, the government made Russian finance a priority; and, because the government had the right to select the securities traded on the bourse, that policy accounts for the large proportion of French total investment that was directed toward Tsarist bonds. In the case of *dirigiste* France, therefore, the risk-taking in response to diminished nominal returns on their traditional *rentes* was taken by the French investing public, rather than by the members of the organized stock exchanges, as was the case of New York and, to a lesser extent, in London.

Berlin

In Germany, the explosion of incorporations that occurred both before and after the founding of the Reich and the receipt of five billion francs in reparations from the defeated French nation led to speculative manias that ended in the *Gründungkrise* of 1873. That explosion was certainly aided and abetted by a law passed on June 11, 1870 – a law that greatly eased the creation of corporations. The passage of that piece of legislation was the high point of a series of attempts to liberalize the marketing of corporate shares, and it sealed the structural interdependence of that German nation's banks and industry – an interdependence that still exists to this day. The rise of new joint-stock banks after the passage of the law is particularly noteworthy. In the first two years of the new German Reich, 107 joint-stock banks were founded – banks with a total capital of 740 million marks (Gömmel 1992: p. 154). By the end of 1873, seventy-three of the newly chartered banks were in liquidation (Gömmel 1992: p. 156).

Faced with a crisis, and in an attempt to protect the earnings of the remaining corporations, the government's initial reaction was to raise customs barriers. In the longer term, however, as it tried to improve the economic robustness of the nation's business organizations, the government moved to restructure the internal organization of the nation's corporations. In 1884, a new law redefined the framework of governance of German corporations. Each corporation was required to adopt an institutional decision-making structure that consisted of three distinct committees, with each committee serving a different function. The managing board of directors (*Vorstand*) and a general assembly of stockholders (*Generalversammlung*) were features that were common to corporations in all four countries. The German law, however, added a third oversight board, the *Aufsichtsrat* – a board with a large majority of its members drawn from outside the firm. Those members represented, not owners and managers, but labor, the government, the general public, and the banks. The *Aufsichtsrat* was peculiar to Germany.

As in France, the stock market crises of the early 1890s led to further major reforms in Germany. Like the French statutes, the German reforms outlawed the informal exchanges – the so-called *Winkelbörsen* – that had sprung up around the formal exchange. They specified that only transfers validated on the formal exchange would have standing in legal disputes. The new law went further, however, by outlawing uncovered, or short-selling, of securities. As a result, trading in corporate securities tended to move, not merely out of Berlin but out of all of Germany, to the more friendly purviews of the Amsterdam and London stock exchanges. In retrospect, it seems that the formation of the *Kommission für den Börsenenquete* – a commission that included only token representation from members of the stock exchange and a commission that was heavily weighted with representatives of agricultural interests eager to do anything to raise prices of farm products – was responsible for this outcome. But, given that the concerns of a wide range of potential interest groups had been represented in the composition of the *Aufsichtsrat* – one of the three committees charged with overseeing the governance of a corporation – the broad composition of the commission reflected political reality, if not economic rationality.

As a result of the legal changes, trading on the German stock exchanges quickly became concentrated on public securities issued by German state and city authorities. At the same time, the great banks continued their efforts to develop new private sector business in adjacent, politically friendly, countries. Both Austria and Italy were initial beneficiaries of the legal changes and the response of German investment banks to those changes. According to Cohen (1992) and Good and Ma (1999), the initial outcomes have been deemed beneficial for both countries, although more recent analyses of the financial sectors in each country suggest that there may have been few long-run benefits.[7] To continue their active trading on the securities held by their customers, the German banks appear to have had increasing recourse to the forward markets available in Amsterdam and the trading facilities of the London Stock Exchange.

In sum, the competitive responses of the regional exchanges in Germany to the growing dominance of the Berlin exchange over the period of continued deflation created an economic environment in which their clients felt comfortable in seeking alternative political jurisdictions for their activities whenever local legislation or regulation constrained them. The main clients, of course, were the great universal banks that arose after 1848 in Prussia. When the legislation of 1898 limited their possibilities for hedging risks, they found it natural to turn to external markets in search of diversified investments and higher returns for themselves and their clients. Extending their banking activities into Italy and the Austro-Hungarian Empire, and their stock trading activities into Amsterdam and London, with investment banking outposts in New York, they were able to offset in large part the effects of suppressive domestic legislation. By 1908, after the ripple effects of the 1907 panic in New York had passed through Berlin, much of the legislation was modified in favor of the great banks. The international diversity of German investors, however, proved a liability during World War I, the consequences of which were obviously not foreseen clearly by Germany's decision makers (see Ferguson 1999, especially chapter 9).

Summary

By the end of the nineteenth century, all four major stock markets (Berlin, London, New York, and Paris) responded in different ways to the widespread deflationary pressures – pressures that affected both the traders and their customers in very similar ways. Not surprisingly, because the policies adopted were quite dissimilar, the economic productivity of the responses differed markedly between countries. France appears to have generated the least productive response – a response that was characterized by increased central government regulation and oversight. Both the German and British

[7] Longer-term results for Italy and Austria are reported in Fohlin (1998) and Tilly (1998).

exchanges seem to have flourished in the aftermath of the microstructure reforms that took effect in the first decade of the twentieth century; but, on closer examination, it appears that the observed resurgence
in London and Berlin was more deeply rooted in the indirect comple-
mentarity that developed between the broker-dominated market in London and the jobber- or bank-dominated market in Berlin, rather than in
the changes in the rules that governed the markets. Despite the trauma
of the 1907 panic on the NYSE and the governmental investigations and
reforms that followed in its aftermath, it would appear that the competitive responses of the NYSE to the challenges of deflation carried the most
promise for the design of efficient capital markets in the decades that were to
follow.

The exchange's original "draconian" listing requirements – a listed firm
not only had to show a history of profitability, but it had to be a representative of an industry with a history of profitability – was reinforced at
the end of the century with the requirement that a listed firm must annually produce audited financial statements. Taken together, the rule changes
speeded up the process of investor education so much so that, by 1914,
American investors were at least as willing to hold the paper securities of
private companies as were investors in the United Kingdom. Moreover, the
innovation of continuous calls, coupled with the belated introduction of the
clearing house, greatly simplified and, therefore, reduced the transaction
costs involved in buying and selling securities. Again, daily settlement, as
opposed to the London Stock Exchange's practice of periodic settlements,
made transactions on the NYSE much more transparent than their London
counterpart, and that difference also helped relieve the uncertainty fears of
investors. Finally, the development of the complementary relationship with
the Curb market made it possible to maintain the blue chip character of
securities traded on the NYSE, while at the same time, providing a market for those securities that could not qualify for the NYSE's imprimatur.
Unfortunately, this rating of the relative efficiency of the microstructure of
the rules circa 1914 still cannot be tested directly. The effects of massive
government war finance required for World War I, to say nothing of the
indirect impact of widespread military mobilization, overshadowed future
developments in all four exchanges, particularly those in Paris and Berlin.
Nevertheless, it is useful to make an overall assessment of the financial
structures of the four powers as they developed along separate paths until
1914.

Table 10.4. *Financial assets in the national balance sheets of France, Germany, Great Britain and the United States in the nineteenth century (percent of national assets)*

	France				
	1850	*1880*		*1913*	*1976*
Claims on FIs	0.8	4.0		9.7	14.8
Corp'n D + E	1.9	7.2		10.6	6.2
TOTAL Fin. Assets	16.2	28.6		39.3	40.9
	Germany				
	1850	*1875*	*1895*	*1913*	*1977*
Claims on FI s	3.4	6.0	11.0	13.0	18.1
Corp'n D + E	1.4	2.7	3.1	4.5	5.2
TOTAL Fin. Assets	15.2	23.5	36.5	39.5	42.6
	Great Britain				
	1850	*1875*	*1895*	*1913*	*1977*
Claims on FI s	5.9	9.5	10.2	11.4	21.5
Corp'n D + E	5.9	8.1	24.3	18.3	6.7
TOTAL Fin. Assets	35.8	37.5	50.9	47.4	52.5
	United States				
	1850	*1880*	*1900*	*1912*	*1978*
Claims on FI s	4.1	5.3	8.3	9.2	13.3
Corp'n D + E	8.3	13.4	12.6	17.3	9.7
TOTAL Fin. Assets	30.0	37.4	39.9	42.9	47.0

Note: FI = Financial intermediaries; Corp'n = Corporation; D + E = debt + equity; Fin. = Financial.
Source: Goldsmith R. W. (1985), *Comparative National Balance Sheets, A Study of Twenty Countries, 1688–1978* (Chicago: University of Chicago Press), pp. 216–7, 225, 232–3, 300–1.

ASSESSMENT

Table 10.4, taken from Goldsmith's (1985) national balance sheets of France, Germany, Great Britain, and the United States, shows the differences between the proportion of claims on financial institutions and of financial claims on nonfinancial institutions to total national assets in the four countries. Already by 1850, the British and American economies were marked with a much higher proportion of financial assets. In terms of the composition of those assets, corporate debt and equity represented a much larger fraction of total national assets than in the two continental countries. The rise of a global capital market in the latter half of the nineteenth century, especially after 1880 when the gold standard was adopted by almost all industrialized or industrializing nations, underwrote an increase in the share of financial assets for all four countries. However, in the case of the continental European countries, it was the increase in claims issued by financial institutions that rose most dramatically – in France and Germany, the fraction more than doubled – and, among the financial institutions, in the case of France, it was the increase of the claims of joint-stock banks that provided the bulk of the impetus. In that country, the increase in bank claims rose 4.5 times between 1880 and 1913. In the case of Germany, although the claims of joint-stock banks accounted for 3.9 of the 7 percent increase, it was the claims of insurance and pensions that grew most rapidly – an increase of 5.7 times between 1875 and 1913.

The role of the formal capital markets in the industrial growth of Great Britain and the United States continued to expand rapidly, even as both countries experienced major innovations in their financial infrastructure. In the case of the United Kingdom, although the importance of all financial assets in national assets increased 1.3 times between 1875 and 1913, that increase was underwritten by the increasing importance of loans by financial institutions (they rose 1.9 times), corporate stocks and bonds (1.7 times), and claims against financial institutions (1.4 times). At the same time, the importance of government debt and trade credit in the national total was declining – by 47 percent and 6 percent, respectively. In the case of the United States, the ratio of all financial to total assets increased by 15 percent over the years 1880 to 1912. That increase was, however, far from uniform across the types of financial assets. The importance of mortgages grew by 54 percent, insurance by 40 percent, loans by financial intermediaries by 36 percent, and corporate stocks and bonds by 29 percent. Formal consumer credit, nonexistent in 1880, accounted for 1 percent of the total in 1912. At the same time, the importance of government debt declined by 61 percent, trade credit by 51 percent, and currency and deposits by 28 percent. In both the United States and the United Kingdom, the financial infrastructure was both expanding and evolving as new institutions emerged.

This brief overview of the distinctive characteristics of the four leading security exchanges in the nineteenth century indicates that, even in the case of the most highly developed and most efficiently functioning markets of the first global economy, differences in legal and political environments led the four to develop different institutions to perform essentially the same tasks. If the legal environment was broadly similar, as it was for Great Britain and the

United States, the political environment led to a different structure of capital markets. Moreover, by the end of the nineteenth century, even for the two countries that had begun the century with very similar sets of statute and common laws, the legal environments had begun to diverge in important ways. For example, in Britain, antitrust was not to become an important issue until the middle of the twentieth century: There were no statutory prohibitions or court decisions regulating the powers of self-governance by trade groups. The absence of such rules clearly favored the freedom of those organizations to make and to enforce contracts among themselves. In the United States, the courts and then the national legislature moved, first, to make such anticompetitive contracts unenforceable and, then, illegal if they were found to infringe on the freedom of new players to enter an industry and vigorously compete with other already established or other newly created firms.

Regional security exchanges flourished in both countries, but in Great Britain before 1912, they were largely complementary and seldom competed with the central exchange in London for primacy in the market for any except local securities. And because of easy and inexpensive entry into the London Stock Exchange, there were no competitive exchanges in London. In the United States, it was not until after the Civil War that the NYSE was able to establish permanently its preeminence over the older exchanges of Philadelphia and Boston and the rising markets in Cincinnati and Chicago. Moreover, it would be another forty years before other New York exchanges ceased to be major competitors – the Curb (later the American) becoming a complementary exchange and the Consolidated finally eliminated from the market. Nor, as the growth of the National Association of Securities Dealers Automated Quotations (NASDAQ) has recently shown, has the NYSE been permanently insulated from competition.

Further, differences in the original definition of property rights in the marketplaces meant that the NYSE had a constant battle to establish and then maintain its primacy as the central marketplace in New York City. Conversely, throughout the century, the London Stock Exchange was able to encompass all the business in London and to place the regional exchanges in a complementary, rather than a competing, role. The complementary role of the provincial exchanges, however, was threatened when, by 1912, the members of the London Stock Exchange had both established minimum commissions and forbidden jobbers to shunt business from other exchanges. Banks and other financial institutions were expressly forbidden from participating in the British exchanges, although the few originally entering as proprietors were grandfathered in. Moreover, the rules of the London Stock Exchange severely limited the size of the brokerage house that could be members; as a result, there were no member firms operating nationwide, let alone world-wide. On the American exchanges, until the regulatory reforms of the 1930s, almost any firm in any business could form a partnership with a brokerage house or simply buy seats for itself. Because there were no limits on size, a brokerage house with a seat on the NYSE could, and did, operate branches in cities across the United States, in London, and on the continent, as well.

On the continent, where the legal environment provided statutory mo-nopolies for the stock exchanges of Paris and Berlin, the political environ-ments in the two countries were sufficiently different that the rules governing the organization and operation of the central exchanges evolved in markedly different ways. In Paris, a small group of *agents de change* – a group that, over the century, became very tightly organized as a self-regulating *Compagnie* – was, when challenged, able to call on the police powers of the state to main-tain their monopoly. As a result, the rules of the Paris bourse remained essentially unchanged from the time of Napoleon until the breakup of the *Compagnie's* monopoly – a breakup that did not occur until the late 1980s; and, even then, the breakup would probably not have occurred had it not been for pressure from the European community. By contrast, in Berlin, where there had always been open access to the exchange, the structure im-posed by the power of the state guaranteed that nonfinancial interest groups – groups with little interest in increasing efficiency – were in a position to alter drastically the rules of the exchange: As a result, their action greatly reduced the efficiency of the Berlin market and, thus, its effectiveness in helping to solve the twin problems of capital accumulation and mobilization in Ger-many.

CONCLUSION

To conclude, the entire deflationary decade of the 1890s provides a labo-ratory in which it is possible to study the distinct natural experiments that were being conducted with respect to institutional arrangements that gov-erned the operation of the global financial market of the time, an experiment that encompassed both the formal financial markets and the array of finan-cial intermediaries that operated on these markets. The tentative conclusion of this chapter is that those experiments that exploited the possibilities of expanding the scope of financial markets as opposed to strengthening the security of the banks succeeded in generating more rapid economic growth for their economies as the twentieth century began. The higher returns available to investors in these rapidly growing economies came at a cost, however, as their banking and/or currency systems remained more vulnerable to financial crises. The lessons for the new global financial markets at the beginning of the twenty-first century may be that self-interested innovations initiated by the leading participants in capital markets, designed to improve the competitiveness of the formal exchanges (New York) or of the major investment houses trading in the exchanges (Berlin), will be more beneficial in the long run to their respective economies than regulatory constraints imposed by governmental authorities (Paris) or self-protective measures initiated by stockbrokers seeking secure commissions (London).

11 The Stock Market and the Business Cycle in Periods of Deflation, (Hyper-) Inflation, and Political Turmoil: Germany, 1913–1926

Martin T. Bohl and Pierre L. Siklos

INTRODUCTION

With the onset of a deflation in stock prices beginning in early 2000, economists and policy makers have begun to worry that this development might eventually spill over into the goods market, possibly leading to a recession, if not outright depression, and that it is symptomatic of a "bad" deflation (see Bordo and Redish in this volume). The fact that political turmoil, and its attendant uncertainties, is also a feature of current events, stemming from the terrorist attacks of September 11, 2001, the subsequent wars in Afghanistan and Iraq, and a general economic malaise in Europe and the United States just to name a few events, only adds to the fears that deflation ought to be avoided at all costs. Implicit in such views is that financial markets in particular, and economies more generally, operate differently in a deflationary environment than in conditions of inflation. Although it is too early to tell how ongoing developments in asset prices will unfold, it may be useful to examine a period in economic history that has all of these elements to try and learn how widely accepted views about the determinants of asset prices, and their potential links to the real economy, fare under conditions of deflation, inflation, or even hyper-inflation.

More precisely, the aim of this chapter is to provide empirical evidence on the long run validity of the present value model of asset price determination and the characteristics of the short run dynamics away from the long run equilibrium. We also investigate the long run and short run behavior of the link between stock prices and the business cycle. In investigating the foregoing relationships, we depart from the relevant literature in two respects. First, we consider a data set of monthly time series covering the period 1913–1926 in Germany. This rather extraordinary period in German history is one that encompasses enormous political turmoil, a powerful asset price deflation, and periods of alternating persistent deflation and (hyper-) inflation in consumer prices. In contrast, much of the existing empirical work on stock market dynamics has focused on periods of inflation only. The empirical findings in this study permit a comparison with the results of studies that consider only inflationary samples. Second, although previous studies assume symmetry in the short run adjustment mechanisms to some long run equilibrium, we allow the possibility of asymmetric adjustment.

The rest of the chapter is organized as follows. First, we provide a brief description of the period in German economic history under investigation, known as the "Great Disorder." A separate section outlines the theory behind the present value model and the structural booms and slumps hypothesis. Next, we discuss the empirical testing methodologies, followed by a reporting of our empirical findings and their implications for the study of deflation.

DATA AND HISTORICAL BACKDROP: STOCK MARKET
PERFORMANCE AND POLITICS IN GERMANY, 1913–1926

The time series used in this chapter are Germany's dividend-price ratio, a dividend-adjusted stock price index, the consumer price index, and the unemployment rate covering the period from January 1913 to December 1926. The stock market data and the consumer price index are from Gielen (1994), whereas the unemployment rate data are taken from Gleitze (1960). The unemployment data are available on an annual basis from 1913 to 1918. Thereafter, the data are available at the monthly frequency for the period from 1919 to 1926. The availability of the monthly unemployment data determines the ending for the sample period in this study. Stock market data are discussed in detail later in connection with the important political events in Germany during the period under study.

Figures 11.1 and 11.2 show, for the period from January 1913 to December 1926, the dividend-price ratio (or dividend yield) for deflation and inflation samples, respectively.[1] Solid circles represent inflation or

---

[1]   Inflation is defined as a positive rate of change in prices. Deflation is therefore defined as a zero or negative rate of change in prices. No allowance is made for measurement problems (see, however, the following section).

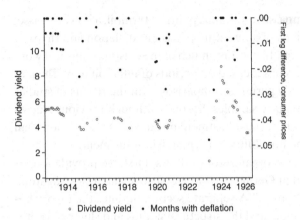

Figure 11.1. Dividend Yields During Deflation: Germany, 1913–1926

deflation in goods prices, whereas dividend yields are shown as plain circles. Notice that episodes of inflation and deflation alternate throughout the
1913–1926 period. The only sustained gap in time when no deflation is evident is in the year and a half period following the end of World War I. Hence,
although deflation is essentially a feature throughout the sample considered,

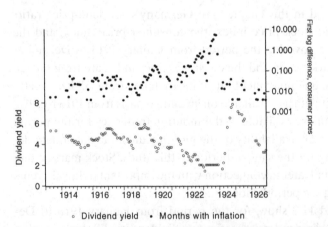

Figure 11.2. Dividend Yields During Inflation: Germany, 1913–1926
Notes to Figures 11.1 and 11.2: Inflation is defined as positive values for the first log
difference in the consumer price index. Zero or negative values are defined as deflation.
For Figure 11.2, logarithmic scaling was used (right-hand scale) because of the inclusion
of the hyper-inflation period.

sustained episodes are a feature of the years 1913–1914, 1917, 1920–1921, and 1925–1926 only.[2]

The correlation between the two time series plotted in Figures 11.1 and 11.2 is negative and significant for the combined inflation and deflation samples (−0.38). When we subdivide the data according to whether there is respectively deflation or inflation, but not both, the correlation is negative when there is inflation only (−0.40), whereas a significantly positive correlation is obtained for the deflation only sample (0.47). We obtain similar signs for the correlations between inflation and unemployment rates as between periods of inflation and deflation in goods prices, although these are not statistically significant (−0.26 for the full sample, −0.27 for the inflation only sample, and −0.19 for the deflation only sample).

Panel A of Figure 11.3 plots the available monthly data for the unemployment rate and dividend yields for a sample that encompasses both periods of deflation, inflation, and hyper-inflation. The theoretical motivation for this relationship is explored later in the chapter when we examine the connection between booms and busts in economic activity and stock market performance. The correlation between the dividend-price ratio and unemployment rates is small. Although the correlation is −0.17 when periods of deflation-only are considered (these are highlighted in the figure), the same correlation is only 0.03, and insignificant, in the months when there is only inflation or for the full available sample. Also interesting is the fact that the cross-correlation between these same two series peaks at the zero lag in the deflation-only sample, indicative of a contemporaneous relationship, whereas dividend yields are mainly highly cross-correlated with future unemployment rate in the inflation-only and hyper-inflation samples.[3]

Panel B of Figure 11.3 extends the data back to 1913 using a proxy for the unemployment rate based on annual estimates. Alternative proxies were estimated, and the correlations reported previously are unaffected by the addition of these additional observations, although, clearly, the proxy is considerably smoother for the 1913–1918 sample than for the subsequent sample. Figures 11.1 to 11.3, as well as the simple correlation coefficients, suggest

[2] Deflation is not just a feature of the current sample considered. There were sustained episodes of deflation previously in 1875–1876, 1878–1879, 1882, 1884–1887, 1892–1897, 1899, and 1903.

[3] Because the focus of the chapter is not the direction of statistical causality; we do not pursue this issue any further.

Panel A: 1919 – 1926

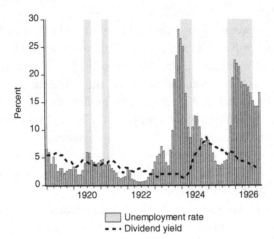

Unemployment rate
- - · Dividend yield

Panel B: 1913 – 1918

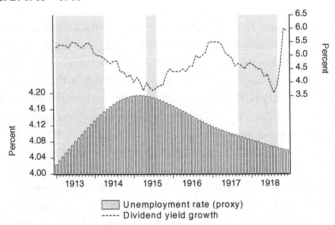

Unemployment rate (proxy)
----- Dividend yield growth

Figure 11.3. Unemployment Rate and Dividend Yields, 1913–1926
Note: See Appendix for the construction of the proxy unemployment rate and the text
for the data sources available at www.wlu.ca/~wwwsbe/faculty/psiklos/deflation.htm. The
shaded areas illustrate periods of sustained deflation (i.e., zero or negative inflation rates
in consumer prices).

that the relationship between consumer price changes and dividend yields
are influenced according to whether we are in a deflationary or inflationary
regime. This result extends, although to a lesser extent, to the relationship
between unemployment rates and dividend yields.

Stock market data used in Figures 11.1 to 11.3 are from Gielen (1994), who relies on a variety of sources to ensure monthly time series without gaps for the 1870–1993 period. Because the period under study is a turbulent one in German history, it is not an easy task to construct complete stock market time series, and the Gielen data are certainly confronted with a number of measurement problems, especially for the period under investigation. Feldman (1993) refers to this period as the Great Disorder. Nevertheless, Gielen's data are widely recognized as the single best source for long-term time series on the German stock market (Bittlingmayer 1998; Jorion and Goetzmann 1999).

For the period that ends with the beginning of World War I, Gielen relies on data found in Donner (1934). Donner reports a monthly nominal share price index and estimates of average yearly dividends. Hence, Gielen's data for the dividend-price ratio relies on an interpolated dividend time series. At the start of World War I, in August 1914, the Berlin stock exchange suspended official transactions to prevent a stock market panic. In November 1917, official trading resumed once again. However, in the meantime, stocks were unofficially traded from office to office and, in mid-1915, the volume of transactions approached the trading volume reached shortly before World War I (Kronenberger 1920).

One consequence of the stock market suspension is the lack of official stock market statistics. Kronenberger (1920) collected monthly stock price data for about 115 companies up to December 1918. Relying on this data, Gielen (1994) is able to construct a simple unweighted stock index. In addition, Kronenberger provides yearly dividend measures from which Gielen estimates, via interpolation, a monthly dividend time series. For the period from January 1919 to December 1926, Gielen relies on official stock price and dividend data contained in various issues of *Wirtschaft und Statistik*, published by the Statistisches Reichsamt.

Figure 11.4 shows the development of real dividend-adjusted German stock prices over the period from 1913 to 1926 and highlights some of the major political and economic events that mark this turbulent period in German economic history. The consumer price index is used to deflate the nominal stock price measure. World War I broke out in August 1914 and was associated with a stock price decline of about 50 percent from February to December 1914. In wartime, real stock prices fell gradually, until mid-1918, and then declined drastically with the signing of the armistice and the abdication

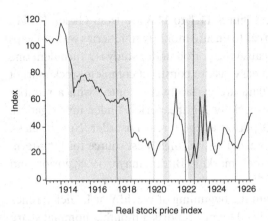

Figure 11.4. Real Stock Price Index
Note: The nominal stock price index was deflated by the consumer price index (see the description in the text). The vertical bars and shaded areas highlight a few key events, such as World War I (August 1914–November 1918), the resumption of stock trading (November 1917), a period of Great Disorder (April 1920–May 1920 and December 1920–May 1921), the suspension of reparations payments (June 1922), the Ruhr invasion (January 1923), the period of hyper-inflation (August 1922–November 1923), the Treaty of Locarno (October 1925), and membership in the League of Nations (September 1926).

of the Kaiser in November 1918. This date corresponds to the end of World War I and the arrival of the Weimar Republic. Germany lost one-eighth of its territory and one-tenth of its population together with a substantial volume of real assets, such as ships, locomotives, and railway wagons.

The further decline in real stock prices from December 1918 to May 1920, was associated with strikes and insurrections in early 1919. In the brief period from March to May 1920, the Kapp Putsch failed, the U.S. Congress refused Germany's desire to join the League of Nations, the Treaty of Versailles was signed, and regional wars in central Germany erupted, as well as fighting in the Ruhr region. Real stock prices reached their lowest level in May 1920. More than two years after the armistice, the Allies, under the London ultimatum of May 1921, set the amount of reparations. The extremely high scheduled reparation payments were the chief bone of contention between the Allies and Germany.

From May 1920 to November 1921, real stock prices increased about 285 percent and declined drastically again during the period from November 1921 to October 1922. Bresciani-Turroni (1937) argues that, after "Black Thursday" on December 1, 1921, stock market investors became more and more cautious and began shifting their attention to foreign exchanges and commodities. Furthermore, German banks restricted credits because they were losing deposits due to inflation. A third explanation for the drastic stock price decrease, according to Bresciani-Turroni, is that the German government imposed significant new taxes and tariffs to reduce its budget deficit.

From the end of 1922, to the termination of the hyper-inflation in November 1923, German stock prices were extremely volatile. The suspension of the reparation payments in June 1922 and the rejection of a moratorium by the Allies are widely regarded as setting the stage for the invasion and occupation of the Ruhr in January 1923 by French and Belgian troops. Bresciani-Turroni (1937) describes the situation of the German stock market during these days as a period of the "most violent fever of speculation" (p. 259). By then, even the rural population was participating in the stock market, "In 1923 the telephone lines that connected Berlin with the agricultural districts were always congested at certain hours, because the country folk sought information on the latest dollar exchange rate and gave stock exchange orders to their bankers" (Bresciani-Turroni 1937: p. 271). Because equities represent claims on real assets and provide the investors with a hedge against rapid inflation, this may explain the growing participation in the German stock market during the hyper-inflation period (Lee, Tang, and Wong 2000).

After the failed Hitler Putsch, and the end of the hyper-inflation in November 1923, stock prices fell until mid-1924 before doubling from June 1924 to January 1925. Possible explanations for the recovery in stock prices include the approval of the Dawes plan in August 1924, which provided for a substantial reduction of the German reparations payments, and the election losses by radical parties in December. From January to December 1925, real stock prices steadily decreased again before reversing course during 1926. Important political events at the time included the October 1925 Treaty of Locarno, which scaled back some allied rights under the Treaty of Versailles, and Germany's membership in the League of Nations beginning in September 1926.[4]

It is against this backdrop that we investigate the performance of asset prices and economic performance to determine whether the links between these variables differ as between periods of inflation and deflation.

---

[4] Stolper (1964), Feldman (1993), and Kolb (1993) provide thorough descriptions of the historical events during the period under investigation.

THE PRESENT VALUE RELATION OF ASSET PRICES, BUBBLES, AND
ASYMMETRIC BOOMS AND SLUMPS

The Present Value Model and Asset Price Bubbles

The basic framework for our analysis is the so-called present value model,
which relates the real stock price, P_t, to its discounted expected future real
dividends, D_t, relying on time-varying expected returns (or discount rates).[5]
The logarithm of the return can be written as,

$$r_{t+1} \equiv p_{t+1} - p_t + \log(1 + \exp(d_{t+1} - p_{t+1})), \tag{11.1}$$

with lowercase letters denoting variables in logs. The application of a first
order Taylor expansion yields the log linear approximation,

$$r_{t+1} \approx k + \rho p_{t+1} + (1 - \rho)d_{t+1} - p_t \tag{11.2}$$

with ρ and k as linearization parameters. Solving forward and taking expectations, we obtain, after some mathematical reformulations, the log dividend-
price ratio,

$$d_t - p_t = -\frac{k}{1 - \rho} + E_t \left[\sum_{i=0}^{\infty} \rho^i (-\Delta d_{t+1+i} + r_{t+1+i}) \right] \tag{11.3}$$

where Δ is the first difference operator.[6] Given that changes in the log dividend and the log discount rate follow a stationary process, the log stock
price and the log dividends are cointegrated with the vector $[1,-1]$ and the
log dividend-price ratio is a stationary process.

   The implication of the present value model (11.3) relies on the assumption of the validity of the transversality condition (see footnote 6) to ensure
a unique solution of the stock price, called the market fundamentals stock
price. If this condition fails to hold, there are an infinite number of solutions.
This provides the opportunity to incorporate a nonfundamental component
into the present value model, permitting one to model deviations of stock
prices from their fundamental value. One interesting case is where a departure from equilibrium produces a bubble in stock prices.[7]

---

[5]   Detailed descriptions of present value models can be found in Campbell and Shiller (1988a;
      1988b), Campbell, Lo, and MacKinlay (1997), and Cochrane (2001).
[6]   We also impose the transversality condition $\lim_{j \to \infty} \rho^j p_{t+j} = 0$ to rule out nonfundamental
      stock price components, and we use $p_t = E_t p_t$.
[7]   Although the bubble solution satisfies the Euler equation, it violates the transversality
      condition and the stock price is nonunique.

Speculative bubbles are mostly defined as nonfundamental stock price increases generated by extraneous events or rumors and driven by self-fulfilling expectations. After the stock price reaches some high level, the bubble bursts and stock prices can resume their upward movement (Blanchard and Watson 1982; Evans 1991; West 1987).[8] Shleifer (2000) provides a model of positive feedback trader behavior in such bubbles. Shleifer's model describes the events occurring during bubble periods more accurately than do models of rational bubbles that focus exclusively on price increases and an eventual crash. In addition, Kirman (1993, 1991) presents a theoretical explanation of how changes in market opinion among nonfundamentalist agents in financial markets may be generated and how these changes may be transmitted into asset prices. Although his model is very different from Shleifer's framework, the Kirman approach also gives rise to bubblelike phenomena in which asset prices exhibit periods of tranquility followed by bubbles and crashes.

Although the above-mentioned frameworks are different theoretical approaches that explain large and persistent departures from the long run equilibrium, all have in common the notion that stock prices may nonfundamentally grow and collapse after reaching high levels. Furthermore, by ruling out non-negative, nonfundamental stock price movements, the models suggest an asymmetry in the behavior of stock prices relative to fundamentals of a particular variety, to be detailed later. Precisely because the historical period under investigation reveals large fluctuations in asset prices, the foregoing situations are relevant to our empirical investigation.

The potential behavior of stock prices previously described can be formally included in the present value model by adding on the right-hand side of equation (3) the term,

$$b_t = \vartheta_t b_{t-1} u_t \qquad (11.4)$$

where b_t denotes the bubble term defined in logarithms, ϑ_t is a random variable with $E\vartheta_t = 1 + r_t$, and u_t is a stationary time series of identically, not necessarily independently, distributed random variables with $E(u_t) = 1$.[9]

---

[8] Unlike speculative bubbles, traditionally defined, Froot and Obstfeld (1991) propose the concept of so-called intrinsic bubbles, which depend exclusively on market fundamentals and not on extraneous events. Although negative speculative bubbles are ruled out in most bubble models, Weil (1990) argues, on theoretical grounds, that it is possible for assets to be undervalued when the economy is in a bubble equilibrium.

[9] This quite general class of bubble processes put forward by Charemza and Deadman (1995) satisfies two conditions that are generally accepted in the literature. First, the bubble process must be a submartingale $E_{t-1}b_t = (1 + r_t)b_{t-1}$. Second, the multiplicative and lognormal formulation for $\vartheta_t = \exp(\theta_t)$ and $u_t = \exp(U_t)$ ensures the non-negativity of the bubble process (4), where $\theta_t \sim IIN(\ln(1 + r_t) - \sigma_\theta^2/2, \sigma_\theta^2)$ and $U_t \sim IIN(-\sigma_U^2/2, \sigma_U^2)$.

If a bubble is present, the right-hand side of equation (11.3) must be augmented by the nonstationary process b_t so that d_t and p_t cannot be cointegrated with the cointegrating vector $[1,-1]$.

Another important characteristic of the bubble model (11.4) is its flexibility to capture processes that eventually burst. Depending on the specific values of r and σ_θ^2, the bubble process can, after a period of stability, accelerate in growth, then collapse, and then restart again. Examination of Figure 11.4 suggests that such forces may have been in play for the institutional and historical reasons described in the preceding section. More importantly, this kind of phenomenon also suggests asymmetric adjustment from a disequilibrium condition. Clearly then, an appropriate econometric test must reject a symmetric type of adjustment when the log dividend-price equilibrium relationship is out of equilibrium.

Structural Booms and Slumps

As pointed out in the introduction, current worries over the impact of deflation in the price of equities originate with the belief that, if current stock prices reflect future economic performance (as proxied by the anticipated flow of future dividends), then such expectations would result in a slump in economic activity. In contrast, rising stock prices might be indicative of future inflation but not necessarily of any recession or depression in economic activity.

Phelps (1994) develops a theoretical link between stock market and real activity, which he terms the structural booms and slumps hypothesis (see also Phelps and Zoega 2001). Phelps argues that there exists a long run relationship between stock market performance and employment growth. The paradigm of the structural slump is characterized by a steep decrease in stock prices followed by a gradual rise in unemployment. Structural slumps are temporary phenomena and do not coincide with a secular rise in productivity. Similarly, structural booms reveal a steep rise in stock prices followed by a reduction in unemployment.

The mechanism is one in which entrepreneurs speculate that, in the case of a structural boom, a jump in future asset returns is anticipated and, consequently, the valuation of these assets should be reflected in the stock market. The resulting rise in the profitability of investment signals a falling unemployment rate. The boom ends when the productivity rise increases investment costs. The slump scenario works symmetrically in theory, although such a relationship need not necessarily hold in practice because other factors may impinge on the evolution of economic activity. Unlike existing attempts to empirically test the booms vs. slumps hypothesis that rely on samples with persistent inflation, the present application encompasses periods of deflation as well as inflation, thereby providing a more direct test of the potential for asymmetry between periods of booms and slumps in asset prices and economic activity.

There is, of course, voluminous literature supporting the notion of asymmetries in business cycles (e.g., Neftci 1984). A good deal of empirical support also exists for the view that asymmetries may partly originate from the differential impact of monetary policies during recessions and booms (e.g., Balke and Wynne 1996). The objective here, then, is to demonstrate empirically the existence of asymmetry in deviations from the long run equilibrium relationship between economic activity and stock market performance that is fundamental to the structural booms and slumps hypothesis. Because there may exist an asymmetric relationship between dividends, reflecting the "fundamentals" in the economy and stock prices, it seems natural to consider that it is paralleled by another asymmetry linking the stock market and the business cycle.

ECONOMETRIC TESTING: COINTEGRATION AND THRESHOLD ADJUSTMENT

The versions of the present value and structural booms and slumps hypotheses we rely on in this study require econometric techniques that are capable of capturing asymmetric adjustments to some long run equilibrium condition. In other words, we need to specify a model that permits asymmetric adjustment around a stationary time series, or a linear cointegrating relationship. Consequently, we first apply the technique of Enders and Granger (1998) to empirically explore the implications of the present value model. Next, the testing framework developed by Enders and Siklos (2001) is used in an investigation of Phelps' booms and slumps hypothesis.

Enders and Granger (1998) point out that conventional unit root tests will be mis-specified if changes of the errors in the augmented Dickey-Fuller test equation are not symmetric. Hence, we can write,

$$\Delta(d - p)_t = \alpha_0 + \alpha_1 t + I_t \rho_1 (d - p)_{t-1} + (1 - I_t)\rho_2 (d - p)_{t-1}$$
$$+ \sum_{i=1}^{l} \gamma_i \Delta(d - p)_{t-1} + \upsilon_t \tag{11.5}$$

where d_t and p_t have been previously defined, and the indicator variable is given by,

$$
I_t = \begin{cases} 1, & \text{if } \Delta(d-p)_{t-1} \geq \tau \\ 0, & \text{if } \Delta(d-p)_{t-1} < \tau \end{cases} . \tag{11.6}
$$

τ denotes the value of the threshold. The model specifies a threshold such that when *changes* in the log dividend-price ratio exceed the threshold τ, this triggers a shift into a different degree of dependence on the past, whereas the resort to lagged dependent variables indicates that the model is autoregressive in nature. Hence, such models are referred to as "momentum" threshold autoregressive models, or MTAR. The model sets up the null hypothesis of a unit root in the log dividend-price ratio, that is, $H_0 : \rho_1 = 0$, $H_0 : \rho_2 = 0$, and $H_0 : \rho_1 = \rho_2 = 0$. If the null hypothesis is rejected, the null hypothesis of symmetric adjustment $H_0 : \rho_1 = \rho_2$ can be tested. In case the null hypothesis $H_0 : \rho_1 = \rho_2$ is not rejected, we can conclude in favor of a linear and symmetric adjustment in the log dividend-price ratio.

The MTAR technique is designed to detect empirically the bubble process outlined previously because the theoretical potential for positive, but not negative, bubbles and the characteristic of run-ups in stock prices before a crash suggest an asymmetry in the development of the log dividend-price ratio. This bubble behavior is captured via changes in $(d-p)_{t-1}$ below the threshold followed by a sharp increase to the threshold, whereas the path of changes in $(d-p)_{t-1}$ above the threshold does not imply the eruption of a bubble followed by a collapse in asset prices.

$\Delta(d-p)_t < \tau$ signals a rise in stock prices relative to dividends followed by a crash where, according to the bubble hypothesis, the departures from present value prices can be large and persistent. In contrast, in the event of a decrease in stock prices relative to dividends, that is, $\Delta(d-p)_t > \tau$, a return back to the equilibrium position is not expected. The implication then is asymmetric behavior in departures from the equilibrium that is indicative of the presence of bubbles that eventually burst. Therefore, if the estimated coefficient $\hat{\rho}_2$ in (11.5) is statistically significant, negative, and larger in absolute value relative to the parameter $\hat{\rho}_1$, such that the null hypothesis of symmetric adjustment $H_0 : \rho_1 = \rho_2$ is rejected, evidence is consistent with the existence of bubbles in stock prices. Hence, a test of the null hypothesis of a unit root against the alternative of stationarity with MTAR adjustment permits an empirical investigation of bubbles in stock prices.

The technique of Enders and Siklos (2001) is ideally suited to finding a long run link between the variables of interest with short run departures that are asymmetric, as found in the vast literature on business cycle movements over time. Because the structural booms and slumps hypothesis outlined in the previous section is bivariate, as is the Enders-Siklos test, it is a suitable approach to testing the hypothesis of interest. The cointegrating regression of Phelps and Zoega (2001) is written as,

$$p_t = \alpha_0 + \alpha_1 u_t + \varepsilon_t \tag{11.7}$$

where p_t is the logarithm of real stock prices and u_t denotes the level of the unemployment rate in percent. We assume that both time series are individually integrated of order one. Relying on (11.7), the auxiliary regression,

$$\Delta\hat{\varepsilon}_t = I_t \rho_1 \hat{\varepsilon}_{t-1} + (1 - I_t)\rho_2 \hat{\varepsilon}_{t-1} + \sum_{i=1}^{l} \gamma_i \Delta\hat{\varepsilon}_{t-i} + \upsilon_t \tag{11.8}$$

is performed using the indicator variable,

$$I_t = \begin{cases} 1, & \text{if } \hat{\varepsilon}_{t-1} \geq \tau \\ 0, & \text{if } \hat{\varepsilon}_{t-1} < \tau \end{cases} \tag{11.9}$$

with τ as the value of the threshold. Although the Enders-Siklos approach also allows specification of the short run adjustment process in an MTAR formulation, investigating Phelps' structural booms and slumps hypothesis suggests a preference for a simple threshold autoregressive, or TAR, specification. The only difference between (11.6) and (11.9) is that the degree of persistence is now influenced by whether we are above or below the equilibrium defined by the threshold τ in levels instead of changes in the levels. In principle, there is nothing to prevent testing the relationship of interest using the MTAR approach (indeed we have done so but do not report the results here), but the TAR framework captures the flavor of Phelps' hypothesis, namely that a large enough deviation between stock prices and unemployment levels is required to trigger the return to an equilibrium position.

Accordingly, the indicator variable in (11.9) depends on the level of $\hat{\varepsilon}_{t-1}$ and not on the previous periods' change in $\hat{\varepsilon}_{t-1}$, as in the MTAR specification (11.6). The adjustment is modeled by $\rho_1\hat{\varepsilon}_{t-1}$ if the residuals from the cointegrating regression (11.7) are above the threshold and by the term $\rho_2\hat{\varepsilon}_{t-1}$ if the residuals are below the threshold. As argued previously, the MTAR specification is used to investigate the existence of speculative bubbles due to its ability to model sharp movements back to the equilibrium position. In the case of the structural booms and slumps hypothesis, the TAR specification seems to be more appropriate because departures from the equilibrium are interpreted as creating forces to restore the long run relationship if the size of the departure is larger than some threshold.

The TAR model, as is true of the MTAR model outlined previously, sets up the null hypothesis of no cointegration $H_0 : \rho_1 = 0$, $H_0 : \rho_2 = 0$ and $H_0 : \rho_1 = \rho_2 = 0$. If the null hypothesis of no cointegration is rejected, the null hypothesis of symmetric adjustment, $H_0 : \rho = \rho_2$, can be tested. The nonrejection of the null hypothesis $H_0 : \rho = \rho_2$ can be considered as evidence of a cointegrating relationship between p_t and u_t with linear and symmetric adjustment, and the rejection of $H_0 : \rho = \rho_2$ refers to the case asymmetric adjustment.

EMPIRICAL RESULTS

MTAR Estimates of the Log Dividend-Price Ratio

The relevant results are shown in Table 11.1. We first describe the empirical results based on the present value model. We consider both the conventional augmented Dickey-Fuller (ADF; 1981) test (ADF) and the MTAR test described in the previous section for the logarithm of the dividend-price ratio time series. We investigate the 1913:1–1926:12 period, as well as the subsamples 1918:12–1926:12 and 1918:12–1923:11. The subsample selections are motivated by the end of World War I in November 1918 and the end of the hyper-inflation in November 1923. In addition, we perform tests for the 1918:12–1926:12 period by excluding observations covering the hyper-inflation sample (August 1922 to November 1923) consistent with the Cagan (1956) definition.

The standard ADF tests provide mixed results. We cannot reject the null hypothesis of a unit root in the logarithm of the dividend-price ratio in five of eight cases considered. Possible explanations for this finding could be the well-known low power of ADF tests in small samples, the existence of outliers, structural breaks, or, as emphasized in this chapter, the presence of asymmetric adjustment. In contrast to the ADF results, all $\hat{F}_C$ statistics are significant and reject the null hypothesis of a unit root in the log dividend-price ratio. This finding can be interpreted as evidence in favor of a cointegrating relationship between p_t and d_t with cointegrating vector $[1,-1]$,

Table 11.1. *Testing for asymmetric adjustment in the dividend-price ratio: ADF vs. MTAR approaches*

		Samples			
		1913:1 −26:12	1918:12 −26:12	1918:12 −1926:12#	1918:12 −23:11
ADF	C	−2.45	−2.05	−3.79[†]	−1.28
	C, T	−2.51	−2.05	−3.86*	−3.16*
$\hat{\tau}$	C	−0.03	−0.11	0.37	−0.11
	C, T	−0.03	−0.10	0.37	−0.09
$\hat{\rho}_1$	C	−0.01 (0.48)	−0.02 (0.72)	0.63 (1.86)	0.02 (0.48)
	C, T	−0.02 (0.58)	−0.02 (0.72)	0.68 (1.91)	−0.27 (2.56)[‡]
$\hat{\rho}_2$	C	−0.13 (3.59)[‡]	−0.21 (3.41)[‡]	−0.12 (4.10)[‡]	−0.34 (3.94)[‡]
	C, T	−0.13 (3.51)[‡]	−0.21 (3.39)[‡]	−0.12 (4.18)[‡]	−0.72 (4.17)[‡]
$\hat{F}_C$	C	6.61[†]	6.09[†]	10.00[‡]	7.87[‡]
	C, T	6.36*	6.02*	10.36[‡]	11.99[‡]
$\hat{F}_A$	C	7.00[‡]	7.71[‡]	4.87[‡]	14.35[‡]
	C, T	6.24[†]	7.58[‡]	5.04[†]	4.90[†]
l	C	1	1	1	—
	C, T	1	1	1	—

Note: ADF indicates *t*-statistics of the augmented Dickey-Fuller test, $\hat{\tau}$ the consistently estimated threshold (Chan 1993), $\hat{\rho}_1$ and $\hat{\rho}_2$ the estimated parameters of the MTAR model with *t*-statistics in parentheses, $\hat{F}_C$ and $\hat{F}_A$ the *F*-statistics for the null hypothesis of no cointegration and symmetry, respectively, and l the lag length. C and T are, respectively, the constant and deterministic trend terms. The regression denoted by # excludes the observations of the hyper-inflation period (August 1922 to November 1923). Lag lengths are selected according to the criteria of statistically significant coefficients at the 5 percent level. *, †, and ‡ denote significant statistics at the 10 percent, 5 percent, and 1 percent level, respectively (MacKinnon 1991; Enders and Granger 1998; Enders and Siklos 2001).

that is, the stationarity of the log dividend-price ratio. Hence, our empirical evidence supports the long run validity of the present value model with time-varying expected returns for the German stock market in this extraordinary period consisting of a mix of inflationary and deflationary periods.

Furthermore, although all the $\hat{\rho}_2$ parameters are statistically significant and negative at the 1 percent level, the $\hat{\rho}_1$ coefficients are, in a majority of cases, insignificantly different from zero. Of particular interest is the high positive $\hat{\rho}_1$ estimated parameter found in the regression for the 1918:12–1926:12 period, excluding the observations for the hyper-inflation period. More importantly, the point estimates for the parameter $\hat{\rho}_2$ are higher in absolute terms compared with the estimated $\hat{\rho}_1$ coefficients, whereas the $\hat{F}_A$ statistics reject the null hypothesis of symmetric adjustment. The findings are insensitive with respect to the chosen deterministic specification or the sample period.

According to the results based on the MTAR model, adjustments to large changes in the log dividend-price ratio below the equilibrium are faster than for short run adjustments above the long run equilibrium. This finding supports our view that, over the period in German economic history considered here, short run stock price increases, relative to fundamentals, were followed by a crash. Hence, in the short run, German share prices exhibit large and persistent deviations from the long run equilibrium driven by speculative bubbles and/or noise trading. However, in the long run, stock prices in Germany, even during the period of the Great Disorder, adhere to fundamentals. The empirical evidence in favor of the long run validity of the present value model of stock prices and supportive for short run bubblelike stock price behavior is also consistent with the findings contained in Bohl and Siklos (2004) for a long time series (1871–2001) of U.S. data that also mixes periods of persistent inflation and deflation in both goods prices and asset prices.

Evidence for Phelps' Booms and Slumps Hypothesis

Table 11.2 presents the cointegration test results based on the TAR approach to investigate the empirical validity of Phelps' structural booms and slumps hypothesis. The chosen samples are identical to those considered in tests of the present value model. With one exception, the $\hat{F}_C$ statistics reject the null hypothesis of no cointegration between the stock price and the unemployment rate. This evidence can be interpreted as indicative of a stable long run relationship between the performance of the stock market and economic activity. As can be seen from the estimated long run cointegrating parameters $\hat{\alpha}_1$, in the majority of cases, increases (decreases) in unemployment are related to stock price decreases (increases). Given a stable relationship between unemployment and real output, business cycle booms (slumps) are related to stock price increases (decreases), which is economically sensible. The fact that the samples considered include periods of deflation and inflation appear not to make any difference to the results.

Based on the t-statistics for the $\hat{\rho}_2$ coefficients and the $\hat{F}_A$-statistics, the hypothesis of symmetric adjustment is uniformly rejected. Furthermore,

Table 11.2. *Cointegration tests for the structural booms and slumps hypothesis: conventional vs. TAR approaches*

	Samples			
	1913:1 −26:12	1918:12 −26:12	1918:12 −1926:12[#]	1918:12 −23:11
$\hat{\alpha}_1$	−0.02	0.009	−0.03	−0.02
CRADF	−2.61	−4.19[†]	−1.85	−3.29[†]
$\hat{\tau}$	−0.52	−0.27	−0.42	−0.30
$\hat{\rho}_1$	−0.01	−0.12	−0.004	−0.13
	(0.51)	(1.88)*	(0.21)	(1.38)
$\hat{\rho}_2$	−0.12	−0.37	−0.06	−0.35
	(3.94)[‡]	(5.04)[‡]	(2.52)[†]	(3.72)[‡]
$\hat{F}_C$	7.88[†]	13.27[‡]	3.21	7.26[†]
$\hat{F}_A$	8.60[‡]	7.45[‡]	2.95*	3.16[†]
l	1, 5	1, 5	1	1, 5

Note: CRADF indicates t-statistics of the cointegrating regression augmented Dickey-Fuller test, $\hat{\tau}$ the estimated threshold (Chan 1993), $\hat{\rho}_1$ and $\hat{\rho}_2$ the estimated parameters of the TAR model with t-statistics in parentheses, $\hat{F}_C$ and $\hat{F}_A$ the F-statistics for the null hypothesis of no cointegration and symmetry, respectively, and l the lag length. The regression denoted by # excludes the observations of the hyper-inflation period (August 1922 to November 1923).*, †, and ‡ denote significant statistics at the 10 percent, 5 percent, and 1 percent level, respectively (MacKinnon 1991; Enders and Siklos 2001).

the values of the $\hat{\rho}_2$ parameters are higher in absolute terms compared with the $\hat{\rho}_1$ coefficients. Hence, real stock prices below the long run equilibrium represent a stronger attractor than when real stock prices are above equilibrium. Deviations from the long run equilibrium relationship between economic activity and stock market performance are therefore asymmetric in nature. The short run asymmetry in the log dividend-price ratio discovered previously seems to be reflected in the asymmetry between economic activity and stock market performance.

Siklos (2002a) provides empirical evidence on Phelps' booms and slumps hypothesis for the United Kingdom and the United States, relying on quarterly data from 1960 to 1999 and using also the TAR technique. Siklos' findings are comparable with the ones in this chapter. Although not providing evidence on the long run relationship between stock prices and the unemployment rate, the short run adjustment mechanism is for both countries asymmetric in nature. In case of the United States, the speed of adjustment below the equilibrium is faster than above the long run relationship, and this is again consistent with the findings for Germany over the period of the Great Disorder. Therefore, alternating periods of deflation and inflation,

combined with tumultuous events, do not upset the fundamental equilibrium relationship in question.

SUMMARY AND CONCLUSIONS

The enormous political instability during the period from 1913 to 1926 in
Germany, combined with powerful asset price deflation tendencies as well
as periods of persistent deflation and (hyper-) inflation in consumer prices,
offers a unique opportunity to study stock market dynamics under extraordinary conditions. Empirical work on stock market issues, such as investigations of the present value model and the relationship between stock price developments and the business cycle, has been almost exclusively undertaken
in samples characterized by positive inflation rates. Indeed, there has been
no specific attempt to ask, Are there differences in the empirical findings
of the studies undertaken for inflationary periods and the extraordinarily
volatile period in German history that mixes inflation, deflation, and even
hyper-inflationary periods?

In the present chapter, we address this question by relying on a present
value model with time-varying expected returns that incorporates a nonfundamental bubblelike process (Campbell and Shiller 1988a, 1988b; Charemza
and Deadman 1995), as well as Phelps' (1994) structural booms and slumps
hypothesis. We then rely on time series techniques designed to capture asymmetries in adjustment mechanisms to the long run equilibrium relationship
(Enders and Granger 1998; Enders and Siklos 2001).

Our principal conclusions are as follows. First, the empirical evidence
supports the long run validity of the present value model with time-varying
expected returns for the German stock market in the politically turbulent
period referred to as the Great Disorder. Nevertheless, in the short run,
German share prices exhibit large and persistent deviations from the long
run equilibrium, which may be driven by speculative bubbles and/or noise
trading activities as nonfundamental factors. Second, the empirical findings
on the booms and slumps hypothesis show that a stable long run relationship
between the performance of the stock market and economic activity exists
despite alternating episodes of deflation and inflation in both consumer and
asset prices. Business cycle booms (slumps) seem to be related in the long
run to stock price increases (decreases), and the short run deviations are
asymmetric in nature.

When comparing our empirical findings with existing results in the relevant literature, we find the differences to be negligible. The long run validity of the present value model as well as evidence in favor of the existence of nonfundamental components in stock prices in the short run have also been reported using U.S. data covering a long time span (Bohl and Siklos 2004). In addition, short run asymmetries in the adjustment mechanism in the stock price-unemployment relationship have been reported in Siklos (2002b) for the United States and the United Kingdom for the post–World War II periods during which neither economy experience any deflation. These findings indicate that periods of inflation and deflation in consumer prices cannot explain asset price and economic performance in Germany in the 1913–1926 sample.

12 Deflationary Pressures and the Role of Gold Stocks: 1929, 1987, and Today

Richard C. K. Burdekin and Marc D. Weidenmier

INTRODUCTION

After the U.S. stock market plunged in October 1929, deflation in asset prices was soon followed by declining goods prices as well. Although this episode has attracted enormous scrutiny over the years, surprisingly little attention has been paid to the fact that one of the very few, if not only, areas of appreciation during the bleak years after 1929 was in the stock prices of gold and silver producers. The largest gold producer at the time, Homestake Mining, enjoyed greater than 500 percent capital appreciation between October 1929 and December 1935, even as the Dow Jones index lost almost two-thirds of its value. These gains occurred in the midst of financial turmoil and massive bank failures, with nearly one-third of all U.S. banks failing between 1930 and 1933. At the same time, the great out-performance of gold stocks over this period proves that gold stocks do not require inflationary conditions in order to prosper.[1] Indeed, the recent strength of gold stocks after 2000 has again occurred under conditions in which the threat of deflation again appears much more imminent than that of inflation – as reflected in the sharp rate cuts eventually taking the federal funds rate target down to 1 percent.

In this chapter, we assess the performance of gold stocks following two more recent stock market crashes (post–October 1987 and post–March 2000) in relation to the experience with Homestake Mining after the 1929 crash.

---

[1] The link between gold and inflation may have been overemphasized in the modern era as well. Mahdavi and Zhou (1997) find the price of gold did not function as a good leading indicator of inflation over the 1970–1994 period. Meanwhile, Jaffe (1989) suggests that returns on the Toronto Stock Exchange gold stock index were not significantly related to changes in the consumer price index over the 1971–1987 period, and Larsen and McQueen (1995) find that gold stocks (albeit not gold bullion itself) were a poor hedge against expected inflation over the 1971–1992 period.

Although no consistent gold stock index is available for the 1930s (hence, our use of Homestake as a single proxy for the industry) for both the later periods, we examine the performance of the Philadelphia XAU index of major precious metal stocks as well as the alternative Standard and Poors (S & P) Gold Index.[2] We have not included data from the 1973–1974 major stock market decline, when gold stocks again gained while the Dow Jones index plunged (losing nearly half its value) because of the disruptive effects arising from Nixon's closing of the "gold window" in August 1971 – that eliminated the last formal link between the dollar and gold – coupled with speculation about possible future sales of government stocks of gold (Salant and Henderson, 1978). The first U.S. government gold auction in December 1974 was, in fact, followed by the restoration of the right of individual Americans to own gold on January 1, 1975 – and there was a temporary reversal of the rise in the gold price at this time.

Just as the benefits of gold stocks as a hedge against inflation are open to question, so too have observers cast doubt on the usefulness of gold as a hedge against overall stock market declines. Chua, Sick, and Woodward (1990) find that the correlation between the Toronto Stock Exchange Gold Index and the broad U.S. S & P 500 index increased markedly between the 1970s and the 1980s. Indeed, they find that the "beta" of the Gold Index (i.e., its co-movement with respect to the S & P 500) rose above unity over the 1980–1988 period, suggesting therefore that gold stocks actually *added* to systematic market risk. Given that the 1970s experience may have been distorted not only by the renewed opening up of the gold market but also by the disruptive effects of both the Hunt brothers' attempt to corner the silver market and the Iranian revolution and energy crisis at the end of the decade,[3] it is not clear how much confidence one should place in conclusions based on 1970s data that "gold-related holdings tend to appreciate when other securities decline in value" (McDonald and Solnik 1977: p. 32).

In this chapter, we find that examination of the performance of gold stocks following the October 1987 market crash (when the Dow Jones index lost nearly 20 percent in single day) really does not offer much, if any, support for

[2] While the XAU and S & P gold indices include multiple gold- and silver-producing companies, each is dominated by two or three large corporations. Newmont Mining, Barrick Gold, and Anglogold together recently accounted for more than two-thirds of the XAU index, for example.

[3] Cheung and Lai (1993) point to the importance of these events and find that the long run properties of gold returns are critically sensitive to the inclusion or exclusion of data from the single year of 1979.

the premise that gold stocks necessarily offer a useful hedge against broad market declines. Over the period surrounding this sharp market, decline we find a positive beta for gold stocks that is quite close to one. Moreover, gold stocks rise with the general market in the first half of 1987 and thereafter decline at the same time that the broad market encounters weakness.[4] It may be premature to write-off the usefulness of gold stocks on the basis of the 1987 experience, however. After all, the market recovery was itself very quick and there were no signs of serious financial sector problems of the kind that emerged after the 1929 crash. That is, although there is abundant evidence that gold stocks do not *consistently* offer offsetting risks or *always* move opposite the overall trend in asset prices, it is still possible that they perform this role under sufficiently extreme circumstances. And the defensive benefits of gold stocks during the Great Depression have been supplemented by the recent trend for gold stocks to rise as the broad market declines. Such an offsetting move in gold stocks is clearly evident if we focus our attention on the post–March 2000 experience when National Association of Securities Dealers Automated Quotations (NASDAQ) stocks reversed their prior steep ascent and began a dramatic fall that was accompanied by a prolonged decline in the broader S & P 500 index.

The common link between the post-1929 and post-2000 experiences may be that, in each case, a severe stock market decline was associated with broader financial sector difficulties and a general loss of confidence on the part of investors.[5] Key concerns in the early 1930s included bank failures, the collapse of many of the investment trusts (that were the predecessors of today's stock market mutual funds), the huge losses incurred by investors on margin, and scandalous revelations of insider trading and stock price manipulation that led to congressional inquiries, new regulation of the banking and securities industries (as under the 1933 Glass-Steagall Act), and the establishment of the Securities Exchange Commission in 1934 (see, for example,

---

[4] This is in contradiction to Murphy's (1992: p. 238) assertion that gold moved inversely with stock markets at the time of the 1987 stock market crash. Although we do find some support for such a negative correlation under the most extreme circumstances it certainly does not seem to be as "common" as Murphy and others have sometimes alleged.

[5] An example of the importance of confidence effects can be seen in the sharp and broad-based decline in small mining stocks when the Bre-X fraud was uncovered in the spring of 1997 (Brown and Burdekin 2000). Although these other stocks had no direct connection with the fraudulent operation at Bre-X in Indonesia, the widespread negative impact showed how important reputation and full disclosure can be – and perhaps foreshadowed the later more general loss of confidence following the Enron collapse and the criminal case against Arthur Andersen, Enron's accountants.

Brooks 1997). Post-2000 worries have centered on, inter alia, the number of high-profile corporate bankruptcies, mounting evidence of bad loans both at home and abroad, terrorism concerns following the events of September 11, 2001, political instability in the Middle East and elsewhere, and a loss of confidence in accounting statements and regulatory oversight in the post-Enron era (which provoked congressional inquiries and public outcry somewhat reminiscent of the post-1929 experience). In short, gold stocks may still be able to prove their "mettle" in the modern era, but it may require especially adverse conditions for these benefits to emerge.

EMPIRICAL ANALYSIS

We begin by examining the post-1929 performance of Homestake Mining and regress returns for Homestake over the 1926–1937 period on returns in the broader market as represented by the S & P 500.[6] Our empirical analysis essentially amounts to an extended event study with excess returns being given by the movement in Homestake's share price relative to the S & P 500. Using monthly data, we find that the coefficient on the S & P 500 is insignificant for Homestake, and this stock seems to move independent of the overall market (see Table 12.1). This inference is robust to alterations in the sample if we narrow or extend the "window" around the 1929 crash. The implied independent performance is consistent with the fact that Homestake takes almost no part either in the huge run-up of the market between 1926 and 1929 or the great crash and final bottoming of the S & P 500 in mid-1932 (see Figure 12.1). The very large abnormal returns for Homestake after the 1929 crash, meanwhile, are shown in Figure 12.2 Homestake's improved stock performance begins well before the abandonment of the gold standard in March 1933 and accompanying nationalization of gold. Homestake even enjoyed an increase in profits between 1929 and 1930 at a time when so much of corporate America was suffering from the overall downturn in economic activity.

As early as the summer of 1931, commodity futures data pointed to investor expectations of sharply rising prices for cotton, wheat, corn, and oats.

---

[6] This particular sample period reflects the beginning of the official monthly data series on the S & P 500 in 1926 and ends in December 1937 so as to leave out the effects of the 1938 Czech crisis that was soon followed by the invasion of Poland and the outbreak of World War II.

Table 12.1. *Gold stocks vs. overall market returns, 1929, 1987, and post-2000*

Dependent variable*	Constant	Market return	Crash	1933	1934	Float
1929 Crash						
Sample Period: Jan. 1926–Dec. 1937						
Homestake Mining	2.532 (.586)§	.036 (.060)				
Homestake Mining	2.202 (1.061)‡	.039 (.061)	.477 (1.275)			
Homestake Mining	2.287 (1.040)†	.009 (.062)	.250 (1.522)	5.979 (2.502)‡	−6.935 (2.427)§	
Homestake Mining	2.113 (.591)§	−.001 (.059)				6.470 (2.282)§
1987 Crash						
Sample Period: Jan. 1985–Dec. 1989						

Dependent variable*	Constant	Market return	Gold return
XAU	.003 (.012)	.541 (.233)‡	
XAU	−.010 (.011)	.949 (.210)§	1.308 (.254)§
SPGOLD	.009 (.014)	.592 (.256)‡	
SPGOLD	−.005 (.012)	1.021 (.233)§	1.374 (.283)§
2000–2002 Market Downturn			

Dependent variable*	Constant	Market return	Gold return	Sept. 11
XAU	.002 (.004)	−.120 (.148)		
XAU	.001 (.003)	−.031 (.111)	1.568 (.134)§	
XAU	−.0001 (.003)	−.029 (.112)	1.562 (.134)§	.004 (.007)
SPGOLD	.002 (.004)	−.377 (.156)‡		
SPGOLD	.001 (.003)	−.281 (.114)‡	1.720 (.136)§	
SPGOLD	.0005 (.003)	−.281 (.114)‡	1.720 (.137)§	.0001 (.007)
GOLDBUG	.005 (.005)	−.314 (.171)†		
GOLDBUG	.003 (.003)	−.220 (.116)†	2.022 (.139)§	
GOLDBUG	.0089 (.003)	−.193 (.115)†	2.006 (.139)§	.011 (.007)

*The dependent variables are all measured in percentage changes (returns). XAU = Philadelphia Index of Precious Metals; SPGOLD = Standard and Poors Gold Index; GOLDBUG = American Stock Exchange "Gold BUGS" Index (see footnote 9, p. 327).
†Significant at the 10 percent level.
‡Significant at the 5 percent level.
§Significant at the 1 percent level.
Market Return = total return on the S & P 500.
Note: Durbin-Watson test statistics were not able to reject the null hypothesis of no first-order autocorrelation for each regression. Standard errors are in parenthesis.

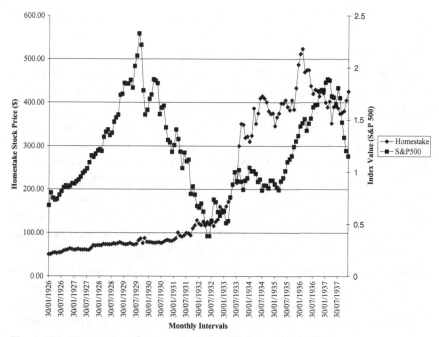

Figure 12.1. Homestake Mining vs. the S & P 500 Index, 1926–1937

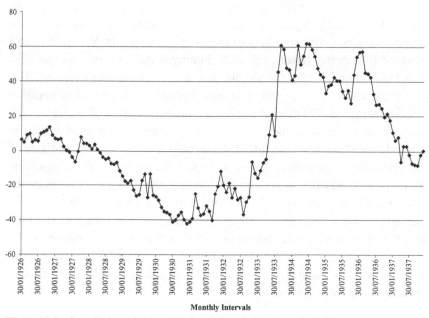

Figure 12.2. Cumulative Abnormal Returns for Homestake Mining, 1926–1937

Although rising commodity prices did not actually surface until 1933 under President Roosevelt's "New Deal" policies, Hamilton (1988: p. 87) stresses that there was a "tremendous increase in uncertainty over the domestic price level" during 1931. Homestake's stock price gains accelerated after the market price of gold was finally allowed to rise in 1933. A reduction in the gold content of the dollar was first authorized under the May 12, 1933, amendment to the Agricultural Adjustment Act. As part of its expansionary policies aimed at raising the price level of commodities, the government began to directly intervene in the gold market with large purchases after October 1933 (Friedman and Schwartz 1963: p. 465). The gold price was eventually re-pegged under the January 1934 Gold Reserve Act when President Roosevelt raised the official gold price from $20.67/ounce to $35/ounce – see also Angell (1934) on the rationale for these moves. This new $35 level actually endured into the 1970s. Meanwhile, the hike in the gold price after 1933 not only offered a boost to gold mining stocks but also fueled large gold inflows into the United States (see Friedman and Schwartz 1963; Kindleberger 1985).

The initial gains in Homestake in the aftermath of the 1929 crash likely reflect a flight to gold and gold stocks in times of severe crisis and financial uncertainty, and this period does appear to demonstrate the potential role for gold as a hedge against overall asset price deflation. If we allow for dummy variables corresponding to the 1929 crash, and the March 1933 and January 1934 policy moves, the 1929 dummy is insignificant and the 1933 and 1934 dummies are individually significant but offsetting in sign. The positive coefficient on the 1933 dummy coupled with the offsetting negative coefficient on the 1934 dummy suggest a temporary period of extra gains for Homestake when the dollar price of gold was allowed to float between the United States' exit from the international gold standard and the re-fixing of the price of gold the following year. We test this inference by defining a third dummy (FLOAT) that is set equal to one for the interim period between March 1933 and January 1934. As expected, this float dummy features a strongly significant positive coefficient (whereas re-estimation with the 1933 and 1934 dummies entered individually showed each to be insignificant). The surge in Homestake's stock price in the latter part of 1933 occurred in the midst of not only a sharply rising U.S. dollar gold price but also considerable market uncertainty. For example,

... all through November ... the government's assault on the dollar continued, with gold purchases made regularly on both the domestic and world markets at ever-higher prices ... Paris and London were jittery, and as a result of the uncertainty international trade was virtually paralyzed ... Matters came to a crisis on the ninth. The dollar on the world market suddenly plunged to under 62 cents as the speculators joined the United States government in trouncing it. ... (Brooks 1997: p. 170–71)

Although Figures 12.1. and 12.2 are consistent with a temporary reversal of Homestake's upward trend after the gold price was re-pegged in 1934, renewed gains set in during 1935–1936. Homestake's financial success is evidenced by its ability to pay each of its workers $50 bonuses in 1935 at a time when so much of the nation's labor force was on the bread lines (*New York Times*, 21 June, 1935: p. 36).

In examining the behavior of gold stocks following the 1987 and 2000 stock market declines, we include the gold price (based on the afternoon close in the New York market) as an additional right-hand-side variable. This was not our chosen procedure for the earlier data, as the gold price was fixed through so much of the 1920s and 1930s (and if we do add the gold bullion price to the earlier regressions, the gold price is indeed always found to be insignificant there). When we now regress returns for the XAU index (or S & P gold index) on S & P 500 returns and the gold price, the estimated coefficient on the gold price is always statistically significant, with a coefficient between one and two that corresponds with the earlier findings of Tufano (1998).[7] The estimated beta coefficient on the S & P 500 for the 1985–1989 sample surrounding the October 1987 crash is positive and significant. This contrasts sharply with the significantly negative beta for the S & P gold and independent movement of the XAU index over the more recent 1999–2002 period (in line also with the trends evident in Figures 12.3. and 12.4). Our findings suggest, therefore, that the potential diversification benefits of gold stocks did not emerge in 1987 but do seem to have become important again over the latest period.

Interestingly, allowing for a "terrorism" dummy set equal to one for all observations after September 11, 2001 – whether entered additively or interactively – does not significantly improve the fit of the 1999–2002 regression. Thus, as the with the changes in gold's official status in the early 1930s, the offsetting movement in gold stocks seems to have been under way already, and it would not seem accurate to tie gold's resurgence to the September 11 events alone. The September 11 effects were themselves

---

[7] Further evidence on the link between gold price movements and returns on gold stocks is provided by Blose and Shieh (1995) – whereas Blose (1996) documents the effects of gold price movements on the returns on gold mutual funds.

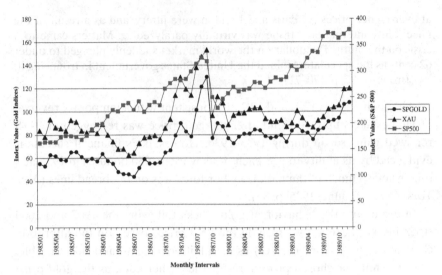

Figure 12.3. S & P 500 vs. Gold Indices, 1985–1989

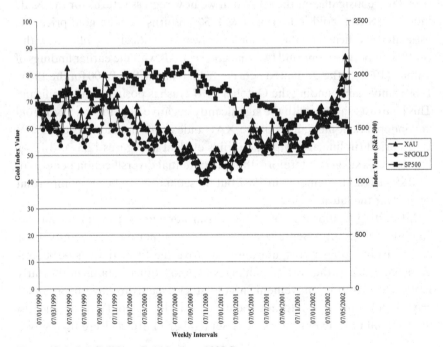

Figure 12.4. S & P 500 vs. Gold Indices, 1999-Present

likely damped insofar as the Federal Reserve acted immediately to supply billions of dollars in funds from its discount window – and may also have formed part of a coordinated effort to support the U.S. stock market when trading resumed on September 17, 2001 (Wachman and Doward 2001). It is generally agreed that the Federal Reserve should intervene to maintain liquidity in financial markets and that the Federal Reserve's reaction was quite insufficient in this regard after the 1929 crash (see, for example, Friedman and Schwartz 1963). A direct focus on stock markets, much less actual intervention, is considerably more controversial, however. Mishkin and White (2002: p. 37) point to a number of potential problems with the central bank focusing too much on stock prices, including the risk of creating moral hazard that "might help facilitate excessive valuation of stocks and help encourage a stock market bubble that might crash later, something that the central bank would rather avoid."

Notwithstanding the importance of overall market trends, gold stock returns over the most recent period cannot be adequately analyzed without considering the role played by hedging. Gold mining companies that hedge sell a portion of their current and future output into forward contracts at a fixed price that typically exceeds the current spot price. One influence on firms' propensity to hedge is the extent of their leverage or debt burden (Adam 2002). Firms with large hedge books can actually be hurt by a rise in the gold price and one major gold mining company, Ashanti Goldfields of Ghana, was threatened with insolvency when a sharp gold price increase in the fall of 1999 caused its hedge book to take on a negative value and made the company vulnerable to margin calls.[8] In the post-2000 period, an index of relatively unhedged gold miners (the American Stock Exchange "Gold BUGS" index) has gained considerably more than the XAU or S & P Gold indices that include heavily-hedged gold mining companies like Barrick (see Figure 12.5).[9]

[8]   The 1999 gold price "spike" reflected the so-called "Washington Agreement" of September 26, 1999, whereby fifteen major European central banks, led by the European Central Bank, agreed to limit their sales of gold to 400 metric tons a year for the following five years (including the amounts already earmarked for sale in the then-ongoing Bank of England gold auctions). This led to a sudden but relatively short-lived surge in the price of gold prior to the more sustained increase that sets in after 2000.

[9]   The American Stock Exchange website defines the Gold BUGS index as a "modified equal dollar weighted index of companies involved in gold mining ... [that] was designed to provide significant exposure to near term movements in gold prices by including companies that do not hedge their gold production beyond 1.5 years." As of June 2002, the Gold BUGS index included 12 stocks, the largest of which were Goldcorp, Newmont Mining, and Freeport-McMoran. Large hedged producers like Barrick, Anglogold, and Placer Dome, although major components of the XAU, are totally excluded from the Gold BUGS index.

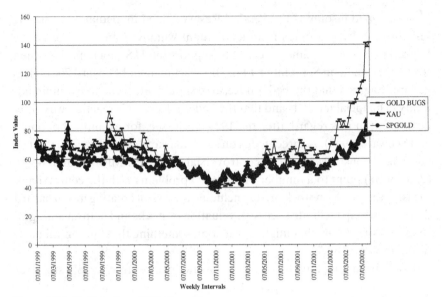

Figure 12.5. Gold Indices, 1999–Present

As shown in Table 12.1, the coefficient on the price of gold for the Gold BUGS index is almost exactly two over 1999–2002 compared with coefficient values of 1.56 for the XAU and 1.72 for the S & P Gold Index. Given that the gold price itself moves opposite to the S & P 500 over this period, the net result remains a stronger inverse relationship with the overall market for the Gold BUGS index than for the other two gold stock indices. This points to the importance of how funds are allocated within this asset class. (There is also a risk that the larger hedged mining companies could suffer a similar fate to that nearly suffered by Ashanti if the broad market decline and rise in gold prices continues into the future.) Finally, just as a rising gold price and a weakening dollar went hand in hand in late 1933 – pending the setting of a new higher fixed gold price – so too did the strength in gold in the first half of 2002 occur in the face of a pronounced weakening of the dollar against the euro and most other major currencies. In that sense, gold stocks may be valued not just as a hedge against falling domestic asset prices but also against a decline in the external value of the nation's currency.

In comparing our three sets of results, the 1987 crash itself clearly differs from both the post-1929 and post-2000 declines in terms of its very short duration and the fact that the long-term uptrend in the stock market remained intact. There was also much less concern about the underlying strength of the economy in 1987 than for the other two episodes. A similarity across all three episodes, however, is that, in each case, gold stocks initially *did* decline along with the general market. Homestake's gains during the Great Depression occurred only after 1930 and recent out-performance by our three indices of gold stocks did not emerge until after 2000 – with each of the indices actually "bottoming" near the end of 2000. The failure of gold stocks to generate meaningful excess returns in the face of the 1987 crash, therefore, fits with the evidence that the gains that occurred in the other episodes were delayed by many months. Accordingly, the evidence presented here does not offer much hope that gold stocks will serve as a very satisfactory hedge against – even very severe – short-term market declines. Rather, it appears that much more drawn out periods of weakness may be required to elicit the countervailing potential of gold and silver stocks.

CONCLUDING REMARKS

Contrary to much conventional wisdom, gold stocks clearly do not require inflation to perform well. Gains in the 1930s and post-2000 were, however, accompanied by declines in the external value of the dollar so that gold stocks did serve as a hedge against a loss of purchasing power abroad as well as a hedge against declining domestic asset prices. Although gold stocks do not always serve as a hedge against asset price deflation and stock market declines, evidence from the post-1929 and post-2000 periods do suggest that they perform this role under sufficiently extreme – and prolonged – conditions of general financial turmoil and distress. These benefits emerge only with a lag, however, and, as in the 1987 case, gold stocks show a tendency to *initially* rise and fall with the overall market.

References

Affärsvärlden (business weekly), (various issues).

Ahearne, A., J. Gagnon, J. Haltmaier, S. Kamin, C. Erceg, J. Faust, L. Guerrieri, C. Hemphill, L. Kole, J. Roush, J. Rogers, N. Sheets, and J. Wright (2002), "Preventing Deflation: Lessons from Japan's Experience in the 1990s," Board of Governors of the Federal Reserve System, International Finance Discussion Papers 729, June.

Alberti, M. (1931), "La vicenda economico monetaria dell'Italia dal 1913 al 1929," in M. Alberti and V. Cornaro (Eds.), *Banche di emissione, moneta e politica monetaria in Italia dal 1948 al 1929* (Milano: GUF).

Alchian, A., and B. Klein (1973), "On a Correct Measure of Inflation," *Journal of Money, Credit and Banking* 5: 173–91.

Alston, L. J., W. A. Grove, and D. C. Wheelock (1994), "Why Do Banks Fail? Evidence From the 1920s," *Explorations in Economic History*, 31 (October): 409–31.

Amirault, D., and B. O'Reilly (2001), "The Zero-Bound on Nominal Interest Rates: How Important Is It?" Bank of Canada working paper 2001–06, April.

Ando, A., and F. Modigliani (1963), "The 'Life Cycle' Hypothesis of Saving: Aggregate Implications and Tests," *American Economic Review* 53: 55–84.

Angell, J. W. (1969 [1936]), *The Behavior of Money: Exploratory Studies.* (New York: McGraw-Hill Book Company), reprinted by Augustus M. Kelley.

Angell, J. W. (1934), "Gold, Banks and the New Deal," *Political Science Quarterly* 49 (December): 481–505.

Asso P. F. (1993), "L'Italia e i prestiti internazionali, 1919–1931," in *Finanza Internazionale, vincolo esterno e cambi. 1919–1939*, Collana Storica della Banca d'Italia, Ricerche per la Storia della Banca d'Italia, volume III, Bari: Laterza, pp. 2–342.

Balke, N., and R. Gordon (1989), "The Estimation of Prewar GNP: Methodology and New Evidence," *Journal of Political Economy* 97 (February): 38–92.

Balke, N. S. and M. A. Wynne (1996), "Are Deep Recessions Followed by Strong Recoveries? Results for the G-7 Countries," *Applied Economics* 28: 889–97.

Ball, L., and D. Romer (1991), "Sticky Prices as Coordination Failure," *American Economic Review* 81: 539–52.

Ballantine, A. A. (1948), "When All the Banks Closed," *Harvard Business Review* 26: 129–43.

Banca d'Italia (1934), *Relazione annuale*, Roma: Banca d'Italia, pp. 34–35.

Banca d'Italia (1935), *Relazione annuale*, Roma: Banca d'Italia, pp. 37–39.

Bank for International Settlements (2001), 71st Annual Report.

Bank for International Settlements (1999), *69th Annual Report* (Basle: Bank for International Settlements).

Bank of Japan (2001), "Minutes of the Monetary Policy Meeting," December 4. Available at www.boj.jp/en/scisahu/01/pb1g011029_f.htm.

Barsky, R. B., and J. B. DeLong (2000), "Forecasting Pre-World War I Inflation: The Fisher Effect and the Gold Standard," *Quarterly Journal of Economics* 106 (August): 815–36.

Batini, N., and E. Nelson (2000), "When the Bubble Bursts: Monetary Policy Rules and Foreign Exchange Market Behavior," mimeo, Bank of England, London.

Bayoumi, T., and B. Eichengreen (1996), "Déjà Vu All Over Again: Lessons From the Gold Standard for European Monetary Unification," in T. Bayoumi, B. Eichengreen, and M. Taylor (Eds.), *Modern Perspectives on the Gold Standard* (Cambridge: Cambridge University Press), pp. 365–87.

Bayoumi, T., and B. Eichengreen (1993), "Shocking Aspects of European Monetary Integration," in Francisco Torres and Francesco Giavazzi (Eds.), *Adjustment and Growth in the European Monetary Union* (New York: Cambridge University Press), pp. 193–229.

Bayoumi, T., and C. Collyns (2000), *Post-Bubble Blues: How Japan Responded to Asset Price Collapse* (Washington: International Monetary Fund).

Bean, C. (2002), "The MPC and the UK Economy: Should We Fear the D-Words?" Speech to the Emmanuel Society, London, 25 November. Available at http://www.bankofengland.co.uk.

Benati, L. (2002), "Investigating Inflation Persistence Across Monetary Regimes," Working Paper, Monetary Assessment and Strategy Division, Bank of England.

Berg, C., and L. Jonung (1999), "Pioneering Price Level Targeting. The Swedish Experience 1931–1937," *Journal of Monetary Economics* 41: 525–52.

Bernanke, B. (1983) "Non-Monetary Effects of the Financial Crisis in the Propagation of the Great Depression," *American Economic Review* 73 (June 1973): 257–76.

Bernanke, B. S. (2002a), "Deflation: Making Sure 'It' Doesn't Happen Here," remarks by Governor Ben S. Bernanke before the National Economists Club, Washington, D.C., November 21, 2002 (available at www.federalreserve.gov/boarddocs/speeches/2002/20021121/default.htm).

Bernanke, B. S. (2002b), "Asset-Price 'Bubbles' and Monetary Policy," speech before the New York Chapter of the National Association for Business Economics, New York. Available at http://www.federalreserve.gov/boarddocs/Speeches/2002/20021015/ default.htm.

Bernanke, B. S. (1995), "The Macroeconomics of the Great Depression: A Comparative Approach," *Journal of Money, Credit and Banking* 27 (February): 1–28.

Bernanke, B., and M. Gertler (2001), "Should Central Banks Respond To Movements in Asset Prices?" *American Economic Review, Papers and Proceedings* 91 (May): 253–7.

Bernanke, B., and M. Gertler (1999), "Monetary Policy and Asset Price Volatility," Federal Reserve Bank of Kansas City *Economic Review* Fourth Quarter: 17–51.

Bernanke, B., and M. Gertler (1989), "Agency Costs, Collateral and Business Fluctuations," *American Economic Review* 79:14–31.

Bernanke, B., M. Gertler, and S. Gilchrist (1998), "The Financial Accelerator in a Quantitative Business Cycle Framework," NBER Working Paper 6455.

Bernanke, B. S., and H. James (1991), "The Gold Standard, Deflation and Financial Crisis in the Great Depression: An International Comparison," in R. G. Hubbard (Ed.), *Financial Markets and Financial Crises*. (Chicago: University of Chicago Press), pp. 33–68.

Bittlingmayer, G. (1998), "Output, Stock Volatility, and Political Uncertainty in a Natural Experiment: Germany, 1880–1940," *Journal of Finance* 53: 2243–57.

Blanchard, O., and D. Quah (1989), "The Dynamic Effects of Aggregate Demand and Supply Disturbances," *American Economic Review* 79 (September): 655–73.

Blanchard, O. J., and M. Watson (1982), "Bubbles, Rational Expectations, and Financial Markets," in P. Wachtel (Ed.), *Crises in the Economic and the Financial Structure* (Lexington Books: Lexington), pp. 295–315.

Blose, L. E. (1996), "Gold Price Risk and the Returns on Gold Mutual Funds," *Journal of Economics and Business* 48 (November/ December): 499–513.

Blose, L. E., and J. C. P. Shieh (1995), "The Impact of Gold Price on the Value of Gold Mining Stock," *Review of Financial Economics* 4 (Spring): 125–39.

Bodenhorn, H. (1995), "A More Perfect Union: Regional Interest Rates in the United States, 1880–1960," in M. D. Bordo and R. Sylla (Eds.), *Anglo-American Financial Systems: Institutions and Markets in the Twentieth Century*. (New York: Irwin Professional Publishing, New York University Solomon Center), pp. 415–53.

Bohl, M. T., and P. L. Siklos (2004), "The Present Value Model of US Stock Prices Redux: A New Testing Strategy and Some Evidence," *Quarterly Review of Economics and Finance* 44 (May): 208–223.

Boissière, G. (1908), *La Compagnies des Agents de Change et le Marché Officiel à la Bourse de Paris* (Paris: Arthur Rousseau).

Booth, J., and M. Pottinger (2001), "China's Deflation Puts Pressure on WTO Nations," *Wall Street Journal*, November 23, p. A2.

Bordo, M. D. (1993), "The Gold Standard, Bretton Woods and Other Monetary Regimes: A Historical Appraisal," in Federal Reserve Bank of St. Louis, *Review* 75 (March/April): 123–91.

Bordo, M. D, T. Ito, and T. Iwaisako (1997), "Banking Crisis and Monetary Policy: Japan in the 1990s and the U.S. in the 1930s," University of Tsukuba (mimeo).

Bordo, M. D., and R. MacDonald (1997), "Violations of the Rules of the Game and the Credibility of the Classical Gold Standard," NBER Working Paper 6115.

Bordo, M. D., A. Redish, and H. Rockoff (1994), "The US Banking System from a Northern Exposure: Stability vs. Efficiency" *Journal of Economic History* 54(2): 325–41.

Borio, C. (1996), "Credit Characteristics and the Monetary Policy Transmission Mechanism in Fourteen Industrial Countries: Facts, Conjectures and Some Econometric Evidence," in Alders et al. (Eds.), *Monetary Policy in a Converging Europe* (Do.drecht: Kluwer Academic), pp. 77–116.

Borio, C., N. Kennedy, and S. D. Prowse (1994), "Exploring Aggregate Asset Price Fluctuations Across Countries: Measurement, Determinants and Monetary Policy Implications," BIS Economic Paper No. 40.

Borio, C., and P. Lowe (2002), "Asset Prices, Financial and Monetary Stability: Exploring the Nexus," BIS Working Paper No. 114.

Brandt, L., and T. J. Sargent (1989), "Interpreting New Evidence about China and U.S. Silver Purchases," *Journal of Monetary Economics* 23 (January): 31–51.

Bresciani-Turroni, C. (1937), *The Economics of Inflation. A Study of Currency Depreciation in Post-War Germany* (London: George Allen & Unwin).

Brooks, J. (1997), *Once in Golconda: A True Drama of Wall Street 1920–1938* (New York: Allworth Press).

Brown. W. O., Jr., and R. C. K. Burdekin (2000), "Fraud and Financial Markets: The 1997 Collapse of the Junior Mining Stocks," *Journal of Economics and Business* 52 (May/June): 277–88.

Brunner, K., and A. H. Meltzer (1968), "What Did We Learn from the Monetary Experience of the United States in the Great Depression?" *Canadian Journal of Economics* 1 (May): 334–48.

Burdekin, R. C. K. (2000), "Ending Inflation in the People's Republic of China: From Mao to the 21st Century," *Cato Journal* 20 (Fall): 223–35.

Burdekin, R. C. K., and P. L. Siklos (1999), "Exchange Rate Regimes and Shifts in Inflation Persistence: Does Nothing Else Matter?" *Journal of Money, Credit, and Banking* 31 (May): 235–47.

Burdekin, R. C. K., and M. D. Weidenmier (2003), "Suppressing Asset Price Inflation: The Confederate Experience, 1861–1865," *Economic Inquiry* 41 (July): 420–32.

Cagan, P. (1956), "The Monetary Dynamics of Hyperinflation," in Milton Friedman (Ed.), *Studies in the Quantity Theory of Money*, (Chicago: Chicago University Press), pp. 25–117.

Calomiris, C. (1993), "Financial Factors in the Great Depression," *Journal of Economic Perspectives* 7: 61–86.

Calomiris, C., and C. Hanes (1994), "Historical Macroeconomics and American Macroeconomic History," NBER Working Paper 4935.

Calomiris, C. W., and R. G. Hubbard, (1989), "Price Flexibility, Credit Availability and Economic fluctuations" *Quarterly Journal of Economics* 104 (3) (August): 429–52.

Calomiris, C. W., and J. R. Mason (2000), "Causes of U.S. Bank Distress During the Depression," NBER Working Paper 7919, September.

Calomiris, C. W., and J. R. Mason (1997), "Contagion and Bank Failures during the Great Depression: The June 1932 Chicago Banking Panic," *American Economic Review* 87 (December): 863–83.

Calomiris, C. W., and D. Wheelock (1998), "Was the Great Depression a Watershed for American Monetary Policy?" in M. D. Bordo, C. Goldin, and E. White (Eds.), *The Defining Moment: The Great Depression and the American Economy in the Twentieth Century* (Chicago: University of Chicago Press), pp. 23–66.

Calomiris, C. W., A. Orphanides, and S. A. Sharpe (1997), "Leverage as a State Variable for Employment, Inventory Accumulation and Fixed Investment," in F. H. Capie and G. E. Wood (Eds.), *Asset Price and the Real Economy.* (London: Macmillan), pp. 169–93.

Campbell, E. (1938), *The Reorganization of the American Railroad System, 1893–1900* (New York: Columbia University Press).

Campbell, J. Y., and R. J. Shiller (1988a), "The Dividend-Price Ratio and Expectations of Future Dividends and Discount Factors," *Review of Financial Studies* 1: 195–227.

Campbell, J. Y., and R. J. Shiller (1988b), "Stock Prices, Earnings, and Expected Dividends," *Journal of Finance* 43: 661–76.

Campbell, J. Y., A. W. Lo, and A. C. MacKinlay (1997), *The Econometrics of Financial Markets* (Princeton, N. J.: Princeton University Press).

Capie, F. H. (1988), "Structure Conduct Performance in British Banking," in P. Cottrell and D. E. Moggridge (Eds.), *Money and Power* (London: Macmillan).

Capie, F. H. (1983), *Depression and Protectionism.* (London: Allen and Unwin).

Capie F. H., and M. Billings (2001), "Profitability in English Banking in the Twentieth Century," *European Review of Economic History* 5 (December): 367–401.

Capie F. H., and M. Collins (1996), "Industrial Lending by English Commercial Banks, 1860–1914: Why Did Banks Refuse Loans," *Business History* 38(1): 26–44.

Capie, F. H., and T. C. Mills (1985), "British Bank Conservatism in the Late 19th Century," *Explorations in Economic History* 32 (July): 409–20.

Capie, F. H., T. C. Mills, and G. E. Wood (1991), "Money, Interest Rates and the Great Depression: Britain from 1870 to 1913," in James Foreman-Peck (Ed.), *New Perspectives on the Late Victorian Economy: Essays in Quantitative Economic History, 1860–1914* (Cambridge University Press), pp. 251–84.

Capie, F. H., T. C. Mills, and G. E. Wood (1986), "What Happened in 1931?" in F. H. Capie and G. E. Wood (Eds.), *Financial Crises and the World Banking System* (New York, St. Martins Press), pp. 120–48.

Capie, F. H. and A. Webber (1985), *A Monetary History of the UK, Vol I: 1870–1982 Data, Sources, Methods* (London: George Allen and Unwin).

Cargill, T. (2001), "Monetary Policy, Deflation and Economic History: Lessons for the Bank of Japan," *Bank of Japan Monetary and Economic Studies* 19 (February).

Cargill, T. F., M. M. Hutchison, and T. Ito (2000), *Financial Policy and Central Banking in Japan* (Cambridge, Mass.: MIT Press).

Cargill, T. F., M. M. Hutchison, and T. Ito (1997), *The Political Economy of Japanese Monetary Policy* (Cambridge, Mass.: MIT Press).

Carlson, M. (2001), "Are Branch Banks Better Survivors: Evidence from the Depression Era?" No 2001–51 in Finance and Economics Discussion Series from the Board of Governors of the Federal Reserve System (U.S.).

Casparsson, R. (1947), *LO under fem årtioenden*, (LO under five decades.) Landsorganisationen.

Cassel, G. (1941), *I förnuftets tjänst.* (In the Service of Reason), Natur och Kultur, Stockholm.

Cecchetti, S. G. (1998), "Understanding the Great Depression: Lessons for Current Policy," in M. Wheeler (Ed.), *The Economics of the Great Depression* (Kalamazoo, Mich.:W. E. Upjohn Institute for Employment Research).

Cecchetti, S. B. H. Genberg, J. Lipsky, and S. Wadhwhani (2000), *Asset Prices and Central Bank Policy* (London: International Center for Monetary and Banking Studies).

Chambers, E., and D. Gordon (1966), "Primary Products and Economic Growth: An Empirical Measurement," *Journal of Political Economy* 74 (4): 315–32.

Chan, K. S. (1993), "Consistency and Limiting Distribution of the Least Squares Estimator of a Threshold Autoregressive Model," *The Annals of Statistics* 21: 520–33.

Chandler, L. V. (1970), *America's Greatest Depression, 1929–1941* (New York: Harper & Row).

Charemza, W. W., and D. F. Deadman (1995), "Speculative Bubbles with Stochastic Explosive Roots: The Failure of Unit Root Testing," *Journal of Empirical Finance* 2: 1453–63.

Chen, N.-K. (2001), "Bank Net Worth, Asset Prices and Economic Activity," *Journal of Monetary Economics* 48: 415–36.

Cheung, Y.-W., and K. S. Lai (1993), "Do Gold Market Returns Have Long Memory?" *The Financial Review* 28 (May): 181–202.

"China Still Troubled by Deflation in October" (in Chinese) November 13, 2002. Available from http://home.donews.com/donews/article/3/ 36342.html.

Choudhry, T. (1996), "Real Stock Prices and the Long-Run Money Demand Function: Evidence from Canada and the USA," *Journal of International Money and Finance* 15 (February): 1–17.

Chua, J. H., G. Sick, and R. S. Woodward (1990), "Diversifying with Gold Stocks," *Financial Analysts Journal* 46 (July–August): 76–9.

Ciocca, P. (1976), "L'economia italiana nel contesto internazionale," in P. Ciocca and G. Toniolo (Eds.), *L'economia italiana nel periodo fascista* (Bologna: Il Mulino).

Clarida, R., and J. Gali (1994), "Sources of Real Exchange-Rate Fluctuations: How Important are Nominal Shocks?" *Carnegie-Rochester Conference Series on Public Policy* 41:1–56.

Cochrane, J. H. (2001), *Asset Pricing* (Princeton, N.J.: Princeton University Press).

Cogley, T. (1999), "Should the Fed Take Deliberate Steps to Deflate Asset Price Bubbles?" *Economic Review of the Federal Reserve Bank of San Francisco* 1: 42–52.

Cogley, T., and T. J. Sargent (2002), "Evolving Post-World War II U.S. Inflation Dynamics," in Ben S. Bernanke and Kenneth Rogoff (Eds.), *NBER Macroeconomics Annual 2001* (Cambridge, Mass.: MIT Press), pp. 331–72.

Cohen, J. S. (1992), "Financing Industrialization in Italy, 1894–1914: The Partial Transformation of a Late Comer," in *Financing Industrialization*, Volume 2 (Brookfield, Vt.: Edward Elgar), pp. 57–76.

Cohen, J. S. (1988), "Was Italian Fascism a Developmental Dictatorship? Some Evidence to the Contrary," *Economic History Review* 41 (1): 95–113.

Collyns, C., and A. Senhadji (2002), "Lending Booms, Real Estate Bubbles and the Asian Crisis," IMF Working Paper 02/20.

Commercial and Financial Chronicle (1933), March 4, pp. 1484–5.

Commercial and Financial Chronicle (1933), March 11, p. 1670.

Cotula, F., and P. Garofalo (1993), "Appendice statistica," in F. Cotula and L. Spaventa (Eds.), *La politica monetaria fra le due guerre 1919–1935* (Bari: Laterza), pp. 811–22.

Cotula, F., and L. Spaventa (1993), "Introduzione," in F. Cotula and L. Spaventa (Eds.), *La politica monetaria fra le due guerre 1919–1935* (Bari: Laterza), pp. 3–206.

Crafts, N. F. R. (1997), "Comment on Eichengreen and Grossman," in F. H. Capie and G. E. Wood (Eds.), *Asset Prices and the Real Economy* (London: Macmillan).

Crafts, N. F. R., S. J. Leybourne, and T. C. Mills (1989), "The Climacteric in Late Victorian Britain and France: A Reappraisal of the Evidence," *Journal of Applied Econometrics* 4 (Apr.–June): 103–17.

Davis, L. E., and R. E. Gallman (2001), *Evolving Financial Markets and International Capital Flows: Britain, the Americas, and Australia, 1865–1914* (Cambridge, U.K.: Cambridge University Press).

De Cecco, M. (Ed.) (1993), *L'Italia e il sistema finanziario internazionale 1919–1936*, Collana Storica della Banca d'Italia- Documenti (Bari: Laterza).

De Geer, H. (1986), *SAF i förhandlingar*. Svenska arbetsgivarföreningen.

Deaton, A. (1992), *Understanding Consumption* (Oxford: Oxford University Press).

Delargy, P., and C. Goodhart (1999), "Financial Crises: Plus ça change, plus c'est la meme chose," Financial Markets Group Special Paper No. 108.

DeLong, J. B. (1997), "America's Peacetime Inflation: the 1970s," in C. D. Romer and D. H. Romer (Eds.), *Reducing Inflation: Motivation and Strategy* (Chicago: University of Chicago Press), pp. 247–78.

DeLong, J. B., and M. Becht (1992), "'Excess Volatility' and the German Stock Market, 1876–1990," NBER Working Paper 4054, April.

Dewey, D. R. (1903), *Financial History of the United States* (New York: Longmans, Green, and Co.).

Dick, T., and J. Floyd (1992), *Canada and the Gold Standard: Balance of Payments Adjustment, 1871–1913* (Cambridge: Cambridge University Press).

Dickey, D. A., and W. A. Fuller (1981), "The Likelihood Ratio Statistics for Autoregressive Time Series with a Unit Root," *Econometrica* 49: 1057–72.

Dickey, G. E. (1977), *Money, Prices and Growth: The American Experience 1869–1896* (New York: Arno Press).

Donner, O. (1934), "Die Kursbildung am Aktienmarkt: Grundlage zur Konjunkturbeobachtung an den Effektenmärkten," *Vierteljahreshefte zur Konjunkturforschung*, Sonderheft 36, (Berlin: Institut für Konjunkturforschung).

Drees, B., and C. Pazarbasioglu (1998), *The Nordic Banking Crises: Pitfalls in Financial Liberalization?* IMF Occasional Paper No. 161 (Washington: International Monetary Fund).

Duisenberg, W. F. (2002), "Testimony Before the Committee on Economic and Monetary Affairs of the European Parliament," October 8. Available from http://www.ecb.int.

Dupasquier, C. R. Lalonde, and P. St-Amant, (1997), "Optimum Currency Areas as Applied to Canada and the United States," in *Exchange Rates and Monetary Policy*, Proceedings of a conference held by the Bank of Canada, October 1996, pp. 131–70.

Economist, The (2002a), "Dial D for Deflation," September 14, from www. economist.com.

Economist, The (2002b), "Of Debt, Deflation and Denial," October 12, from www.economist.com.

Economist, The (1999a), "Could It Happen Again?" February 20, pp. 19–22.

Economist, The (1999b), "What's Your Problem?" September 25, pp. 26–30.

Economist, The (1997), "Deflation and All That," November 15, pp. 77–8.

Eichengreen, B. (2002), "Still Fettered After All These Years," NBER Working Paper No. 9276.

Eichengreen, B. (1992a), *Golden Fetters: The Gold Standard and the Great Depression, 1919–1939* (New York: Oxford University Press).

Eichengreen, B. (1992b), "Designing a Central Bank for Europe: A Cautionary Tale from the Early Years of the Federal Reserve System," in M. B. Canzoneri, V. Grilli, and P. R. Masson (Eds.), *Establishing a Central Bank: Issues in Europe and Lessons from the US* (Cambridge: Cambridge University Press), pp. 13–33.

Eichengreen, B., and M. D. Bordo (2002), "Crises Now and Then: What Lessons from the Last Era of Financial Globalization," NBER Working Paper No. 8716.

Eichengreen, B., and R. S. Grossman (1997), "Debt-Deflation and Financial Instability: Two Historical Explorations," in F. H. Capie and G. E. Wood (Eds.), *Asset Prices and the Real Economy* (London, Macmillan), pp. 65–96.

Enders, W., and C. W. J. Granger (1998), "Unit-Root Tests and Asymmetric Adjustment With an Example Using the Term Structure of Interest Rates," *Journal of Business and Economic Statistics* 16: 304–11.

Enders, W., and P. L. Siklos (2001), "Cointegration and Threshold Adjustment," *Journal of Business and Economic Statistics* 19: 166–176.

Engle, R. F., and C. W. J. Granger (1987), "Co-Integration and Error Correction: Representation, Estimation and Testing," *Econometrica* 55 (March): 251–76.

Evans, G. W. (1991), "Pitfalls in Testing for Explosive Bubbles in Asset Prices," *American Economic Review* 81: 922–30.

Fackföreningsrörelsen (Swedish Trade Union Federation's monthly journal), (1931), p. 368.

Fatum, R., and M. M. Hutchison (2002), "Is Foreign Exchange Market Intervention An Alternative to Monetary Policy? Evidence from Japan," Santa Cruz Center for International Economics, UC Santa Cruz Working Paper, March 2002.

Feinstein, C. H. (1989), "Wages and the Paradox of the 1880s: Comment" *Explorations in Economic History* 26 (April): 237–47.

Feinstein, C. H. (1972), *National Income, Expenditure and Output of the United Kingdom, 1855–1965*, (Cambridge: Cambridge University Press).

Feldman, G. D. (1993), *The Great Disorder: Politics, Economics, and Society in the German Inflation 1914–1924* (New York: Oxford University Press).

Fels, R. (1950), "Interregional Payments: A Comment," *Quarterly Journal of Economics* 64 (3) (August): 488–9.

Ferguson, N. (1999), *The Pity of War* (New York: Basic Books).

Ferri, G., and P. Garofalo (1994), "La crisi finanziaria nella grande depressione in Italia," in *Il mercato del credito e la borsa, i sistemi di compensazione e statistiche storiche (salari industriali e occupazione)*, Collana storica della Banca d'Italia–Contributi, ricerche per la storia della Banca d'Italia, Volume V (Bari: Laterza), pp. 97–151.

Filardo, A. J. (2000), "Monetary Policy and Asset Prices," *Federal Reserve Bank of Kansas City Review* 85(3).

Filosa, R., G. M. Rey, and B. Sitzia (1976), "Uno schema di analisi quantitativa dell'economia italiana durante il fascismo," in P. Ciocca e G. Toniolo (Eds.), *L'economia italiana nel periodo fascista* (Bologna: Il Mulino).

Fischer, S. (2001), "Comments on Kuttner and Posen," *Brookings Papers on Economic Activity* (2): 161–6.

Fischer, S. (1986), "Contracts, Credibility, and Disinflation," in S. Fischer (Ed.), *Indexing, Inflation and Economic Policy* (Cambridge, Mass.: MIT Press), pp. 221–40.

Fisher, I. (1935), *Stabilizing Money: A History of the Movement* (London: Allen and Unwin).

Fisher, I. (1933), "The Debt-Deflation Theory of Great Depressions," *Econometrica* 1 (October): 337–57.

Fisher, I. (1930), *The Theory of Interest* (New York: Macmillan).

Fisher, I. (1911), *The Purchasing Power of Money: Its Determination and Relation to Credit, Interest and Crises* (New York: Macmillan).

Fisher, I. (1907), *The Rate of Interest* (New York: Macmillan).

Fisher, I. (1896), *Appreciation and Interest*, Publications of the American Economic Association 3rd series, Vol 11 (4).

Fohlin, C. (1998), "Fiduciary and Firm Liquidity Constraints: The Italian Experience with German-Style Universal Banking," *Explorations in Economic History* 35 (January): 83–107.

Fratianni, M., and M. Artis (1996), "The Lira and the Pound in the 1992 Currency Crisis: Fundamentals or Speculation? *Open Economies Review* 7: 573–589.

Fratianni, M., and F. Spinelli (2001), *Storia monetaria d'Italia: lira e politica monetaria dall'Unita' all'Unione europea* (Milano: Etas).

Fratianni, M., and F. Spinelli (1997), *A Monetary History of Italy* (Cambridge: Cambridge University Press).

Fratianni, M., and J. von Hagen (1992), *The European Monetary System and European Monetary Union* (Boulder-London: Westview).

Fregert, K. (2000), "The Great Depression in Sweden as Wage Coordination Failure," *European Review of Economic History* 4: 341–60.

Fregert, K. (1994), *Wage Contracts, Policy Regimes and Business Cycles. A Contractual History of Sweden 1908–1990*, Lund Economic Studies 54.

Fregert, K., and S. Magnusson (1994), "Den höga arbetslösheten under 1920-talet: Kan det hända igen?" *Ekonomisk Debatt*, nr 8.

Friedman, M. (1992), *Money Mischief: Episodes in Monetary History* (New York: Harcourt Brace Jovanovitch).

Friedman, M., and A. J. Schwartz (1982), *Monetary Trends in the United States and the United Kingdom. Their Relation to Income, Prices, and Interest Rates, 1867–1975* (Chicago: University of Chicago Press).

Friedman, M., and A. J. Schwartz (1970), *Monetary Statistics of the United States: Estimates Sources, Methods* (New York: Columbia University).

Friedman, M., and A. J. Schwartz (1963), *A Monetary History of the United States 1867–1960* (Princeton: Princeton University Press).

Froot, K., and M. Obstfeld (1991), "Intrinsic Bubbles: The Case of Stock Prices," *American Economic Review* 81: 1189–214.

Fuhrer, J. C. (1997), "The (Un)Importance of Forward-Looking Behavior in Price Specifications," *Journal of Money, Credit, and Banking* 29 (August): 338–50.

Fukao, M. (2000), *Life Insurance Crisis* (Kensho Seiho Kiki), Nikkei Shinbun Sha.

Galbraith, J. (1958), *The Great Crash* (Boston: Houghlin Mifflin).

Garber, P. (2000), *Famous First Bubbles: The Fundamentals of Early Manias* (Cambridge: MIT Press).

Gelsomino, C. O. (1994), "Da istituto di emissione a banca delle banche: le operazioni di credito della Banca d'Italia tra le due guerre mondiali," in *Il mercato del credito e la borsa, i sistemi di compensazione e statistiche storiche (salari industriali e occupazione)*, Collana storica della Banca d'Italia – Contributi, ricerche per la storia della Banca d'Italia, Volume V (Bari: Laterza).

Gerlach, S., and W. Peng (2002), "Bank Lending and Property Prices in Hong Kong," mimeo, Hong Kong Monetary Authority.

Gertler, M., M. Goodfriend, O., Issing, and L. Spaventa, (1998), *Asset Prices and Monetary Policy: Four Views*, Centre for Economic Policy Research (CEPR) and Bank for International Settlements (BIS).

Gielen, G. (1994), *Können Aktienkurse noch steigen? Langfristige Trendanalyse des deutschen Aktienmarktes* (Wiesbaden: Gabler).

Gigliobianco, A. (1993), "La Sezione speciale autonoma del Consorzio per sovvensioni su valori industriali," in G. Guarino and G. Toniolo (Eds.), *La Banca d'Italia e il sistema bancario, 1919–1936* (Bari: Laterza), pp. 171–87.

Gleitze, B. (1960), *Wirtschafts- und Sozialstatistisches Handbuch*, Köln.

Goldenweiser, E. A. (1951), *American Monetary Policy* (New York: McGraw-Hill).

Goldsmith, R. (1985), *Comparative National Balance Sheets, A Study of Twenty Countries, 1688 to 1978* (Chicago: University of Chicago Press).

Gömmel, R. (1992), "Entstehung und Entwicklung der Effektenbörse im 19. Jahrhundert bis 1914," in H. Pohl (Ed.), *Deutsche Börsengeschichte* (Frankfurt am Main: Fritz Knapp Verlag, 1992), pp. 135–210.

Good, D. F., and T. Ma (1999), "The Economic Growth of Central and Eastern Europe in Comparative Perspective, 1870–1989," *European Review of Economic History* 3 (August): 103–37.

Goodhart, C. (1995), "Price Stability and Financial Fragility," in: K. Sawamoto, Z. Nakajima and H. Taguchi (Eds.), *Financial Stability in a Changing Environment* (New York: St. Martin's Press), pp. 263–302.

Goodhart, C. A. E. (1969), *The New York Money Market and the Finance of Trade, 1900–1913* (Cambridge, Mass.: Harvard University Press).

Gordon, R. (1986), *The American Business Cycle: Continuity and Change* (Chicago: University of Chicago Press).

Greasley, D. (1989), "British Wages and and Income, 1856–1913: A Revision" *Explorations in Economic History* 26 (April): 248–59.

Greasley, D. (1986), "British Economic Growth: the Paradox of the 1880s and the Timing of the Climacteric," *Explorations in Economic History* 23 (October): 416–44.

Greenspan, A. (1998), "Problems of Price Measurement," remarks at the Annual Meeting of the American Economic Association and the American Finance Association, Chicago, IL, January 3. Available at http://www.federalreserve.gov/boarddocs/speeches/1998/default.htm.

Gregor, A. J. (1979), *Italian fascism and developmental dictatorship* (Princeton: Princeton University Press).

Grifone, P. (1971), *Il capitale finanziario in Italia* (Torino: Einaudi).

Gualerni, G. (1982), *Lo stato industriale in Italia 1890–1940* (Milano: Etas libri).

Guarino, G., and G. Toniolo (Eds.) (1993), *La Banca d'Italia e il sistema bancario, 1919–1936* (Bari: Laterza).

Guarnieri, F. (1953), *Battaglie economiche tra le due grandi guerre* (2 volumes), (Milano: Garzanti).

Guildhall Library, City of London, MS 1400/65 (1896), "Minutes and Related Papers of the Committee for General Purposes: February 15, 1897.

Hallendorff, C. (1927), *Svenska arbetsgifvarföreningen 1902–1927* (The Swedish Employer's Federation, Norstedts).

Hamilton, J. D. (1988), "Role of the International Gold Standard in Propagating the Great Depression," *Contemporary Policy Issues* 6 (April): 67–89.

Hamilton, J. D. (1987), "Monetary Factors in the Great Depression," *Journal of Monetary Economics* 19: 145–70.

Harley, C. K. (1977), "The Interest Rate and Prices in Britain, 1873–1913: A Study of the Gibson Paradox," *Explorations in Economic History* 14 (January): 69–89.

Harley, C. K. (1976), "Goschen's Conversion of the National Debt and the Yield on Consols," *Economic History Review* 29 (February): 101–6.

Hart, O., and J. Moore (1994), "A Theory of Debt Based on the Inalienability of Human Capital," *Quarterly Journal of Economics* 109(4): 841–79.

Hartland-Thunberg, P. (1950a), *Balance of Interregional Payments of New England* (Providence: Brown University).

Hartland-Thunberg, P. (1950b), "Interregional Payments: Reply," *Quarterly Journal of Economics* 64 (August): 489–90.

Hartland-Thunberg, P. (1949), "Interregional Payments Compared with International Payments," *Quarterly Journal of Economics*, 63 (August): 392–407.

Hayami, M. (2001), "Recent Economic Developments and Monetary Policy," Speech given by the Governor of Japan at the Research Institute of Japan, 7 March 2001. Available at http://www.boj.or.jp/en/press/φ3/press_f.htm.

Hayek, F. (1931), *Prices and Production* (London: George Routledge and Sons).

Heckscher, E. (1926), "Penningväsende och penningpolitik från krigsutbrottet tilll den internationella guldmyntfotens återställelse [The monetary system and monetary policy from the outbreak of the war until the restoration of the international goldstandard]," in E. Heckscher (Ed.), *Bidrag till Sveriges ekonomiska och social historia under och efter världskriget.* [Contributions to the economic and social history of Sweden during the world war]. (Stockholm: Norstedts).

Heim, C. E. (1998), "Uneven Impacts of the Great Depression: Industries, Regions, and Nations," in M. Wheeler (Ed.), The Economics of the Great Depression (Kalamazoo, MI: W. E. Upjohn Institute for Employment Research), pp. 29–61.

Hessius, K. (1999), "The New Economy and the Long Boom," Speech delivered at Mjardeni Science Park, Linköping, 29 October. Available at http//www.riksbank.com/upload/3475/991029e.pdf.

Hetzel, R. L. (1999), "Japanese Monetary Policy: A Quantity Theory Perspective," *Federal Reserve Bank of Richmond Economic Quarterly* 85 (Winter): 1–25.

Hilbers, P., Q. Lei, and L. Zacho (2001), "Real Estate Market Developments and Financial Sector Soundness," IMF Working Paper 01/129.

Historical Statistics of the United States: Orillemal Edition (2003), *Colonial Times to the Present* (Cambridge. Mass.: Cambridge University Press).

Hofmann, B. (2001), "The Determinants of Private Sector Credit in Industrialised Countries: Do Property Prices Matter?" BIS Working Paper No. 112.

Homer, S., and R. Sylla (1991), *History of Interest Rates*, 3rd edition (New Brunswick, NJ: Rutgers University Press).

Hoover, C. B., and B. U. Ratchford (1951), *Economic Resources and Policies of the South* (New York: Macmillan).

Hoshi, T., and A. Kashyap (2000), "The Japanese Banking Crisis: Where Did it Come from and How Will it End?" Ben S. Bernanlee and Julio S. Rotemberg (Eds.), *NBER. Macroeconomics Annual 1999* (Cambridge, Mass.: The MIT Press), pp. 129–201.

Hubbard, R. G., and A. Kashyap (1992), "Internet Net Worth and the Investment Process: An Application to US Agriculture," *Journal of Political Economy* 100: 506–34.

Hutchison, M., and K. McDill (1999), "Are All Banking Crises Alike? The Japanese Experience in International Comparison," NBER Working Paper No. 7253.

Industria (Swedish Employers' Federation's monthly journal) (1931), nr 23., p. 648.

International Monetary Fund (various issues) *World Economic Outlook* (Washington, DC.: International Monetary Fund).

International Monetary Fund (2003), "Deflation: Determinants, Risks, and Policy Options," *Findings of an Interdepartmental Task Force*, Washington, D.C., April 30.

International Monetary Fund (2000), "Asset Prices and the Business Cycle," *World Economic Outlook*, Chapter III, May.

Inwood, K., and J. Irwin (2000), "The Patterns of Net Migration by Canadians During the Late Nineteenth Century," working paper, University of Guelph.

Ip, G. (2003), "In a Shift, Fed Signals Concern Over Deflation," *Wall Street Journal*, May 7, pp. A1, A10.

Ip, G. (2002), "Inflation Subdued, Top Hawk at Fed Frets Over the Opposite," *Wall Street Journal*, May 8, pp. A1, A12.

Ito, T. (2002), "Is Foreign Exchange Intervention Effective? The Japanese experiences in the 1990s," NBER Working Paper 8914.

Ito, T., and T. Iwaisako (1996), "Explaining Asset Bubbles in Japan," *Bank of Japan Monetary and Economic Studies* 14 (July): 143–93.

Jaffe, J. F. (1989), "Gold and Gold Stocks as Investments for Institutional Portfolios," *Financial Analysts Journal* 45 (March–April): 53–9.

James, J. (1984), "Public Debt Management and Nineteenth Century American Economic Growth," *Explorations in Economic History* 21 (April): 192–217.

Jao, Y. C. (2001), *The Asian Financial Crisis and the Ordeal of Hong Kong* (Westport, Conn.: Quoram Books).

Japan, Ministry of Foreign Affairs (2002), "Opening Statement by Prime Minister Junichiro Koizumi at the Press Conference on the Passage of the Fiscal Year 2002 Budget," Available at www.mofa.go.jp/policy/economy/japan/pm0203.html.

Jonung, L. (1999), *Med backspegeln som kompass – om stabiliseringspolitiken som läroprocess*, Rapport till ESO, Ds 1999:9, Finansdepartmentet, Stockholm. (Forthcoming as: Looking Ahead Through the Rear-View Mirror. Swedish Stabilization Policy 1975–1995.)

Jonung, L. (1979), "Knut Wicksell's Norm of Price Stabilization and Swedish Monetary Policy in the 1930s," *Journal of Monetary Economics* 5: 459–96.

Jonung, L. (1978), "The Depression in Sweden and the United States – A Comparison of Causes and Policies," mimeo, March.

Jorion, P., and W. N. Goetzmann (1999), "Global Stock Markets in the Twentieth Century," *Journal of Finance* 54: 953–80.

Kahneman, D., and A. Tversky (1979), "Prospect Theory: An Analysis of Decision Under Risk," *Econometrica* 47 (March): 263–91.

Kaminsky, G. L., and C. M. Reinhart (1999), "The Twin Crises: The Causes of Banking and Balance-of-Payments Problems," *American Economic Review* 89 (June): 473–500.

Kashyap, A., and T. Hoshi (2001), *Corporate Financing and Governance in Japan: The Road to the Future* (Cambridge, Mass.: The MIT Press).

Keating, J., and J. Nye (1998), "Permanent and Transitory Shocks in Real Output: Estimates from Nineteenth-Century and Postwar Economies," *Journal of Money Credit and Banking* 30 (May): 231–51.

Kennedy, S. E. (1973), *The Banking Crisis of 1933* (Lexington: University Press of Kentucky).

Keynes, J. M. (1936), *The General Theory of Employment, Interest and Money* (London: Macmillan).

Keynes, J. M. (1931), "The Consequences for the Banks of the Collapse in Money Values," in *Essays in Persuasion* (London: Macmillan), pp. 168–78.

Keynes, J. M. (1930), *A Treatise on Money* (London: Macmillan).

Keynes, J. M. (1923), *A Tract on Monetary Reform* (London: Macmillan).

Kindleberger, C. (1995), *Manias, Panics, and Crashes* (New York: John Wiley and Sons).

Kindleberger, C. (1989), *Manias, Panics and Crashes*, (Revised Edition; New York: Basic Books).

Kindleberger, C. (1985), "Keynesianism vs. Monetarism in the 1930s Depression and Recovery," in *Keynesianism vs. Monetarism and Other Essays in Financial History* (London: George Allen & Unwin), pp. 287–92.

Kindleberger, C., and J. Laffargue. (1978), "Introduction" in: C. Kindleberger and J. Laffargue (Eds.), *Financial Crises: Theory, History and Policy* (Cambridge: Cambridge University Press), pp. 1–12.

King, M. (1994), "Debt Deflation: Theory and Evidence," *European Economic Review* 38: 419–45.

Kirman, A. P. (1993), "Ants, Rationality, and Recruitment," *Quarterly Journal of Economics* 108: 137–56.

Kirman, A. P. (1991), "Epidemics of Opinion and Speculative Bubbles in Financial Markets," in Mark P. Taylor (Ed.), *Money and Financial Markets* (Cambridge: Basil Blackwell), pp. 354–68.

Kiyotaki, N., and J. Moore (1997), "Credit Cycles," *Journal of Political Economy* 105 (April): 211–48.

Kock, K. (1961), *Kreditmarknad och räntepolitik 1924–1958* (Uppsala: Sveriges Allmänna Hypoteksbank).

Kolb, E. (1993), *Die Weimarer Republik*, 3. Auflage (München: R. Oldenbourg Verlag).

Krantz, O., and C-A. Nilsson (1975), *Swedish National Product 1861–1970*. (Lund: Gleerups).

Kronenberger, F. (1920), "Die Preisbewegung der Effekten in Deutschland während des Krieges," *Betriebs- und Finanzwirtschaftliche Forschungen*, Heft 2 (Berlin: Verlag von Emil Ebering).

Krugman, P. R. (1998), "It's Baaack: Japan's Slump and the Return of the Liquidity Trap," *Brookings Papers on Economic Activity* 2: 137–205.

Kuttner, K. N., and A. S. Posen (2001), "The Great Recession: Lessons for Macroeconomic Policy from Japan," *Brookings Papers on Economic Activity* 2: 93–185.

Laidler, D. E. W. (1999), *Fabricating the Keynesian Revolution* (New York: Cambridge University Press).

Landsorganisationens verksamhetsberättelse (Annual report of the Swedish Trade Union Federation) (1921), p. 82.

Larsen, A. B., and G. R. McQueen (1995), "REITS, Real Estate, and Inflation: Lessons from the Gold Market," *Journal of Real Estate Finance and Economics* 10 (May): 285–97.

Lastrapes, W. D. (1998), "International Evidence on Equity Prices, Interest Rates and Money," *Journal of International Money and Finance* 17 (June): 377–406.

Laughlin, J. L. (1933), *The Federal Reserve Act: Its Origins and Problems* (New York: MacMillan).

Lee, S. R., D. P. Tang, and K. M. Wong (2000), "Stock Returns During the German Hyperinflation," *Quarterly Review of Economics and Finance* 40: 375–86.

Lindert, P. H. (1988), "Long-Run Trends in American Farmland Values," *Agricultural History* 62 (Summer), reprinted in I. D. Koval'chenko and V. Tishkov (Eds.), *Agrarnaya istoria rossii i SShA v XIX - nachale XX veka* (1990), pp. 87–123, and in M. Rothstein and D. Field (Eds.), *Quantitative Studies in Agrarian History* (1993), pp. 42–82.

Lushkin, D. (2001), "Still Think Deflation's Just a Bugaboo?" *Dow Jones Newswires*, November 21. Available at http://interactive.wsj.com/archive/retrieve.cgi?id=BT-CO-20011121–004007.djm.

MacKinnon, J. G. (1991), "Critical Values for Cointegration Tests," in Robert F. Engle and Clive W. J. Granger (Eds.), *Long-Run Economic Relationships* (Oxford: Oxford University Press), pp. 267–76.

Mahdavi, S., and S. Zhou. (1997), "Gold and Commodity Prices as Leading Indicators of Inflation: Tests of Long-Run Relationship and Predictive Performance." *Journal of Economics and Business* 49 (September/October): 475–89.

Mattesini, F. and B. Quintieri (1997), "Italy and the Great Depression: An Analysis of the Italian Economy, 1929–1936," *Explorations in Economic History* 34: 265–94.

McDonald, J. G., and B. H. Solnik (1977), "Valuation and Strategy for Gold Stocks," *Journal of Portfolio Management* 3 (Spring): 29–33.

McKinnon, R., and K. Ohno (2001), "The Foreign Exchange Origins of Japan's Economic Slump and Low Interest Liquidity Trap," *The World Economy* 24 (June): 279–315.

Meltzer, A. H. (2003), *A History of the Federal Reserve, Volume I: 1913–1951* (Chicago: University of Chicago Press).

Meltzer, A. H. (1988), *Keynes' Monetary Theory: A Different Interpretation* (New York: Cambridge University Press).

Menichella, D. (1956), "The Contribution of the Banking System to Monetary Equilibrium and Economic Stability: The Italian Experience," Banca Nazionale del Lavoro *Quarterly Review* 9 (January–June): 5–21.

Metcalf, C., A. Redish, and R. Shearer, (1998), "New Estimates of the Canadian Money Stock, 1871–1967," *Canadian Journal of Economics* 31 (February): 104–24.

Meyer, R. H. (1970), *Banker's Diplomacy. Monetary Stabilization in the Twenties* (New York: Columbia University Press).

Michie, R. C. (1999), *The London Stock Exchange: A History* (Oxford: Oxford University Press).

Michie, R. C. (1987), *The London and New York Stock Exchanges, 1850–1914* (London: Allen & Unwin).

Migone, G. (1971), *Problemi di storia nei rapporti tra Italia e Stati Uniti* (Torino: Rosenberg e Sellier).

Miller, V. (1998), "Banking Crises, Currency Crises, and Macroeconomic Uncertainty: The Double Drain with a Cross-Border Twist: More on the Relationship Between Banking and Currency Crises," *The American Economic Review Papers and Proceedings* 88 (May): 439–43.

Mills, T. C., and G. E. Wood (1992), "Money and Interest Rates in Britain from 1870 to 1913," in S. R. Broadberry and N. E. Crofts (Eds.), *Britain in the International Economy* (Cambridge: Cambridge University Press), pp. 199–217.

Minford, P. (1994), "The Political Economy of the Exchange Rate Mechanism," *Open Economies Review* 5: 235–47.

Minsky, H. (1982), "Can 'It' Happen Again?" *Essays on Instability and Finance* (New York: M. E. Sharpe).

Mishkin, F. S. (1991), "Asymmetric Information and Financial Crises: A Historical Perspective," in R. G. Hubbard (Ed.) *Financial Markets and Financial Crises* (Chicago: University of Chicago Press), pp. 69–108.

Mishkin, F. S., and E. N. White (2002), "U.S. Stock Market Crashes and Their Aftermath: Implications for Monetary Policy," NBER Working Paper 8992 (June).

Mitchell, B. (1998), *Historical Statistics*. (London: Macmillan).

Miyao, R. (2002), "The Effects of Monetary Policy in Japan," *Journal of Money, Credit, and Banking* 34 (May): 376–92.

Mochi, C. (1982), "Commercio e turismo," in *Annali dell'economia italiana*, vol. 8, tomo 2: 1930–1938. Milano: IPSOA.

Morgan, E. V., and W. A. Thomas (1962), *The Stock Exchange, Its History and Functions* (London: Elek Books).

Muellbauer, J. (1994), "The Assessment: Consumer Expenditure," *Oxford Review of Economic Policy* 10: 1–41.

Mundell, R. A. (2000), "A Reconsideration of the Twentieth Century," *American Economic Review* 90 (June): 327–40.

Murphy, R. (1992), "The Monetary Role of Gold," *Interdisciplinary Science Reviews* 17 (September): 234–38.

Navin, T., and M. Sears (1955), "The Rise of the Market for Industrial Securities, 1887–1902," *Business History Review* 29: 105–138.

Neal, L. (1969), "Investment Behavior by American Railroads: 1897–1914," *Review of Economics and Statistics* 51: 126–35.

Neftci, S. (1984), "Are Economic Time Series Asymmetric Over the Business Cycle?" *Journal of Political Economy* 92: 307–28.

New York State (1909), *Report of Governor Hughes' Committee on Speculation and Commodities*, June 7.

New York Times (1921), "Two Kinds of Deflation," January 19.

New York Times (1921), "McKenna, Deplores Hasty Deflation," January 29.

New York Times (1921), "Our Deflation Seen as Peril," November 27.

New York Times (1935), 21 June, p. 36.

Norrie, K., and D. Owram (1996), *A History of the Canadian Economy* (Toronto: Harcourt Brace and Co.).

Olley, R. (n.d.), "Construction wage rates in Ontario, 1864–1903," mimeo, Kingston.

Organization of Economic Cooperation and Development (2000), *Economic Outlook* 68, December 2000.

Orphanides, A., and V. Wieland (1998), "Price Stability and Monetary Policy Effectiveness When Nominal Interest Rates are Bounded at Zero," Board of Governors of the Federal Reserve System, June.

Östlind, A. (1945), *Svensk samhällsekonomi 1914–1922* [The Swedish economy 1914–1922] (Stockholm: Svenska Bankföreningen).

Paradisi, M. (1976), "Il commercio con l'estero e la struttura industriale," in P. Ciocca and G. Toniolo (Eds.), *L'economia italiana nel periodo fascista* (Bologna: Il Mulino).

Parker, R. E., and J. S. Fackler (2001), "Was Debt Deflation Operative during the Great Depression? A Note," Working Paper 0102, East Carolina University, January.

Phelps, E. S. (1994), *Structural Slumps: The Modern Equilibrium Theory of Unemployment, Interest and Assets* (Cambridge, Mass.: Harvard University Press).

Phelps, E. S., and G. Zoega (2001), "Structural Booms," *Economic Policy* 32: 83–126.

Poole, W., and R. H. Rasche (2002), "Flation," *Review* of the Federal Reserve Bank of St. Louis 84 (November/December 2002): 1–6.

Posen, A. (1998), *Restoring Japan's Economic Growth* (Washington, DC: Institute for International Economics).

Rawski, T. G. (1993), "Milton Friedman, Silver, and China," *Journal of Political Economy* 101: 755–8.

Rey, G. M. (1991), *I conti economici dell'Italia: una sintesi delle fonti ufficiali, 1890–1970* (Bari: Laterza).

Rey, G. M. (1978), "Una sintesi dell'economia italiana durante il fascismo," in G. Toniolo (Ed.), *L'econmia italiana 1861–1940* (Bari: Laterza).

Riksbankens årsbok (Yearbook of Riksbanken) (various issues).

Roach, S. S. (2002), "The Costs of Bursting Bubbles," *New York Times* Week in Review, September 22, p. 13.

Romer, C. (1992), "What Ended the Great Depression?" *Journal of Economic History* 52: 757–84.

Romer, C. (1990), "The Great Crash and the Onset of the Great Depression," *Quarterly Journal of Economics* 105 (August): 597–624.

Roselli, A. (2000), *Il governatore Vincenzo Azzolini 1931–1944* (Bari: Laterza).

Rosenbloom, J. L., and W. A. Sundstrom (1997), "The Sources of Regional Variation in the Severity of the Great Depression: Evidence from the U.S. Manufacturing, 1919–1937," NBER Working Paper 688.

Salant, S. W., and D. W. Henderson (1978). "Market Anticipations of Government Policies and the Price of Gold," *Journal of Political Economy* 86 (August): 627–48.

Sargent, T. (1994), "The Ends of Four Big Inflations," in M. Parkin (Ed.), *The Theory of Inflation* (Aldershot, U.K.: Edward Elgar), pp. 433–89.

Schinasi, G., and M. Hargreaves (1993), "Boom and Bust in Asset Markets in the 1980s: Causes and Consequences," in Staff Studies for the World Economic Outlook (Washington, DC: International Monetary Fund).

Schwartz, A. J. (1997), "Comment on Eichengreen and Grossman," in F. H. Capie and G. E. Wood (Eds.), *Asset Prices and the Real Economy* (London, Macmillan), pp. 100–5.

Schwartz, A. J. (Ed.) (1991), *Commodity Monies* (Cheltenham: Edward Elgar).

Schwartz, C. F., and R. E. Graham, Jr. (1956), *Personal Income by States Since 1929* (Washington, DC: U.S. Govt. Print. Office).

Selgin, G. (1995), "The 'Productivity Norm' versus Zero Inflation in the History of Economic Thought," *History of Political Economy* 27 (Winter): 705–35.

Shilling, A. G. (2001), "The Phillips Curve and Postwar Inflation are History: Central Banks are Fighting the Last War," *Business Economics* 36 (July 2001): 40–5.

Shleifer, A. (2000), *Inefficient Markets. An Introduction to Behavioral Finance* (Oxford: Oxford University Press).

Siklos, P. L. (2002a), "Asymmetric Adjustment from Structural Booms and Slumps," *Economics Letters* 77: 329–33.

Siklos, P. L. (2002b), *The Changing Face of Central Banking: Evolutionary Trends Since World War II* (New York: Cambridge University Press).

Smiley, G. (1981), "Regional Variation in Bank Loan Rates in the Interwar Years," *The Journal of Economic History* 41 (December): 889–901.

Snowden, K. (1990), "Historical Returns and Security Market Developments, 1872–1925," *Explorations in Economic History* 27 (October): 381–420.

Snowden, K. (1987), "American Stock Market Development and Performance, 1871–1929," *Explorations in Economic History* 24 (October): 327–353.

Snowdon, B., and H. R. Vane (1999), *Conversations with Leading Economists: Interpreting Modern Macroeconomics* (Northampton, Mass.: Edward Elgar).

Snyder, C. (1935), "The Problem of Monetary and Economic Stability," *Quarterly Journal of Economics* 49 (February): 173–205.

Sobel, R. (1965), *The Big Board: A History of the New York Stock Exchange* (New York & London: The Free Press).

Sociala Meddelanden (monthly publication from Socialstyrelsen (The National Board of Welfare and Health)), (various issues).

Statens offentliga statistik: Arbetsinställelser och kollektivavtal (Labor conflicts and collective agreements), Statistics Sweden.

Statistisk årsbok (Yearbook of Statistics Sweden), (various issues).

Sprague, O. M. W. (1968 [1910]), History of Crises Under the National Banking System (New York: A. M. Kelley).

Stevens, G. (2002), "Inflation, Deflation, and All That," address to Australian Business Economists 2002 Forecasting Conference Dinner, December 4, Sydney. Available from http://www.rba.gov.au/Speeches/sp_dg_041202.html.

Stolper, G. (1964), *Deutsche Wirtschaft seit 1870* (Tübingen: J. C. B. Mohr [Paul Siebeck]).

Storaci, M. (1993), "L'Italia e il blocco dell'oro (1933–1935)," in *Finanza Internazionale, vincolo esterno e cambi. 1919–1939*, Collana Storica della Banca d'Italia, Ricerche per la Storia della Banca d'Italia, volume III (Roma-Bari: Laterza).

Summers, L. H. (1983), "The Nonadjustment of Nominal Interest Rates," in J. Tobin (Ed.), *Macroeconomics, Prices, and Quantities: Essays in Memory of Arthur Okun* (Washington, DC: The Brookings Institution), pp. 201–40.

Supino, C. (1929), *Storia della circolazione cartacea in Italia dal 1860 al 1928* (Milano: Societa' Editorale Libraria).

Sylla, R. (1991), "Financial Disturbances and Depressions: The View from Economic History," paper presented at "The Crisis in Finance," a Conference of the Jerome Levy Institute, Bard College, Annandale-on-Hudson, NY.

References   349

Takebe, M. (2001a), "Japan Takenaka: Govt, BOJ To Cooperate to Fight Inflation," *Dow Jones Newswire*, November 22. Available from http://interactive.wsj.
com/archive/retrieve.cgi?id=DI-CO-20011122-001668.djm.
Takebe, M. (2001b), "Japan Govt. to Coordinate with BOJ to Tackle Deflation," *Dow Jones Newswire*, November 22. Available from http://interactive.
wsj.com/archive/retrieve.cgi?id=DI-CO-20011122-001991.djm.
Tattara, G., and G. Toniolo (1976), "L'industria manifatturiera: cicli, politiche e mu-
tamenti di struttura (1921–37)," in P. Ciocca and G. Toniolo (Eds.), *L'economia
italiana nel periodo fascista* (Bologna: Il Mulino).
Taylor, J. (1979), "Aggregate dynamics and staggered contracts," *Journal of Political
Economy* 88: 1–23.
Temin, P. (1989), *Lessons from the Great Depression* (Cambridge: MIT Press).
Temin, P. (1976), *Did Monetary Forces Cause the Great Depression?* (New York:
Norton).
Thomas, W. A. (1973), *The Provincial Stock Exchanges* (London: Frank Cass).
Thorsell, W. (2001), "The Costs of Getting to Perfection," *Globe and Mail*, February
2, p. A15.
Tilly, R. (1998), "Universal Banking in Historical Perspective," *Journal of Institu-
tional and Theoretical Economics* 54 (March): 7–32.
Toniolo, G. (1993), "Il profilo economico," in G. Guarino and G. Toniolo (Eds.), *La
Banca d'Italia e il sistema bancario 1919–1936* (Bari: Laterza), pp. 5–101.
Tufano, P. (1998), "The Determinants of Stock Price Exposure: Financial Engineering
and the Gold Mining Industry," *Journal of Finance* 53 (June): 1015–52.
U.S. Bureau of the Census (1960), *Historical Abstracts of the United States: Colonial
Times to 1957*.
U.S. Board of Governors of the Federal Reserve System (1943), *Banking and Mon-
etary Statistics* (Washington, D.C.: Board of Governors of the Federal Reserve
System).
U.S. Bureau of the Census (1975), *Historical Statistics of the United States, Colonial
Times to 1970, Bicentennial Edition* (Washington, D.C.: Governments Printing
Office).
Urquhart, M. (1993), *Gross National Product, Canada, 1870–1926, The Derivation
of the Estimates* (Montreal: McGill-Queens University Press).
Vidal, E. (1910), *The History and Methods of the Paris Bourse* (Washington, D.C.:
Government Printing Office).
Viner, J. (1933), "Balanced Deflation, Inflation, or More Depression," *The Day and
Hour Series of the University of Minnesota* 3, April (Minneapolis: University of
Minnesota Press).
Volpi, G. (1928), "La riforma monetaria illustrata dal ministro delle Finanze (discorso
fatto in Senato il 17 febbraio 1928)," *Giornale degli economisti*, Serie IV, XLIII,
LXVII, 247–68.
Wachman, R., and J. Doward (2001), "Fed to Prop Up Wall Street," *The Observer*
(September 16).
Waite, W. C. (1942), "Indexes of the Terms of Trade, Between Areas in the United
States," *The Review of Economic Statistics* 24 (February): 22–30.

Wallis, J. J. (1987), "Employment, Politics, and Economic Recovery During the Great Depression," *Review of Economics and Statistics* 69: 516–20.

Wanniski, J. (2001), "The Deflation Monster." Available at http://www.gilder.com <http://www.gilder.com.

Watson, K. (1996), "Banks and Industrial Finance: The Experience of Brewers, 1880–1913," *Economic History Review* 49 (February): 58–81.

Weil, P. (1990), "On the Possibility of Price Decreasing Bubbles." *Econometrica* 58: 1467–74.

Weinstein, M. (1981), "Some Macroeconomic Impacts of the National Recovery Act, 1933–35," in K. Bruner (Ed.), *The Great Depression Revisited* (Boston, Martina Nijhoff), pp. 262–81.

West, K. D. (1987), "A Specification Test for Speculative Bubbles." *Quarterly Journal of Economics* 102: 553–80.

Wheelock, D. C. (1998), "National Monetary Policy by Regional Design: The Evolving Role of the Federal Reserve Banks in Regional Federal Reserve System Policy," Federal Reserve Bank of St. Louis, Working Paper, 1998–010B.

Wheelock, D. C. (1992), "Regulation and Bank Failures: New Evidence from the Agricultural Collapse of the 1920s," *The Journal of Economic History* 52 (December): 806–25.

White, E. N. (2000), "Banking and Finance in the Twentieth Century," in Stanley Engerman and Robert Gallman (Eds.), *The Cambridge Economic History of the United States, Vol. III* (Cambridge: Cambridge University Press) pp. 743–802.

White, E. N. (1990), "The Stock Market Boom and Crash of 1929 Revisited," *Journal of Economic Perspectives* 4 (Spring): 67–83.

White, E. N. (1984), "A Reinterpretation of the Banking Crisis of 1930," *Journal of Economic History* 44 (March): 119–38.

White, E. N. (1983), *The Regulation and Reform of the American Banking System, 1900–1929*. Princeton: Princeton University Press.

Wicker, E. (2000), *Banking Panics of the Gilded Age* (New York: Cambridge University Press).

Wicker, E. (1996), *The Banking Panics of the Great Depression* (New York: Cambridge University Press).

Wicksell, K. (1907) "The Influence of the Rate of Interest on Prices," *Economic Journal* 17 (June): 13–20.

Wigmore, B. (1987), "Was the Bank Holiday of 1933 a Run on the Dollar Rather than the Banks?" *The Journal of Economic History* 47 (September): 739–56.

Williamson, J. (1974), *Late 19th Century American Development: A General Equilibrium History* (New York: Cambridge University Press).

Wilson, J. G. (1969), "The Stock Exchange Clearing House," in Edmund Clarence Stedman (Ed.), *The New York Stock Exchange: Its History, Its Contribution to National Prosperity, and Its Relation to American Finance at the Outset of the Twentieth Century* (New York: Greenwood Press), pp. 432–3.

Wright, G. (1996), *Old South, New South: Revolutions in the Southern Economy Since the Civil War* (Baton Rouge: Louisiana State University Press).

Yates, T. (2002), "Monetary Policy and the Zero Bound to Interest Rates: A Review," ECB working paper No. 190, October.

Yuan, M. (2002), "An Analysis of the Co-Existence of the Increasing Growth Rate and Aggravating Deflation," (in Chinese), September 19. Available at http://www.forumcn.com.

Zamagni, V. (1994), "Una ricostruzione dell'andamento mensile dei salari industriali e dell'occupazione," in *Il mercato del credito e la borsa, i sistemi di compensazione e statistiche storiche (salari industriali e occupazione)*, Collana storica della Banca d'Italia – Contributi, ricerche per la storia della Banca d'Italia, Volume V (Bari: Laterza), pp. 349–78.

Index

Burdekin, R.C.K., 12
Bureau of the Census (USA), 171

Cagan, P., 312
Calomiris, C., 39, 56, 83
Campbell, E., 276
Campbell, J.Y., 316
Canada, 139, 182
    inter-war period, *see* Great Depression;
        Canadian experience
    pre-1914 experience, 191–195, 196–203,
        208–216
Capie, F.H., 65, 70, 75, 79–80, 81, 82
Cargill, T., 9, 17, 242, 243, 244, 246, 260, 262,
    265, 266
Carlson, M., 59
Cassel, G., 97–99, 113, 115, 118–119
Cecchetti, S.G., 133, 151, 169, 235, 236
central bank policy, *see* monetary policy
Charemza, W.W., 316
China, People's Republic of
    deflation experience, 1, 9–10, 17–20, 61
Chua, J.H., 319
Ciocca, P., 224
classical gold standard, *see* exchange rate
    systems and Great Depression
Cogley, T., 18
Cohen, J.S., 290
Collins, M., 81
Collyns, C., 138, 177
collateral constraints, *see* Deflation;
    collateral constraints
commodity prices, *see* prices; commodity
consols, *see* United Kingdom *and* Great
    Depression
consumer prices, *see* prices; consumer
Crafts, N.F.R., 81
credit crunch, *see* Deflation; collateral
    constraints
currency boards, *see* exchange rate systems

Davidson, D., 97–99, 118–119
Davis, L.E., 277
De Cecco, M., 224
Deadman, D.F., 316
debt-deflation, *see* Great Depression;
    debt-deflation process
debt issuance, *see* budget deficits
deficits
    balance of payments, 31–32, 43–50
    budget, *see* budget deficits

deflation
    anticipated vs. unanticipated, 8–9, 12–14,
        68–80, 84–86, 105–112, 125–128
    induced by monetary tightening, 6–7,
        17–20, 185–186
    collateral constraints, 3, 17, 81, 136–137,
        138, 147, 149–158, 168, 175–176, 182,
        244, 246, 247–249, 250–258, 260, 275
    during the nineteenth century, *see* Canada;
        pre-1914 experience, United Kingdom;
        pre-1914 experience and United States;
        pre-1914 experience
    during the inter-war period, *see* Great
        Depression
    in Argentina, 1, 9
    in China, *see* China; deflation experience
    in Hong Kong, 1, 9, 61, 166, 168
    in Japan, *see* Japan, deflation experience
    in Singapore, 1, 61, 166, 168
    in Taiwan, 1, 61
    international transmission of, 10–12, 16,
        113, 115, 116, 118, 229, 239, 264
    self-sustaining, 4–5, 83, 84
    supply-side explanations of, 6, 7–8, 9–10,
        14–16, 191–197, 199–216
    wealth effects of, 3–4, 5
Delargy, P., 170
DeLong, J.B., 8, 13
Denmark, 139
    inter-war period, *see* Great Depression;
        Danish experience
Dewey, D.R., 271
Dickey, D.A., 312
Dickey, G.E., 8
Dodge, D., Governor of the Bank of
    Canada, 5
dollar, currency
    Australian, *see* Australia
    Canadian, *see* Canada *and* Great
        Depression
    New Zealand, *see* New Zealand
    United States, *see* United States *and* Great
        Depression
Donner, O., 303

Eichengreen, B., 14, 31, 35, 80–81, 199, 200,
    223, 229, 262
Enders, W., 309, 311, 316
euro, currency, *see* European Central Bank;
    and the euro